W9-AVI-723

BUGIALLI
ON
PASTA

by Giuliano Bugialli

ILLUSTRATIONS BY GLENN WOLFF
PHOTOGRAPHS BY JOHN DOMINIS

SIMON AND SCHUSTER
New York   London   Toronto   Sydney   Tokyo

Simon and Schuster
Simon & Schuster Building
Rockefeller Center
1230 Avenue of the Americas
New York, New York 10020

Copyright © 1988 by Giuliano Bugialli Enterprises, Inc.
Photographs copyright © 1988 by John Dominis
All rights reserved
including the right of reproduction
in whole or in part in any form.

SIMON AND SCHUSTER and colophon are registered trademarks
of Simon & Schuster Inc.

DESIGNED BY BARBARA MARKS
Manufactured in the United States of America

10 9 8 7 6 5 4 3 2

Library of Congress Cataloging in Publication Data

Bugialli, Giuliano.
    Bugialli on pasta / by Giuliano Bugialli.
        p.   cm.
    Includes index.
    1. Cookery (Pasta)   2. Cookery, Italian.   I. Title.
TX809.P38B83   1988   88-27460
641.8'22—dc19   CIP
ISBN 0-671-62024-X

To
Audrey

CONTENTS

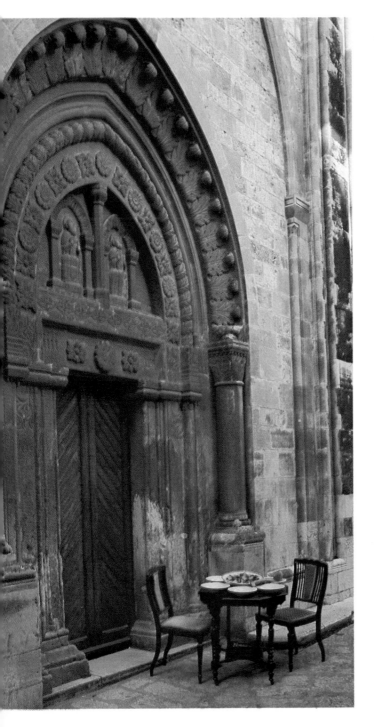

Apulian pasta with
Cathedral of
Conversano behind.

A letter from the great Rossini, composer of The Barber of Seville, *thanking a friend for sending his usual order of Italian olive oil to him in Paris.*
Original: Collection of Giuliano Bugialli

INTRODUCTION

Pasta has been basic to the Italian diet for at least a century and a half, and many pasta dishes have origins that go back much further. The enormous growth in pasta's popularity outside of Italy is a phenomenon of recent years. The discovery of its healthful qualities has led to a burst of innovation and creativity in its pairing with other ingredients.

The purpose of this book is to provide a model of traditional Italian pasta dishes that have stood the test of centuries in Italy. I hope these may give you some guidelines for classic combinations and proper blending of ingredients, so that you can avoid the trial and error of undirected "creativity." Innovation without such guidelines has produced some bizarre combinations that might have temporary shock value, but which don't endure for an educated palate. As in all cooking—or any creative work, for that matter—a foundation of basic techniques, methods, and information must be established. Some combinations now being touted as new and innovative were in fact rejected ages ago in Italy. For example, although goat cheese has existed in Italy for thousands of years, there is not a single traditional dish that uses it cooked. This is not because no one has ever thought of cooking it, but because the change in taste and strong smell of the heated cheese has been consciously rejected. It is my opinion that cooked goat cheese is a culinary travesty, with or without pasta.

I cite the example of a more positive guideline. Just about all dishes that combine pasta with zucchini alone require that the vegetable be fried first. Certainly this is the result of centuries of trial and error. Another idea worth pondering

is that all dishes combining only shrimp with pasta seem to be from the last fifty years. Why was there a traditional aversion to this combination, and why have a few such dishes come to be accepted in recent regional cooking?

In this book I systematically present and concentrate on some pasta dishes that are especially relevant to current gastronomy—pasta and beans, pasta and vegetables, pasta with fish, and so on—and make comparisons of the various preparations of such combinations in several different regions. For example, the diverse ways of combining pasta with eggplant, in both Sicily and other regions, is interesting in itself and provides a fair number of quite different and all valid recipes. The same is true of other vegetables, beans, fish, and like ingredients.

This is the first of my books in which I am able to emphasize dried pasta recipes and to give recipes incorporating a really large selection of them. Fresh pasta is not overlooked, however, and here you will find many special regional examples. The chapter on fresh pasta provides illustrated techniques for its preparation, though that is not the main thrust of this book. Needless to say, no one book can be complete on the subject of regional pastas. I have included many recipes that as far as I know have not been published before or have been published in versions I consider inauthentic.

Arriving at an authentic version of a recipe with a long tradition requires work. The dish as prepared at one regional restaurant or by one family from an area is not necessarily an authentic version of that region's preparation. It is important to compare many different sources, printed and oral, *especially* the oldest available ones. Local restaurant versions are often unreliable, and a single family's version may not be typical. Let us not forget that even some Italian grandmothers are poor cooks. Most of all, I have avoided idiosyncratic versions of dishes made by myself or others. You will not find here Spaghetti Caruso or Chicken with Noodles Tetrazzini.

Several other grain dishes, such as *gran farro*, Italian couscous, and *gnocchi* are included because, aside from being wonderful dishes, they help us understand the evolution of pasta from ancient Roman times. (Marco Polo did *not* introduce pasta to Italy from China.*) If this book helps you to understand some general principles of pasta selection, or assists you in matching various types of pasta with sauces and knowing which ingredients form appropriate combinations, I will feel I have accomplished my goal and have helped you move on to make your own creations rest on an intelligent, solid basis. The recipes themselves, of course, form a collection of wonderful dishes and need no other justification. I hope you enjoy them.

CHOOSING THE SHAPES OF DRIED PASTA

It is fun and enlightening to match the exact regional type of dried pasta with its traditional sauce. But how does one find order among the hundreds of named pasta shapes? To add to the confusion, the same shape may have different names in different regions, and may differ even from one manufacturer of dried pasta to another. And then, the slightest difference in length or twist may give the pasta yet another name.

And what if it is not possible to find the exact pasta you need? What criteria should you use in choosing a substitute? Can we find some general categories to guide us? Here I attempt to show the main functional types of dried pasta, so as to remove some of the mystique. I help you choose substitutes by creating basic categories by general shape, with a brief guide as to how each is used.

LONG PASTA

Among the many different names are *spaghetti, vermicelli, bigoli, ciriole, bavette, linguine, fidelini, spaghettini, capellini.*† Formerly some of these were defined by their length. *Spaghetti* was longer than it is today, *bigoli* were extremely long. But, with the standardization in box size for shelf marketing, now they all tend to be of the same length. The few differences that remain are in thickness and whether they are rounded or flattened. (Apropos of nothing, it is interesting to note that flattened *linguine* have achieved an importance outside of Italy that they never had at home.)

All of these types of traditional regional pastas have associations with specific sauces, but except for their varied thicknesses, they take the sauce in basically the same way. Naturally, the delicate *capellini* require a lighter sauce than the thick *ciriole*. It is also worth mentioning that the most commonly used pasta of this type, *spaghetti*, is now generally less thick than it used to be and is closer to *spaghettini*.

Medium-thick, long pastas can be substituted one for another if you can't find the specific one. If you can't find *capellini*, use the thinnest substitute; for *ciriole*, use the thickest.

---

* While during the early days of the Roman Empire wheat was imported into Italy from Egypt and the northwestern African coast (then called the province of Africa), by the later days of the empire Sicily had become the granary of the Mediterranean world. Wheat cultivation transformed that green and wooded island into the starker landscape and climate we know today. Most authorities now feel that pasta came into being in Sicily; it was a way of preserving the milled wheat by mixing it with water and drying it in the sun. Fresh egg pasta is documented in central and northern Italy from at least the Middle Ages. Factory-made pasta came into being in the early nineteenth century, and dried pasta started its triumphant march northward during the following century. The journey is being completed in our day, as pasta becomes a staple elsewhere in the world, across the Alps and the oceans.

† *Capelli d'angelo* resemble *capellini*, but are classically dried in the shape of nests.

LONG PASTA WITH HOLE

Perciatelli or *bucatini* are a bit thicker than *spaghetti*, but their main characteristic is an almost imperceptible hole through their entire length. The first name is Neapolitan, the second Roman, for the same pasta. There are many other such instances of the same pasta parading under different regional names. Don't let this confuse you. And of course do not take a manufacturer's name for a type as holy writ.

WIDE PASTA

Long, flat pasta from ½ inch to several inches wide include *tagliatelle* (*fettuccine*, the same), *pappardelle, trenette, laganelle, reginelle, lasagnette, lasagne.* They may have straight or curled sides. Most of these appear more often as fresh pasta, and some manufacturers' versions of *tagliatelle* or *trenette* may not resemble the traditional fresh versions very much. Some of these appear at times as dried egg pasta. The main differences among them are in their width and a bit of their thickness. It is these qualities that should determine the closest substitute.

SHORT TUBULAR PASTA

Ranging from about 2 to 3 inches long, with a hole from ½ inch to 1 inch wide, these pastas include *penne, sedanini, denti di cavallo, rigatoni,* and so on. They may have smooth or ridged surfaces, but this difference is not as important as you might think in the traditional pairings with a sauce. Both smoothed and ridged *penne* are used with the same sauces in Tuscany.

SHORT PASTA—OTHER

Included here are bow- or butterfly-shaped *farfalle,* ring-shaped Sicilian *anellini,* twisted *fusilli,* shell-shaped *chiocciole,* and the like. Their shapes retain the sauce just as the hole does in tubular pasta, and they are often used interchangeably with that type.

PASTA PRIMARILY FOR BROTHS OR MINESTRONI

In this category are all the very small pastine, such as *grandinine, stelline,* and so forth; the very short tubular ones, *ditalini, avemarie, paternostri;* and smaller versions of above-mentioned butterflies (*farfalline*) or of shells (*chioccioline*).

The word *maccherone* (not spelled "macaroni" in Italian) is sometimes used as generic term for pasta, especially in the Naples area and in ancient cookbooks. Most commercial producers use the term to refer to a medium-length tubular pasta with ridges, in length between *penne* and *rigatoni.* The elbow shape for *maccherone* is less used. The spelling "macaroni" has existed in English, however, since the eighteenth century.

■   ■   ■

Except for regional specialties, Italians do not hesitate to interchange the pastas within each of these categories.

USE OF CHEESE ON PASTA

Cheese, grated or occasionally sliced very thin, is often added to pasta before serving. However, in Italy it is not added all the time; indeed, it is used much less often than many people think. Generally cheese is not used with fish, game, or mushroom sauces—though there are a few exceptions—and rarely in dishes with hot red pepper. And on many other dishes, cheese should not be sprinkled mindlessly, since they are better without it.

Depending on the region, there is much variety in the cheeses used. The incomparable Parmigiano is used all over Italy, but numerous pecorinos, *bitto* from Valtellina, *latteria* from Friuli, *caciocavallo,* and others are preferred locally for regional dishes. To sum up, one should not indiscriminately sprinkle Parmigiano over everything if all dishes are not to melt into an unappealing sameness.

There is no basis, however, to the recently developed misconception that Parmigiano is rarely used in recipes employing olive oil. It and other cheeses are combined with butter or oil, depending on the region.

A Note on Ricotta

Since most containers of ricotta sold in markets have a net weight of 15 ounces rather than 1 pound, it is more convenient to use that amount.

A Note on Olive Oil

First-pressing, extra-virgin olive oil and even some good ones with a little extra acidity are now available from many parts of Italy. When possible, it is best to use the olive oil of a specific region in preparing a regional dish: Liguria, Tuscany, Umbria, Lazio, Apulia, Calabria, and Sicily are the principal olive-oil producing regions. The production from other regions is negligible and their dishes reflect this, since they usually employ butter rather than oil.

A special exception is Campania, around the Naples area, which though surrounded by other olive-oil regions produces little of its own olive oil and traditionally has used lard as its shortening in local recipes. The olive trees of Gaeta in Campania produce wonderful olives for eating. Recently in southern Italy, there has been a tendency to lighten some dishes by substituting oil for the lard, or occasionally to use lighter oil from central Italy instead of their own excellent but fuller-bodied oil.

BUGIALLI
ON
PASTA

BASIC TECHNIQUE FOR MAKING FRESH PASTA

HOW TO PREPARE THE DOUGH AND KNEAD IT

1. *Place the flour in a mound on a pasta board. Use a fork to make a well in the center.*

2. *Put the eggs, and other ingredients specified in the recipe, in the well.*

3. *With a fork, first mix together the eggs and other ingredients,*

4. *then begin to incorporate the flour from the inner rim of the well, always incorporating fresh flour from the lower part, pushing it under the dough that is forming to keep it from sticking to the board. Remove pieces of the dough attached to the fork.*

5. *Put the pieces of the dough together with your hands.*

6. *Scrape the board with a pastry scraper, gathering together all the unincorporated flour as well as the pieces of dough coated with flour.*

7. *Place this flour with the pieces of dough in a sifter. Resting the sifter on the board and using one hand, "clean" the flour by moving the sifter back and forth.*

   The globules of dough will remain in the sifter screen and will not filter through. Discard

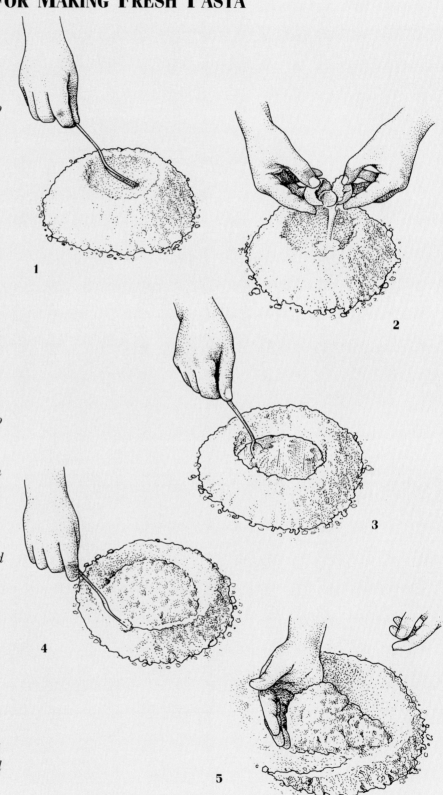

them because, being already coated with flour, they will not integrate into the wet dough and will cause lumps which make holes when the dough is stretched.

8. Start kneading the dough using the palm of the hand,

9. and folding the dough over with the other hand, absorbing the leftover flour from the board. Do not sprinkle the flour over the dough.

Continue kneading, for about 5 minutes, absorbing the flour until the dough is no longer wet and all but 4 or 5 tablespoons have been incorporated (the remaining flour will be used for second kneading of the dough). If you intend to stretch the dough by machine, knead for only 2 to 3 minutes. The amount of flour left over will remain about the same.

10. A ball of elastic and smooth dough should be the result of kneading the dough for this length of time. You can now do the additional kneading and stretching of the dough either by hand or with a pasta machine. (See pages 16– 19 and 20–21.)

HOW TO STRETCH THE DOUGH BY HAND WITH A ROLLING PIN

Take the ball of dough that has been kneaded for 5 minutes and continue kneading for about 10 minutes longer, incorporating some, but not all, of the flour that remained from before.

The following drawings demonstrate the technique of using the long Italian-style rolling pin. The American ball-bearing rolling pin may also be used.

1. *Place the center of the long rolling pin over the ball of dough. Rest the palms of your hands a bit from the ends (if using the ball-bearing type, do not grasp the rolling pin by the handles).*

2. *Gently roll the pin forward,*

3. *then backward. This is the basic motion, and should be repeated until the dough is elastic, that is, until the dough springs back when pulled.*

To stretch to an even thickness,

4. *fold the edge over the rolling pin,*

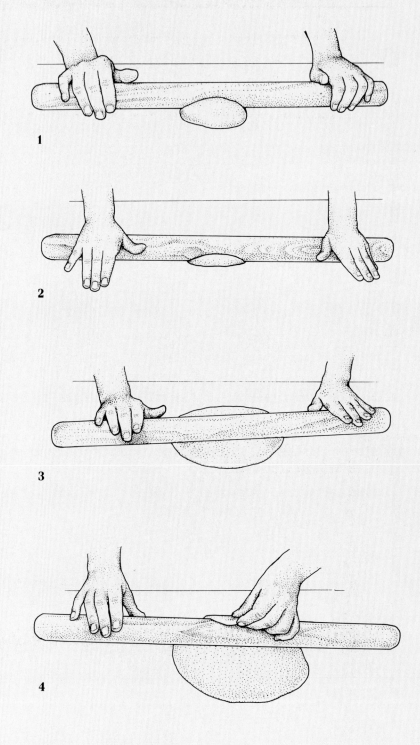

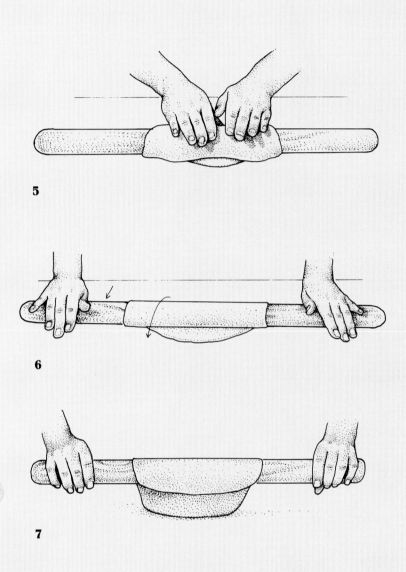

5. *and roll up the sheet of dough around the pin, moving the fingers of your hands outward along the edge of the pasta sheet to even the edges out.*

6. *Move your hands outward almost to the edges of the pin. With a quick jerky movement, roll the pin away from you so that the edge of the pasta sheet slaps against the board. This movement stretches the edge of the sheet as thin as the rest.*

7. *Flip the rolling pin over so that the edge of the pasta sheet is facing toward you rather than away from you.*

8. *Unroll the sheet away from you, so that the underside will now be on top.*

To stretch the pasta evenly, it is important to alternate back-and-forth motion with side-to-side motion. This can be accomplished first,

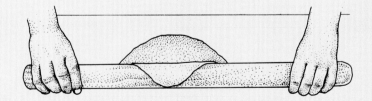

5

6

7

8

9. *turning your body sideways. Let one end of the long rolling pin overlap the end of the pasta board. Loosely hold this end with one hand. Rest the palm of the other hand, as before, on the rolling pin, but closer to the center. With this hand, roll the pin from side to side until the layer of pasta is stretched out to a little less than ⅛ inch thick.*

10. *Roll up the sheet in order to reverse it again. However, in this position, it is not possible to make the slapping movement. Simply flip the pin over and unroll the sheet on the other side.*

Keep alternating the two kinds of movements until the pasta is stretched large and less than ¹⁄₁₆ inch thick.

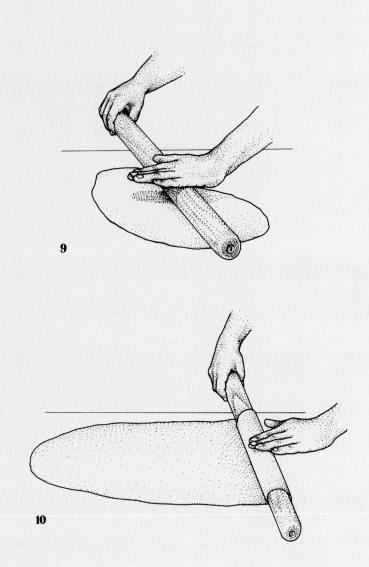

9

10

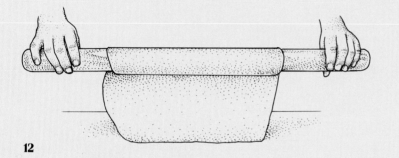

11. This is the rolled up sheet of pasta, larger and thinner than before. Again, move the fingers outward along the edge to even out the sheet.

12. This is the largest sheet of pasta being unrolled and reversed.

13. The pasta stretched evenly to its final thickness, less that $\frac{1}{16}$ inch thick.

11

12

13

HOW TO STRETCH THE DOUGH WITH A HAND PASTA MACHINE

The machine has two parts (detachable or in one piece), one for rolling and stretching the dough in layers, the other for cutting.

The different brands of pasta machines vary in the number of notches controlling the rollers for stretching. They even vary in the final thinness achieved. On some, the last notch produces such a thin sheet (close to $1/32$ inch) that it is impossible to use without breaking the pasta. Get to know your own machine and whether the last or next to the last produces the slightly less than $1/16$ inch thickness desirable for most pasta.

NOTE: *If the pasta dough is made with more than 2 eggs, divide the dough into 1-cup portions before you flatten it in preparation for putting it between the rollers.*

1. *With the palm of your hand, flatten the ball of dough so it can fit between the rollers (about $1/2$ inch thick).*

2. *Set the wheel for the rollers at the widest setting. Turning the handle, pass the dough through the rollers.*

3. *With your hand, remove the layer of dough from underneath the pasta machine.*

4. *Holding the layer of dough with both your hands, gently flour one side of the dough by drawing it across the flour on the board.*

5. *Fold the dough into thirds,*

6. *and press down with your fingers, starting from one open side toward the opposite open side, so that the three layers will be melded together and no*

20

air will remain inside between the three layers of dough.

Using the same wide setting of the rollers, insert the open end of the folded layer of dough through the rollers. Repeat the rolling and folding 8 to 10 times, until the dough is very smooth and elastic.

It is now ready to be stretched. Move the rollers to a narrower setting, following the manufacturer's instructions for the particular type of machine. Roll out a layer of pasta.

7. Flour the layer of pasta on both sides by drawing it across the flour on the board.

8. When feeding the layer of pasta into the machine, the position of your body is very important. Stand sideways in relation to the table, holding the handle of the machine with your right hand. Hold the other hand up sideways, keeping the four fingers together and holding the thumb out. Let the sheet of pasta rest over your hand between the first finger and outstretched thumb.

Pass the dough through the rollers once; do not fold any more. Move the wheel to the next notch, passing the dough through the rollers just once. After passing each time,

sprinkle the layer of pasta with a little flour. Each successive notch will produce a thinner layer of pasta. Repeat this procedure until the layer reaches the thickness desired. The specific thickness of each kind of pasta is indicated in the individual recipes.

9. Still letting the pasta hang over one hand, pull it out to its full length. It is now ready to be cut into different shapes with the pasta machine.

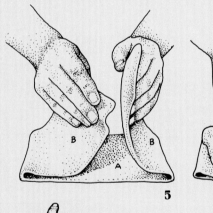

5

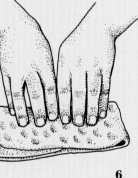

6

7

8

9

Pasta and beans in the
style of Monferrato and
Piacenza, with a view of
the intensely colored
terra-cotta rooftops of
Piacenza in Emilia-
Romagna. A special
homemade regional
pasta is used for this
dish and appears on
page 190.

PASTA AND BEANS

Every part of Italy has its pasta and beans* *minestre* and *minestroni*. Today we are reaffirming the wisdom of this combination, for it provides an almost balanced diet in itself, containing protein and carbohydrates, without cholesterol or fat. This was understood through folk wisdom many centuries ago, and it may be that these dishes were among the first uses of pasta. Devoto, Italy's leading modern etymologist, traces the origin of the word *maccherone* from "*macco*," the ancient dish *macco di fave*, with which we begin this book. In any case, attempts have been made to trace the origins of *maccherone* from a word in Venetian dialect, spelled with a single *c*. (The difference between single and double consonants in Italian is very basic etymology.) It makes more sense to expect the word to come from southern Italy, where pasta originated, rather than from the North, where it arrived much later.

The combination of fava beans with pasta uses one of the very few bean types that is indigenous to the Eastern Hemisphere, most beans having come to Europe from Latin America via the colonists. Dishes using fava beans, along with chick-peas and lentils, are probably the oldest of this type. Dried peas were once used extensively in an analogous way, but when fresh peas came to be used in cooking during the Renaissance—probably for the first time in Europe—they changed the function of that vegetable in the *cucina* as a whole. The great diversity in approach to this basic combination yields an opportunity to see at a glance the regional variety in Italian cooking. We see this diversity also in other chapters showing combinations of pasta with various categories of ingredients.

Important Note: Apparently, methods of drying beans have changed in the past decade. I have noticed from my own experience that cooking times seem to be drastically shorter, though even now these times vary considerably. Do not be surprised

* Beans, lentils, and chick-peas are all legumes.

if my suggested cooking times are shorter than in earlier books by myself or others. Of course, variation still depends on the source of the beans and the time of year they are used, since beans picked in early Autumn continue to dry through the year. For all these reasons, it is best to test the beans from time to time during cooking to be sure the suggested time is correct for that particular batch. Also, bear in mind that Italians like beans a little firm, even a bit al dente.

If you wish to speed up the soaking process, a tablespoon of flour added to the water introduces some fermentation, which hastens the softening a bit.

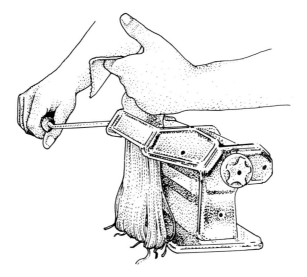

FROM CALABRIA

SERVES 8 TO 10

MACCO DI FAVE

FAVA BEAN SOUP WITH *MACCHERONI*

1 pound dried fava beans
Coarse-grained salt
1 very large ripe, fresh
    tomato; or 4 ounces
    canned tomatoes,
    preferably imported
    Italian, drained and
    seeded
2½ quarts cold water
2 medium-sized red
    onions, peeled and thinly
    sliced
1 pound dried *spaghetti*,
    preferably imported
    Italian
¼ cup olive oil
Salt and freshly ground
    black pepper to taste

TO COOK THE PASTA:
Coarse-grained salt

TO SERVE:
6 to 8 tablespoons freshly
    grated pecorino romano
    cheese (optional)

Macco, or purée of dried or fresh fava beans, survives in different regions: Pescia in Tuscany, in Apulia, in Raffadali in Sicily with homemade **pasta di casa,** *onions, cabbage, and ground pork (it is sometimes made with lentil rather than fava purée); and in Sardinia, where it is even more elaborate than in Sicily. But it is Calabria that is the center of this ancient dish, where it appears in the classically simple version that follows.*

Fava beans **(Vicia faba l.)** *are now considered to have originated in the Middle Eastern Mediterranean. The bean was domesticated about 5000 B.C. From Mesopotamia, it traveled across the northern coast of the Mediterranean as far as Italy and Provence. Interestingly, from Egypt, it crossed North Africa and went from there to Spain. This route from Africa to Spain was established millennia before the Arab conquests, and many foodstuffs thought by some to have been introduced by the Arabs in fact reached Europe by the time of the Roman Empire. Fava beans reached India from the West, one of a group of important foods that went from West to East.*

Dried fava beans are available year-round. They have tough outer skins that must be peeled off after soaking. Fresh fava beans —called **baccelli** *when still in the pod, small and tender—are eaten raw, with their skins, dipped in salt or with pecorino cheese. The vernacular phrase,* **"cacio e baccelli"** *(cheese and fresh fava beans), is used to mean "perfectly matched."*

Soak the dried beans in cold water overnight. The next morning, rinse the beans very well and remove the skins, placing the peeled beans in a bowl of fresh cold water. Let beans soak while you blanch the fresh tomato in salted boiling water, then peel and seed it. Drain the beans and rinse many times under cold running water. Place the beans in a medium-sized stockpot, add the 2½ quarts cold water, then add the fresh or canned tomatoes. Add the onions to the stockpot along with coarse salt to taste. Place the stockpot over medium heat; when the water reaches a boil, cover and simmer for 1 hour.

When the beans are almost done (they should be almost dissolved), bring a large quantity of cold water to a boil, add coarse salt to taste, and then add the *spaghetti*, broken in thirds. Cook the pasta for 8 to 11 minutes depending on the brand; that is, 1 minute less than for normal al dente. Drain the pasta and add it to the simmering soup along with the oil. Let cook for 1 minute more, then taste for salt and pepper. Let the soup rest off the heat for a few minutes before serving. If using cheese, sprinkle a little on each portion.

VARIATIONS
1. Add 1 tablespoon of sugar to the water when boiling the fava beans.
2. Purée the contents of the stockpot before adding the pasta.

MINESTRONE CON FAVE
MINESTRONE WITH FAVA BEANS

*Minestrone con fave is on the border between a **pasta e fagioli** dish and a **minestrone**. It contains only Swiss chard in addition to its two main ingredients. A **minestrone** is a soup of vegetables and beans, usually with pasta, sometimes with rice, and occasionally without either. Most **minestroni** contain both beans and pasta, but they are not its main ingredients. Vegetables are the primary feature and so, with this one exception, I have not included this large category of recipes in the book. This soup is really a simpler version of the very elaborate **macco** of Sardinia called **favata**, which contains fresh meat from several parts of the pig, cut into strips and pieces, as well as ground and cured pork. Sausages, **pancetta**, and **guancia** (cheek) are among the possibilities. Like the Sicilian **macco**, this dish has cabbage and onions along with the fava purée. Instead of pasta, Sardinian bread, **carta di musica** (music paper), is used.*

1 pound dried fava beans
6 ounces very fatty *prosciutto or pancetta,* in 1 piece
3 tablespoons olive oil
12 ounces Swiss chard, large stems removed
15 large sprigs Italian parsley, leaves only
1 medium-sized red onion, peeled
3 quarts plus 1 cup cold water
5 ripe, large, fresh tomatoes; peeled and seeded; or 7 canned tomatoes, seeded
Salt and freshly ground black pepper
½ pound dried short tubular pasta, preferably imported Italian

Soak the fava beans in cold water overnight. The next morning, drain and peel them; rinse the beans in cold water and drain again. Cut the *prosciutto* or *pancetta* into small pieces and put in a large stockpot. Add the oil and place the stockpot over low heat; sauté for 5 minutes. Coarsely chop the chard and parsley together on a board. Thinly slice the onion. Add the chopped ingredients and onion to the pot, mix well, and put in the cold water, tomatoes and beans. When the soup reaches a boil, simmer, uncovered, for 1 hour, mixing with a wooden spoon every so often.

Season soup with salt and pepper to taste, then add the pasta, stir well, and cook for 9 to 12 minutes depending on the brand or until al dente. Taste for salt and pepper, remove from stove, and let rest for 10 minutes before serving.

FROM APULIA

SERVES 6 TO 8

FOR THE LENTILS:
1½ cups dried lentils
2½ quarts cold water
5 tablespoons olive oil
½ teaspoon hot red pepper
   flakes
Salt and freshly ground
   black pepper

FOR THE PASTA:
1 pound dried *orecchiette*
        or
2 cups unbleached all-
   purpose flour
1 cup semolina flour
1 cup cold water
Pinch of salt

TO COOK THE PASTA:
Coarse-grained salt

TO SERVE:
6 to 8 teaspoons olive oil

PASTA E LENTICCHIE

PASTA WITH LENTILS

*Lentils (**Lens culinaris** or **esculenta**) have been found at archeological sites 7,000 years old, in the Middle East. In the Old Testament, Esau sold his birthright to Jacob for a plate of lentils. The symbolism is that the lentils were worth only a pittance, because they were so common.*

Lentils usually develop two to a pod. To my knowledge, they have always been eaten dried. Their convex shape has caused the words "lens" to be applied to eyeglasses. Puréed lentils are a staple of the Middle Eastern diet, especially in India. Lentils are rarely puréed in Italy today. But centuries ago the purées were more common in Italy also, and do still survive in a few dishes such as this one. Generally speaking, however, an enormous number of lentil dishes were developed in Italy during the Second World War to substitute for many foodstuffs that were impossible to obtain. I recall as a child eating not only lentil soups and sauces but even lentil bread, main dishes, and desserts in which sugar beets provided the sweetener. Toasted lentils were even used in place of coffee. It has taken Italians decades to be able to face lentils again.

Nothing could be simpler than this dish containing just pasta and lentils, flavored with only a little olive oil and hot pepper—a holding to basics which is typical of Apulia.

Soak the lentils in a bowl of cold water for 1 hour. Discard the lentils floating on top, then drain and rinse the rest. Put the lentils with the 2½ quarts cold water in a flameproof casserole over medium heat. Cover the casserole and when the water reaches a boil, simmer until the lentils are soft but still whole, about 45 minutes. Drain, saving the cooking water.

If using fresh pasta, prepare it with the ingredients and quantities listed, following the directions on page 14. Shape into *orecchiette* following the accompanying illustrations. Let rest on cotton dish towels until ready to use.

Pass the lentils through a food mill, using the disc with the smallest holes, into a medium-sized bowl. Bring the casserole with the cooking water back to a boil. Meanwhile, heat the oil in a large skillet over medium heat, and when the oil is warm, add the lentil purée, then the pepper flakes and salt and pepper to taste. Sauté for 5 minutes, stirring very well to be sure that the lentils do not stick to the pan. When the cooking water reaches a boil, add coarse salt to taste, then add the pasta. Cook the dried pasta for 9 to 12 minutes depending on the brand, or fresh pasta for 5 to 10 minutes depending on dryness. Drain the pasta and add to the skillet with

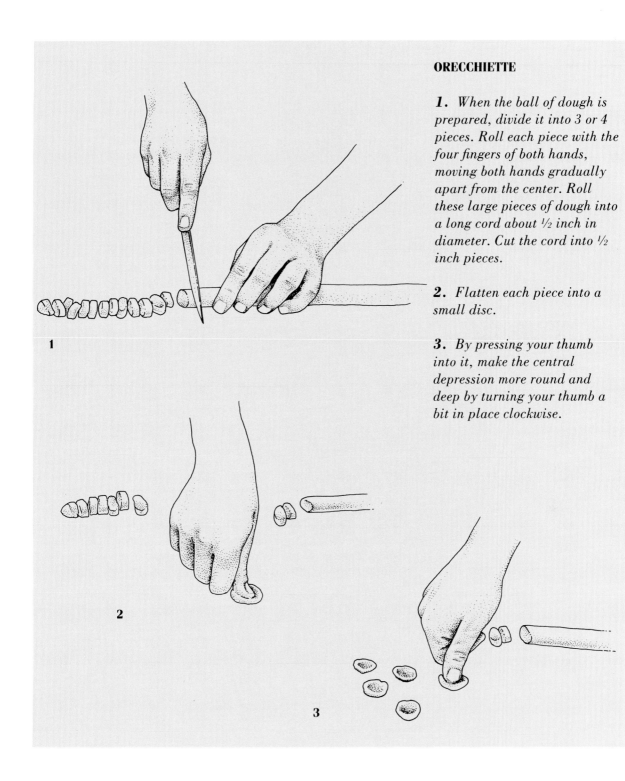

ORECCHIETTE

1. *When the ball of dough is prepared, divide it into 3 or 4 pieces. Roll each piece with the four fingers of both hands, moving both hands gradually apart from the center. Roll these large pieces of dough into a long cord about ½ inch in diameter. Cut the cord into ½ inch pieces.*

2. *Flatten each piece into a small disc.*

3. *By pressing your thumb into it, make the central depression more round and deep by turning your thumb a bit in place clockwise.*

the puréed lentils, mix very well, and sautée for 30 seconds more to distribute the pasta and lentils evenly. Serve, adding 1 teaspoon of oil to each portion.

PASTA E CECI ALLA ROMANA

PASTA WITH CHICK-PEAS, ROMAN STYLE

FOR THE CHICK-PEAS:
2 cups dried chick-peas
2½ quarts cold water
**1 medium-sized sprig fresh
 rosemary; or 1 heaping
 tablespoon rosemary
 leaves, tied into a small
 cheesecloth bag**
Coarse-grained salt

FOR THE SAUCE:
½ cup olive oil
**2 large cloves garlic,
 peeled but left whole**
**1 tablespoon rosemary
 leaves, fresh or
 preserved in salt**
3 tablespoons tomato paste
**Salt and freshly ground
 black pepper**

FOR THE PASTA:
**½ pound dried *tagliatelle*,
 preferably imported
 Italian**

Ceci (Cicer arietinum), or chick-peas, probably originated in southeastern Turkey, but there are no known survivors of the original, wild form of the plant. The varieties presently known likely are domesticated mutations. The Mediterranean chick-pea is larger and is white to dark yellow in color, while the type used in India and Persia is smaller and brown.

*Following are three recipes for **pasta e ceci**: from Rome, Naples, and Lecce (Apulia), all seats of ancient Greek and Roman culture. The Tuscans, famous in Italy as "bean eaters," have in addition to their many **Phaseolus vulgaris** bean dishes quite a few using chick-peas. (For one, see Recipe Appendix.)*

*This first, Roman version of pasta with chick-peas shares certain traditional ingredients of the Tuscan dish, but here the rosemary taste is much stronger, tomato paste is used instead of tomatoes, and the pasta is dried **tagliatelle** instead of the very short tubular **avemarie** or **ditalini**.*

Soak the chick-peas in cold water overnight. The next morning, drain and rinse them under cold running water. Place a medium-sized stockpot with the chick-peas, 2½ quarts cold water, and rosemary over medium heat. When the water reaches a boil, cover and cook chick-peas for 1 to 2 hours depending on their dryness; they should be cooked but still firm. Add coarse salt to taste, cover again, and simmer for 15 minutes more.

Prepare the sauce. Heat the oil with the garlic and rosemary leaves in a small saucepan over medium heat for 5 minutes. Remove 1 cup of the chick-pea broth, dissolve the tomato paste in it, and add the mixture to the pan. Season with salt and abundant black pepper, and cook over high heat for 10 minutes. Pass the sauce through a wire strainer into the stockpot, discarding the garlic and rosemary. Also remove and discard the rosemary from the broth. Add pasta and cook, simmer, uncovered, until done—about 5 minutes, depending on the brand. Taste for salt and pepper, and let the soup rest for 5 minutes off the heat before serving.

VARIATIONS
   1. The garlic for the sauce can be finely chopped instead of left whole.
   2. Cut 4 ounces of *guanciale* (cured pork cheek) or *pancetta* into small pieces and sauté it with the garlic when making the sauce.

PASTA E CECI DI MAGRO, OR LAMPI E TUONI

PASTA WITH CHICK-PEAS, NEAPOLITAN STYLE

*The Neapolitan dish—called, with the local earthy humor, **Lampi e tuoni** (lightning and thunder)—is flavored with parsley and hot red pepper. The pasta is **laganelle**, a form of **lasagnette** or narrow **lasagne** that resembles **tagliatelle** but is made without eggs. The dialect form "**lagane**"* comes from **laganum**, the Latin word for **lasagne**, another indication that pasta existed in Italy when Latin was spoken, before Marco Polo.*

Soak the chick-peas in cold water overnight. The next morning, drain the chick-peas and put them in a flameproof casserole with the 2½ quarts cold water. Set casserole over medium heat, cover, and bring to a boil.

Meanwhile, finely chop the garlic and coarsely chop the parsley on a board, then mix them together. Warm the oil in a small saucepan over medium heat, add the chopped ingredients, and sauté for 3 minutes.

When the water in the casserole reaches a boil, add the sautéed herbs, cover, and simmer until the chick-peas are cooked but still firm—from 1 to 2 hours, depending on the dryness of the beans.

Remove the casserole from the heat. Scoop out 1 cup of the cooked beans and pass them through a food mill, using the disc with the smallest holes, into a small bowl. Add some of the cooking water if necessary to help purée the beans more easily. Pour the purée back into the casserole and return to medium heat. Taste for salt and pepper, and add the red pepper flakes. When the broth returns to a boil, add the pasta and cook for 9 to 12 minutes depending on the brand. When the pasta is cooked, cover the casserole, remove from heat, and rest it for at least 15 minutes before serving.

NOTE:

Fresh *laganelle* can be made using the ingredients and quantities for *Pasta e fagioli alla monferrina* (page 39), and then cutting it into *tagliatelle*. The cooking time for fresh pasta is the same as for that recipe.

1½ cups dried chick-peas
2½ quarts cold water
3 large cloves garlic, peeled
15 large sprigs Italian parsley, leaves only
5 tablespoons olive oil
Salt and freshly ground black pepper
½ teaspoon hot red pepper flakes
½ pound dried *laganelle* or *lasagnette*

---

* *Laganelle* is, of course, a diminutive form.

**FROM LECCE
(APULIA)**

SERVES 6 TO 8

FOR THE CHICK-PEAS:
1½ cups dried chick-peas
3 quarts cold water
1 large stalk celery
1 medium-sized red onion,
   peeled and left whole
1 large carrot, scraped and
   left whole
2 large cloves garlic,
   peeled and left whole
2 bay leaves
Salt and freshly ground
   black pepper

FOR THE PASTA:
1 scant cup semolina flour
1 scant cup unbleached
   all-purpose flour
½ cup lukewarm water
Pinch of salt

TO FRY THE PASTA:
1 quart vegetable oil,
   preferably mixed corn
   and sunflower oil

FOR THE SOUP:
2 medium-sized red
   onions, peeled
6 tablespoons olive oil
Salt and freshly ground
   black pepper
½ teaspoon hot red pepper
   flakes

TO SERVE:
6 to 8 teaspoons olive oil

PASTA E CECI ALLA LECCESE

PASTA AND CHICK-PEAS, LECCE STYLE

*In Lecce, the chick-peas are cooked with vegetables and aromatic herbs. It is traditional to use fresh, short **tagliatelle,** and in another unique touch, half the pasta is fried before adding it to the **minestra.***

Soak the chick-peas in cold water overnight. The next morning, drain and rinse them under cold running water. Put the 3 quarts cold water in a large stockpot and add the chick-peas along with the celery, onion, carrot, garlic, and bay leaves. Cover the pot, place it over medium heat, and simmer until chick-peas are cooked but still firm—from 1 to 2 hours, depending on dryness. Just before they are finished, season with salt and pepper. Drain the chick-peas, saving the cooking broth and discarding the aromatic vegetables. Transfer to a crockery or glass bowl, covered.

While the chick-peas are cooking, prepare the pasta with the ingredients and quantities listed following instructions on page 14. Stretch the layer to ⅟₁₆ inch thick—on the pasta machine, take to next to last notch, following the techniques on page 16. With a knife, cut the sheet of pasta into strips about 3 inches wide, then cut each strip into ½-inch pieces. Spread out pasta on cotton dish towels and let rest until needed.

Heat the vegetable oil in a deep-fat fryer over medium heat. When the oil is hot (about 375 degrees), fry a few pieces of pasta at a time until lightly golden, about 30 seconds. Continue frying until half the pasta is cooked; leave the other half uncooked. Put the fried pasta on paper towels to drain off any excess grease.

Prepare the soup. Finely slice the onions and place them in a bowl of cold water for 15 minutes. Warm the oil in the stockpot over medium heat; drain the onions and add them to the pot. Lower the heat and sauté onions until translucent, about 15 minutes. Add salt, pepper, and the red pepper flakes, then pour in the reserved cooking broth from the chick-peas. Bring the soup to a boil. Add the chick-peas, and when the soup returns to a boil, add the unfried pasta; after 1 minute more, add the fried pasta. Cook for 1 to 3 minutes depending on the dryness of the pasta. Remove from the heat, cover the pot, and let rest 5 minutes before serving. Pour a teaspoon of olive oil on each portion just before serving.

VARIATION
Use 4 large cloves of garlic, peeled and coarsely chopped, in the soup instead of the onions.

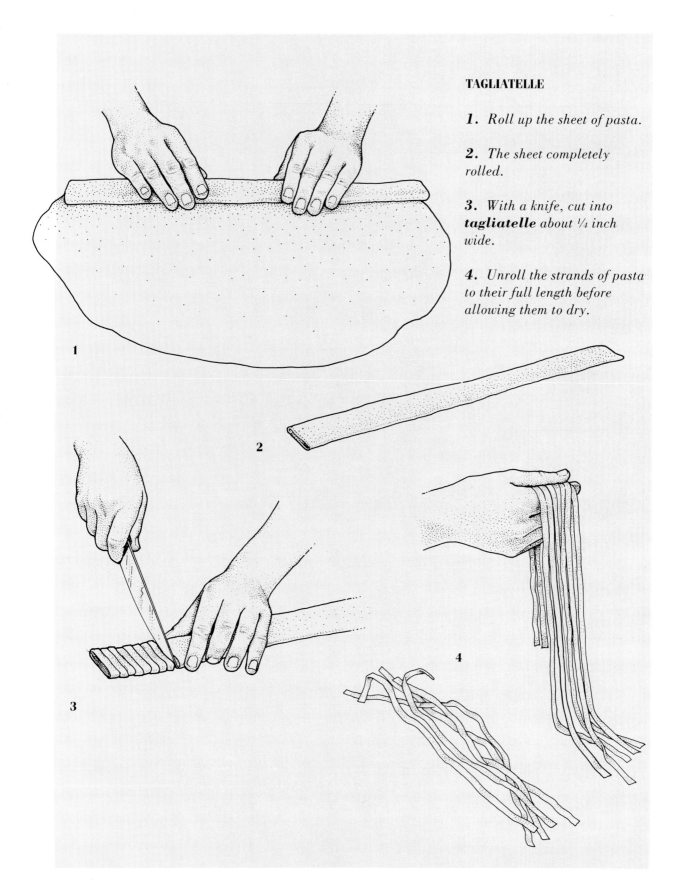

TAGLIATELLE

1. *Roll up the sheet of pasta.*

2. *The sheet completely rolled.*

3. *With a knife, cut into* **tagliatelle** *about ¼ inch wide.*

4. *Unroll the strands of pasta to their full length before allowing them to dry.*

TAGLIATELLE OR TAGLIERINI

1. *With a scalloped pastry cutter, cut the layer of pasta into pieces about 15 inches long. Let pieces rest on cotton dish towels until a thin film forms on the surface.*

2. *For* **tagliatelle,** *insert the layer of pasta into the wider cutter.*

3. *For* **taglierini,** *insert the layer of pasta into the narrower cutter.*

4. **Tagliatelle** *and* **taglierini**

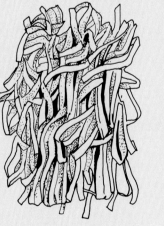

1

2

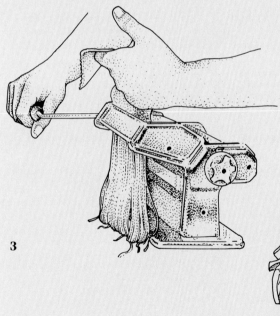

3

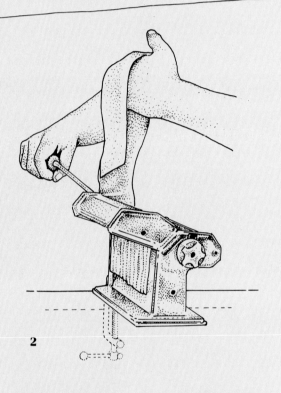

4

BEANS

With the colonization of the New World, the bean repertory of Europe expanded enormously. *Cannellini* (white kidney beans), red kidney beans, *borlotti*, navy beans, great northern beans, cranberry beans, Michigan beans, Lamon beans all belong to the species *Phaseolus vulgaris*. Spanish beans, similar to but larger and flatter than *cannellini*, are from the related *Phaseolus coccineus*. Because one does not find classifications that specify the differences among all the beans belonging to this same large category, in practical terms it is sometimes difficult to know if two beans called by different names, but which resemble one another very much, are really the same. For example, *borlotti*, Roman beans, and cranberry beans resemble one another. It seems that the first two are the same. The last is different, yet it has the same red streaks on a white-to-yellow background and turns dark red when cooked, as the other two do. When you look them up in a reference work, all simply are called *Phaseolus vulgaris*.

All this becomes a real problem when you must decide what to substitute for *borlotti* outside Italy, since even the dried ones are very difficult to obtain. (The special Venetian type of *borlotti* called Lamon are still more difficult to find, if not impossible.) Let us hope that this will change, because the particular bean adds much to the character of each local *pasta e fagioli* dish. Dried *cannellini* are exported and are widely available. It is strange that lima beans are almost never used in Italy.

PASSATO DI FAGIOLI ALLA FIORENTINA
PURÉED BEAN SOUP WITH PASTA

FOR THE BEANS:
1 pound dried *cannellini* (white kidney beans)
5 large leaves sage, fresh or preserved in salt
1 heaping teaspoon rosemary leaves, fresh or preserved in salt
2 large cloves garlic, peeled but left whole
3 tablespoons olive oil
6 cups cold water

FOR THE SAUCE:
2 medium-sized cloves garlic, peeled
6 tablespoons olive oil
2 tablespoons tomato paste
½ teaspoon hot red pepper flakes
1 teaspoon rosemary leaves, fresh or preserved in salt
Salt and freshly ground black pepper

FOR THE PASTA:
½ pound dried short tubular pasta such as *ditalini, paternostri*, or *avemarie*, preferably imported Italian

TO COOK THE PASTA:
Coarse-grained salt

TO SERVE:
Freshly ground black pepper
6 to 8 teaspoons olive oil (optional)

*This Passato di fagioli alla fiorentina differs from the Tuscan puréed bean soup in my book **The Fine Art of Italian Cooking**, in that the beans here are baked with flavorings rather than boiled before being puréed. This dish is additionally flavored with sage along with the rosemary, and with tomato paste (there are no tomatoes at all in the other version). In this Florentine version, the pasta is smaller and is cooked before being added to the soup. It's a good example of how two bean purées from the same locality can differ a great deal in flavor. It is well worth making both of them.*

Soak the beans in cold water overnight. The next morning, preheat the oven to 375 degrees. Drain the beans and place them in a medium-sized casserole, preferably terra-cotta or enamel, along with the sage, rosemary, garlic, olive oil, and cold water. Cover the casserole and bake until the beans are very soft, about 2 hours.

When the beans are ready, prepare the sauce. Coarsely chop the garlic. Place the oil in a small saucepan over medium heat; when the oil is warm, add the garlic and sauté for 2 minutes. Add the tomato paste, red pepper flakes, rosemary, and salt and pepper to taste. Meanwhile, transfer the casserole of beans from the oven to the top of the stove over medium heat. Remove cover, taste for salt and pepper, and mix well. Add the prepared sauce and simmer for 10 minutes more.

Remove as many rosemary leaves as possible from the bean mixture, then pass the contents of the casserole through a food mill, using the disc with smallest holes, into a second casserole. Place this casserole over low heat to simmer for 15 minutes more, tasting for salt and pepper.

Bring a large pot of cold water to a boil. When the water reaches a boil, add coarse salt to taste, then add the pasta and cook until al dente—for 9 to 12 minutes depending on the brand. Drain the pasta, then add it to the casserole and cook for 1 minute more before serving. (The bean purée can be prepared in advance and the pasta added at the last moment. If so, then add some broth to thin the purée, since it will thicken as it stands.)

Serve with a twist of black pepper and, if you wish, a teaspoon of olive oil over each portion.

PASTA E FAGIOLI ALLA NAPOLETANA

PASTA AND BEANS, NAPLES STYLE

*The Neapolitan pasta and beans uses **cannellini**, as does the Tuscan dish found in **The Fine Art of Italian Cooking**. Here some of the cooked beans are puréed to thicken the soup, whereas the Tuscan version uses potato to accomplish this, leaving the beans whole. Celery, parsley, and oregano replace the **prosciutto** rind and onion, and the dish is flavored with hot red pepper rather than grated cheese. (These two ingredients are usually mutually exclusive.) Both versions include some tomato. In the Neapolitan version, the pasta is precooked rather than cooked directly in the soup.*

Soak the beans in cold water overnight. The next morning, drain the beans and put them in a heavy, flameproof casserole with the 2 quarts cold water. Set casserole over medium heat. When the water reaches a boil, lower the heat, cover the casserole, and simmer until the beans are cooked but still firm—from 45 minutes to 1 hour, depending on the dryness of the beans.

Meanwhile, finely chop the garlic, red pepper flakes, celery, parsley, and oregano all together on a board. Warm the oil in a large saucepan over medium heat, add the chopped ingredients, and sauté for 5 minutes. Add the tomatoes and simmer for 20 minutes, stirring every so often with a wooden spoon and being careful to leave the tomatoes in large pieces.

When the beans are done, pour the contents of the saucepan into the casserole with the beans and simmer for 1 minute more. Remove 2 cups of the cooked beans, and with herbs but no liquid, pass them through a food mill using the disc with medium-sized holes, back into the casserole.

Bring a large quantity of cold water to a boil. Add coarse salt to taste, then add the pasta and cook until slightly firmer than normal al dente—8 to 11 minutes depending on the brand. Drain the pasta and add it to the casserole containing all the other ingredients. Taste for salt and pepper. Reheat the soup until it returns to a boil, stir very well, simmer for 30 seconds more, then cover the pot and remove it from the heat. Let the soup rest, covered, for at least 30 minutes before serving.

NOTE:
The soup is even better if prepared one day in advance and reheated at the last moment before serving.

2 cups dried *cannellini* (white kidney beans)
2 quarts cold water
3 medium-sized cloves garlic, peeled
½ teaspoon hot red pepper flakes
1 large stalk celery
10 sprigs Italian parsley, leaves only
½ teaspoon dried oregano
¼ cup olive oil
5 medium-sized ripe, fresh tomatoes, peeled and seeded; or 7 canned whole tomatoes, preferably imported Italian, seeded
½ pound dried *rigatoni* or another tubular pasta, preferably imported Italian
Salt and freshly ground black pepper

TO COOK THE PASTA:
Coarse-grained salt

**FROM BOLOGNA
(EMILIA-
ROMAGNA)**

SERVES 6 TO 8

1½ cups dried *borlotti* or
   cranberry beans
2 quarts cold water
4 ounces unsmoked pork
   rind or *prosciutto*, in
   one piece
8 large sage leaves, fresh
   or preserved in salt
2 large cloves garlic,
   peeled
10 sprigs Italian parsley,
   leaves only
1 medium-sized red onion,
   peeled
6 tablespoons olive oil
Salt and freshly ground
   black pepper
6 ounces any dried short
   tubular pasta about 1
   inch long and ¼ to ½
   inch wide, such as *mezze
   maniche*, *mezze penne*,
   paternostri, *ditaloni*

TO SERVE:
6 to 8 heaping tablespoons
   freshly grated
   Parmigiano cheese

PASTA E FAGIOLI ALLA BOLOGNESE
PASTA WITH *BORLOTTI* BEANS, BOLOGNA STYLE

The Bologna and the Monferrato (Piedmont) version that follows employ **borlotti** *beans (from the Milanese dialect word* **borlot**), *which are light in color and streaked with red. They are also called Roman beans, and are sometimes available fresh in some localities. Cranberry beans, fresh or dried, are most available in some places and can be substituted; though not identical in taste, they are close.*

Neither of these northern versions include tomatoes. It is possible that tomatoes are added to some versions in small amounts to add color, though **borlotti** *beans emit their own dark red coloring to the soup. The Bologna version of pasta and beans, though made with different beans, does share some ingredients with the earlier Tuscany recipe—pork rind, onions with the garlic—but the sage and parsley are added. Like the Tuscan version, the beans are not puréed; the soup is not even thickened with potato.*

Soak the beans in cold water overnight. The next morning, rinse and drain the beans then place them in a medium-sized heavy casserole with the 2 quarts of cold water over medium heat. Meanwhile, cut the pork rind or *prosciutto* into cubes smaller than ½ inch. When the water reaches a boil, add the pork cubes and cover the casserole. Simmer until the beans are cooked but still quite firm—for 45 minutes to 1 hour, depending on the dryness of the beans.

Finely chop the sage, garlic, parsley, and onion all together on a board. Warm the oil in a small saucepan and add the chopped ingredients; sauté for 5 minutes.

When the beans are done, drain them over a large pot, then set the beans aside. Place the pot over medium heat, and when the cooking water reaches a boil, add the sautéed vegetables; simmer for 15 minutes, then taste for salt and pepper. Add the pasta and cook until al dente—for 9 to 12 minutes, depending on the brand. Five minutes before the pasta is cooked, add the beans to pot and stir very well. When the pasta is ready, cover the casserole and let the soup rest for 15 minutes before serving. Serve, sprinkling Parmigiano over each serving.

PASTA E FAGIOLI ALLA MONFERRINA

PASTA WITH BEANS, MONFERRATO STYLE

FROM PIEDMONT

SERVES 6 TO 8

*This very interesting Monferrato pasta and bean soup includes smoked **pancetta,** an ingredient usually restricted to the far north of Italy. A small amount of beans is puréed with the potato and basil, and added to the parsley, sage, and celery. Most pasta and beans soups employ dried pasta, but this is one of the few in which fresh pasta is preferred, though dried may be used in a pinch.*

Soak the beans in cold water overnight. The next day, if you are using fresh pasta, prepare the dough with the ingredients and quantities listed, following the directions on page 14, then stretch layer to slightly less than 1/16 inch thick—next to the last notch on most machines. Cut into *tagliatelle* (see page 33) and let rest on a floured cotton dish towel until needed.

Finely chop the bacon, basil, parsley, sage, garlic, onion, and celery all together on a board. Peel the potatoes and put them in a bowl of cold water. Place a medium-sized flameproof casserole with the butter and oil on medium heat, and when the butter is melted, add the chopped ingredients; sauté for 5 minutes. Bring 2 quarts cold water to a boil in a large pot. Drain and rinse the beans, and add them to casserole along with the boiling water and the sautéed ingredients. Cut the potatoes in half and add to casserole. Simmer, covered, for 45 minutes to 1 hour depending on the dryness of the beans; the beans should be cooked but still firm.

Remove the casserole from the heat. Pass the potatoes and 1 cup of the beans through a food mill, using the disc with medium-sized holes, into a bowl, then add to casserole. Return the casserole to medium heat, taste for salt and pepper, and stir very well. When the soup returns to a boil, add the pasta. Cook the fresh pasta for 30 to 45 seconds depending on dryness; if using dried pasta, cook 9 to 12 minutes depending on the brand. When the pasta is cooked, remove the casserole from heat, cover, and let rest for 15 minutes before serving. This pasta with beans is also very good eaten at room temperature after a few hours or reheated the next day.

1½ cups dried *borlotti* or cranberry beans

FOR THE PASTA:
1½ cups unbleached all-purpose flour
½ cup lukewarm water
Pinch of salt
or
½ pound dried egg *tagliatelle*

FOR THE SOUP:
2 ounces bacon, or smoked *pancetta*
4 large basil leaves, fresh or preserved in salt
10 large sprigs Italian parsley, leaves only
4 large sage leaves, fresh or preserved in salt
1 large clove garlic, peeled
1 medium-sized red onion, peeled
1 large celery stalk
2 medium-sized potatoes (not new potatoes), about 12 ounces
2 tablespoon (1 ounce) sweet butter
4 tablespoons olive oil
2 quarts cold water
Salt and freshly ground black pepper

FROM VICENZA
(VENETO)

SERVES 8

FOR THE SOUP:
½ pound dried *borlotti*
  (Roman beans) or
  cranberry beans
  (substitutes for Lamon
  beans)
2½ quarts cold water
1 large potato (not new
  potato), about ½ pound
4 ounces *pancetta*
3 medium celery stalks
2 large cloves garlic,
  peeled
5 large leaves sage, fresh
  or preserved in salt
15 large sprigs Italian
  parsley, leaves only
1 large yellow onion,
  peeled
4 ounces ripe, fresh
  tomatoes; or 4 ounces
  canned tomatoes,
  preferably imported
  Italian, drained
Salt and freshly ground
  black pepper

FOR THE PASTA:
1½ cups unbleached all-
  purpose flour
2 extra-large eggs
Pinch of salt

TO SERVE:
8 teaspoons olive oil

PASTA E FAGIOLI ALLA VICENTINA
PASTA AND BEANS, VICENZA VERSION

*The Veneto is particularly celebrated for its pasta and bean dishes;
and Venice, Padua, and other cities in the region each have famous
versions, but older printed sources point to Vicenza as the origin for
the Veneto type. A special kind of **borlotti** from the locality of
Lamon is the pride of the bean lovers of this area, who feel it is best
of all beans. Veneto pasta and beans dishes usually employ fresh
pasta.*

Soak the beans in cold water overnight. The next morning, put the
2½ quarts cold water in a medium-sized flameproof casserole,
drain the beans, and add them to the casserole. Peel the potato
and put it whole into the casserole. Cut the *pancetta* into tiny
pieces, and finely chop the celery, garlic, sage, parsley, and onion
all together on a board. If using fresh tomatoes, cut them into
pieces. Pass fresh or canned tomatoes through a food mill, using
the disc with smallest holes, and add them, together with the
chopped ingredients, to the casserole. Cover the casserole and
place it over medium heat; let mixture simmer until beans are
cooked but still firm, about 1 hour.

Prepare the pasta with the ingredients and quantities listed,
following the directions on page 14. Stretch layer to ¹⁄₁₆ inch thick
—on the pasta machine, take to next to last notch—then cut into
short *tagliatelle* (see page 33), about 4 inches long. Let pasta rest
on a cotton dish towel until needed.

Season beans to taste with salt and pepper. Take out the potato
and ¾ cup beans, and pass them together through a food mill,
using the disc with smallest holes, into a bowl. Return the purée to
the casserole, still over medium heat. Mix well and taste for salt
and pepper.

Add the pasta to the casserole and cook for 2 to 4 minutes
depending on dryness. Let the soup rest for 5 minutes before serving, then pour a teaspoon of oil over each portion.

VARIATIONS
1. A pinch of ground cinnamon can be added to the casserole.
For a thicker soup, dissolve 2 tablespoons of flour in a cup of broth
and add it to the casserole.

2. 20 sprigs of Italian parsley can be chopped together with 2
medium-sized cloves garlic, and the resultant *buttuto* sprinkled
over the soup when it is finished cooking.

3. Freshly grated Parmigiano cheese can be sprinkled over each serving. All but ½ cup of the beans can be puréed along with the potato to make a thicker soup.

PASTA E FAGIOLI CON L'OCCHIO
PASTA WITH BLACK-EYED PEAS

A literal translation of **fagioli con l'occhio** *is "beans with the eye," quite similar to our black-eyed peas,* which are native to Central Africa and have found their way to both Europe and America. They are particularly appreciated in "bean-eating'" Tuscany as well as the southern United States. In this Tuscan dish, black-eyed peas are flavored with* **pancetta,** *rosemary, and a little tomato (no garlic or onion), and 1 cup of the beans are puréed to thicken the soup.*

Soak the peas in cold water overnight. The next morning drain and rinse them. Put the peas in a flameproof casserole with the 2 quarts cold water and place over medium heat, cover, and simmer until they are cooked but still very firm, 45 minutes to 1 hour depending on the dryness of the beans.

Meanwhile, cut the *pancetta* or *prosciutto* into small pieces on a board. Warm the oil in a small saucepan over low heat; add the rosemary leaves and sauté for 5 minutes. If using fresh tomatoes, cut them into 1-inch pieces. Pass fresh or canned tomatoes through a food mill, using the disc with the smallest holes, into a small bowl.

Use a slotted spoon to remove the rosemary from the oil, and discard it. Immediately add the *pancetta* to the oil and sauté for 3 minutes. Add the tomatoes, lower the heat, and simmer for 10 minutes. Season with salt and pepper.

While the beans are still simmering, add the tomato sauce and simmer for 1 minute more. Remove the casserole from heat, take out 1 cup of the beans, and pass them through a food mill, using the disc with the smallest holes, into a small bowl. Put the puréed beans back into the casserole, and place it back over medium heat. Taste for salt and pepper. When the broth in the casserole returns to a boil, add the pasta and cook it in the bean broth for 9 to 12 minutes depending on the brand. Remove casserole from heat, cover, and let rest for 15 minutes before serving.

1 ½ cups dried black-eyed peas
2 quarts cold water
2 ounces *pancetta* or *prosciutto*, in one piece
2 tablespoons olive oil
1 tablespoon rosemary leaves, fresh or preserved in salt
½ pound very ripe, fresh tomatoes; or ½ pound canned tomatoes, preferably imported Italian, drained
Salt and freshly ground black pepper
½ pound dried *ditali* or any other short tubular pasta about 1 inch long and ¼ inch wide

* Technically, the plant is called cowpeas *(Vigna unguiculata)* and the seeds are called black-eyed peas.

FROM CALABRIA

SERVES 12

MILLECOSEDDE

MIXED BEANS WITH PASTA, CALABRIAN STYLE

½ cup dried lentils
½ cup dried *cannellini*
   (white kidney beans)
½ cup dried *borlotti* or
   cranberry beans
½ cup dried fava beans
½ cup dried chick-peas
½ ounce dried porcini
   mushrooms
1 pound savoy cabbage,
   cleaned
2 medium-sized red
   onions, peeled
2 medium-sized stalks
   celery
4 quarts cold water
Coarse-grained salt
4 teaspoons olive oil
1 pound dried long pasta,
   such as *spaghetti* or
   linguine, preferably
   imported Italian
Salt and freshly ground
   black pepper

TO SERVE:
12 teaspoons olive oil

We end this chapter appropriately with a **minestra** *combining five different types of legumes. A Calabrian dish, its most unusual feature aside from the mixed beans is the flavoring from dried wild mushrooms. This is among the pasta and bean dishes which also feature vegetables—here, cabbage and celery as well as the more usual onions. I consider the dish in the pasta-and-bean category rather than a* **minestrone** *because its beans are so much more central than its vegetables. Long pasta is used, broken into thirds.*

Soak the lentils, beans, and chick-peas in 5 different bowls of cold water overnight. The next morning, soak the mushrooms in a bowl of lukewarm water for 30 minutes. Rinse the beans, remove and discard the skins from the fava beans, and put all the beans in a large stockpot. Slice the cabbage into ½-inch strips, coarsely chop the onions and celery, and add the vegetables to the pot. Drain the mushrooms, making sure no sand is attached to the stems, and add them to the pot. Add the 4 quarts cold water, cover, and place the pot over medium heat. When the water reaches a boil, simmer for 1 hour.

When all the vegetables and legumes are almost cooked, add coarse salt to taste, then add the oil, mixing very well. When the soup reaches a boil again, add the pasta broken into thirds, and cook for 9 to 12 minutes depending on the brand. As the pasta cooks, stir the mixture several times to prevent it from sticking to the bottom of the pot. Taste for salt and pepper. When the pasta is cooked, even the least tender beans will be completely cooked and others will be puréed to form a quite thick *minestra*. Remove the pot from heat and let mixture rest for 10 minutes before serving. Pour 1 teaspoon of olive oil over each serving.

This *minestra* may be eaten at room temperature or prepared in advance and reheated.

RECIPE APPENDIX

Pasta-and-Beans Recipes in Other Bugialli Books

PASTA E CECI (Pasta and Chick-Peas) *FA* p. 128
PASSATO DI CECI CON TAGLIERINI (*Taglierini* in Chick-Pea Soup) *CT* p.138
PASTA E FAGIOLI (Pasta and Bean Soup) *FA*, p. 127
CAVATELLI CON FAGIOLI (Pasta and Beans Puglia Style) *FI* p. 94
PASSATO DI FAGIOLI (Tuscan Puréed Bean Soup) *FA* p. 119

FA   *The Fine Art of Italian Cooking*
CT   *Giuliano Bugialli's Classic Techniques of Italian Cooking*
FI   *Giuliano Bugialli's Foods of Italy*

Pasta aglio
e olio

PASTA AND VEGETABLES

If I may reveal my own most personal taste, I would say that a dish made with pasta and vegetables is the most satisfying thing I can eat. It is just the right combination of taste, texture, nourishment, and lightness. I feel completely satisfied afterward, and any dishes that might follow are simply an embellishment.

Strangely, this feeling does not come out of my own Tuscan background, although such dishes do exist there; it was the rich contribution of southern Italy that opened my eyes to the wide repertory of these combinations. And what a joy to be able to make, for example, artichokes with pasta in four or five different ways, each reflecting its own region and yielding a completely new flavor.

Let us begin with that incomparable ingredient, garlic.

PASTA AGLIO E OLIO

PASTA WITH GARLIC AND OIL

FROM ALL OVER
ITALY

SERVES 4 TO 6

The most basic dressing for pasta is that of olive oil with garlic.
Aglio e olio *is the simplest of vegetable or herb dressings for pasta,
and it is still the most used, in many small variations, all over
Italy. It seems reasonable to regard it as possibly the oldest of all
dressings. We can see that many other dressings evolved from it.
The addition of parsley, basil, rosemary, oregano, mint, black pepper, and hot red pepper flakes all contribute to manifold small
variations on the theme. I cannot state strongly enough that grated
cheese is* **never** *added to any* ***aglio-olio*** *preparation.*

*Here are the fundamental recipe and six variations, including
the most classic of herbs—parsley, rosemary, and basil.*

**2 large cloves garlic,
   peeled**
**1 pound dried *spaghetti*,
   preferably imported
   Italian**
¾ cup extra-virgin olive oil
**½ teaspoon hot red pepper
   flakes**
**Salt and freshly ground
   black pepper**
**25 large sprigs Italian
   parsley, leaves only**

TO COOK THE PASTA:
Coarse-grained salt

Coarsely chop the garlic on a board. Bring a large pot of cold water
to a boil, add the coarse salt to taste, then add the pasta and cook
it until al dente, for 9 to 12 minutes depending on the brand.

Meanwhile, place a small saucepan with the oil over low heat;
when the oil is warm, add the chopped garlic and sauté for 2 minutes. Add the red pepper flakes and salt and black pepper to taste,
and sauté until garlic is lightly golden, about 2 minutes. Coarsely
chop the parsley on a board.

When the pasta is ready, drain and transfer it to a large,
warmed serving dish; pour the oil with the garlic over, toss very
well, add the parsley, and serve immediately.

VARIATIONS

1. Garlic can be chopped and sautéed, but removed before
the oil is added to pasta.

2. Garlic can be left whole, sautéed, then removed or left in
the serving dish.

3. Rather than sautéing the garlic, it can be grated raw over
the pasta already tossed with oil, salt, pepper, and red pepper
flakes in the serving dish.

4. Parsley can be left out.

5. Garlic can be left whole, sautéed with 1 heaping tablespoon
of rosemary leaves, fresh or preserved in salt. Discard garlic and
rosemary and toss with the oil.

6. Ten large leaves of fresh basil, torn into thirds, can be
added to either of the first 2 variations.

**24 large cloves garlic,
   peeled but left whole**
**24 large fresh basil leaves,
   left whole**
**1 pound dried *spaghetti*,
   preferably imported
   Italian**
¾ cup extra-virgin olive oil
**½ teaspoon hot red pepper
   flakes**
**Salt and freshly ground
   black pepper**

TO COOK THE PASTA:
Coarse-grained salt

PASTA AGLIO OLIO E BASILICO
PASTA WITH UNCOOKED GARLIC AND BASIL

We have seen the addition of fresh, uncooked basil in two variations of the fundamental recipe. There are in addition two special treatments with basil that deserve to be regarded as separate recipes.

*A wonderful treatment that always evokes a tremendous response from my guests is the use of a very large amount of both garlic and basil, both uncooked and mixed with the oil and pasta. The fresh flavors suffuse the oil in a remarkably light way. This treatment is related to the Tuscan method of preparing **Pasta alla puttanesca**, in which uncooked tomatoes are also added with the garlic and basil. But as with **Maccheroni alla marinara** (page 101), the tomatoes were likely added to a previous **aglio e olio** recipe.*

Wash and dry the garlic and basil, place on a large serving platter, and set aside until needed.

Bring a large pot of cold water to a boil, add coarse salt to taste, then add the pasta and cook until al dente, for 9 to 12 minutes depending on the brand. Meanwhile, place a small saucepan with the oil over low heat; when the oil is warm, add the red pepper flakes and salt and pepper to taste, then let the oil become very hot. When the pasta is ready, drain and transfer it to the prepared serving platter, placing it over the uncooked garlic and basil. Pour the still-hot oil over, toss very well, and serve immediately.

Drawing of a potted basil plant from Mattioli's famous book on botany, one of the first such printed books Siena 1536. (From original edition, collection Giuliano Bugialli.)

HERBS

Three recipes here are dominated by the flavor of a single herb or a combination of them. *Rigatoni al basilico* stresses sautéed whole basil leaves. Such leaves are most often eaten uncooked or used to flavor tomatoes, thus the flavor of the sautéed leaves used in this dish is really unique.

A sauce that does use the basil in the normal way is the beloved *Pesto alla genovese*. (See Recipe Appendix for other versions of this sauce.) However, *pesto* does not refer only to the sauces made with basil, but really applies to any combination of herbs ground with a mortar and pestle, in Liguria and elsewhere. Even in Liguria there are other pestos, such as this favorite made with mint leaves. (See also the Sicilian pesto based on uncooked tomatoes and basil, page 107.)

SERVES 4 TO 6

¾ **cup olive oil**
2 medium-sized cloves
   garlic, peeled
40 large fresh basil leaves,
   left whole
Salt and freshly ground
   black pepper
1 pound dried *rigatoni*,
   preferably imported
   Italian

TO COOK THE PASTA:
Coarse-grained salt

RIGATONI AL BASILICO

RIGATONI WITH SAUTÉED BASIL

Here we shift the emphasis from the garlic to the basil, so that we really have a basil sauce flavored with garlic. This shift of emphasis is accomplished by sautéing the basil, thereby emphasizing its flavor, and also by reducing the amount of garlic.

*In the early nineteenth century, when ripe, red tomatoes exploded on the southern Italian scene, they were added to the fundamental **aglio e olio** to form the so-called **marinara** preparation, which in its classic form does not necessarily have to do with fish or seafood. See the discussion of its real meaning in the introduction to **Maccheroni alla marinara** (page 101).*

Place the oil in a large skillet over low heat. Meanwhile, coarsely chop the garlic and place the basil leaves in a bowl of cold water. Bring a large pot of cold water to a boil.

When the oil is warm, add the chopped garlic and sauté for 2 minutes, then drain the basil and add it to the skillet. Season with salt and abundant pepper, and sauté for 15 minutes more over very low heat.

When the water reaches a boil, add coarse salt to taste, then add the pasta and cook it for 8 to 11 minutes according to the brand; that is, 1 minute less than for normal al dente. Drain pasta, add it to the skillet, raise the heat to medium, and sauté, continuously mixing with a wooden spoon, for another minute. Taste for salt and pepper, stir again, and remove from heat. Transfer pasta to a warmed serving dish and serve immediately.

TAGLIATELLE VERDI ALLA MENTA

GREEN *TAGLIATELLE* WITH MINT PESTO

Perhaps it is not generally known abroad how much fresh mint is used in Italy. The mint flavor here is combined with small amounts of parsley and basil, and is accentuated by the butter, cream, and Parmigiano, in lieu of the creamy local ricotta **prescinsus,** *while the more usual garlic and nuts are omitted.*

If fresh pasta is to be used, prepare it with the ingredients and quantities listed, following the directions on page 14. Stretch layer to a little more than 1/16 inch—on the pasta machine, take to next to last notch. Cut into *tagliatelle*, see page 33. Let the pasta rest on a cotton dish towel until needed.

Prepare the pesto. Place the parsley, basil, mint, and coarse salt in a stone mortar and use a marble pestle to coarsely grind all the ingredients together. Transfer the mixture to a crockery or glass bowl, then add the butter, cream, and Parmigiano; mix very well with a wooden spoon and season with salt and pepper. Place the bowl, covered, in the refrigerator until needed.

Bring a large pot of cold water to a boil, add coarse salt to taste, then add the fresh pasta and cook for 30 seconds to 1 minute depending on dryness; if dried pasta is used, cook it until al dente 9 to 12 minutes depending on the brand. Drain and transfer the pasta to a large, warmed serving platter, toss it with the butter, then pour the prepared sauce over, toss again, and sprinkle with the mint leaves. Serve immediately.

FOR THE PASTA:
3 1/2 cups unbleached all-purpose flour
3 extra-large eggs
2 heaping tablespoons cooked, drained, and finely chopped spinach
Pinch of salt
or
1 pound dried green *tagliatelle*, preferably imported Italian

FOR THE MINT PESTO:
15 large sprigs Italian parsley, leaves only
5 large fresh basil leaves
15 large fresh mint leaves
1 teaspoon coarse-grained salt
5 tablespoons (2 1/2 ounces) sweet butter, at room temperature
1 1/2 cups heavy cream
1/4 cup freshly grated Parmigiano cheese
Salt and freshly ground black pepper

TO COOK THE PASTA:
Coarse-grained salt

TO SERVE:
4 tablespoons (2 ounces) sweet butter, cut into pieces
15 large fresh mint leaves

FROM TUSCANY

SERVES 8 TO 10

NASTRI ALLA BORRACCINA

RIBBONS OF PASTA WITH SIX-HERB SAUCE

FOR THE SAUCE:
2 medium-sized cloves
    garlic, peeled
2 tablespoons rosemary
    leaves, fresh or
    preserved in salt; or 2
    tablespoons rosemary
    leaves, dried and
    blanched
10 large sage leaves, fresh
    or preserved in salt
10 large fresh mint leaves
1 teaspoon dried
    marjoram
2 cups dry white wine
4 bay leaves
Coarse-grained salt
2 pounds fresh spinach,
    leaves only, carefully
    washed
½ cup olive oil
10 tablespoons (5 ounces)
    sweet butter
Salt and freshly ground
    black pepper
2 cups beef broth,
    preferably homemade

FOR THE PASTA:
4 cups unbleached all-
    purpose flour
4 extra-large eggs
4 teaspoons vegetable or
    olive oil
Pinch of salt

TO COOK THE PASTA:
Coarse-grained salt

Borraccina sauce is a "moss" made by chopping many herbs extremely fine so they emit an incredible fresh perfume, like the woods after a rain. Body is added to this delicate Tuscan sauce by including some cooked spinach. *Borraccina* sauce should be used with fresh pasta only.

Prepare the sauce. Finely chop the garlic, rosemary, sage, mint, and marjoram on a board. Place the chopped ingredients in a crockery or glass bowl, then add the wine along with the bay leaves. Let the ingredients marinate for 2 hours.

Prepare the pasta with the ingredients and quantities listed, following the instructions on page 14. Stretch layer to ¹⁄₁₆ inch thick —on the pasta machine, take to next to last notch, then with a scalloped pastry wheel, cut the layers of dough into strips 4 inches long and 1 inch wide (see illustration page 230). Let the pasta rest on a dry cotton dish towel until needed.

Bring a large quantity of cold water to a boil, add coarse salt to taste, then add the spinach and cook for 10 minutes. Drain the spinach until cool under cold running water, squeeze dry, and finely chop on a board.

Place a heavy saucepan with the oil and 6 tablespoons of the butter over medium heat. When the butter is melted, add the chopped spinach and sauté for 2 minutes. Discard the bay leaves from the marinated mixture and add the remaining contents of the bowl to the pan. Cook for 20 minutes, stirring and mixing all ingredients together. Taste for salt and peppper.

Heat the broth in a small saucepan, and when it is hot, add it to the pan with the herb sauce; reduce it over medium heat for 25 minutes.

Bring a large quantity of cold water to a boil, add coarse salt to taste, then add the pasta and cook for 30 seconds to 1 minute depending on dryness. Drain the pasta, transfer it to a warmed serving platter, and toss very well with the remaining butter. Add the sauce, mix very well, and serve immediately.

MOLLICA

Bread with the crust removed, or the inside of the bread, is called the "crumb" of the bread in English and *mollica* in Italian. It is, of course, not the same thing as bread crumbs. Both of these played an enormous role in medieval cooking and continue to be used as an ingredient in some traditional Italian dishes. Bread crumbs, or *pangrattato*, are understood to be grated bread, therefore considerably hardened. In Italy today, it is also understood that the crumbs are toasted after grating. Most of the time these crumbs remain unseasoned, to allow for greatest versatility in combination with other ingredients.

Pasta sauced with oil and bread crumbs or *mollica* is probably as old and as fundamental a combination as pasta with garlic. The simplest form of this is *Spaghetti con briciolata* (see Recipe Appendix), a combination of pasta, oil, and bread crumbs, sometimes with a little fresh parsley added at the end. The two recipes given here—a Tuscan one with bread crumbs and a Sicilian with *mollica* as a starting point—each use garlic and abundant parsley. They are therefore combinations of oil with both garlic and bread crumbs. These recipes may sound old-fashioned to you, but try them. They remain very valid.

Bread crumbs were used in medieval recipes as a thickener in place of modern grated cheese or flour, which only emerged in the fifteenth century. *Mollica* was much used in stuffings, and to a lesser degree, still is.

FROM TUSCANY

SERVES 4 TO 6

2 large cloves garlic, peeled
1 pound dried short tubular pasta such as *penne* or *penne rigate*, preferably imported Italian
¾ cup extra-virgin olive oil
3 tablespoons unseasoned bread crumbs, preferably homemade
Salt and freshly ground black pepper
25 large sprigs Italian parsley, leaves only

TO COOK THE PASTA:
Coarse-grained salt

PASTA CON PANGRATTATO
PASTA WITH GARLIC AND BREAD CRUMBS

Coarsely chop the garlic on a board. Bring a large pot of cold water to a boil, add coarse salt to taste, then add the pasta and cook until al dente, 9 to 12 minutes depending on the brand.

Meanwhile, place a small saucepan with the oil over low heat, and when the oil is warm, add the garlic and sauté for 2 minutes. Add the bread crumbs, season to taste with salt and pepper, and sauté until the bread crumbs are slightly golden, 1 minute. Coarsely chop the parsley on a board.

When the pasta is ready, drain and transfer it to a large warmed serving dish; pour the oil with the garlic and bread crumbs over, toss very well, add the parsley, and serve.

VARIATIONS

   1. The 2 cloves of garlic can be peeled and left whole, sautéed, then discarded.
   2. Parsley can be omitted.

NOTE:

The Sicilian dish *pasta cu la muddica* (in Italian, *pasta con la mollica*) is similar to this Tuscan one. However, the *mollica*, or "crumb,"—bread inside only, without crust—is baked in the oven with oil poured over it until very crisp. Then it is made into bread *crumbs*, which are sautéed in oil as in the Tuscan version. (More complicated Sicilian versions also use tomatoes and anchovies.)

The Tuscan recipe *Spaghetti con briciolata* in my book *The Fine Art of Italian Cooking* does not contain garlic. That particular bread-crumb sauce is always paired with *spaghetti*.

PASTA CACIO E PEPE
PASTA WITH GRATED CHEESE AND BLACK PEPPER

FROM ROME

SERVES 4 TO 6

1 pound dried *spaghetti* or *vermicelli*, preferably imported Italian
1 tablespoon olive oil
6 tablespoons (3 ounces) sweet butter
Salt
¾ cup freshly grated Parmigiano cheese
Freshly ground black pepper

TO COOK THE PASTA:
Coarse-grained salt

We have discussed categories of oil with garlic or with bread crumbs. The third simple category is of oil (or, in this case, butter) and abundant grated cheese or ricotta. This category always is flavored with much black pepper—enough to be mentioned in the name of the dish and to serve as the main aromatic ingredient in place of the garlic. Butter can be substituted for oil in this category because of its relation to the cheese (though not in the other two).

Bring a large pot of cold water to a boil over medium heat, and when the water reaches a boil, add the pasta and cook it for 9 to 12 minutes depending on the brand. As the pasta cooks, heat the oil in a small saucepan over low heat; when the oil is warm, add the butter and let it melt completely but do not let it brown. Season to taste with salt.

When the pasta is ready, drain it and place on a warmed serving platter. Pour over the hot oil and butter, sprinkle with Parmigiano, and toss very well. Grind abundant black pepper over, toss again, and serve immediately. More black pepper and cheese can be served at table.

VARIATIONS
1. Omit olive oil and increase butter to 7 tablespoons.
2. Use 7 tablespoons of warmed olive oil and omit the butter.
3. Mix 2 ounces of ricotta with 2 tablespoons of oil or butter and 2 tablespoons of ricotta salata. Omit the grated Parmigiano, although some may be served at table. (The selection of a very good ricotta is essential. In Italy I use sheep's milk or buffalo milk ricotta. Since these types are not widely available outside Italy, the readily available ricotta salata, often made of sheep's milk, flavors the more common cow's milk ricotta.

NOTE:
I use mostly butter in this recipe, since I prefer it in combination with cheese in this very exposed form, rather than with oil. Of course, oil is a legitimate option.

MUSHROOMS

In Italy it is assumed that "mushrooms" means wild mushrooms, of many different types, varying according to the locale. Pasta is happily combined with different kinds of fresh mushrooms when they are in season. However, dried wild ones, especially porcini, are even more commonly used, both in sauces in which they are the dominant ingredient as well as in many dishes in which they are merely a flavoring for the main ingredients.

The following two mushroom sauces, from Tuscany and Liguria respectively, are based on dried porcini; and their differing treatments give insight into the varying approaches in those regions.

FROM TUSCANY

SERVES 6

PASTA AI FUNGHI ALLA CHIANTIGIANA
PASTA WITH MUSHROOMS, CHIANTI STYLE

FOR THE SAUCE:
**2 ounces dried porcini
   mushrooms
1 medium-sized red onion,
   peeled
2 medium-sized cloves
   garlic, peeled
20 medium-sized sprigs
   Italian parsley, leaves
   only
4 tablespoons olive oil**

This Tuscan mushroom sauce employs olive oil, wine, and a touch of tomato paste, with parsley as the herb. The aromatic vegetables are simply chopped. Typically Tuscan is the dry Vinsanto from the Chianti, which when unavailable can be substituted with a dry Marsala.

Prepare the sauce. Soak the mushrooms in lukewarm water for 30 minutes. Drain the mushrooms, saving 2 cups of the soaking water, then clean them very well to remove all sand attached to the stems. Strain the mushroom water by passing it through several layers of paper towels. Finely chop the mushrooms, onion, garlic, and parsley all together on a board. Heat the oil in a medium-sized saucepan over medium heat, and when the oil is warm, add the chopped ingredients. Sauté for 15 minutes, mixing every so often with a wooden spoon. Then add the wine and let it evaporate for 5 minutes. Meanwhile, dissolve the tomato paste in the 2 cups of reserved mushroom water, and add them to pan. Cover and cook over low heat for 1 hour, mixing occasionally with a wooden spoon. Season to taste with salt and pepper, raise the heat, and reduce the sauce by half, about 10 minutes more.

If using fresh pasta, prepare it with the ingredients listed, following the directions on page 14. Stretch layer to ⅛ inch, and cut into *spaghetti*, see below. Let rest on cotton dish towels until ready to use.

Bring a large pot of cold water to a boil, add coarse salt to taste, then add the pasta. If using dried *spaghetti*, cook it for 8 to 11 minutes depending on the brand—that is, 1 minute less than normal for al dente. If using fresh *spaghetti*, cook it for 1 to 3 minutes depending on dryness. Drain and transfer pasta to a large bowl with the butter, mix well, then place in a large skillet together with the sauce and sauté over high heat for 1 minute more. Place pasta on a warmed serving dish and serve immediately.

½ cup dry Vinsanto or dry Marsala
5 tablespoons tomato paste
Salt and freshly ground black pepper

FOR THE PASTA:
1 pound dried *spaghetti*
        or
3 cups unbleached all-purpose flour
4 extra-large eggs
Pinch of salt

TO COOK THE PASTA:
Coarse-grained salt

TO SERVE:
2 tablespoons (1 ounce) sweet butter

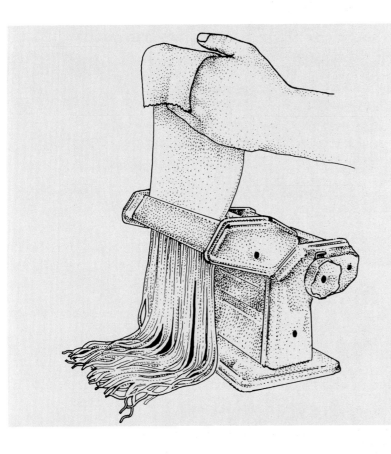

SPAGHETTI

To cut **spaghetti,** *insert the thick pasta layer into the* **taglierini** *cutter (narrower cutter)*

FROM LIGURIA

SERVES 4 TO 6

PASTA CON INTINGOLO DI FUNGHI ALLA GENOVESE
PASTA WITH MUSHROOM PESTO

FOR THE SAUCE:
- 1 ounce dried porcini mushrooms
- 1 medium-sized red onion, peeled
- 2 medium-sized cloves garlic, peeled
- 3 tablespoons pine nuts (pignolis)
- 1 tablespoon rosemary leaves, fresh or preserved in salt
- 4 tablespoons (2 ounces) sweet butter
- 8 tablespoons olive oil
- 1 pound ripe, fresh tomatoes; or 1 pound canned tomatoes, preferably imported Italian, drained
- Salt and freshly ground black pepper
- 2 anchovies in salt, or 4 anchovy fillets in oil, drained
- 1 pound flat dried pasta such as *tagliatelle* or *lasagnette*

TO COOK THE PASTA:
Coarse-grained salt

This Ligurian sauce is a real pesto in which the mushrooms, vegetables, herbs—in this case rosemary—and pignolis are ground with a mortar and pestle, combined with tomatoes, and flavored with anchovies. Butter is used with the oil, a northern touch. Especially Ligurian is the combination of rosemary with mushrooms, which is not done in central Italy.

Prepare the sauce. Soak the mushrooms in lukewarm water for 30 minutes, then drain and clean them thoroughly to remove all sand attached to the stems; discard the soaking water. Finely chop the mushrooms, onion, garlic, pine nuts, and rosemary all together on a board (or as originally done, with a mortar and pestle, or use a food processor). Place the butter and 5 tablespoons of the oil in a medium-sized flameproof casserole over medium heat. When the oil is warm but the butter not yet completely melted, add the chopped ingredients and sauté for 15 minutes, stirring every so often with a wooden spoon. Meanwhile, if using fresh tomatoes, cut them into pieces. Pass fresh or canned tomatoes through a food mill, using the disc with smallest holes, into a crockery or glass bowl. Add the tomatoes to the casserole, season to taste with salt and pepper, and simmer for 15 minutes more. Be sure to mix every so often so the mushrooms do not stick to the bottom of the casserole.

Bring a large pot of cold water to a boil, add coarse salt to taste, then add the pasta and cook it for 9 to 12 minutes depending on the brand.

While the pasta cooks, put a small saucepan with remaining oil over low heat. If using anchovies in salt, clean and fillet them under cold running water. When the oil is warm, remove pan from heat, add the anchovy fillets, and use a fork to mash them into the oil. Add this paste to the casserole, and mix well over high heat for 1 minute.

When the pasta is ready, drain and transfer it to a large bowl, pour the sauce over, and mix well again. Transfer to a large, warmed dish and serve immediately.

MINESTRONE O ZUPPA DI FUNGHI ALLA CONTADINA

TUSCAN WILD MUSHROOM *MINESTRONE* OR SOUP

*This wonderful mushroom dish made with fresh pasta is **Mine-strone o zuppa di funghi alla contadina,** though it is not a true minestrone because it has no beans. The soup is thickened instead with riced potatoes.*

Soak the mushrooms in the lukewarm water for 30 minutes. Meanwhile, bring a medium-sized pot of cold water to a boil, add coarse salt to taste, then add the potatoes and cook until very soft, for 30 to 45 minutes depending on size. Drain the mushrooms, saving the soaking water. Clean the mushrooms well, removing all the sand attached to the stems. Strain the soaking water by passing it several times through layers of paper towels.

Cut the *prosciutto* or *pancetta* into small pieces. Heat the oil in a medium-sized stockpot over low heat, and when the oil is warm, add *prosciutto* or *pancetta* and garlic, then sauté for 5 minutes. Pour in the mushroom water and enough additional cold broth to total 3 quarts liquid; bring to a boil and simmer, uncovered, for 30 minutes.

Meanwhile, peel the potatoes and pass them through a food mill, using the disc with smallest holes (rather than a potato ricer), into a small bowl. Add the mushrooms to the stockpot and simmer for another 30 minutes, tasting for salt and pepper. Add the potatoes and stir well with a wooden spoon to dissolve them completely in the broth. Put in the tomato paste and simmer for 30 minutes, tasting again for salt and pepper.

If using fresh pasta, prepare it with the ingredients and quantities listed, following the directions on page 14. Stretch layer to about 1/16 inch thick—on the pasta machine, take to next to last notch. Cut the sheets into 3-inch long pieces, using a pastry cutter, then with the machine cut them into 3-inch long *tagliatelle* (see page 33). When the broth is ready, add the pasta and cook for 1 to 3 minutes depending on dryness. With the addition of the pasta the soup is a *minestrone* without beans.

If using croutons, ladle the soup into individual bowls and place the croutons on top. When croutons are added instead of pasta, you have a *zuppa.*

FOR THE *MINESTRONE:*
1½ ounces dried porcini mushrooms
6 cups lukewarm water
Coarse-grained salt
1½ pounds potatoes (not new potatoes)
4 ounces *prosciutto* or *pancetta*, in one piece
¼ cup olive oil
3 large cloves garlic, peeled and finely chopped
About 7 cups cold chicken or beef broth, preferably homemade
Salt and freshly ground black pepper
2 tablespoons tomato paste

FOR THE PASTA:
2 cups unbleached all-purpose flour
3 extra-large eggs
Pinch of salt

FOR THE *ZUPPA:*
2 cups homemade croutons, fried or toasted

FROM UMBRIA

SERVES 4 TO 6

1 ounce black truffles,
   fresh or canned
¾ cup olive oil
1 large clove garlic, peeled
   but left whole
2 anchovies preserved in
   salt; or 4 anchovy fillets
   packed in oil, drained
Salt and freshly ground
   black pepper
1 pound dried *spaghetti*,
   preferably imported
   Italian

TO COOK THE PASTA:
Coarse-grained salt

TO SERVE:
20 large sprigs Italian
   parsley, leaves only

SPAGHETTI ALLA NURSINA
SPAGHETTI WITH BLACK TRUFFLES

Umbria is the home of Italian black truffles, and Norcia is the center. While white truffles are characteristically used raw, the black ones are most often cooked for a long time in order to bring out their nutty flavor, as in various galantines. However, when black truffles are combined with anchovies, which strongly heighten their flavor, it is not necessary to have such a long cooking time.

If working with fresh truffles, use a small brush to clean them very well. Finely chop the truffles on a board. Place a small saucepan with the oil over low heat. When the oil is warm, add the garlic and sauté until golden brown, about 5 minutes. Meanwhile, bring a large pot of cold water to a boil.

If anchovies in salt are used, clean them under cold running water, removing bones and excess salt. When the garlic is done, discard it, remove the saucepan from the heat, and add the anchovy fillets to the hot oil, using a fork to mash them into the oil. Add the chopped truffles and mix very well. Taste for salt and pepper.

When the water reaches a boil, add coarse salt to taste, then add the pasta and cook until al dente, for 9 to 12 minutes depending on the brand. As the pasta cooks, coarsely chop the parsley on a board. Just 1 minute before the pasta is ready, put the pan with the sauce over medium heat. Drain the pasta; transfer to a large, warmed serving platter, pour the sauce over, and toss very well. Sprinkle the parsley all over and serve immediately.

ORECCHIETTE CON RUCHETTA E PATATE
PASTA WITH ARUGULA AND POTATOES

FROM APULIA

SERVES 6

Here is the first of two recipes in this book in which the arugula is cooked. The other, on page 276, is the Apulian **Cavatieddi con la rucola**. Arugula is best known as a salad green, but it is also excellent when cooked and often used that way in Apulia. The dried* **orecchiette** *are quite firm and form an interesting texture with the cooked green and the potatoes. The dish is flavored with garlic and hot red pepper flakes, but no tomatoes.*

Peel the potatoes and cut them into ¾-inch cubes. Place the potatoes and arugula in a bowl of cold water and set aside for 30 minutes.

Bring a large pot of cold water to a boil, add coarse salt to taste, then drain the vegetables and add them to the pot. When the water returns to a boil, add the pasta, mix very well, and cook until al dente, for 9 to 12 minutes depending on the brand. By then the potatoes also should be completely cooked but still firm.

Coarsely chop the garlic on a board. Place the oil in a small saucepan over medium heat, and when the oil is warm, add the garlic and sauté until lightly golden, about 1 minute. Add salt, pepper, and the red pepper flakes. Drain the pasta and vegetables, then transfer to a large, warmed serving platter. Pour the sauce over, toss very well, and serve immediately.

1 pound potatoes (not new potatoes)
1 pound arugula (rocket), cleaned
1 pound dried *orecchiette*, preferably imported Italian

TO COOK THE VEGETABLES AND PASTA:
Coarse-grained salt

FOR THE SAUCE:
2 large cloves garlic, peeled
¾ cup olive oil
Salt and freshly ground black pepper
1 teaspoon hot red pepper flakes

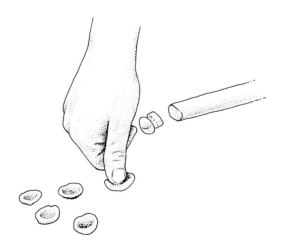

*Arugula is also known in English as "rocket".

**Pasta alla
panzanella**

FROM SIENA
(TUSCANY)

SERVES 4 TO 6

FOR THE SAUCE:
1 large red onion, cleaned
1½ pounds ripe (but not overripe) fresh tomatoes
1 medium-sized clove garlic, peeled
¾ to 1 cup olive oil
Salt and freshly ground black pepper

FOR THE PASTA:
3 cups unbleached all-purpose flour
4 extra-large eggs
Pinch of salt
or
1 pound dried *penne* or any other tubular pasta 2 inches long and ¼ inch wide, preferably imported Italian

TO SERVE:
4 bunches arugula (rocket), about 1 pound, large stems removed and leaves thoroughly washed
15 large fresh basil leaves

TO COOK THE PASTA:
Coarse-grained salt

PASTA ALLA PANZANELLA
PASTA IN THE MANNER OF *PANZANELLA*

Pasta alla panzanella *belongs to a type of dish much more appreciated in Italy than the cold pasta salads popular elsewhere. Here, a cold sauce is used with hot pasta. Cold sauces are also combined in Italy with hot main courses and even desserts.* ***Panzanella*** *is the traditional Tuscan bread salad, mixing the crumbled bread with fresh tomatoes, basil, and onions, and dressed with olive oil and vinegar. In Siena, the uncooked sauce has been adapted to pasta and fresh arugula is added.*

Arugula is not typically Tuscan, but because Siena is close to the border of Lazio, the green is better known there than in Florence.

Prepare the sauce. Coarsely chop the onion and put it in a bowl of cold water for 30 minutes. Cut the tomatoes into 1-inch pieces without removing the seeds and put them in a crockery or glass bowl. Drain the onion and place it over the tomatoes. Finely chop the garlic on a board, and scatter it over the onion. Top with olive oil and season to taste with salt and pepper. Cover the bowl and refrigerate for at least 1 hour.

If fresh pasta is to be used, prepare it with the ingredients and quantities listed, following the directions on page 14. Stretch the layer of pasta to ⅛ inch thick. Cut it into *spaghetti* (see illustration on page 57).

Use 2 bunches arugula to make a bed on each of the individual serving plates. Bring a large pot of cold water to a boil, add coarse salt to taste, and add the pasta. Cook fresh pasta 1 to 3 minutes depending on the dryness; cook dried pasta for 9 to 12 minutes depending on the brand.

Remove the sauce from the refrigerator and mix well. Arrange the remaining arugula and the basil leaves on a large platter. When the pasta is ready, drain it and place over. Immediately distribute the cold sauce over the pasta. Mix everything and serve, placing the mixed pasta on the prepared plates over the beds of arugula.

COMBINED VEGETABLE SAUCES

Combined vegetable sauces are prepared in two different ways. In the first, very contemporary mode, each vegetable is cooked separately and then they are all combined with the pasta. The obvious advantage is that each can receive its optimum cooking time. Each vegetable also retains its own flavor and there is a minimum of blending, which may be a disadvantage. The second, older method is to cook all the vegetables together in order to achieve a new flavor that none could produce individually. One must be more careful about the vegetables selected in this second method, because not all necessarily blend together well with others. The best blends—indeed, those most used in combination, even as the basis for meat sauces—are of carrots, celery, and onions. Spinach and chard do not create problems, nor do peas, zucchini, and artichokes. Much care must be taken with the cabbage family and with fennel, because of their strong dominant personalities. Of the cabbage family, I would select only cauliflower for blending; cabbage itself and broccoli I would avoid. Broccoli is much used in combination when it can be cooked separately, as in the first method, but it will not produce a good result when cooked with other vegetables.

Neither of the two mixed-vegetable sauces which follow attempts to preserve the perfect cooking time of each individual vegetable, and certainly they do not take an oriental-style al dente approach to the vegetables.

FROM TUSCANY

SERVES 6

SPAGHETTI CON SALSA DI VERDURE
SPAGHETTI WITH TUSCAN DICED VEGETABLE SAUCE

1 large artichoke
1 large lemon, cut in half
2 medium-sized zucchini
1 large stalk celery
1 medium-sized red onion,
    peeled
1 medium-sized carrot,
    scraped
20 large sprigs Italian
    parsley, leaves only
6 tablespoons olive oil
1 pound ripe, fresh
    tomatoes; or 1 pound
    canned tomatoes,
    preferably imported
    Italian, drained
Salt and freshly ground
    black pepper
¼ teaspoon hot red pepper
    flakes
½ teaspoon dried oregano
½ cup chicken or beef
    broth, preferably
    homemade
1 pound dried *spaghetti*,
    preferably imported
    Italian

TO COOK THE PASTA
Coarse-grained salt

This modern diced vegetable sauce combines artichokes, zucchini, celery, onions, and carrots, cooking them all for the same amount of time so that the tender zucchini will become almost a purée while the artichokes and carrots will remain firm. This is exactly as should be, as you will agree when you taste it. Unusual flavoring for this Tuscan dish is the oregano mixed with the hot red pepper flakes.

Place the artichoke in a bowl of cold water with the lemon halves; put the zucchini and celery in a large, second bowl of cold water and soak both for 30 minutes.

Finely chop the onion, carrot, and parsley on a board. Place the oil in a heavy, medium-sized flameproof casserole over low heat, and when the oil is warm, add the chopped ingredients and sauté for 10 minutes.

Clean the artichoke following the directions on page 67 and cut it into 1-inch pieces. Cut the zucchini lengthwise into quarters, then into ½-inch pieces. Cut the celery into similar-sized pieces. Add the vegetables to the casserole, sauté for 2 minutes, then cover and cook over medium heat for 20 minutes, stirring every so often with a wooden spoon.

If using fresh tomatoes, cut them into pieces. Pass fresh or canned tomatoes through a food mill, using the disc with smallest holes, into a crockery or glass bowl. Add tomatoes to the casserole and season with salt, pepper, red pepper flakes, and oregano. Cover and cook for 20 minutes more. Add the broth, cover, reduce heat, and simmer for 15 minutes. Uncover, raise the heat, and cook for 15 minutes; taste for salt and pepper. (The sauce may be prepared a day in advance, refrigerated in a covered crockery or glass bowl, and reheated before using.)

Bring a large pot of cold water to a boil, add coarse salt to taste, then add the pasta and cook for 9 to 12 minutes depending on the brand. As the pasta cooks, warm a large serving dish and ladle some of the sauce onto it. Drain the pasta, transfer it to the prepared platter, add the remaining sauce, mix well, and serve hot.

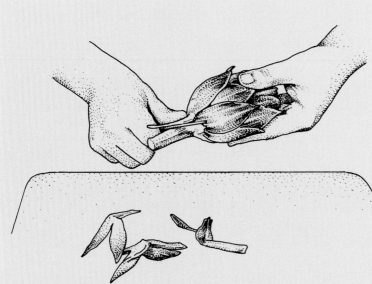

ARTICHOKES

1. *Trim off all of the darker outer ring. The inner core is the best part because it has the real taste of the artichoke.*

1

2. *Remove as many rows of the outer leaves as necessary to arrive at those tender inner rows where you can clearly see the separation between the green at the top and the light yellow at the bottom.*

Then remove the top green part. Press your thumb on the bottom of each leaf, the white part, to hold it in place, and with the other hand, tear off the top green part. As each new row is uncovered the tender yellow part of the leaves will be bigger. When you reach the rows in which only the very tips of the leaves are green, cut off all the tips together with a knife.

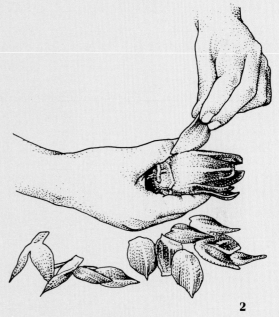

2

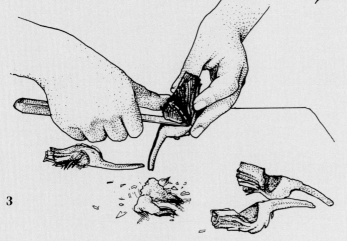

3

3. *It is best to cut the artichoke into quarters lengthwise, in order to remove the choke. Draw the tip of the knife blade across just below the choke to draw it out.*

FROM TUSCANY

SERVES 6

PASTA ALLE ERBE

SPAGHETTI WITH SPRING VEGETABLES

FOR THE SAUCE:
2 large artichokes
1 large lemon, cut in half
½ pound Swiss chard, large stems removed
1 pound very thin asparagus
1 pound unshelled peas
1 tablespoon unbleached all-purpose flour
10 scallions
4 ounces *pancetta* or *prosciutto*, in 1 piece
½ cup olive oil
About 1 cup chicken broth, preferably homemade
Salt and freshly ground black pepper

FOR THE PASTA:
3 cups unbleached all-purpose flour
4 extra-large eggs
Pinch of salt
        or
1 pound dried *spaghetti*, preferably imported Italian

TO COOK THE PASTA:
Coarse-grained salt

TO SERVE:
15 large sprigs Italian parsley, leaves only

*Spaghetti with Spring Vegetables comes from a Renaissance Florentine cookbook, and it combines many seasonal vegetables: small peas, thin asparagus, and spring onions or scallions—all flavored with the **pancetta** so popular in Michelangelo's Florence. This really was a pasta primavera, and remains very valid alongside its modern counterparts. Again, the vegetables are not miniaturized, nor are they undercooked and very crisp. It is time to revive this dish still compatible to contemporary taste.*

Place the artichokes in a bowl of cold water with the lemon halves and set aside for 30 minutes. Place the chard and asparagus in 2 separate bowls of cold water and set aside for 30 minutes. Shell the peas and place them in a third bowl of cold water together with the flour; set aside for 30 minutes.

Cut off and discard the very green parts of the scallions and cut the white portions into pieces less than ½ inch long. Cut the *pancetta* or *prosciutto* into ½-inch cubes. Clean the artichokes according to instructions on page 67, cutting them into quarters, then cutting each quarter into thirds. Place artichoke pieces back in the water with the lemon. Cut the green leaves of chard into 1-inch strips. Trim off and discard the white parts of the asparagus, and cut the green parts into 1-inch pieces. Drain and rinse the peas under cold running water.

Place the *pancetta* or *prosciutto* in a medium-sized saucepan with the oil over medium heat and sauté for 5 minutes; add the scallions and sauté for 5 minutes more. Drain and add the artichokes, asparagus, peas, and Swiss chard; cook, covered, for 30 minutes, adding broth as more liquid is needed and stirring every so often with a wooden spoon. Taste for salt and pepper. At that time the vegetables should all be cooked but some softer than others, however this will produce the appropriate sauce.

If fresh pasta is to be used, prepare it with the ingredients and quantities listed, according to directions on page 14. Stretch layer to ⅛ inch thick, cutting into *spaghetti*, see illustration page 57. Bring a large pot of cold water to a boil, add coarse salt to taste, add the pasta, stir with a wooden spoon, and cover the pot to bring the water back to a boil as soon as possible. Cook the fresh pasta for 1 to 3 minutes depending on dryness, or dried pasta for 9 to 12 minutes depending on the brand.

Coarsely chop the parsley on a board. When the pasta is ready, drain and transfer it to the pan with the sauce. Mix very well and cook for 20 seconds more. Transfer to a large, warmed serving platter and serve with the chopped parsley sprinkled over the individual servings. (No cheese should be added.)

SPAGHETTI AL LIMONE

SPAGHETTI WITH LEMON CREAM SAUCE

*The flavor of lemon, so versatile it enhances so many different kinds of dishes, even has its application to pasta. Lately, in the search for new varieties of flavored fresh pasta, it has become popular to put grated lemon peel into the dough itself. One must be careful in doing this with thin **tagliatelle** dressed with a butter-cream sauce, because the extremely tart taste that develops when the lemon peel is cooked is not balanced by the delicate butter and cream and does not succeed in combining with them. With this pasta and sauce, it is better if the grated lemon peel is placed in the butter-cream sauce itself, pleasantly flavoring the **alla panna** which absorbs the oil of the lemon skin. In this way the sauce can be used with plain fresh pasta or even with dried pasta to produce a good result. (See page 307 for **Fiocchietti al pomodoro**, a pasta made with lemon peel. The dish works because the pasta is thicker and short; nutmeg as well as lemon flavors the pasta, and the two recommended sauces are hearty enough to absorb and stand up to the lemon oils.)*

If using fresh pasta, prepare the pasta with the ingredients and quantities listed, following the directions on page 14. Stretch layer to ⅛ inch thick, cutting into *spaghetti*, see illustration page 57. Let the pasta rest on cotton dish towels until needed.

Bring a large pot of cold water to a boil, and put a large skillet with the butter in it over the pot so that the butter melts as the water heats. When the water reaches a boil and the butter is melted, remove the skillet and add coarse salt to taste to the pot. Then add the pasta and cook fresh pasta for 1 to 3 minutes depending on the dryness, or dried pasta for 9 to 12 minutes depending on the brand. Drain pasta and add to the skillet. Immediately put the skillet over medium heat, add the cream, lemon peel, salt and pepper to taste, and nutmeg. Mix very well and let the sauce reduce for 2 minutes. Add the Parmigiano, mix very well, and transfer to a warmed serving platter. Sprinkle with parsley leaves and serve immediately.

FROM ALL OVER ITALY

SERVES 4 TO 6

FOR THE PASTA:
3 cups unbleached all-purpose flour
3 extra-large eggs
3 teaspoons vegetable or olive oil
Pinch of salt
or
1 pound dried *spaghetti*, preferably imported Italian

TO COOK THE PASTA:
Coarse-grained salt

FOR THE SAUCE:
12 tablespoons (6 ounces) sweet butter
2 cups heavy cream
Grated peel of 2 large lemons with thick skin
Salt and freshly ground white pepper
Pinch of freshly grated nutmeg
1 cup freshly grated Parmigiano cheese

TO SERVE:
15 large sprigs Italian parsley, leaves only

ASPARAGUS

Asparagus has a very limited spring season in Italy, and the use of those grown in hothouses is rare. Though only available for a short period, Italian asparagus has a very distinctive flavor and appears in a variety of forms. Cultivated asparagus is preferred almost pencil-thin and young. In addition, wild asparagus may still be found, even thinner and with an aggressive flavor. Subtly flavored white asparagus is grown in a number of areas. And finally, there is the rare and exquisite snow asparagus, which peeps out from the snow covering the pre-Alpine hills and mountains. When the season comes, one eats asparagus every day and then relishes the memory of it for a year until it reappears. Asparagus is used with both risotto and pasta, imparting a strong flavor.

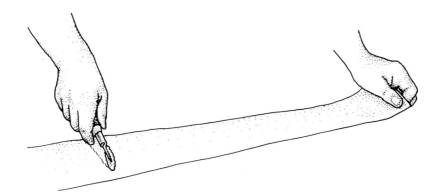

PASTA CON ASPARAGI

PASTA WITH ASPARAGUS

This version of Pasta with Asparagus from Umbria also employs tomatoes; the northern versions do not, relying on the distinctive flavor of the vegetable itself. With the cultivated asparagus one finds, often raised in hothouses, the version with tomatoes is perhaps preferable. Should you have the good fortune to obtain wild or snow asparagus, I suggest you omit the tomatoes.

Place a large pot of cold water for the pasta over medium heat.

Prepare the sauce. Cut off the asparagus tips and place them in a bowl of cold water and put the tender green stems in a second bowl, both to soak until needed. Put the remaining white sections of asparagus in the pot of water for the pasta. When the pasta water reaches a boil, add coarse salt to taste and cook the asparagus ends for 20 minutes.

If using fresh tomatoes, blanch them in a small pot of salted boiling water, then remove the skins and seeds, and cut them into 1-inch squares. If using canned tomatoes, pass them through a food mill, using the disc with smallest holes, into a glass or crockery bowl.

Place a large skillet with the oil over medium heat, and when the oil is warm, drain the green stems of asparagus, add them to the skillet, and sauté for 4 minutes. Then drain and add the asparagus tips, and sauté for 2 minutes more. Add the tomatoes, lower the heat, season to taste with salt and pepper, cover, and cook for 10 minutes, stirring every so often with a wooden spoon.

Meanwhile, remove the white asparagus ends from the boiling pasta water, using a strainer-skimmer, and discard them. Add the pasta to the asparagus-flavored water, and cook it for 8 to 11 minutes depending on the brand; that is, 1 minute less than for normal al dente. Drain the pasta, add it to the skillet containing the sauce, mix gently but thoroughly, and let the pasta absorb the sauce for 1 minute. Remove from heat, transfer to a warmed serving platter, and serve with or without the cheese.

NOTE:
In Italy, wild asparagus are preferred for this dish.

2½ pounds pencil-thin asparagus to yield about 6 ounces tips plus ½ pound stems
Coarse-grained salt
1½ pounds ripe, fresh tomatoes; or 1 pound canned tomatoes, preferably imported Italian, drained
½ cup olive oil
Salt and freshly ground black pepper
1 pound dried *spaghetti*, preferably imported Italian

TO SERVE:
4 to 6 tablespoons freshly grated pecorino sardo or pecorino romano cheese (optional)

EGGPLANT

Pasta combined with eggplant is exclusively associated with southern Italy and especially with Sicily, where a whole series of dishes called *Pasta alla norma* developed. This category is said to have originated in Catania, the birthplace of the composer Bellini, whose popular opera *Norma* is widely assumed to have given its name to the dish. In fact, *norma* is spelled with a small *n* and the word is taken from the Sicilian language, not from Italian. It actually means "pasta in the normal way." And so we can see from this how important the combination is to the Sicilians.

There are many, many dishes throughout Sicily using eggplant as the base for a pasta sauce. In an area in which beef is not much used, it is as though eggplant sauce plays the role that meat sauce does in such areas as Emilia-Romagna, where meat is more abundant.

I have included three versions of *Pasta alla norma*. In the first, not containing tomatoes, the peeled eggplant is sautéed until it almost dissolves into a purée. In the second, the eggplant discs are fried and then placed over the pasta with a tomato sauce. In the third, the very thin slices or discs of eggplant are broiled and combined with the tomato sauce and pasta. The three preparations result in very different dishes.

Note that Italian eggplants are smaller than regular eggplants but not as small as Japanese or miniature.

PASTA ALLA NORMA I

PASTA WITH EGGPLANT, FIRST VERSION

2 pounds Italian eggplants
Coarse-grained salt
¼ cup olive oil
2 large cloves garlic,
 peeled
Salt and freshly ground
 black pepper
½ cup cold water
1 pound dried *rigatoni* or
 ***spaghetti*, preferably**
 imported Italian

Peel the eggplants and slice them crosswise into discs less than ½ inch thick. Place the eggplant in a bowl, lightly sprinkling coarse salt on each layer. Let stand for 30 minutes, with a weight on them (such as a plate with a can of tomatoes on top).

Rinse the eggplant very well and pat dry with paper towels. Heat the oil in a medium-sized flameproof casserole over medium heat; add the garlic and sauté for 2 minutes. Add the eggplant and sauté for 15 minutes. Taste for salt and pepper. Pour in cold water, cover, and cook for 20 minutes more, stirring every so often with a wooden spoon.

Bring a large pot of cold water to a boil. When the water

reaches a boil, add coarse salt to taste, then add the pasta and cook until al dente, for 9 to 12 minutes depending on the brand. Coarsely chop the parsley on a board. Remove the garlic from the eggplant and discard. Drain the pasta, transfer to a large, warmed serving dish, and pour the eggplant sauce over. Toss very well, sprinkle the parsley over, and serve with more freshly ground black pepper. (Do not add any cheese.)

TO COOK THE PASTA:
Coarse-grained salt

TO SERVE
15 large sprigs Italian parsley, leaves only

Pasta alla norma II
PASTA WITH EGGPLANT, SECOND VERSION

FROM SICILY

SERVES 4 TO 6

Peel the eggplants and slice them crosswise into discs less than ½ inch thick. Place the eggplant in a bowl, lightly sprinkling coarse salt on each layer. Let stand for 30 minutes with a weight on them (such as a plate with a can of tomatoes on top.)

Start the sauce. Heat the olive oil in a medium-sized saucepan over medium heat; add the garlic and sauté for 3 minutes. If using fresh tomatoes, cut them into 1-inch pieces. Add fresh or canned tomatoes to saucepan and simmer for 25 minutes, stirring every so often with a wooden spoon. Taste for salt and pepper. Pass the contents of pan through a food mill, using the disc with the smallest holes, into a medium-sized crockery or glass bowl. Return the tomato purée to the saucepan and reduce for 5 minutes.

Heat the vegetable oil and olive oil together in a deep-fat fryer over medium heat. Rinse the eggplant very well and pat dry with paper towels. When the oil is hot (about 400 degrees), add some of the eggplant and cook until lightly golden on each side, about 2 minutes. Using a strainer-skimmer, transfer the cooked eggplant to a serving dish lined with paper towels. Fry the rest of the eggplant in the same way.

Bring a large pot of cold water to a boil. When the water reaches a boil, add coarse salt to taste, then add the pasta and cook until al dente, 9 to 12 minutes depending on the brand. Reheat the tomato sauce and add the basil leaves. Drain the pasta, transfer to a large serving dish, and pour the sauce over. Toss very well, add the eggplant, and serve, with grated ricotta salata sprinkled over each portion.

2 pounds Italian eggplants
Coarse-grained salt
1 quart vegetable oil
¼ cup olive oil
1 pound dried *rigatoni* or *spaghetti*, preferably imported Italian

FOR THE SAUCE:
⅓ cup olive oil
2 medium-sized cloves garlic, peeled
1½ pounds ripe, fresh tomatoes; or 1½ pounds canned tomatoes, preferably imported Italian, drained
Salt and freshly ground black pepper
10 large basil leaves, fresh or preserved in salt, torn into thirds

TO COOK THE PASTA:
Coarse-grained salt

TO SERVE:
4 to 6 tablespoons freshly grated ricotta salata

FROM SICILY

SERVES 4 TO 6

PASTA ALLA NORMA III

PASTA WITH EGGPLANT, THIRD VERSION

1 ½ pounds Italian
   eggplants
2 medium-sized cloves
   garlic, peeled
½ cup olive oil
Salt and freshly ground
   black pepper
1 pound *rigatoni* or
   spaghetti, preferably
   imported Italian

FOR THE SAUCE:
1 medium-sized red onion,
   peeled
½ cup olive oil
1 ½ pounds ripe, fresh
   tomatoes, or 1 ½ pounds
   canned tomatoes,
   preferably imported
   Italian, drained
Salt and freshly ground
   black pepper
10 large basil leaves, fresh
   or preserved in salt, torn
   into thirds

TO COOK THE PASTA:
Coarse-grained salt

TO SERVE:
4 to 6 tablespoons freshly
   grated ricotta salata

Wash the eggplants well but do not peel them. Slice the eggplants crosswise into discs less than ¼ inch thick. Place the eggplant in a crockery or glass bowl. Coarsely chop the garlic on a board and sprinkle it over the eggplant, then add ¼ cup of the oil and salt and pepper to taste. Mix very well and let rest for 5 minutes.

Preheat the broiler. Using tongs, transfer the eggplant directly from the bowl to the broiler rack; broil for about 20 minutes or more if eggplants are very large and tough. Transfer slices back to the same bowl with some leftover oil. Pour over the remaining oil and mix well.

Prepare the sauce. Finely chop the onion on a board. Place the oil in a medium-sized saucepan over medium heat, and when the oil is warm, add the chopped onion and sauté for 5 minutes. If using fresh tomatoes, cut them into 1-inch pieces. Add fresh or canned tomatoes to the saucepan and simmer for 25 minutes, mixing every so often. Season with salt and pepper. Pass the contents of the saucepan through a food mill, using the disc with the smallest holes, into a crockery or glass bowl.

Bring a large quantity of cold water to a boil, add coarse salt to taste, then add the pasta and cook until al dente, for 9 to 12 minutes depending on the brand.

Transfer the tomato sauce to a large skillet, add the basil, and reduce over low heat until the pasta is ready. Drain the pasta, add the sauce, mix well, then add the grilled eggplant. Mix, and transfer to a warmed serving dish. Serve with the cheese sprinkled over.

PASTA ALLE MELANZANE
PASTA WITH EGGPLANT SAUCE

F R O M   A P U L I A

SERVES 4 TO 6

The recipe from Apulia, **Pasta alle melanzane,** *combines eggplant cubes and sweet pepper rings with the pasta, flavored with onion, garlic, and hot red pepper flakes. Apulia sometimes has quite peppery dishes, like its neighbor, Calabria. This is in contrast to Sicily, where—contrary to some assumptions—dishes are preferred more on the sweet side than on the hot. It is not usual for Sicilian recipes to employ hot red pepper flakes.*

Clean the peppers, but do not cut into their sides; remove stems, cores, and seeds through the stem end. Cut the peppers into rings less than 1 inch wide, and soak them in a bowl of cold water for 30 minutes. Clean the eggplants and remove their stems; cut them, unpeeled, into 1-inch cubes and soak them in a bowl of cold water with a little coarse salt for 10 minutes. Coarsely chop the onion and garlic together on a board.

Pour the oil into a medium-sized flameproof casserole, add the chopped onion and garlic, then drain the pepper rings and place them on top. Drain and rinse the eggplant cubes very well under cold running water, pat them dry with paper towels, and arrange them over the peppers. Cover the casserole and put it over medium heat; cook for 15 minutes without stirring. Add cold water, salt and pepper to taste, and red pepper flakes, then cover again and cook for 20 minutes more, stirring every so often with a wooden spoon.

Bring a large pot of cold water to a boil, add coarse salt to taste, then add the pasta and cook until al dente, for 9 to 12 minutes depending on the brand. Drain the pasta, transfer it to a warmed serving platter, pour the sauce over, mix, and serve. (Cheese is not used with this dish.)

2 sweet bell peppers, any color
2 medium-sized Italian eggplants (about 1 pound total)
Coarse-grained salt
1 medium-sized red onion, peeled
1 large clove garlic, peeled
⅓ cup olive oil
½ cup cold water
Salt and freshly ground black pepper
½ teaspoon hot red pepper flakes
1 pound dried short tubular pasta such as *rigatoni* or *penne rigate*

TO COOK THE PASTA:
Coarse-grained salt

MELANZANE RIPIENE DI PASTA

EGGPLANT STUFFED WITH PASTA

FROM SICILY

SERVES 8

FOR THE TOMATO
SAUCE:

**1 medium-sized carrot,
scraped**

1 small red onion, peeled

1 large stalk celery

**1 medium-sized clove
garlic, peeled**

**1½ pounds fresh, ripe
tomatoes; or 1½ pound
canned tomatoes,
preferably imported
Italian, drained**

¼ cup olive oil

**Salt and freshly ground
black pepper**

**10 large basil leaves, fresh
or preserved in salt**

FOR THE SHELLS:

**8 small, round white
Sicilian or purple
eggplants (about 10
ounces each)**

Coarse-grained salt

FOR THE FILLING:

**6 ounces dried *cavatappi*
(twisted tubular pasta),
preferably imported
Italian**

**4 tablespoons freshly
grated pecorino sardo or
Parmigiano cheese**

1 cup cold water

**Salt and freshly ground
black pepper**

TO COOK THE PASTA:

Coarse-grained salt

*The fascinating **Melanzane ripiene di pasta,** again from Sicily, consists of small eggplants, preferably the whitish purple ones so characteristic of the island, emptied of their pulp to make a container for pasta and sauce. The stuffed eggplants are then baked in a tomato sauce. The presentation is attractive, and the dish is appropriate for a fancier dinner.*

It is worth mentioning that tomatoes grown in Sicily are less sweet than the Neapolitan type, though it is probably not possible to duplicate their precise quality in making these tomato sauces.

Begin the sauce. Cut the carrot, onion, celery, garlic, and tomatoes into large pieces, and put them in a medium-sized saucepan. Add the oil, place the pan over medium heat, cover, and cook for 45 minutes, stirring with a wooden spoon every so often. When ready, pass the contents of the pan through a food mill, using the disc with the smallest holes, into a medium-sized flameproof casserole. Return the sauce to the pan, season with salt and pepper, and reduce over medium heat for 30 minutes.

Meanwhile, wash the eggplants very well, slice 1 inch off the stem ends, and cut off enough of the bottom ends to flatten them. Use a melon-ball cutter to scoop out the pulp, making a "container" uniformly ½ inch thick around. Save 1 pound of the pulp. Soak the eggplant shells in a bowl of cold water for 10 minutes.

Bring a large pot of cold water to a boil, add coarse salt to taste, then add the eggplant shells and simmer for 8 minutes. Use a strainer-skimmer to transfer the eggplant shells to a bowl of cold water; let stand for a few minutes, then place them upside down on paper towels to drain completely.

Finish the sauce. Cut the reserved eggplant pulp into small pieces and put it in the casserole along with the tomato sauce and the basil. Place the casserole over medium heat and cook for 35 minutes, then season with salt and pepper. Pass the mixture through a food mill, using the disc with the smallest holes, into a medium-sized saucepan. Place this pan over medium heat and reduce mixture until you have about 4 cups of sauce, about 10 minutes.

Preheat the oven to 375 degrees. Bring a medium-sized stockpot of cold water to a boil. Add coarse salt to taste, then add the pasta and cook it for 4 to 7 minutes depending upon the brand; that is, 5 minutes less than for pasta cooked normal al dente. Drain the pasta and mix with 3 cups of the sauce and the grated cheese. Use

a tablespoon of oil to coat a 13½- x 8¾-inch glass baking dish, then add the cold water to the remaining sauce and pour it into the dish. Arrange the eggplant shells in the dish, sprinkle the insides with a little salt and pepper, then fill each eggplant shell with the sauced pasta. (Be sure there is a good amount of sauce inside each eggplant to allow it to cook.) Cover the dish with aluminum foil and bake for 1 hour. Remove from the oven and serve. Each portion consists of 1 stuffed eggplant and some sauce poured over the pasta filling.

The whitish type of Sicilian eggplant is the one usually used for stuffing. Notice the picturesque Sicilian puppets in the background.

Peppers

Pasta is combined with peppers in as many different ways as it is with eggplant, and each region of the South has one or more treatments of its own. Bell peppers are most commonly used, but in a variety of colors: green, red, yellow, orange. Green peppers are as common as the others in Italy, but no more so. Fortunately, the yellow and orangish peppers so popular there have become widely available outside the peninsula in recent years, and they add variety, not only in color but also in flavor and texture, being somewhat more delicate than the green ones. Sweet red peppers found in Italy, like elsewhere, are not the same as pimientos. They are slightly less sweet, so be sure to try to find red peppers, not pimientos for these dishes.

FROM CAMPANIA

SERVES 4 TO 6

1½ pounds small or 2
  pounds large, light-
  green "Italian" (frying)
  peppers
¾ cup olive oil
1¾ pounds fresh, ripe
  tomatoes, or 1¾ pounds
  canned tomatoes,
  preferably imported
  Italian, drained
2 large cloves garlic,
  peeled but left whole
Salt and freshly ground
  black pepper
5 large basil leaves, fresh
  or preserved in salt
1 pound dried *perciatelli*,
  bucatini, or *spaghetti*,
  preferably imported
  Italian

TO COOK THE PASTA:
Coarse-grained salt

Perciatelli ai Peperoncini Verdi
PERCIATELLI WITH "ITALIAN" PEPPERS

In Campania, the Naples area, there exists a special, smaller light green pepper, sometimes referred to as an Italian pepper, which is marvelous combined with pasta. Longer and thinner than those of the bell shape, they are also less meaty and perhaps more delicate than green bell peppers. Classic recipes do exist for dishes in which the peppers are used with their skins. The Neapolitan or Italian peppers have delicate skins that do not separate in cooking.

If using small peppers, put them in a bowl of cold water, without removing seeds and stems, for 30 minutes. If using larger peppers, remove stems and larger seeds before soaking them.

Place a large skillet with the oil over medium heat; when the oil is warm, drain the peppers and add to the skillet. Cover the skillet and sauté for 15 minutes, turning peppers over 2 or 3 times until they are cooked but still firm. Use a strainer-skimmer to transfer the peppers to a crockery or glass bowl. If using fresh tomatoes, cut into pieces. Add the fresh or canned tomatoes and the garlic to the pan juices. Simmer the tomatoes for 25 minutes, stirring every so often with a wooden spoon.

Pass the contents of the skillet through a food mill, using the disc with smallest holes, into a crockery or glass bowl. Pour the purée back into the skillet and place over medium heat. Put the peppers back in, taste for salt and pepper, and add the basil leaves. Simmer the sauce for 10 minutes more.

Meanwhile, bring a large pot of cold water to a boil, add coarse salt to taste, then add the pasta and cook for 8 to 11 minutes depending on the brand; that is, 1 minute less than for normal al dente. Drain the pasta, add it to the skillet with the sauce, mix well, and sauté for 1 minute more. Transfer to a warmed serving platter and serve.

BELL PEPPERS

In all three of the bell pepper recipes included here the vegetable is used with the skin removed. The best method of removing the skins is to first roast the peppers—over an open flame is ideal—until the skins are charred, and peel when cool enough to handle. I personally avoid the methods of frying or broiling to accomplish this; when fried, the peppers absorb too much fat, and the broiled ones retain a smoky taste.

TECHNIQUE FOR SKINNING PEPPERS

Preheat the oven to 375 degrees. Place a baking dish half full of cold water on a lower shelf of the oven.

After a few minutes, put the whole peppers on the shelf above the steaming water. Roast the peppers for about forty minutes, turning them over three or four times.

Remove the peppers from the oven and put them into a plastic bag. Let them stand until they are lukewarm (approximately fifteen minutes).

Put the peppers in a large bowl of cold water and peel them, removing the stems and seeds.

With all the combinations of pasta and peppers, one really begins by preparing a *peperonata* and using it as the sauce. *Peperonata* is a pepper stew that exists in many versions all over Italy, including in northern regions which do not combine it with pasta.

The first two versions, from Sicily and Calabria respectively, have several points of interest. First, they reverse the normal roles of the two regions with regard to hot red pepper flakes. Here, it is the Sicilian version that employs it and the Calabrian that omits it. These usages are equally rare in both regions. Also, the Sicilian version uses no tomatoes. The use of tomatoes is much more characteristic of the Naples region, and even our Calabrian recipe is influenced more by Naples than by Sicily. The dish without tomatoes is expressed in its purest, simplest form in this Sicilian recipe using only olive oil and black pepper, and not even garlic. There are versions without tomato from other parts of Italy, but none so pure.

The Calabrian dish, Pasta in *Peperonata* Sauce, is fascinating, in that it is traditionally combined with a second dish, the Sweet Bell Pepper *Frittata*. After cooking, the peppers are removed from the sauce and used in the preparation of an Italian omelet, or *frittata,* which is eaten after the pasta course; this is unusual in Italy. (A more typical approach is in *Lasagne* with Duck, in which the duck is cooked in the sauce and then removed. It is not served during the same meal, but rather reserved for another meal or snack.)

The Neapolitan recipe employs tomatoes, of course, combining bell peppers with onion and basil. Other versions use Italian peppers with garlic and basil. The previously mentioned Calabrese recipe contains parsley and garlic.

From all this, we are reminded once again of how carefully each ingredient is weighed in Italian regional cooking and, indeed, how much different is the flavor resulting from these small variations. Each ingredient has its role and its logic. There are no arbitrary improvisations or substitutions in these recipes, which have developed over a period of at least a century.

PASTA AI PEPERONI

FROM SICILY

SERVES 4 TO 6

PASTA WITH SWEET BELL PEPPERS

6 very large or 8 medium-sized sweet bell peppers of different colors
½ cup extra-virgin olive oil from southern Italy
Salt and freshly ground black pepper
¾ teaspoon hot red pepper flakes
1 pound dried tubular pasta such as *rigatoni,* preferably imported Italian

TO COOK THE PASTA:
Coarse-grained salt

Roast the peppers following directions on page 79, and remove the skins. Cut the peppers into 1-inch strips. Heat the oil in a large skillet over medium heat, add the peppers, and sauté for 2 minutes. Add salt, pepper, and red pepper flakes, mix very well, cover, and cook over low heat for 20 minutes, stirring every so often with a wooden spoon.

Bring a large pot of cold water to a boil, add coarse salt to taste, then add the pasta and cook until al dente, for 9 to 12 minutes depending on the brand. Drain pasta and add to the peppers. Mix very well, incorporating the peppers, which by now should have a very creamy texture. Transfer to a warmed serving dish and serve immediately.

Pasta ai peperoni

PASTA E PEPERONI ALLA CALABRESE

PASTA IN *PEPERONATA* SAUCE, WITH SWEET BELL PEPPER *FRITTATA*

**8 large sweet bell peppers
    of different colors
1 medium-sized red onion,
    peeled
10 large sprigs Italian
    parsley, leaves only
1 large clove garlic, peeled
5 tablespoons olive oil
1½ pounds ripe, fresh
    tomatoes; or 1½ pounds
    canned tomatoes,
    preferably imported
    Italian, drained
Salt and freshly ground
    black pepper
1 pound dried *rigatoni*,
    preferably imported
    Italian**

TO COOK THE PASTA:
Coarse-grained salt

FOR THE *FRITTATA:*
**6 extra-large eggs
Salt and freshly ground
    black pepper**

Roast the peppers following directions on page 79, and remove their skins, seeds, and stems. Cut the peppers into ½-inch strips and put them between layers of paper towels to dry.

Finely chop the onion, parsley, and garlic all together on a board. Heat the oil in a large skillet over medium heat; add the chopped ingredients and sauté for 5 minutes. If using fresh tomatoes, cut them into 1-inch pieces. Pass fresh or canned tomatoes through a food mill, using the disc with the smallest holes, into a crockery or glass bowl. Add tomatoes to the skillet and sauté for 5 minutes more. Taste for salt and pepper. Add the peppers, cover the skillet, and simmer for 20 minutes, stirring every so often with a wooden spoon. Pour the skillet mixture into a colander and set over a large bowl; drain well. Set mixture aside in the colander for later use in the *frittata*. Transfer the pepper juices to the skillet and put it over low heat.

Bring a large pot of cold water to a boil. When water in pot reaches a boil, add coarse salt to taste, then add the pasta and cook until al dente, for 9 to 12 minutes depending on the brand. While the pasta is cooking, in a 10-inch omelet pan prepare a *frittata* using the strained peppers and the 6 eggs, seasoned with salt and pepper. Cook until golden on both sides, about 2 minutes on each side. Set aside.

Drain the pasta, add it to the skillet with the sauce, and mix very well to incorporate all the sauce with the pasta. Transfer to a warmed serving platter and serve immediately. Serve the *frittata* at room temperature as a second course.

NOTE: TO PREPARE *FRITTATA*

Break the eggs into a large crockery bowl. With a fork, break the yolks of the eggs and beat them lightly so no air bubbles or foam begins to form. Place a 10-inch omelet pan over medium heat. Add 1 scant tablespoon of olive or vegetable oil to the pan. When the oil is hot, add the beaten eggs and reserved pepper mixture.

Keep puncturing the bottom with a fork as the eggs set to allow the liquid on top to move through to the bottom.

When the eggs are well set and the *frittata* is well detached from the bottom of the pan, put a plate, upside down, over the pan. Holding the plate firmly, reverse the pan and turn the *frittata* out onto the plate. Return the pan to the heat and carefully slide the *frittata* into the pan and cook the other side.

When the eggs are well set on the second side (about 1 minute), reverse the *frittata* onto a serving dish.

PASTA CON LA PEPERONATA ALLA NAPOLETANA

PASTA WITH SWEET BELL PEPPERS, NAPLES STYLE

FROM NAPLES

SERVES 4 TO 6

Roast the peppers following directions on page 79, and remove their skins, stems and seeds. Cut the peppers into 1-inch strips. Place the strips between layers of paper towels and pat them dry.

Coarsely chop the onion and place it in a small bowl of cold water for 30 minutes. If using fresh tomatoes, cut them into 1-inch pieces. Pass fresh or canned tomatoes through a food mill, using the disc with the smallest holes, into a crockery or glass bowl. Place a flameproof casserole with the oil over medium heat; when the oil is warm, drain the onion and add it to the casserole. Sauté for 4 minutes, then cover and cook for 15 minutes more. Add the tomatoes and basil leaves. Cover and cook for 20 minutes, stirring every so often. Taste for salt and pepper. Add the peppers, mix very well, and cook, uncovered, for 10 minutes more.

Meanwhile, bring a large pot of cold water to a boil. When the water reaches a boil, add coarse salt to taste, then add the pasta and cook until al dente, for 9 to 12 minutes depending on the brand. Drain the pasta and add it to the casserole. Mix all the ingredients very well. Let the sauce be absorbed by the pasta for 30 seconds, then transfer from casserole to a large, warmed serving dish and serve immediately.

8 medium-sized sweet bell peppers of different colors
1 medium-sized red onion, peeled
1 pound very ripe, fresh tomatoes; or 1 pound canned tomatoes, preferably imported Italian, drained
4 tablespoons olive oil
5 large basil leaves, fresh or preserved in salt, torn into thirds
Salt and freshly ground black pepper
1 pound dried *conchiglie*, *fusilli* or any short pasta, not tubular

TO COOK THE PASTA:
Coarse-grained salt

BROCCOLI AND CAULIFLOWER

Broccoli means "hard flower" in Italian and is used in the area south of Rome to mean any vegetable with a hard flower top, such as white, green, or purple cauliflower. *Cime di rape (broccolirab, in dialect)* is also known as *broccoletti*. Most often in Sicily and southern Italy the word refers to some type of cauliflower. The word is used so interchangeably, however, that dishes that most often involve cauliflower might just as well have broccoli itself, if that should be more available. There are in addition species of broccoli (in the Italian sense of the word) that exist locally and are not available outside of the region. These would be used locally when available in place of other types of "broccoli."

PASTA E BROCCOLI

PASTA AND BROCCOLI

FROM SOUTHERN ITALY

SERVES 4 TO 6

1 large bunch broccoli, with at least 4 stems
Coarse-grained salt
1 pound dried *cavatappi* or *fusilli*, preferably imported Italian
2 large cloves garlic, peeled
¾ cup olive oil
Salt and freshly ground black pepper
½ to ¾ teaspoon hot red pepper flakes
4 heaping tablespoons capers packed in wine vinegar, drained

TO SERVE:
20 large sprigs Italian parsley, leaves only, coarsely chopped

*In this version of pasta and broccoli found all over southern Italy, the anchovy is omitted in favor of capers, garlic, and parsley, and is made with short pasta rather than **spaghetti**. However, the main difference in preparation is that the vegetable stems and flowers are cooked together with the pasta, rather than before. Like the other, the pasta and vegetables are then sautéed with their seasonings. The classic **Spaghetti** with Broccoli is flavored with anchovy and red pepper flakes (see Recipe Appendix).*

Clean the broccoli, discarding the tough bottom stems, and separate the stems from the flowerets; place them in 2 different bowls of cold water for 30 minutes.

Bring a large pot of cold water to a boil, add coarse salt to taste, then add the pasta and immediately afterward the broccoli stems. The pasta should be cooked al dente in from 9 to 12 minutes depending on the brand. Two minutes after adding the stems, add the flowerets. All three—pasta, stems, and flowerets—should emerge properly cooked at the end of the pasta cooking time.

Meanwhile, mince the garlic. Place the oil in a small saucepan over medium heat; when the oil is warm, add the garlic and sauté until lightly golden, about 1 minute. Season with salt, pepper, and the red pepper flakes. Add the capers and sauté for 2 minutes more. By that time, the pasta and broccoli should be cooked.

Drain the contents of the stockpot, transfer to a large warmed serving dish, pour the sauce over, mix well, sprinkle the parsley over, and serve immediately.

PASTA CON BROCCOLI SALTATI

PASTA WITH SAUTÉED CAULIFLOWER

It should not surprise you to see the recipe here, **Pasta con broc-coli saltati,** *translated as Pasta with Sautéed Cauliflower.*

Clean the cauliflower, detach all the flowerets, and discard everything else. Soak the flowerets in a bowl of cold water for 30 minutes. Peel the potatoes, cut them into 1-inch cubes, and put them in a second bowl of cold water.

Bring a large pot of cold water to a boil, add coarse salt to taste, then drain the cauliflower and add it to the pot. Cook for 3 minutes, then use a strainer-skimmer to transfer the flowerets to a platter. Place a towel dampened with cold water over the cauliflower. Drain the potatoes, add them to the boiling cauliflower water, and cook for 5 minutes. Again use a strainer-skimmer to transfer them to the platter with the cauliflower. Save the cooking water for later use.

Prepare the sauce. If using fresh tomatoes, cut them into pieces. Put the fresh or canned tomatoes in a medium-sized saucepan along with the garlic and oil, and place pan over medium heat; cook for 15 minutes. Season with salt and pepper and cook for 5 minutes more. Pass the contents of the saucepan through a food mill, using the disc with the smallest holes, into a second saucepan. Set aside.

Reheat the cauliflower-potato cooking water to a boil, taste for salt, then add the pasta and cook until al dente, for 9 to 12 minutes depending on the brand. As the pasta cooks, heat the oil in a large skillet over medium heat, and when the oil is hot, add the whole cloves of garlic together with the potatoes and cauliflower. Season with salt and pepper, and sauté, mixing every so often with a wooden spoon.

Reheat the tomato sauce. When the pasta is ready, drain it and transfer it to a large bowl, pour the sauce over, sprinkle with the cheese, and mix very well. Then transfer the pasta and sauce to a large, warmed serving platter. Use a strainer-skimmer to transfer the sautéed vegetables from the skillet onto the platter of pasta. Serve very hot.

NOTE:
In Sicily, "broccoli" usually means cauliflower.

1 medium-sized cauliflower (see Note), to yield 1½ pounds flowerets
½ pound potatoes (not new potatoes)
Coarse-grained salt
1 pound dried pasta such as *spaghetti*, preferably imported Italian
½ cup olive oil
2 medium-sized cloves garlic, peeled but left whole
Salt and freshly ground black pepper
½ cup freshly grated pecorino Siciliano or romano cheese

FOR THE SAUCE:
1½ pounds ripe, fresh tomatoes, or 1½ pounds canned tomatoes, preferably imported Italian, drained
1 medium-sized clove garlic, peeled but left whole
½ cup olive oil
Salt and freshly ground black pepper

TO COOK THE PASTA:
Coarse-grained salt

FROM APULIA

SERVES 4 TO 6

PASTA AL CAVOLFIORE
PASTA AND CAULIFLOWER

1 medium-sized cauliflower
Coarse-grained salt
1 pound dried pasta such
as *orecchiette* or any
other short tubular pasta

FOR THE SAUCE:
1½ pounds ripe, fresh
tomatoes, or 1½ pounds
canned tomatoes,
preferably imported
Italian, drained
20 large sprigs Italian
parsley, leaves only
2 large cloves garlic,
peeled
½ cup olive oil
Salt and freshly ground
black pepper
½ cup freshly grated
pecorino romano or
pecorino sardo cheese

The dishes made with cauliflower demonstrate perfectly how to use almost the same ingredients and by varied treatments change the entire flavor of the dish. Both the Sicilian and Apulian versions of pasta with cauliflower use tomatoes, garlic, olive oil, and black pepper. But the Sicilians sauté the cauliflower together with potatoes, which don't exist in the other version, in the oil and garlic before adding it to the tomato sauce. In the Apulian version the boiled cauliflower is simply added to the tomato sauce itself, along with parsley. The difference is accentuated by using two different kinds of pasta and two different pecorino sheep's cheeses.

Remove all the leaves from the cauliflower and use a knife to detach all the flowerets, discarding the rest. Soak the flowerets in a bowl of cold water for 30 minutes. Bring a large pot of cold water to a boil, add coarse salt to taste, then add the cauliflower and cook until cooked but still very firm, 10 to 15 minutes. Use a strainer-skimmer to transfer the cauliflower to a crockery or glass bowl, saving the cooking water. Cover the bowl and let stand until needed.

Begin the sauce. If using fresh tomatoes, cut them into pieces. Pass fresh or canned tomatoes through a food mill, using the disc with smallest holes, into a crockery or glass bowl. Finely chop the parsley and garlic together on a board. Heat the oil in a large skillet over low heat, and when warm, add the chopped ingredients and sauté for 5 minutes. Add the tomatoes, season with salt and pepper, and simmer for 10 minutes.

Meanwhile, bring the cauliflower water back to a boil. Add the pasta and cook for 8 to 11 minutes according to the brand; that is, 1 minute less than for normal al dente. When the pasta is ready, place the cauliflower in the skillet with the sauce still on low heat. Drain the pasta, raise the heat, and add the pasta to the skillet. Mix gently but thoroughly. Taste for salt and pepper, and add the grated cheese. Mix well and let cook for 1 minute more, mixing constantly with 2 spoons. Transfer the pasta to a warmed serving dish and serve immediately.

VARIATIONS (all or some may be used at the same time)
   1. ½ cup dry white wine can be added to the sauce and evaporated away.
   2. Parsley or cheese can be omitted.
   3. Green or purple cauliflower can be used instead of white.
   4. A large pinch of hot red pepper flakes can be added.

PASTA CHI VRUCCOLI ARRIMINATA

MACCHERONI WITH CAULIFLOWER AND SAFFRON

*This recipe, **Pasta chi vruccoli arriminata**, also from Sicily, combines the pasta and cauliflower with onions, raisins, saffron, and **pignolis** to make one of the classics of the island. This dish is as typical of Sicily as **Pasta con le sarde**.*

Place the cauliflower in a bowl of cold water and soak for 30 minutes. Bring a large pot of cold water to a boil, add coarse salt to taste, and when the water returns to a boil, add the cauliflower and cook for 5 minutes. Transfer the cauliflower, whole, to a bowl of cold water to cool for 30 minutes. Detach the individual flowerets from the head, and place them on paper towels to drain well. Discard the rest of the cauliflower.

Soak the raisins in a small bowl of lukewarm water for 30 minutes. Meanwhile, slice the onion into thin rings. Heat the oil in a heavy saucepan over low heat, and when warm, add the onion and sauté for 5 minutes. Then add the saffron along with the broth. Season with salt and pepper to taste and simmer for 10 minutes.

Bring a stockpot of cold water to a boil; add coarse salt to taste. While the water is heating, transfer the onion-saffron mixture to a large skillet and put it over medium heat. If you are using whole anchovies packed in salt, fillet under cold running water. Add anchovy fillets to the skillet along with the cauliflower and pine nuts. Drain the raisins and pat them dry with paper towels, then add them to skillet and cook for 5 minutes, stirring all the ingredients together.

When stockpot of water is boiling, add the pasta and cook for 9 to 12 minutes depending on the brand. Drain and transfer pasta to the skillet. Mix very well over medium heat for 1 minute, then transfer contents to a large, warmed serving platter. Sprinkle the cheese and basil leaves over and serve immediately.

VARIATIONS
   1. Saffron can be omitted.
   2. 4 large cloves of garlic, finely chopped, can be substituted for the red onion. Saffron can be used or omitted here as well.

1 large cauliflower, cleaned and left whole
Coarse-grained salt
4 tablespoons raisins
1 large red onion, peeled
¾ cup olive oil
½ teaspoon ground saffron
1 cup hot chicken or beef broth, preferably homemade
Salt and freshly ground black pepper
4 whole anchovies in salt; or 8 anchovy fillets packed in oil, drained
4 tablespoons pine nuts (*pignolis*)
1 pound dried *maccheroni*, preferably imported Italian

TO COOK THE PASTA:
Coarse-grained salt

TO SERVE:
½ cup freshly grated pecorino siciliano or Parmigiano cheese
10 large fresh basil leaves, torn into thirds

PASTA E CARCIOFI

PASTA AND ARTICHOKES

3 large artichokes
1 large lemon, cut in half
2 medium-sized cloves
    garlic, peeled
½ cup olive oil
½ cup dry white wine
Salt and freshly ground
    black pepper
1 cup lukewarm water
1 pound dried *rigatoni*,
    preferably imported
    Italian

TO COOK THE PASTA:
Coarse-grained salt

TO BAKE:
2 tablespoons (1 ounce)
    sweet butter
15 large sprigs Italian
    parsley, leaves only
4 ounces provolone cheese

In this Sicilian recipe the artichokes are cut into thin slices so that they almost dissolve into the sauce. A special feature is the use of white wine. It is often asserted that artichokes kill the bouquet of wine, yet there exist a number of traditional recipes in which the vegetable itself is cooked in white wine. While no herb is used in the cooking, parsley, which goes so well with artichokes, is added uncooked at the end, along with small cubes of provolone, blending in its distinct flavor and replacing the usual grated cheese.

Place the artichokes in a bowl of cold water. Squeeze the lemon halves over and soak, for 30 minutes. Meanwhile, finely chop the garlic on a board.

Clean the artichokes following instructions on page 67, cutting them into quarters, then cutting each quarter into thin slices, and put them back in the lemon water. Heat the oil in a medium-sized flameproof casserole over medium heat; when the oil is warm, add the garlic and sauté for 5 minutes. Pour in the wine, and boil, letting it evaporate for 10 minutes. Season to taste with salt and pepper, then add the water, cover the pan, and cook for 20 minutes, stirring every so often with a wooden spoon.

Bring a large pot of cold water to a boil. Preheat the oven to 375 degrees. When the water reaches a boil, add coarse salt to taste, then add the pasta and cook for 8 to 11 minutes, depending on the brand; that is, 1 minute less than for normal al dente.

Use the 2 tablespoons of butter to heavily coat a 13½- x 8¾-inch glass baking dish. Coarsely chop the parsley on a board, and cut the cheese into cubes smaller than ½ inch. Drain the pasta, transfer it to a large bowl, add the artichokes with their juice, then sprinkle on the chopped parsley and the provolone cubes. Mix gently but thoroughly, then transfer to the prepared baking dish and bake for 10 minutes. Remove from the oven and serve immediately.

Pasta ai Carciofi

PASTA WITH ARTICHOKES

In this dish from Apulia, the artichokes are cut into eighths so that the pieces are fully discernible in the sauce. Parsley is cooked with the garlic, and the grated pecorino is added at the end.

Place the artichokes and the lemon halves in a bowl of cold water and set aside for 30 minutes. Clean the artichokes following the instructions on page 67, and cut them into eighths. Put the artichoke pieces back in the lemon water until needed. Finely chop the garlic and 10 sprigs of the parsley together on a board.

Heat the oil in a heavy, medium-sized flameproof casserole, preferably of terra-cotta or enamel, over medium heat. When the oil is warm, add the chopped ingredients and sauté for 2 minutes. Drain the artichokes and add them to the casserole. Mix very well, cover, and cook for 20 minutes, adding up to 1 cup of cold water as needed. Taste for salt and pepper. Meanwhile, coarsely chop the remaining parsley.

Bring a large pot of cold water to a boil, add coarse salt to taste, then add the pasta. Cook until al dente, for 9 to 12 minutes depending on the brand. Drain the pasta and place it in the casserole with the sauce. Mix very well, remove from the heat, add the cheese, and mix again. Transfer to a warmed serving dish and serve immediately with a twist of black pepper on each serving.

4 large artichokes
1 large lemon, cut in half
3 medium-sized cloves garlic, peeled
25 large sprigs Italian parsley, leaves only
½ cup olive oil
1 cup cold water, approximately
Salt and freshly ground black pepper
1 pound dried *rigatoni* or any other large, ridged tubular pasta; or 1 pound dried *spaghetti*
½ cup freshly grated pecorino romano cheese

TO COOK THE PASTA:
Coarse-grained salt

FROM SICILY

SERVES 4 TO 6

PASTA CON I CARCIOFI

PASTA WITH ARTICHOKES AND EGGS

1 large lemon, cut in half
3 large artichokes
1 medium-sized red onion,
    peeled
½ cup olive oil
Salt and freshly ground
    black pepper
1 cup lukewarm water
2 extra-large eggs
2 tablespoons freshly
    grated pecorino siciliano
    or romano cheese
1 pound dried *rigatoni*,
    preferably imported
    Italian

TO COOK THE PASTA:
Coarse-grained salt

*In Pasta with Artichokes and Eggs, as in the other Sicilian version, the vegetable is cut into small pieces which almost dissolve. They are sautéed together with onions. Two eggs are mixed with the grated pecorino (as in **Pasta alla carbonara**) and mixed gently with the hot pasta before the cooked artichokes are added.*

Squeeze the lemon into a bowl of cold water and drop in the lemon halves. Add the artichokes to soak for 30 minutes. Meanwhile, finely chop the onion on a board. Clean the artichokes following the instructions on page 67, and cut them into quarters. Then cut each quarter into thin slices and return to the lemon water.

Heat the oil in a medium-sized flameproof casserole over medium heat; when the oil is warm, add the onion and sauté for 5 minutes. Drain the artichokes and add to casserole, mix very well, and sauté for 4 minutes more. Season to taste with salt and pepper, and add the water. Cover the casserole and cook for 30 minutes, stirring every so often with a wooden spoon. When finished, the liquid should be completely absorbed and the artichokes very soft.

Bring a large pot of cold water to a boil. Mix the eggs with the cheese and salt and pepper to taste in a large serving bowl. When the water reaches a boil, add coarse salt to taste, then add the pasta and cook until al dente, for 9 to 12 minutes depending on the brand. Drain the pasta, transfer to the bowl with the egg mixture, mix gently but thoroughly, then add the artichokes with their juice. Mix again and serve with a few twists of black pepper.

PASTA CON CARCIOFI A FUNGETIELLO

PASTA WITH ARTICHOKES IN PIQUANT SAUCE

FROM NAPLES

SERVES 6

In this Neapolitan recipe, the artichokes also are cut into larger pieces and olives and capers added for a piquant touch. The favorite Neapolitan **perciatelli**—*thick* **spaghetti** *with the tiny hole inside—are preferred. No cheese would be sprinkled over a piquant dish such as this. None of these four dishes employs tomatoes, not even the Neapolitan version.*

Clean the artichokes according to directions on page 67, cut them into eighths, and soak in cold water with the lemon halves squeezed in and with the flour stirred in. After 30 minutes, drain artichokes and rinse many times to completely remove the flour. Discard the lemon.

Place the oil in a heavy casserole, preferably of terra-cotta or enamel, over medium heat. When the oil is warm, add the garlic and sauté for 10 minutes.

Pit the olives and cut them into quarters. Rinse the capers under cold running water. Add the olives, capers, and salt and pepper to taste, then pour in ¼ cup of the water. Lower the heat, cover, and cook for 15 minutes, stirring every so often with a wooden spoon. Add the remaining water, taste for salt and pepper, and cook, covered, for 10 minutes more.

Meanwhile, bring a large pot of cold water to a boil, add coarse salt to taste, then add the pasta and cook for 8 to 11 minutes depending on the brand; that is, 1 minute less than for normal al dente. Drain the pasta, add it to the casserole, mix well, and sauté for 1 minute more. Add the parsley, mix well, and serve immediately.

4 large artichokes
1 large lemon, cut in half
1 tablespoon unbleached all-purpose flour
¾ cup olive oil
2 large cloves garlic, peeled but left whole
6 ounces large black Greek olives in brine, drained
5 heaping tablespoons capers in wine vinegar, drained
Salt and freshly ground black pepper
½ cup lukewarm water
1 pound dried *perciatelli* or any other long pasta, preferably imported Italian
20 large sprigs Italian parsley, leaves only

TO COOK THE PASTA:
Coarse-grained salt

PASTA RIPIENA DI CARCIOFI
PASTA STUFFED WITH ARTICHOKES

*This stuffed pasta from the Veneto alone among these artichoke recipes requires fresh pasta, since it is a type of **lasagne** with only top and bottom layers of pasta. The artichoke stuffing becomes almost a purée, with eggs, cheese, and some of the **balsamella** added to the vegetable, then flavored with nutmeg. The rest of the **balsamella** is placed on top along with the unusual use of a small amount of tomato sauce. This wonderful dish is useful for a more formal presentation.*

FOR THE PASTA:
2 cups unbleached all-purpose flour
2 extra-large eggs
2 teaspoons olive oil or vegetable oil
Pinch of salt

FOR COOKING THE PASTA:
Coarse-grained salt
2 tablespoons olive or vegetable oil

FOR THE STUFFING:
6 large artichokes, yields 2 pounds cleaned
1 lemon, cut in half
20 large sprigs Italian parsley, leaves only
3 medium-sized cloves garlic, peeled
4 tablespoons olive oil
4 tablespoons (2 ounces) sweet butter
Salt and freshly ground black pepper
1 cup cold water
4 extra-large eggs
1 cup freshly grated Parmigiano cheese
Freshly grated nutmeg

FOR THE *BALSAMELLA* (BÉCHAMEL):
8 tablespoons (4 ounces) sweet butter
¼ cup unbleached all-purpose flour
3½ cups milk
Salt, freshly ground black pepper, and freshly grated nutmeg

Prepare the pasta with the ingredients and quantities listed, following the instructions on page 14. Stretch layer to 1/16 inch thick—on the pasta machine, take to next to last notch. Cut the pasta into squares as for *lasagne*. Preboil the squares in a large amount of salted boiling water for two seconds. Transfer the pasta to a large bowl of cold water to which the oil has been added. Cool the pasta in the water, then transfer to wet cotton dish towels until needed.

Prepare the stuffing. Soak the artichokes in a bowl of cold water with the lemon halves for 30 minutes. Clean the artichokes (page 67), and cut them into pieces no larger than an almond. Place the artichoke pieces back in the acidulated water until needed. Coarsely chop the parsley and finely chop the garlic separately on a board. Place a medium-sized saucepan with the oil and butter over medium heat. When the butter is melted, add the chopped ingredients and sauté for 2 minutes. Drain the artichokes and add to casserole, season with salt and pepper, cover, and cook for 15 minutes. Add the cold water, cover again, and cook artichokes for 10 minutes more, by which time they should be very soft. Transfer to a large dish and let rest until completely cooled, about 30 minutes.

As the artichokes cool, prepare the *balsamella* with the ingredients and quantities listed (see note), then transfer the sauce to a crockery or glass bowl and let it rest with a piece of buttered waxed paper directly against its surface until cool.

Prepare the tomato sauce. If fresh tomatoes are used, cut them into 1-inch pieces. Place fresh or canned tomatoes in a small saucepan with 4 tablespoons of the butter and the basil over medium heat; cook for 20 minutes. Pass tomatoes through a food mill, using the disc with smallest holes, into a bowl, then return the sauce to the pan, season with salt and pepper, and simmer until sauce is quite thick, about 15 minutes. Let rest until needed.

Assemble the dish. Preheat the oven to 375 degrees. With the remaining tablespoon of butter, heavily butter a jelly-roll pan, bottom and sides.

Finish the stuffing. Transfer artichokes to a large bowl, add the eggs to the artichokes, then the Parmigiano, and mix very well; add half the *balsamella*, taste for salt and pepper, season with nutmeg, and mix again. Line the jelly-roll pan with the pasta and let the squares hang over the sides 2 inches all around. Pour the stuffing into the pan, level it, then cover with the remaining pasta squares. Fold the overlapping pieces of pasta inward, spread the remaining *balsamella* over, and sprinkle the tomato sauce on top. Bake for 25 minutes. Allow to cool for a few minutes before serving.

NOTE: TO PREPARE *BALSAMELLA*

Melt the butter in a heavy saucepan, preferably copper or enamel, over low heat. When the butter reaches the frothing point, add the flour all at once. Mix very well with a wooden spoon.

Cook until the flour is completely incorporated (1 to 3 minutes, depending on the quantities). If any lumps form, dissolve them by crushing them against the side of the pan with a wooden spoon. Remove the pan from the heat and let stand for 10 to 15 minutes.

While the butter-flour mixture is standing, heat the milk in another pan until it is very close to the boiling point. Put the saucepan with the butter-flour mixture over low heat and add all of the hot milk at once. Stir until the sauce is smooth.

When the sauce reaches the boiling point, add the salt and continue to stir gently while the sauce cooks slowly for about 10 minutes longer. Remove from the heat and transfer the sauce to a crockery bowl pressing a piece of buttered wax paper over the sauce to prevent a skin from forming. Let the sauce cool completely.

FOR THE TOMATO SAUCE:

1 ½ pounds ripe, fresh tomatoes, or 1 ½ pounds canned tomatoes, preferably imported Italian, drained

5 tablespoons (2 ½ ounces) sweet butter

4 large basil leaves, fresh or preserved in salt

Salt and freshly ground black pepper

PASTA ALLE PATATE

PASTA WITH POTATOES

1 pound potatoes (not new potatoes)
Coarse-grained salt
2 large cloves garlic, peeled
½ cup olive oil
Salt and freshly ground black pepper
½ teaspoon hot red pepper flakes
1 pound dried *spaghetti*, preferably imported Italian
¼ cup cold water
30 large sprigs Italian parsley, leaves only

In Tuscany, pasta is combined with potatoes in several ways. Since the carbohydrate horror is now outdated, it is understood that pasta has some protein and potatoes have valuable vitamins and minerals, and so we are not faced with a completely unbalanced dish.

*If the potatoes are boiled, as in the basic recipe for the **Pasta alle patate**, the pasta is then cooked in the potato water and the two are sautéed together with olive oil and garlic; fresh parsley and red pepper flakes are added at the end. The result is a warming and most satisfying dish. In one variation, the potatoes can be sautéed without boiling; in another, the potatoes are mashed before being incorporated.*

Peel the potatoes, then cut them into ½-inch slices, placing them in a bowl of cold water until needed. Bring a large quantity of cold water to a boil, add coarse salt to taste, then drain the potatoes, add them to the boiling water, and cook for 2 minutes. Use a strainer-skimmer to transfer the potatoes to a serving dish; reserve the potato water for later use.

Finely chop the garlic on a board. Place the oil in a large skillet over medium heat. When the oil is warm, add the potatoes; season with salt, pepper, and red pepper flakes; and sauté for 5 minutes, mixing every so often with a wooden spoon.

Meanwhile, bring the potato water back to a boil, add the pasta, and cook for 8 to 11 minutes depending on the brand; that is, 1 minute less than for normal al dente. As the pasta cooks, finish the potato sauce. Add the cold water to the skillet with the potatoes, cover, and cook for 10 minutes more. Coarsely chop the parsley on a board. When pasta is ready, drain and place it in the skillet with the potatoes. Raise the heat to high, mix well, and sauté for 1 minute more. Sprinkle the parsley over, mix well again, then transfer to a large, warmed platter and serve immediately.

VARIATIONS

1. The sliced potatoes can be added to the skillet raw instead of parboiled. In this case, ¼ cup of lukewarm chicken or beef broth should be added to the skillet after 2 minutes, to help cook the potatoes. The ¼ cup cold water is still added later, and the pasta is then cooked in fresh water rather than the potato water.

2. With either the original recipe or the above variation, once cooked, the potatoes can be passed through a food mill.

SPAGHETTI AL FINOCCHIO

SPAGHETTI WITH FRESH FENNEL

FROM SICILY

SERVES 4 TO 6

Recipes for fennel "bulbs" with pasta are very rare, but there is this wonderful one from Sicily, in which the fennel is cooked in tomato with oil, oregano, and red pepper flakes, and then puréed. The result is a tomato sauce flavored with lightly sautéed, puréed fennel. It is interesting to speculate as to why fennel is not traditionally used more in combination with pasta. Is there something in the texture that was not favored, and is this overcome by puréeing the fennel?

Clean the fennel, discarding the tough outer leaves and the dark green stems but not the feathery leafy parts; you should have about ¾ pound. Cut fennel into 1-inch pieces and put in a bowl of cold water for 30 minutes. If using fresh tomatoes, cut them into small pieces. Put fresh or canned tomatoes in a medium-sized flameproof casserole; drain the fennel and add it to the casserole along with the water and a little salt. Place casserole over medium heat and cook for 30 minutes.

Pass casserole contents through a food mill, using the disc with medium-sized holes, into a crockery or glass bowl. Place a medium-sized skillet with the oil, red pepper flakes, and oregano over low heat, and sauté for 1 minute. Add the puréed sauce, taste for salt and pepper, and reduce liquid for 10 minutes.

Bring a large pot of cold water to a boil, add coarse salt to taste, then add the pasta and cook for 8 to 11 minutes depending on the brand; that is, 1 minute less than for normal al dente. Drain the pasta, transfer it to the skillet, raise the heat, and sauté for 1 minute more, mixing with 2 forks to incorporate all the sauce. Transfer to a warmed serving platter and serve hot.

1 medium-sized bulb fennel (about 1¼ pounds), with green top leaves
1½ pounds ripe, fresh tomatoes; or 1½ pounds canned tomatoes, preferably imported Italian, drained
1 cup lukewarm water
Salt
6 tablespoons olive oil
½ teaspoon hot red pepper flakes
½ teaspoon dried oregano
Freshly ground black pepper
1 pound dried *spaghetti*, preferably imported Italian

TO COOK THE PASTA:
Coarse-grained salt

FROM TUSCANY

SERVES 4 TO 6

PENNE ALLE CIPOLLE

PASTA WITH ONION SAUCE

2 pounds red onions,
  peeled
8 tablespoons (4 ounces)
  sweet butter
2 tablespoons olive oil
2 cups dry white wine
1 cup cold water
Salt and freshly ground
  black pepper
1 pound dried tubular
  pasta, such as plain or
  ridged *penne*, preferably
  imported Italian

TO COOK THE PASTA:
Coarse-grained salt

TO SERVE:
**25 large sprigs Italian
  parsley, leaves only
Freshly ground black
  pepper**

A simple onion sauce is a favorite both in Tuscany and around Naples. The sweetness of the red onions is accentuated by white wine and, in Tuscany, by mixing some butter with the olive oil. In the Naples area the traditional lard is used instead.

Cut the onions into quarters and soak them in a bowl of cold water for 30 minutes. Drain and coarsely chop onions on a board. Place a large skillet with the onions, butter, and oil over medium heat. Cover and sauté for 10 minutes. Stir very well, lower the heat, add the first cup of wine, cover, and simmer for 1½ hours, stirring every so often with a wooden spoon. Add the remaining wine and finally the cold water, ½ cup at a time every 30 minutes. When all the liquid is added, season to taste with salt and abundant black pepper.

Bring a large pot of cold water to a boil, add coarse salt to taste, then add the pasta and cook until al dente, for 9 to 12 minutes depending on the brand.

As the pasta cooks, coarsely chop the parsley on a board. Drain the pasta, add it to the skillet with the sauce, and sauté for 30 seconds, mixing constantly and incorporating all the sauce with the pasta. Transfer to a large, warmed serving platter, sprinkle with more black pepper, then add the parsley and serve immediately.

NOTE:
In Campania, lard is substituted for butter, along with the small amount of oil; *perciatelli* is used rather than *penne*.

Sedanini al Sedano

PASTA WITH CELERY

*Another combination that appeals to the aesthetic Tuscans is celery cut into pieces the same size and shape as the dried pasta called **sedanini** (which in fact means "small celery pieces") and combined with that same pasta. With or without pasta, the frequent use of cooked celery as a vegetable is particularly Tuscan.*

Clean the celery, removing and discarding the tough outer stalks. Cut the tender white inner stalks into pieces the same length and width as the pasta. Weigh out 1 pound (see Note) of the cut-up celery and place it in a bowl of cold water to soak for 30 minutes.

Bring a large pot of cold water to a boil, add coarse salt to taste, then add the celery and boil until vegetable is fully cooked but still firm, about 5 to 8 minutes. Use a strainer-skimmer to transfer the celery pieces to a crockery or glass bowl; reserve the cooking water. Coarsely chop the garlic on a board. Place the oil in a large skillet over medium heat, and when the oil is warm, add the garlic and sauté for 30 seconds. Add the celery, then season with salt, pepper, and the red pepper flakes; mix very well and sauté for 5 minutes more.

Return the celery water to a boil, add the pasta and cook 7 to 10 minutes depending on the brand, or 2 minutes less than for normal al dente. As the pasta cooks, coarsely chop the parsley on a board. Drain the pasta, transfer it to the skillet with the celery, and sauté over medium heat for 2 minutes more, mixing very well. Transfer to a warmed platter, add the parsley, toss very well, and serve.

NOTE:
If you do not have a kitchen scale, 1 pound of the cut-up celery is approximately 2 cups.

2 large bunches celery
Coarse-grained salt
1 large clove garlic, peeled
½ cup olive oil
Salt and freshly ground
 black pepper
½ teaspoon hot red pepper
 flakes
1 pound dried *sedanini*
 (ridged tubular pasta
 similar to *rigatoni*, but
 smaller, also called
 fischiotti)

TO SERVE:
20 large sprigs Italian
 parsley, leaves only.

FROM APULIA

SERVES 4 TO 6

SEDANINI ALLA CRUDAIOLA
PASTA WITH UNCOOKED VEGETABLE SAUCE

1½ pounds fresh ripe
   tomatoes
Coarse-grained salt
2 medium-sized cloves
   garlic, peeled
½ teaspoon hot red pepper
   flakes, to be added to
   marinade (optional)
Juice of a medium-sized
   lemon
4 medium-sized inner
   white celery stalks, well
   scraped
½ cup olive oil
Salt and freshly ground
   black pepper
1 pound dried *sedanini*
   pasta, preferably
   imported Italian

TO COOK THE PASTA:
Coarse-grained salt

TO SERVE:
20 large sprigs Italian
   parsley, leaves only
15 large fresh basil leaves,
   left whole

*From Apulia we have the refreshing **Sedanini alla crudaiola**, in which the pasta is combined with uncooked celery and herbs; again, a cold sauce combined with a hot pasta.*

Blanch the tomatoes in salted boiling water, then remove the skins and seeds, leaving the tomato fillets whole. Place tomatoes in a crockery or glass bowl along with the garlic and hot red pepper flakes if used and pour the lemon juice over. Cut the celery into pieces the same size as the pasta and put them, along with the oil, in the bowl. Season with salt to taste and abundant black pepper, but do not mix. Cover the bowl and refrigerate for at least 1 hour or until needed.

Bring a large pot of cold water to a boil over medium heat, add coarse salt to taste, then add the pasta and cook it for 9 to 12 minutes depending on the brand. Meanwhile, mix the tomatoes with the other ingredients and coarsely chop the parsley. When the pasta is ready, drain and transfer it to a large serving platter, then pour the sauce over. Mix the pasta and sauce together very well, then sprinkle the parsley and basil all over, mix again, and serve.

TOMATOES

The pairing of pasta and tomatoes is legendary, yet it has existed only since the second quarter of the nineteenth century. It occurred, as one might guess, in and around Naples; the earliest printed recipe I have found is *Maccheroni all' Ultima Moda 1841 alla Napoletana* (see Recipe Appendix). Only fried green tomato dishes existed before that in Italy, specifically in Florence, dating back to the sixteenth century.

The two most classic tomato sauces are *Pommarola* (Summer Tomato Sauce) and *Sugo scappato* (Winter Tomato Sauce). They are made with aromatic vegetables and herbs. The summer version, using fresh tomatoes, has the vegetables simply simmered in the tomatoes. In the winter version, made with canned tomatoes, the vegetables are sautéed first (see Recipe Appendix).

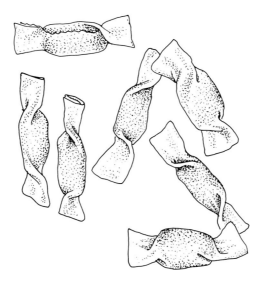

FROM CAMPANIA

SERVES 4 TO 6

2 large cloves garlic,
   peeled
20 large sprigs Italian
   parsley, leaves only
½ cup olive oil
2 pounds fresh, ripe
   tomatoes; or 2 pounds
   canned tomatoes,
   preferably imported
   Italian, drained
Salt and freshly ground
   black pepper
1 pound dried *vermicelli*
   or *perciatelli*,
   preferably imported
   Italian

TO COOK THE PASTA:
Coarse-grained salt

MACCHERONI ALLA MARINARA
PASTA MARINARA STYLE

*"Alla marinara" is a very popular treatment, though some versions have strayed very far from the original. Fundamentally, **alla marinara** simply means to add tomatoes to the basic olive oil and garlic, **aglio e olio**. This must have originated sometime in the nineteenth century, when ripe tomatoes came to play a dominant role in Neapolitan cooking, before spreading north. In Italy, even pizza **alla marinara** still means only tomatoes, oil, and garlic. The phrase refers to sailors or to fisherman, and, like "alla pescatora," means made in a quick and simple way, with just the few ingredients easily available to them. Because this basic dressing became popular to use with mussels and clams with pasta, some mistakenly think the phrase means "with seafood."*

*Here is the basic recipe with a few variations. Another variation, the popular red sauce for **spaghetti** with clams, which is simply "marinara" with the addition of the delicious "fruit of the sea" will be found on page 129. In Italy, no one ever refers to "marinara sauce," because it never appears independently. The sauce is always prepared quickly, together with the dish it is adorning. The greatest distortion of "alla marinara" is to add cheese, whether grated Parmigiano or pecorino or mozzarella, coarsely grated or in slices. In Italy, it is always understood that when you order "alla marinara," whether pasta or pizza, cheese is **not** an ingredient. And, of course, grated cheese should not be served with any dish in this category.*

Finely chop the garlic and coarsely chop the parsley separately on a board, then combine them. Place the oil in a medium-sized flame-proof casserole over medium heat; when the oil is warm, add the chopped ingredients and sauté for 2 minutes. If using fresh tomatoes, cut them into 1-inch pieces. Add fresh or canned tomatoes to the casserole and cook for 25 minutes more, stirring every so often with a wooden spoon. Pass the contents of the casserole through a food mill, using the disc with smallest holes, into a crockery or glass bowl. Then return sauce to the casserole, season with salt and pepper, and reduce over medium heat for 10 minutes.

Meanwhile, bring a large pot of cold water to a boil, add coarse salt to taste, then add the pasta and cook until al dente, 9 to 12 minutes depending on the brand. As the pasta cooks, reheat the sauce. Drain the pasta, transfer it to a warmed serving dish, pour the sauce over, toss well, and serve.

VARIATIONS

1. Peel and seed the tomatoes before adding them to the casserole, then do not pass the tomatoes through the food mill. Increase the cooking time to 35 minutes.

2. Leaves from 15 sprigs of Italian parsley, coarsely chopped, can be sprinkled over the pasta before serving with any of the versions.

3. Capers and olives can be added to the sauce when it is reheated. Use 4 tablespoons of capers in wine vinegar, drained, and 10 large Greek black olives, preserved in brine, pitted and cut into thirds. Capers and olives can be added to the above versions.

SPAGHETTI ALL'ARRABBIATA

SPAGHETTI WITH VERY SPICY TOMATO SAUCE

FROM ALL OVER ITALY

SERVES 4 TO 6

Tomato sauce with just olive oil and lots of hot red pepper flakes exists under a variety of names, one of the most picturesque being this **Spaghetti all'arrabbiata,** *which means "angry"* **spaghetti.** *Pasta sauces which are dominated by hot red pepper also often contain meat such as* **pancetta** *or* **prosciutto** *(see Recipe Appendix).*

If fresh tomatoes are used, cut them into pieces. Place fresh or canned tomatoes with the oil in a medium-sized saucepan over medium heat and cook for 25 minutes, stirring every so often with a wooden spoon. Season to taste with salt and pepper. Pass the mixture through a food mill, using the disc with smallest holes, into a second saucepan. Return the tomatoes to medium heat, add the red pepper flakes, and simmer for 15 minutes more.

Bring a large pot of cold water to a boil, add coarse salt to taste, then add the pasta and cook until al dente—from 9 to 12 minutes, depending on the brand.

Coarsely chop the parsley on a board. Drain the pasta, transfer to a warmed serving platter, pour the sauce over, mix very well, sprinkle the parsley over, and serve immediately.

VARIATION

Use 15 large fresh basil leaves, torn into thirds, instead of parsley.

1½ pounds ripe fresh tomatoes; or 1½ pounds canned tomatoes, preferably imported Italian, drained
4 tablespoons olive oil
Salt and freshly ground black pepper
½ teaspoon to ¾ teaspoon hot red pepper flakes
1 pound dried *spaghetti*, preferably imported Italian

TO COOK THE PASTA:
Coarse-grained salt

TO SERVE:
20 large sprigs Italian parsley, leaves only.

FROM TUSCANY

SERVES 4

1¼ pounds ripe, fresh
  tomatoes
2 tablespoons olive oil
2 large basil leaves, fresh
  or preserved in salt
Salt and freshly ground
  black pepper
½ pound dried *capelli
  d'angelo* or *capellini*
  (made with or without
  eggs), preferably
  imported Italian

TO COOK THE PASTA:
Coarse-grained salt

TO SERVE:
2 tablespoons (1 ounce)
  sweet butter, in 4 pieces
4 large fresh basil leaves
4 tablespoons freshly
  grated Parmigiano
  cheese (optional)

CAPELLI D'ANGELO AL POMODORO E BASILICO

ANGEL-HAIR PASTA WITH TOMATO SAUCE AND BASIL

*The flavor of ripe, fresh tomatoes in season is so satisfying that it is possible to add very little else to make a wonderful pasta dish. This simple treatment, incorporating a little olive oil and basil and a bit of butter melted onto the hot pasta, works well with many kinds of pasta, but best of all with the thinnest of all, **capelli d'angelo**. This "angel-hair" pasta has become very popular in recent years and, like **tortellini**, is put into all kinds of dishes where it does not belong. (The difference between **capellini** and **capelli d'angelo** is that the latter are arranged in small nests, while **capellini** are simply very fine long pasta.) In Italy, this fine pasta is used very little; indeed, one must really search to find a traditional regional dish that employs it. Again, it is important to ponder why this is so. Surely its use must have occurred to cooks and it must have been tried and rejected many times over the last two centuries.*

Prepare the fresh tomato sauce *alla toscana* (see Note). Cut fresh tomatoes into medium-sized pieces. Put in a flameproof casserole with the oil and basil leaves. Place the tomato casserole over medium heat and simmer, stirring every so often with a wooden spoon, for 25 minutes. Pass contents of casserole through a food mill, using the disc with smallest holes, into a crockery or glass bowl. Pour the strained sauce back into the casserole and reduce over low heat for 5 minutes more. Taste for salt and pepper.

Bring a large pot of cold water to a boil, add coarse salt to taste, then add the pasta and cook for 3 to 5 minutes depending on the brand. Pour half the sauce into a warmed crockery or glass bowl. Drain the pasta, transfer it to the bowl containing the sauce, pour the remaining sauce over, then mix very well. Serve immediately, placing ½ tablespoon of the butter and a basil leaf over each serving. Serve with cheese, if desired.

NOTE:

A slightly different *Sugo di pomodoro fresco* is given in my book, *The Fine Art of Italian Cooking.*

OTHER TOMATO INTERPRETATIONS

Another classic Neapolitan tomato sauce includes onions (though not carrots, celery, or garlic), basil, and the traditional lard as shortening. To accommodate modern taste, olive oil usually is substituted for the latter, but you might want to at least try it the old way. The favorite Neapolitan pasta is *vermicelli*, but *spaghetti* can be used if not available. Cheese is usually grated over the finished dish.

In the Neapolitan version of *alla puttanesca* garlic is substituted for the onions and the piquant ingredients—olives, capers, anchovies, and hot pepper flakes—are added. A little tomato paste is authentic in this recipe. Another famous *alla puttanesca* is Tuscan (see Recipe Appendix). Its special characteristic is that the tomatoes, garlic, and basil are all uncooked, simply marinated in the olive oil, then chilled and combined with hot pasta, which releases their incredible flavors.

Penne alla pizza, also from Naples, uses the Pommarola type of tomato sauce previously mentioned, with aromatic vegetables and herbs. The pasta with its sauce and olives is spread on a baking dish and covered, like many types of pizza, with pieces of mozzarella and baked for 15 minutes. The result is pasta "in the manner of pizza."

Three recipes then follow which characterize their individual regions. From Trapani in Sicily we have the special pesto made by combining fresh tomatoes, garlic and basil with the very typical Sicilian almonds (rather than *pignolis* and/or walnuts, used in the pesto of other regions). This Sicilian pesto will almost certainly become as popular as the Ligurian version once it is well known.

In Piedmont, the secret ingredient in the tomato sauce is eggs, mixed with the Parmigiano. Butter is preferred in this region, which has no olive oil of its own. It's a special dish, again characteristic of its region.

The combination of spicy and creamy is mediated well by using a tomato base. The most successful sauce of this type that I know can be found at the excellent traditional trattoria in Florence, La Vecchia Bettola. A little grain alcohol is added, and while it cooks off, it accentuates the bite of the red pepper flakes. When grain alcohol is not available, an unflavored vodka can be substituted.

1 medium-sized red onion,
　　peeled
8 tablespoons lard or olive
　　oil
1½ pounds ripe, fresh
　　tomatoes; or 1½ pounds
　　canned tomatoes,
　　preferably imported
　　Italian, drained
Salt and freshly ground
　　black pepper
1 pound dried *vermicelli*
　　or *spaghetti*, preferably
　　imported Italian
10 large fresh basil leaves

TO COOK THE PASTA:
Coarse-grained salt

TO SERVE:
Freshly grated pecorino
　　romano or Parmigiano
　　cheese

VERMICELLI CON SALSA DI POMODORO ALLA NAPOLETANA

VERMICELLI WITH NEAPOLITAN TOMATO SAUCE

Cut the onion into quarters. Place the lard or oil in a medium-sized, flameproof casserole over medium heat; when the lard is melted or oil is warm, add the onion and sauté until the outer layers are translucent, about 5 minutes. If using fresh tomatoes, cut them into 1-inch pieces. Add fresh or canned tomatoes to the casserole and cook for 25 minutes, seasoning to taste with salt and pepper. Remove and discard the onion, then pass the contents of the casserole through a food mill, using the disc with smallest holes, into a second flameproof casserole. Place the second casserole over low heat and reduce sauce for 10 minutes.

Bring a large pot of cold water to a boil, add coarse salt to taste, then add the pasta and cook for 9 to 12 minutes depending on the brand (see Note). As the pasta cooks, tear the basil leaves into thirds and add them to the sauce. Drain the pasta and transfer it to a large, warmed serving platter; add the sauce, toss well, and serve hot, sprinkling cheese over each serving.

NOTE:
In Naples, pasta is eaten very al dente, cooked about 2 minutes less than indicated here.

SPAGHETTI ALLA PUTTANESCA ALLA NAPOLETANA

SPAGHETTI ALLA PUTTANESCA, CAMPANIA STYLE

FROM CAMPANIA

SERVES 4 TO 6

If using fresh tomatoes, blanch them in boiling salted water, remove the skins, and cut them into pieces. Pass fresh or canned tomatoes through a food mill, using the disc with smallest holes, into a crockery or glass bowl.

Coarsely chop the garlic on a board. Heat the oil in a medium-sized saucepan over medium heat; when the oil is warm, add the garlic and sauté until lightly golden, about 10 minutes. Meanwhile, pit the olives and cut them into quarters. If using anchovies preserved in salt, fillet them under cold running water, discarding bones and washing away excess salt. Cut anchovy fillets into 1-inch pieces. Add the tomatoes to the pan, then the olives, anchovies, capers, and tomato paste. Mix well and season to taste with salt, pepper, and the red pepper flakes. Cook for 15 minutes over medium heat, stirring every so often with a wooden spoon.

Meanwhile, bring a large pot of cold water to a boil, add coarse salt to taste, then add the pasta and cook until al dente, for 9 to 12 minutes depending on the brand. Drain the pasta, place it in a large bowl, pour the sauce over, and mix well. Transfer to a warmed serving dish and serve immediately.

1½ pounds ripe, fresh tomatoes; or 1½ pounds canned tomatoes, preferably imported Italian, drained
Coarse-grained salt
2 medium-sized cloves garlic, peeled
½ cup olive oil
½ pound large black Greek olives in brine
3 anchovies in salt, or 6 anchovy fillets packed in oil, drained
4 heaping tablespoons capers in wine vinegar, drained
2 tablespoons tomato paste
Salt and freshly ground black pepper
½ teaspoon hot red pepper flakes
1 pound dried *spaghetti*, preferably imported Italian

TO COOK THE PASTA:
Coarse-grained salt

FROM CAMPANIA

SERVES 6 TO 8

PENNE ALLA PIZZA
PASTA IN THE STYLE OF PIZZA

**1 medium-sized stalk
  celery**
**½ medium-sized red onion,
  peeled**
1 large clove garlic, peeled
**10 large sprigs Italian
  parsley, leaves only**
**2 medium-sized carrots,
  scraped**
**20 large basil leaves, fresh
  or preserved in salt**
**2 pounds ripe, fresh
  tomatoes; or 2 pounds
  canned tomatoes,
  preferably imported
  Italian, drained**
**Salt and freshly ground
  black pepper**
3 tablespoons olive oil
**1 pound dried *penne*,
  preferably imported
  Italian**

TO COOK THE PASTA:
Coarse-grained salt

TO BAKE:
1 tablespoon olive oil
**8 ounces mozzarella
  cheese, cut into about
  ¼-inch thick slices**
1 teaspoon dried oregano
**30 black Greek olives in
  oil, drained and pitted**
**Salt and freshly ground
  black pepper**
**2 tablespoons (1 ounce)
  sweet butter, cut into
  small pieces**

Coarsely chop the celery, onion, garlic, parsley, carrots, and 5 of the basil leaves all together on a board. Put chopped ingredients in a medium-sized saucepan. If using fresh tomatoes, cut them into pieces. Add fresh or canned tomatoes to pan, cover, and cook, over low heat for 1 hour, stirring every so often with a wooden spoon. Pass the contents of the pan through a food mill, using the disc with the smallest holes, into a second saucepan. Add salt and pepper to taste and the oil; cook for 10 minutes longer.

Meanwhile, bring a large pot of cold water to a boil and preheat the oven to 375 degrees. When the water reaches a boil, add coarse salt to taste, then add the pasta and cook it for 8 to 11 minutes depending on the brand; that is, 1 minute less than for normal al dente.

Use the tablespoon of oil to heavily coat a 13½- x 8¾-inch glass baking dish. Drain the pasta and place it in a large bowl. Add the still-hot tomato sauce, the mozzarella, oregano, olives, remaining basil leaves torn into thirds, and salt and pepper to taste. Gently but thoroughly mix all the ingredients, then place in the oiled dish. Spread the butter pieces over the pasta, cover the dish with aluminum foil, and bake 15 minutes. Serve hot directly from the dish.

PASTA CON PESTO ALLA TRAPANESE

PASTA WITH SICILIAN PESTO

Bring a medium-sized saucepan of cold water to a boil over medium heat, and when the water reaches a boil add coarse salt to taste, then add the tomatoes. Blanch them, then remove the seeds and put the tomatoes in a crockery or glass bowl until needed.

With a mortar and pestle, finely grind the almonds with the garlic; when the texture is very creamy, add the basil and grind until basil is completely incorporated. Transfer mixture to a large crockery or glass bowl. Pass the tomatoes through a food mill, using the disc with the smallest holes, into the bowl containing the mixture. Season to taste with salt and pepper, add the olive oil, and mix all the ingredients with a wooden spoon. Cover the bowl and refrigerate until needed. (The pesto sauce can be prepared several hours before serving and kept covered, in the refrigerator.)

If using fresh pasta, prepare it with the ingredients listed and follow the directions on page 14. Stretch layer to 1/8 inch thick, cutting into *spaghetti*, see illustration page 57. Let pasta rest on cotton dish towels or paper towels until needed.

Bring a large pot of cold water to a boil, and when the water reaches a boil, add coarse salt to taste, then add the pasta and cook until al dente, for 9 to 12 minutes depending on the brand. (If using fresh pasta, cook for 1 to 3 minutes depending on dryness.) Drain the pasta, and transfer it to a large, warmed serving platter; pour the sauce over, mix very well, and serve immediately.

NOTE:

The pesto can be made in a food processor. Place the almonds, garlic, and olive oil in the bowl and, using the metal blade, grind until very fine. Then add the basil, salt, and pepper, and grind again until texture is very creamy.

Coarse-grained salt
1½ pounds ripe, fresh tomatoes
4½ ounces blanched almonds
4 medium-sized cloves garlic, peeled
25 large basil leaves
Salt and freshly ground black pepper
½ cup olive oil
1 pound dried *bucatini*, *linguini*, or *spaghetti*, preferably imported Italian
or
3 cups unbleached all-purpose flour
4 extra-large eggs
Pinch of salt

TO COOK THE PASTA:
Coarse-grained salt

SPAGHETTI ALLA PIEMONTESE

SPAGHETTI, PIEDMONT STYLE

FROM PIEDMONT

SERVES 4 TO 6

1 pound very ripe, fresh
    tomatoes; or 1 pound
    canned tomatoes,
    preferably imported
    Italian, drained
8 tablespoons (4 ounces)
    sweet butter
1 tablespoon olive oil
Salt and freshly ground
    black pepper
3 extra-large eggs
1 cup freshly grated
    Parmigiano cheese
1 pound dried *spaghetti*,
    preferably imported
    Italian

TO COOK THE PASTA:
Coarse-grained salt

If using fresh tomatoes, cut them into 1-inch pieces. Pass fresh or canned tomatoes through a food mill, using the disc with the smallest holes, into a crockery or glass bowl. Place a saucepan with the butter and oil over medium heat, and when the butter is melted, add the tomatoes and simmer for 15 minutes. Taste for salt and pepper.

Bring a large pot of cold water to a boil. Meanwhile, mix the eggs and Parmigiano very well in a small crockery or glass bowl and set aside until needed. When the water reaches a boil, add coarse salt to taste, then add the pasta and cook until al dente, for 9 to 12 minutes depending on the brand.

As the pasta cooks, place 1 cup of the tomato sauce in a large serving dish and place it over the boiling water, partially covering the top of the pot. Drain the pasta, transfer it to the heated serving dish, and pour over the remaining sauce. Mix very well, then add the egg mixture, toss thoroughly, and serve immediately.

PENNE ALLA BETTOLA

PENNE WITH SPICY TOMATO-CREAM SAUCE

FROM FLORENCE

SERVES 4 TO 6

2 medium-sized cloves
    garlic, peeled
5 tablespoons olive oil
1½ pounds ripe, fresh
    tomatoes; or 1½ pounds
    canned tomatoes,
    preferably Italian
    imported, drained
Salt and freshly ground
    black pepper
½ teaspoon hot red pepper
    flakes

Coarsely chop the garlic on a board. Heat the oil in a medium-sized saucepan over medium heat, and when the oil is warm, add the chopped garlic and sauté for 3 minutes. If using fresh tomatoes, cut them into 1-inch pieces. Add fresh or canned tomatoes to pan and cook for 20 minutes. Season to taste with salt and pepper, then add the red pepper flakes. Pass the contents of the pan through a food mill, using the disc with the smallest holes, into a large skillet.

Bring a large pot of cold water to a boil. Meanwhile, place the skillet over low heat and simmer sauce as you cook the pasta. Add coarse salt to the boiling water, then add the pasta and cook for 8 to 11 minutes depending on the brand, that is, 1 minute less than for normal al dente.

Meanwhile, coarsely chop the parsley on a board. Drain the pasta and add it to the skillet with the tomato sauce. Add the alcohol or vodka, mix very well, and raise the heat to medium. Sauté for 1 minute, stirring the pasta vigorously with a wooden spoon. Add the cream; taste for salt and pepper. Mix for 30 seconds to allow the cream to get well absorbed into the pasta, then sprinkle on the parsley, transfer pasta to a warmed serving dish, and serve immediately.

1 pound dried *penne*, preferably imported Italian
15 large sprigs Italian parsley, leaves only
2 tablespoons pure grain alcohol, or vodka
1 cup heavy cream

TO COOK THE PASTA:
Coarse-grained salt

ZUCCHINI

Most zucchini and pasta recipes come from southern Italy, and I have not found a single one from those regions in which the zucchini are not cut into discs and fried in olive oil. Included here are two Sicilian recipes with their variations, as well as another from Calabria—all three of which are typical of the treatment in the southern regions.

In the first, the fried zucchini are tossed together with the pasta and sprinkled with grated cheese. In this recipe, as in the following one, some of the oil suffused with the zucchini flavor serves as the sauce. In the second version, first a pasta with bread crumbs is prepared, and then the fried zucchini discs are arranged either on top or on the side. No cheese is added.

In the third recipe, from Calabria, ricotta is used instead of grated cheese or bread crumbs, and the flavor of basil is added. The zucchini are fried in the lighter vegetable oil and only the olive oil used to brown the garlic is added. Again it is unlikely that it never occurred to cooks in these several centuries that zucchini might be sautéed or boiled or whatever when combined with pasta. Clearly these methods were eliminated as a consensus was reached that the zucchini worked best when fried.

In Lucca (Tuscany), *ravioli* are dressed with a sauce in which coarsely grated zucchini are cooked together with tomatoes and olive oil. The *ravioli* and sauce are alternated in layers to make a most attractive presentation. Butter, basil, and Parmigiano are added at the end.

FROM SICILY

SERVES 4 TO 6

PASTA E ZUCCHINE
PASTA AND ZUCCHINI

2 pounds small, thin
zucchini (not miniature)
2 cups extra-virgin olive
oil, preferably from
southern Italy
Salt and freshly ground
black pepper
1 pound dried *spaghetti*,
preferably imported
Italian
4 to 6 tablespoons
unseasoned bread
crumbs, preferably
homemade

TO COOK THE PASTA:
Coarse-grained salt

Cut off and discard the ends of the zucchini, then soak them in a bowl of cold water for 30 minutes. Place a large pot of cold water over high heat and a large skillet with the oil over medium heat. Remove the zucchini from the water, pat very dry with paper towels, then cut into ¼-inch-thick discs. When the oil is hot (about 400 degrees), raise the heat, add the zucchini, and cook until golden on both sides, about 3 minutes, mixing frequently with a strainer-skimmer.

When the water reaches a boil, add coarse salt to taste, then add the pasta and cook until al dente, 9 to 12 minutes depending on the brand. Use the strainer-skimmer to transfer the zucchini to a serving dish lined with paper towels to drain off excess oil. Season with salt and pepper to taste and cover dish to keep the zucchini warm.

Take ¾ cup of the hot oil from the zucchini, pour it into a small saucepan, and let it cool for 2 minutes. Add the bread crumbs, put pan over low heat, season with salt and pepper, and sauté the bread crumbs until lightly golden, for 1 minute. Transfer bread crumbs with strainer-skimmer to a dish, saving oil for later use.

Drain the pasta and arrange it on a large, warmed serving dish, pour the hot oil from the bread crumbs over, toss well, place the zucchini over the pasta, then sprinkle the bread crumbs over and serve hot.

VARIATIONS
1. Use 1 pound of zucchini instead of 2.
2. Instead of placing the fried zucchini over the pasta, serve a portion separately on the same plate.

PASTA ALLE ZUCCHINE

PASTA WITH ZUCCHINI, SICILIAN STYLE

1 pound small, thin zucchini (not miniature)
2 cups extra-virgin, full-bodied olive oil, preferably from southern Italy
1 pound dried *spaghetti*, preferably imported Italian
Salt and freshly ground black pepper
½ cup freshly grated pecorino romano or Parmigiano cheese

TO COOK THE PASTA:
Coarse-grained salt

Cut off and discard the ends of the zucchini, and soak zucchini in a bowl of cold water for 30 minutes. Bring a large pot of cold water to a boil, and place a large, heavy skillet with the oil on medium heat. Remove the zucchini from the water, pat dry with paper towels, then cut into ¼-inch-thick discs. When the oil is hot (about 400 degrees), raise the heat, add the zucchini, and cook until golden on both sides, about 3 minutes, mixing frequently with a strainer-skimmer.

When the water reaches a boil, add coarse salt to taste, and then add the pasta and cook until al dente, 9 to 12 minutes depending on the brand. When the zucchini are ready, use the strainer-skimmer to transfer them to a serving dish lined with paper towels to drain off excess oil. Take ¾ cup of the hot oil from the zucchini and pour it into a large serving bowl. Add salt and pepper to taste. At that point the pasta should be ready; drain it and place in the bowl with the oil. Sprinkle the cheese over, then add the zucchini, toss very well but gently, and serve immediately.

VARIATIONS

1. Cheese can be omitted.

2. Leaves of 20 sprigs of Italian parsley, coarsely chopped, can be added to the bowl over the zucchini and tossed together with the other ingredients.

3. A large clove of garlic, peeled, can be added whole while frying the zucchini and discarded, or chopped and can be added sautéed in the oil used to dress the pasta. This is not a very typical preparation.

4. Any combination of the above.

NOTE:

Olive oil is no longer exclusively used for frying in Italy; most have switched to the lighter vegetable oils, and use a little olive oil for flavor in sautéing. But this dish really depends on the flavor of olive oil-permeated zucchini. The flavor need not be heavy if the oil is fresh, and not reused, as was once the custom. The zucchini should be completely cooked, not half cooked and crisp.

FROM LUCCA
(TUSCANY)

SERVES 6 TO 8

FOR THE STUFFING:
**15 ounces whole-milk
ricotta**
2 extra-large egg yolks
**4 tablespoons freshly
grated Parmigiano
cheese**
**Salt and freshly ground
black pepper**

FOR THE PASTA:
**4 cups unbleached all-
purpose flour**
5 extra-large eggs
Pinch of salt

FOR THE SAUCE:
1½ pounds thin zucchini
1 large lemon
**1 pound ripe, fresh
tomatoes; or 1 pound
canned tomatoes,
preferably imported
Italian, drained and
seeded**
Coarse-grained salt
½ cup olive oil
**Salt and freshly ground
black pepper**

TO COOK THE PASTA:
Coarse-grained salt

TO SERVE:
**4 tablespoons (2 ounces)
sweet butter**
6 large fresh basil leaves
**6 to 8 tablespoons freshly
grated Parmigiano
cheese**
**Freshly ground black
pepper**

RAVIOLI ALLE ZUCCHINE
RAVIOLI WITH ZUCCHINI SAUCE

Prepare the stuffing. Use a cheesecloth to drain the ricotta very well, then place the ricotta in a crockery or a glass bowl. Add the egg yolks, Parmigiano, and salt and pepper to taste, and mix with a wooden spoon. Cover the bowl and refrigerate until needed.

Prepare the pasta with the ingredients and quantities listed, following the directions on page 14. Stretch layer to less than 1/16 inch thick—the finest setting on the pasta machine. Prepare *ravioli* with a rectangular shape (2 x 3 inches; see illustrations, page 113), and use ½ tablespoon of the stuffing for each. Let the *ravioli* rest on cotton dish towels until needed.

Prepare the sauce. Clean and wash the zucchini well, then use a hand grater to coarsely grate them into a crockery or glass bowl. Squeeze the lemon and add 2 tablespoons of the juice to the bowl; mix well and let rest for 5 minutes. Meanwhile, if using fresh tomatoes, bring a small saucepan of cold water to a boil, add coarse salt to taste, then add the tomatoes. Blanch for 2 minutes, then remove from the water. Peel and seed the tomatoes. Heat the oil in a medium-sized saucepan over medium heat. Drain and rinse the zucchini under cold running water. When the oil is warm, add the zucchini along with the fresh or canned tomatoes without cutting them up. Sauté for 2 minutes, stirring every so often.

Bring a large pot of cold water to a boil and add coarse salt to taste. Melt the butter in a small saucepan set over the pot of boiling water. Raise the heat on the zucchini sauce, and season it with salt and pepper. Add the *ravioli* to the boiling water and cook for 1 to 3 minutes depending on dryness. Use a strainer-skimmer to transfer the cooked *ravioli* to a warmed serving dish.

Make a layer of *ravioli* on the serving dish, then pour one-third of the melted butter and one-third of the zucchini sauce over them. Sprinkle with 2 basil leaves torn into thirds. Repeat the same order —pasta, butter, sauce and basil—2 more times. Serve, sprinkling each individual portion with some Parmigiano and a twist of black pepper.

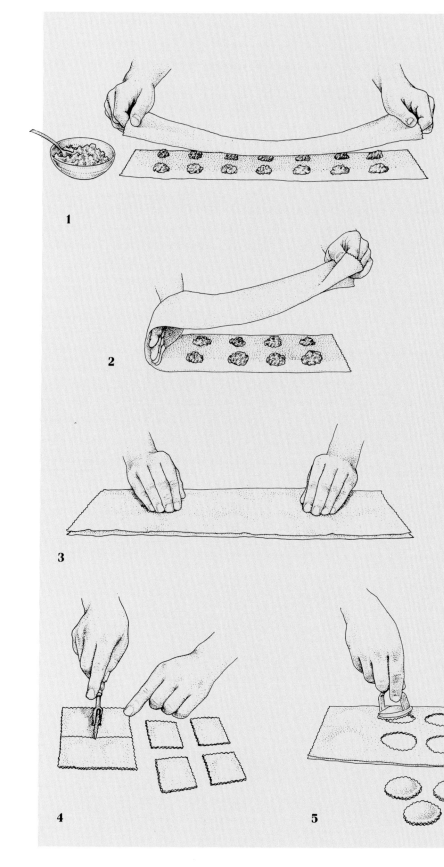

TORTELLI, RAVIOLI, AND MEZZELUNE

1. **Tortelli** may be squares, rounds, rectangles or half-moons of two layers of pasta filled with a little stuffing and sealed. They are sometimes called **ravioli.** After pasta is made, stretch the layer to the thickness required by the recipe. Place dots of the filling on the bottom layer and fit a second layer of pasta over the first.

2. It is also possible to place the dots of filling on half of one layer of pasta and to fold the other half over.

3. With the tips of your fingers, press down the edges along the center of the two overlapped layers of pasta to remove the air.

4. Then, for square or rectangular shaped **tortelli** or **ravioli,** use a scalloped pastry cutter to cut them into these shapes.

5. If you want round **tortelli** or **ravioli,** use a large or small **ravioli** cutter.

113

PASTA CON LE ZUCCHINE

PASTA WITH ZUCCHINI, CALABRIAN STYLE

1 pound small, thin
  zucchini (not miniature),
  cleaned
Coarse-grained salt
1 quart vegetable oil
½ cup olive oil
4 large cloves garlic,
  peeled but left whole
1 pound dried *vermicelli*,
  preferably imported
  Italian
4 ounces ricotta
Salt and freshly ground
  black pepper
10 large leaves fresh basil,
  torn into thirds

TO COOK THE PASTA:
Coarse-grained salt

Slice the zucchini into discs about ¼ inch thick and place them on a large platter. Sprinkle 2 tablespoons of coarse salt over and let stand for 30 minutes.

Rinse the zucchini under cold running water and pat dry with paper towels to drain off excess oil. Heat the vegetable oil in a large skillet over medium heat. When the oil is hot, add the zucchini and fry until lightly golden on both sides, about 4 minutes. Meanwhile, bring a large pot of cold water to a boil over medium heat.

With a slotted spoon, transfer the cooked zucchini to a platter lined with paper towels to remove excess oil. Remove and discard all but ¼ cup of the cooking oil, add the olive oil to the skillet, and sauté the garlic until lightly golden, 5 minutes.

Add coarse salt to the pasta pot, then add the pasta and cook it until al dente, for 9 to 12 minutes depending on the brand. Drain the pasta and place it in a large bowl. Add the ricotta and salt and pepper to taste, then add the hot oil from the garlic and mix very well. (Discard the garlic.) Arrange the fried zucchini over, sprinkle with the basil leaves, and serve very hot.

RECIPE APPENDIX

Pasta and Vegetable Recipes in Other Bugialli Books

TRENETTE AL PESTO (*Trenette* with Basil Sauce) *FA* p. 153
SPAGHETTI CON BRICIOLATA (*Spaghetti* with Bread Crumb Sauce) *FA* p. 158
PASTA ALLA PUTTANESCA (Pasta with a Sauce of Uncooked Tomatoes and Herbs) *FA* p. 159
TORTELLI ALLA MENTA (*Tortelli* with Fresh Mint) *FA* p. 168
TORTELLI DELLA VIGILIA ("Half-moon" *Tortelli* Stuffed with Spinach and Ricotta) *FA* p. 169
TORTELLI DI ZUCCA ALLA MODENESE (Pumpkin *Tortelli*, Modena Style) *FA* p. 174
CANNELLONI DELLA VIGILIA (*Cannelloni* Stuffed with Spinach and Ricotta) *FA* p. 184
CANNELLONI CON RICOTTA (*Cannelloni* Stuffed with Ricotta and Parsley) *FA* p. 185
ROTOLO DI PASTA RIPIENO (Stuffed Pasta Roll) *FA* p. 198
ORECCHIETTE CON CIME DI RAPE (*Orecchiette* with Broccolirab) *CT* p. 153
SPAGHETTI AL POMODORO AL FORNO (*Spaghetti* in Sauce with Baked Tomatoes) *CT* p. 139
TAGLIATELLE CON SUGO DI ASPARAGI (*Tagliatelle* with Asparagus Sauce) *CT* p. 133
TRENETTE CON SALSA DI CARCIOFI (*Trenette* with Artichoke Sauce) *CT* p. 149
TAGLIATELLE CON SALSA DI NOCI (*Tagliatelle* in Walnut Sauce) *CT* p. 136
TORTELLI DI MELE (Apple *Tortelli* for Christmas Eve) *CT* p. 171
CANNELLONI CON PUNTE DI ASPARAGI (*Cannelloni* Stuffed with Asparagus) *CT* p. 156
LASAGNE CON MELANZANE (*Lasagne* with Eggplant) *CT* p. 163
LASAGNE CON PESTO (*Lasagne* with Pesto) *CT* p. 159
MACCHERONI "ALL'ULTIMA MODA 1841" (Pasta "in the Latest Style," Naples 1841) *CT* p. 182
SPAGHETTI CON BROCCOLI (*Spaghetti* with Broccoli) *CT* p. 183
SPAGHETTI DELL'ORTOLANO (Thin *Spaghetti* with Aromatic Herbs and Vegetables) *CT* p. 184
POMODORI RIPIENI DI PASTA (Tomatoes Stuffed with *Macaroni*) *CT* p. 387
PISELLI E PATERNOSTRI (Peas and *Paternostri*) *FI* p. 57
SPAGHETTI ALLA SANGIOVANNINO (*Spaghetti* with Air-dried Cherry Tomatoes) *FI* p. 108
ORECCHIETTE CON CAVOLFIORE (*Orecchiette* with Cauliflower) *FI* p. 110
LUMACHELLE AL TARTUFO (*Lumachelle* Pasta with Black Truffle Sauce) *FI* p. 116
PASTA AL CARTOCCIO (*Spaghetti* Baked in Parchment Paper) *FI* p. 118
TAGLIERINI AL POMODORO FRESCO (*Taglierini* with Fresh Tomato Sauce) *FA* p. 145

Vegetable Sauces for Pasta in Other Bugialli Books

POMMAROLA (Summer Tomato Sauce) *FA* p. 70
SUGO SCAPPATO (Winter Tomato Sauce) *FA* p. 71

FA The Fine Art of Italian Cooking
CT Giuliano Bugialli's Classic Techniques of Italian Cooking
FI Giuliano Bugialli's Foods of Italy

**Minestra di pasta
all' aragosta**

CHAPTER 3

PASTA WITH FISH

PESCE AZZURRO

The category of fish known as *pesce azzurro*, literally "blue fish," which has no connection with the North Atlantic bluefish, includes mackerel and two smaller fish, sardines and anchovies. These two small types traditionally were preserved in salt and used to flavor many dishes. Their flavor is probably the descendent of that ancient Roman pungent fish sauce called *garum*, which we find in Apicius. Sardines in their salted form were once used as much as anchovies, but they have all but disappeared. Flavoring pasta with these fish, filleted and crushed into a paste, may well have been the original wedding of fish with pasta. Indeed, when the Milanese took the original Venetian salted sardine dish and substituted fresh sardines, it was a noteworthy enough event that the use of fresh sardines with pasta is known as *alla milanese* to this day in parts of Sicily, where the dish still flourishes. (See page 212 for the Venetian *Bigoli scuri in salsa*, using the salted sardines or anchovies and the Milanese version with fresh sardines.)

Fresh anchovies are abundant in the Mediterranean, but are not usually found in most areas of the Atlantic. However, even in Italy, fresh anchovies are not traditionally combined with pasta. They are eaten freshly marinated as an appetizer, or are baked, fried, or broiled (see Recipe Appendix).

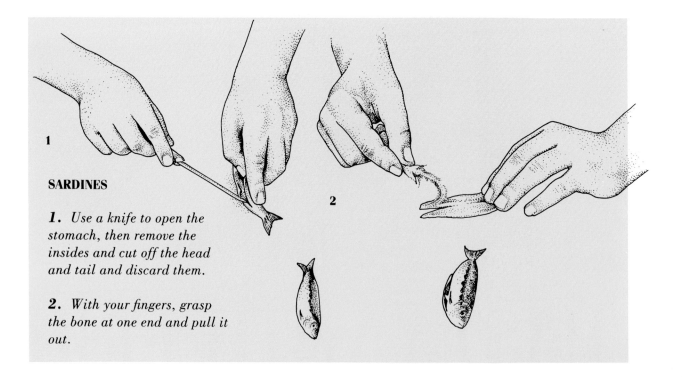

SARDINES

1. *Use a knife to open the stomach, then remove the insides and cut off the head and tail and discard them.*

2. *With your fingers, grasp the bone at one end and pull it out.*

PASTA ALLE SARDE II

PASTA WITH FRESH SARDINES, SECOND VERSION

*This version of **Pasta alle sarde** differs a bit from the one in my **Classic Techniques of Italian Cooking**. Preserved anchovies are combined with the fresh sardines and an onion is added; the **pignolis** are more abundant and a little saffron is added; the wine vinegar is omitted, and the pasta is the substantial, thick **perciatelli** with the hole through them. Dried wild fennel is sufficiently available now outside of Sicily that no substitute is necessary. The dried herb looks like woody small stalks and yields intense flavor when cooked.*

In a large stockpot, bring the cold water to a boil, add coarse salt to taste, then add the dried fennel and the fennel tops and cook for 20 minutes. With a strainer-skimmer, transfer the herbs from the water onto a plate. Save the water for later use, discard the cooked dried fennel, and save the fresh green tops.

Coarsely chop the onion with the cooked fennel tops on a board and set aside until needed. Clean the sardines, discarding the heads, tails, and bones (you should have ½ pound meat), and soak the fillets in a bowl of cold water with a little coarse salt. If using anchovies preserved in salt, clean them under cold running water, then remove the heads, bones, and excess salt. Set aside.

Place a medium-sized flameproof casserole with the oil over medium heat, and when the oil is warm, add the chopped onion and fennel tops. Sauté for 5 minutes, then add the raisins, pine nuts, and anchovies, using a fork to mash the anchovies. Taste for salt and pepper, add the saffron, and cook over low heat for 10 minutes more.

Meanwhile, reheat the fennel water to a boil, taste for salt, add the pasta, and cook until al dente for 9 to 12 minutes depending on the brand. Four minutes before the pasta is to finish cooking, add the sardines to the sauce; mix very well and cook over low heat until the pasta is ready. Drain the pasta, transfer it to a large warmed platter, add the sauce, mix well using 2 forks, and serve immediately.

VARIATION

Sprinkle 3 tablespoons of toasted bread crumbs over the pasta when it is on the serving platter.

3½ quarts cold water
Coarse-grained salt
¼ ounce dried wild fennel
2 ounces green tops of fennel (Florence fennel) bulbs
1 medium-sized red onion, peeled
1 pound fresh sardines
4 whole anchovies in salt; or 8 anchovy fillets packed in oil, drained
¾ cup olive oil
3 tablespoons raisins
3 tablespoons pine nuts (*pignolis*)
Salt and freshly ground black pepper
Large pinch of ground saffron
1 pound dried *perciatelli* or *bucatini*, preferably imported Italian

FROM LIVORNO
(TUSCANY)

SERVES 4 TO 6

1 pound several different
   kinds of saltwater fish
Coarse-grained salt
2 large red onions, peeled
   and cut into large pieces
2 medium-sized stalks
   celery, cut into 2-inch
   pieces
10 large sprigs Italian
   parsley, leaves only
2 cups cold water
½ cup olive oil
4 tablespoons tomato paste
½ cup chicken or beef
   broth, preferably
   homemade
Salt and freshly ground
   black pepper
1 pound dried *bavette*
   pasta, preferably
   imported Italian

TO COOK THE PASTA:
Coarse-grained salt

TO SERVE:
15 large sprigs Italian
   parsley, leaves only

BAVETTE SUL PESCE

BAVETTE WITH FISH SAUCE, LIVORNO STYLE

The two most famous sauces made from a puréed combination of saltwater fish come from Genoa and from Livorno. The Genoese **Passato di pesce,** *generally eaten with* **spaghetti,** *is very pure, with no broth or tomato added to the water. This sauce is reduced for a long time, and the purity of the fish flavor is enhanced only by parsley, rosemary, and onion.* In this, as in the Livorno version here, the fish is sautéed in olive oil before being puréed and reduced. The tomato and broth are added as well as celery and the rosemary is omitted. The preferred pasta is* **bavette,** *long and flat like* **linguine** *and available as a dried pasta.*

Cut the fish into small pieces, leaving bones, of about 2 inches and put them in a bowl of cold water with coarse salt to soak for 30 minutes. Soak the onions, celery, and parsley in another bowl of cold water for the same period.

Bring the 2 cups cold water to a boil in a small saucepan over medium heat, and when the water reaches a boil, add coarse salt to taste. Drain the vegetables and add the celery, parsley, and 1 onion. Simmer for 15 minutes. Drain the fish, rinse it under cold running water, and add it to the saucepan with the vegetables. Cover and cook for 10 minutes more, then set aside to rest, covered, for 15 minutes.

Remove and discard the bones from the fish, then pass the fish along with the rest of the contents of the pan through a food mill, using the disc with the largest holes, into a small bowl. If the mixture does not pass through the mill easily, add up to 1 cup of hot water to thin it.

Finely chop the remaining onion on a board. Place a medium-sized saucepan with the oil over medium heat. When the oil is warm, add the onion and sauté until translucent, about 10 minutes. Dissolve the tomato paste in the broth and add it to the pan. Simmer for 10 minutes, then add the fish mixture and simmer for 15 minutes longer. Pass the contents of the saucepan through a food mill, using the disc with the smallest holes, into a bowl. Return the contents of the bowl to the saucepan, taste for salt and pepper, and simmer over medium heat for 10 minutes more.

Bring a large pot of cold water to a boil, and when the water reaches a boil, add coarse salt to taste, then add the pasta and cook for 7 to 10 minutes depending on the brand; that is, 2 minutes less than for normal al dente. Transfer the sautéed mixture to a large skillet and place over high heat. Drain the pasta, add it to the skillet, and sauté for a minute or so. Let the sauce assimilate with the pasta, mixing with 2 forks. Transfer to a large, warmed serving dish, sprinkle with the parsley, and serve.

* See Recipe Appendix.

PASTA CON PESCE SPADA
PASTA WITH SWORDFISH

One would expect Sicily to have a fish sauce made with its favorite swordfish. Aromatic vegetables and herbs, basil, and parsley are chopped and sautéed, and the swordfish is cut into 1-inch squares without skin or bone. Tomatoes, olives, and capers are added to this tasty sauce, which is used to dress short tubular pasta as in this recipe.

Finely chop the parsley, garlic, carrots, celery, and basil all together on a board. Place the oil in a medium-sized flameproof casserole over medium heat, and when the oil is warm, add the chopped ingredients. Sauté for 5 minutes, stirring every so often with a wooden spoon. If using fresh tomatoes, cut them into pieces. Pass the fresh or canned tomatoes through a food mill, using the disc with smallest holes, into a crockery or glass bowl. Add the tomatoes to the pot and simmer for 20 minutes; add the capers and olives and cook for 5 minutes more.

Remove the skin from the fish, cut the flesh into 1-inch cubes, and add them to the sauce. Simmer for 15 minutes, mixing every so often with a wooden spoon and mashing the fish pieces to incorporate them. Taste for salt and pepper.

Meanwhile, bring a large pot of cold water to a boil, add coarse salt to taste, then add the pasta and cook for 9 to 12 minutes depending on the brand. Drain the pasta, place it on a warmed serving platter, add the sauce, mix well, and serve.

VARIATIONS

1. Sprinkle leaves of 25 sprigs of Italian parsley over the dish before serving.

2. A large pinch of dried oregano can be added along with salt and pepper.

FOR THE SAUCE:
15 large sprigs Italian parsley, leaves only
4 large cloves garlic, peeled
2 medium-sized carrots, scraped
3 large stalks celery
5 large basil leaves, fresh or preserved in salt
¼ cup olive oil
1 pound ripe, fresh tomatoes; or 1 pound canned tomatoes, preferably imported Italian, drained
4 tablespoons capers in wine vinegar, drained
15 large green olives in brine, drained, pitted, and cut into thirds
½ pound swordfish steak, in 1 piece
Salt and freshly ground black pepper
1 pound dried short tubular pasta, such as *rigatoni* or *penne*, preferably imported Italian

TO COOK THE PASTA:
Coarse-grained salt

FROM THE
MARCHES

SERVES 6 TO 8

FOR THE STUFFING:
15 ounces ricotta
3 extra-large egg yolks
½ cup freshly grated
    Parmigiano cheese
20 large sprigs Italian
    parsley, leaves only
Salt and freshly ground
    black pepper
Freshly grated nutmeg

FOR THE PASTA:
3 cups unbleached all-
    purpose flour
4 extra-large eggs
Pinch of salt

FOR THE SAUCE:
1 medium-sized carrot,
    scraped
1 medium-sized stalk
    celery
1 medium-sized red onion,
    peeled
1 medium-sized clove
    garlic, peeled
15 large sprigs Italian
    parsley, leaves only
½ cup olive oil
1½ pounds ripe, fresh
    tomatoes; or 1½ pounds
    canned tomatoes,
    preferably imported
    Italian, drained
¾ cup dry white wine
Salt and freshly ground
    black pepper
1 pound sole fillets

TO COOK THE PASTA:
Coarse-grained salt

RAVIOLI AL SUGO DI FILETTI DI SOGLIOLA
RAVIOLI WITH SAUCE OF SOLE FILLET

*In the Marches on the Adriatic, we have a sauce made with sole fillets. Again, the aromatic vegetables and herbs are sautéed and tomatoes and white wine are added. Basil is omitted, and the abundant garlic of the Sicilian fish sauce is reduced to a single clove. Interestingly, the sauce is used to dress a stuffed pasta, **ravioli**, filled simply with ricotta, egg yolks, Parmigiano, and parsley. This recipe is one of the rare exceptions to the avoidance of grated cheese in combination with fish; but here the cheese is a binder for the stuffing, and again no grated cheese would be sprinkled over at the end.*

Prepare the stuffing. Put the ricotta, egg yolks, and Parmigiano in a crockery or glass bowl; mix the ingredients with a wooden spoon. Finely chop the parsley on a board, then add it to bowl and season to taste with salt, pepper, and nutmeg. Mix well, cover the bowl, and refrigerate until needed.

Prepare the pasta with the ingredients and quantities listed, following the directions on page 14. Stretch layer to less than 1/16 inch thick—almost the finest setting on the pasta machine. Prepare *ravioli* about 2½ inches square (see page 113). Use a heaping teaspoon of the stuffing for each square, and let them sit on cotton towels until needed.

Prepare the sauce. Finely chop the carrot, celery, onion, garlic, and parsley all together on a board. Heat the olive oil in a medium-sized flameproof casserole, preferably terra-cotta or enamel, over low heat. Add the chopped ingredients and sauté for 10 minutes, stirring every so often with a wooden spoon.

If fresh tomatoes are used, cut them into pieces. Pass the fresh or canned tomatoes through a food mill, using the disc with smallest holes, into a crockery or glass bowl. Pour the wine into the casserole, raise the heat to medium, and let the wine evaporate for 2 minutes. Add the tomatoes, season with salt and pepper, lower the heat, and simmer for 25 minutes. Add the whole sole fillets, sprinkle with a little salt and pepper, cover, and simmer for 15 minutes.

Meanwhile, bring a large pot of cold water to a boil, add coarse salt to taste, then gently drop in the *ravioli* one by one; cook them for 1 to 3 minutes, depending on dryness. Have a large, warmed serving platter on hand and ladle one-fourth of the sauce and fish onto it. Use a strainer-skimmer to transfer some of the cooked *ravioli* from the pot to the prepared platter. Ladle more sauce over each layer as you make 3 more. Serve hot.

PASTA CON BOTTARGA

PASTA WITH PRESSED TUNA CAVIAR

FROM SICILY

SERVES 4 TO 6

Bottarga *is made by pressing salted tuna or mullet caviar eggs. This becomes a solid mass, which can be sliced and used for flavorings. It is a unique and wonderful flavor, especially popular in Sardinia and Sicily, where these fish are plentiful, but also used elsewhere in Italy. It travels well and could be available outside of Italy should the demand arise.* **Bottarga,** *chopped with garlic and mixed with olive oil and black pepper, makes a simple, wonderful lusty uncooked sauce for pasta.*

Fresh tuna roe or caviar is still popular in Sardinia and Sicily in combination with pasta. The outer membrane is removed and the fresh eggs lightly sautéed in olive oil and butter. Older cookbooks show that the roe of a number of fish were prized for various dishes —sturgeon, then available in many Italian rivers, being among them. This Sicilian **Pasta con bottarga** *is an eloquent testimony to the taste of those generations.*

Finely chop half the *bottarga* with the parsley on a board, then transfer to a crockery or glass bowl. Finely chop the garlic on the board, then add the remaining *bottarga* and coarsely chop also, continuing to chop the garlic with it. Mix into the bowl with the other ingredients, then start adding the oil, a little at a time, mixing continuously with a wooden spoon and seasoning with pepper. Cover and refrigerate this sauce until needed.

Bring a large pot of cold water to a boil, add coarse salt to taste, then add the pasta and cook until al dente, for 9 to 12 minutes depending on the brand. Meanwhile, coarsely chop the 10 sprigs parsley. Drain the pasta, transfer to a large serving platter, add the sauce, toss very well, and serve with the chopped parsley and a twist of black pepper on top.

4 ounces *bottarga* (pressed salted tuna or mullet caviar, imported from Italy), thinly sliced
20 large sprigs Italian parsley, leaves only
2 large cloves garlic, peeled
¾ cup olive oil
Freshly ground black pepper
1 pound dried *spaghetti*, preferably imported Italian

TO COOK THE PASTA:
Coarse-grained salt

TO SERVE:
10 large sprigs Italian parsley, leaves only
Freshly ground black pepper

CLAMS, MUSSELS, SHRIMP, AND CALAMARI

The most common types of seafood sauce for pasta are those using a mixture such as clams, mussels, shrimp, and calamari, or simply the two versions involving just clams. The most common ingredients are olive oil, parsley, garlic, and white wine. Tomatoes have come to be widely used in these sauces; but particularly in northern areas there are some who still object to the sweetness of tomatoes in combination with shellfish. They usually make their sauce with a *battuto* of parsley and garlic, and with white wine—a kind of green sauce sautéed in olive oil. But as we can see from the following recipes, the use of tomato has all but conquered these sauces, the *bianco* version of pasta with clams remaining popular.

The ink of the cuttlefish (*seppie*) or ink-squid is used with *spaghetti* in Tuscany. (The Venetian version with rice is equally celebrated.) The ink is extracted and cooked into a sauce that exploits the spicy, peppery flavor of the ink itself (see Recipe Appendix). The color is really brownish, like sepia drawings of the old masters, which are made with this very ink (notice the derivation of *sepia* from *seppie*). It has become fashionably chic to make a black pasta by putting this ink or some substitute thereof directly into the dough. I find this questionable, as very little flavor is retained, and the color, though trendy, is not really attractive. Indeed, it is often so black that I wonder if the brownish ink is really the coloring agent in those instances.

FROM LIGURIA

SERVES 8 TO 10

LASAGNE DI GAMBERI E MUSCOLI
LASAGNE WITH SHRIMP AND MUSSELS

*In Liguria, shrimp and mussels are used in combination with **lasagne,** the two chopped to produce a pinkish color for the stuffing. Typically northern is the addition of butter to the oil for sautéing and additional butter in the tomato sauce with basil flavoring, a Ligurian must.*

FOR THE PASTA:
4 cups unbleached all-purpose flour
2 extra-large eggs
¾ cup lukewarm water
Pinch of salt

Prepare the pasta with the ingredients and quantities listed, following the directions on page 14. Stretch layer to ¹⁄₁₆ inch thick—on the pasta machine, take to next to last notch. Cut the pasta sheet into *lasagne* squares, precook in salted water, transfer to cold water with oil, remove and let rest on dampened cotton dish towels until needed.

Place the shrimp and mussels in separate bowls of cold water with a little coarse salt added to each; let soak for 30 minutes.

Meanwhile, begin the tomato sauce. If fresh tomatoes are used, cut them into pieces. Put fresh or canned tomatoes in a medium-sized saucepan with the butter and basil, and cook over medium heat for 30 minutes.

Bring a large pot of cold water to a boil, add coarse salt and the lemon cut in half. Drain the shrimp, add to the boiling water, and simmer for 3 minutes. Drain the shrimp, rinse with cold water, then shell and devein them. Drain the mussels, put them in a large skillet with 3 tablespoons of the olive oil, cover, and place over high heat. Most of the mussels should open in about 10 minutes; discard any that do not. Shell the mussels and place the meat in a crockery or glass bowl.

Finely chop the onion, garlic, and parsley together on a board. Put the remaining oil and the butter in a medium-sized heavy casserole; when the butter is melted, add the chopped ingredients and sauté for 5 minutes. Add the shrimp and mussels, mix well, and cook for 1 minute more. Pour in the wine, raise the heat to medium-high, and let evaporate for 5 minutes. Season the mixture with salt, pepper, and a large pinch of hot red pepper flakes. Remove the chopped ingredients and the seafood with a slotted spoon, and finely chop them on a board or in a food processor. Set aside the casserole with the reserved juices.

Finish the sauce. Pass the tomato sauce through a food mill, using the disc with the smallest holes, into a second saucepan. Season with salt and pepper. Reduce the sauce over medium heat for 15 minutes more. Add 1½ cups of the reduced tomato sauce to the shrimp-mussel mixture, then place everything back in the casserole with the leftover juices. Simmer for 2 minutes more, mixing with a wooden spoon. Transfer to a bowl and set aside until cool.

Preheat the oven to 375 degrees.

Oil a 13½- x 8¾-inch glass baking dish. Make a layer of pasta on the bottom of the pan, place some of the fish sauce over it, then put on more pasta and some of the tomato sauce. Keep alternating layers of pasta, fish sauce, pasta, and tomato sauce. The top layer of pasta should be covered with tomato sauce; reserve at least ½ cup of the tomato sauce for this layer. Bake for 30 minutes, remove from oven, and let rest for 2 minutes before serving.

TO COOK THE PASTA:
Coarse-grained salt
2 tablespoons olive or vegetable oil

FOR THE STUFFING:
2½ pounds medium-sized shrimp, unshelled
1½ pounds mussels
Coarse-grained salt
1 large lemon, cut in half
7 tablespoons olive oil
1 medium-sized red onion, peeled
2 large cloves garlic, peeled
20 large sprigs Italian parsley, leaves only
4 tablespoons (2 ounces) sweet butter
1 cup dry white wine
Salt and freshly ground black pepper
Pinch of hot red pepper flakes

FOR THE TOMATO SAUCE:
3 pounds ripe, fresh tomatoes, or 3 pounds canned tomatoes, preferably imported Italian, drained
4 tablespoons (2 ounces) sweet butter
4 large basil leaves, fresh or preserved in salt
Salt and freshly ground black pepper

LASAGNE

1. *Line the baking dish with the pasta squares and allow about 1 inch to hang out over the edges all around the dish.*

2. *Make a layer of stuffing, then add another layer of pasta, this time covering only the inside of the dish.*

3 and 4. *According to the individual recipe, keep alternating a layer of stuffing (in some recipes there are more than one) with layers of pasta.*

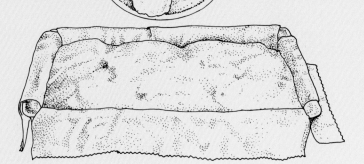

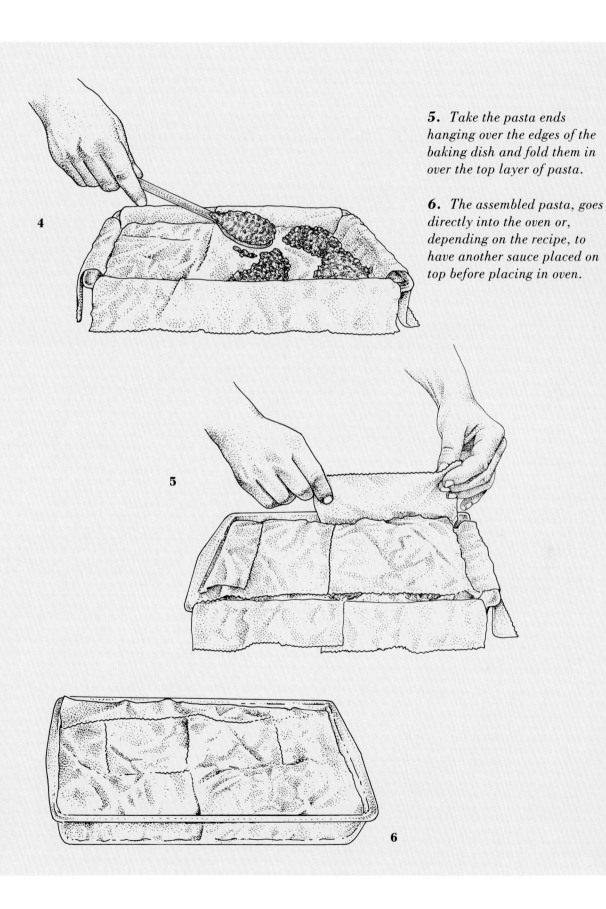

5. *Take the pasta ends hanging over the edges of the baking dish and fold them in over the top layer of pasta.*

6. *The assembled pasta, goes directly into the oven or, depending on the recipe, to have another sauce placed on top before placing in oven.*

4

5

6

FROM CAMPANIA

SERVES 4 TO 6

½ pound small shrimp,
    unshelled
1 pound very small squid
    (calamari), cleaned and
    cut into ½-inch rings
1 pound mussels,
    unshelled
1 pound small clams
    (littlenecks), unshelled
Coarse-grained salt
2 cups cold water
2 large cloves garlic,
    peeled
¾ cup olive oil
2 pounds canned
    tomatoes, preferably
    imported Italian,
    undrained
Salt and freshly ground
    black pepper
½ cup dry white wine
1 pound dried *perciatelli*,
    preferably imported
    Italian
20 large sprigs Italian
    parsley, leaves only

TO COOK THE PASTA:
Coarse-grained salt

PASTA ALLA POSILLIPO

PASTA WITH MIXED SEAFOOD

Pasta alla posillipo from the Naples area combines shrimp, squid, mussels, and clams with the other ingredients (tomatoes, of course, in Naples). The squid must be cooked a long time, here by using some of the water from cooking the shrimp shells and then combining the shrimp with the squid. The clams and mussels are cooked separately, and then they are all combined. (Spaghetti della pina combines clams and mussels, adds lemon peel and basil, and instead of white wine, uses red wine vinegar. See Recipe Appendix.)

Place the shrimp, squid, mussels, and clams in 4 different bowls of cold water with a little coarse salt added to each, and soak for 30 minutes.

Drain the shrimp and rinse under cold running water, then shell them. Place the shrimp in a small bowl; put the shells in a small saucepan. Pour the 2 cups cold water over shells, place saucepan over medium heat, and simmer for 30 minutes. Strain the broth (it should yield about 1 cup), discard the shells, and set aside until needed.

Coarsely chop the garlic on a board. Place a small saucepan with ¼ cup of the oil over medium heat. When the oil is warm, add the garlic, sauté for 2 minutes, then add the tomatoes and simmer for 30 minutes, seasoning to taste with salt and pepper. Pass the contents of the saucepan through a food mill, using the disc with smallest holes, into a flameproof casserole. Set casserole over low heat to reduce liquid for 15 minutes.

Meanwhile, drain the squid and rinse under cold running water. Place another medium-sized saucepan with ¼ cup of oil over low heat. When the oil is warm, add the squid and sauté for 5 minutes. Pour in the wine and let it evaporate for 5 minutes. Add ½ cup of broth from the shrimp shells, cover, and cook for 10 minutes. Season with salt and pepper, and keep adding the shrimp broth until the squid is tender, for 10 to 20 minutes, depending on the size of the squid.

Bring a large pot of cold water to a boil and add coarse salt to taste. Once the squid are cooked, add the pasta to the boiling water and cook for 8 to 11 minutes depending on the brand; that is, 1 minute less than for normal al dente. As the pasta cooks, drain the mussels and clams, scrub them under cold water, then place in a large skillet with the remaining ¼ cup of olive oil. Place over high heat, cover, and cook for 10 minutes, by which time they should be opened. (Discard any that remain unopened.)

Add the shrimp to the pan with the squid and cook for 3 minutes. When the pasta is ready, drain it, transfer to the skillet with the mussels and clams, add the tomato sauce with the shrimp and squid, then mix very well and let cook for 1 minute more to allow the pasta to absorb some of the sauce. Transfer to a warmed serving platter, sprinkle the whole parsley leaves over, and serve.

NOTE:
See note on page 132 regarding tomatoes.

MACCHERONI ALLE VONGOLE

PASTA WITH CLAMS

*Maccheroni with Clams exists in two classic versions, each marvelously simple. For **in bianco,** the clams are simply added to a basic **aglio-olio;** for the "red" version, the clams are combined with a basic marinara. The white version is certainly the older, and even suggests itself as the very first pasta with a shellfish combination. As we see elsewhere in this book, "alla marinara" itself develops right out of **aglio-olio,** so only the addition of tomato is necessary to make the white version into the red one we have here.*

Scrub the clams very well; soak them in a bowl of cold water with a little coarse salt for 30 minutes.

To prepare the sauce and cook the pasta, follow the recipe for *Maccheroni alla marinara*, page 100. Add the clams to the simmering tomatoes when the pasta is added to the boiling water, and cook them at the same time as the pasta, for 9 to 12 minutes. Remove any clams that do not open. Serve the pasta with the clams in the shells.

For the "white" version, add the clams to the oil together with the garlic and cook for 10 minutes. Sprinkle with chopped parsley.

NOTE:
Grated cheese is never added to this dish in Italy.

FROM CAMPANIA

SERVES 4 TO 6

2 pounds very small clams, in their shells
Coarse-grained salt
2 large cloves garlic, peeled
20 large sprigs Italian parsley, leaves only
½ cup olive oil
2 pounds ripe, fresh tomatoes; or 2 pounds canned tomatoes, preferably imported Italian, drained
Salt and freshly ground black pepper
1 pound dried *perciatelli* or *vermicelli*, preferably imported Italian

TO COOK THE PASTA:
Coarse-grained salt

VERMICELLI CON CALAMARI
VERMICELLI WITH SQUID

3 pounds calamari (yields
   2 pounds cleaned)
Coarse-grained salt
1 large lemon, cut in half
¾ cup olive oil
3 heaping tablespoons
   tomato paste, preferably
   imported Italian
10 large basil leaves, fresh
   or preserved in salt, torn
   into thirds
Salt and freshly ground
   black pepper
1 pound dried *vermicelli*,
   preferably imported
   Italian

TO COOK THE PASTA:
Coarse-grained salt

Pasta with squid alone is well documented, and we give here the Calabrian version with lemon, basil, and just a little tomato. Squid must be cleaned well, removing the outer skin completely, and cooked for a long time to become really tender. Naturally, the smaller, more tender squid are preferable, though the baby ones should be reserved for frying.

Clean calamari following directions on following page. Cut the bodies of the cleaned calamari into rings about ½ inch thick, and cut the tentacles into strips not longer than 3 inches. Place the calamari in a bowl of cold water, add 1 tablespoon of coarse salt, and soak for 30 minutes.

Place a medium-sized stockpot of cold water over high heat, and when the water reaches a boil, add coarse salt and the lemon halves. Drain and rinse the calamari very well, add them to the boiling water, cover, lower the heat, and simmer for 25 minutes. By that time the calamari should be cooked but still a little chewy. Let calamari rest, covered, in the pot for 30 minutes. Drain the calamari.

Place a large, heavy skillet with the oil over medium heat, and when the oil is warm, add the tomato paste and sauté for 2 minutes. Add the drained calamari and the basil leaves, then add salt and pepper to taste. Cover and cook over low heat for 15 minutes.

Bring a large pot of cold water to a boil, add coarse salt, then add the pasta and cook for 8 to 11 minutes depending on the brand; that is, 1 minute less than for normal al dente. Drain the pasta, add it to skillet, and mix well. Taste for salt and pepper, and sauté, continuously mixing with a wooden spoon until almost all the sauce is incorporated and the pasta is perfectly cooked. Transfer to a warmed serving dish and serve immediately.

*Squid (**calamari**) or cuttlefish (**seppie**) are cleaned in basically the same way. This drawing, though it shows a cuttlefish, labels the main parts of the fish, which would be the same for the squid.*

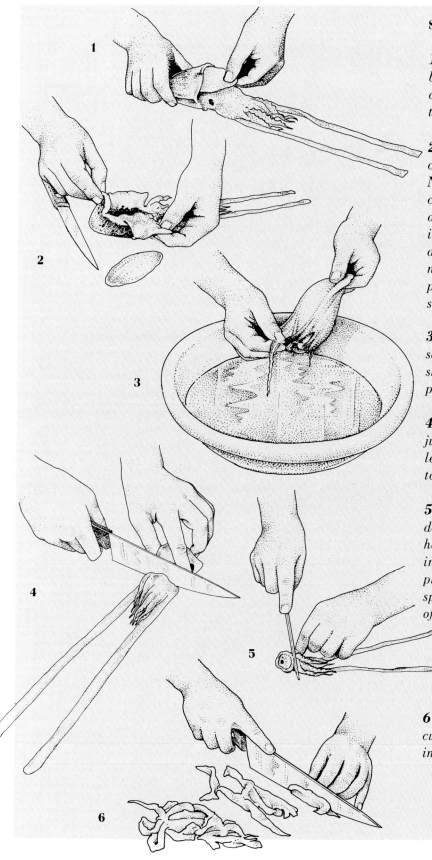

SQUID AND CUTTLEFISH

1. *Pull out the large white bone in the stomach or casing of the cuttlefish, or the long translucent bone of the squid.*

2. *If using the ink sac of the cuttlefish, as in* **Couscous Nero,** *page 330, use a knife to cut open the stomach or casing on the side where the bone was, in order to not break the delicate sac. If using squid, do not cut open the stomach, but pull out the head from the stomach.*

3. *For both cuttlefish and squid, the tough dark outer skin of the stomach must be pulled off in cold water.*

4. *For both, cut the head off just below the eyes and discard, leaving the tentacles attached to the lower part of the head.*

5. *Turn the lower part upside down. The tentacles will now hang over the sides and the inside of the lower head will be pulled open to reveal a black spot which is the mouth. Cut it off.*

6. *Slice the stomach of the cuttlefish into strips, the squids into rings.*

FROM SICILY

SERVES 6 TO 8

2 medium-sized stalks
celery
1 medium-sized red onion,
peeled
2 medium-sized carrots,
scraped
5 large sprigs Italian
parsley, leaves only
1 lobster (about 1¼
pounds), boiled
2 pounds canned
tomatoes, preferably
imported Italian,
undrained
1 heaping teaspoon coarse-
grained salt
2 quarts cold water
Salt and freshly ground
black pepper
6 ounces dried *spaghetti*,
broken into thirds

MINESTRA DI PASTA ALL'ARAGOSTA
LOBSTER SOUP WITH PASTA

This delicious Lobster Soup with Pasta is made with aromatic veg-etables including parsley and with tomato. Water is added to make a soup rather than a sauce, and the **spaghetti** *is broken into thirds. The rich flavor is obtained by simmering the lobster shells in the liquid for an hour and a half, then adding the lobster meat. The pasta is cooked in the broth.*

Cut the celery, onion, and carrots into large pieces and put them, along with the parsley leaves, in a bowl of cold water to soak for 30 minutes. Remove all the meat from the lobster (you should have 6 ounces); cut the larger parts into 1-inch pieces, then put all the meat in a crockery or glass bowl and refrigerate, covered, until needed.

Place the lobster shells in a medium-sized flameproof casse-role, drain the vegetables, and add them to the casserole. Add the tomatoes, the coarse salt, and the cold water. Place casserole over medium heat, uncovered. Simmer for 1½ hours without stirring or mixing.

Remove and discard the lobster shells, then pass the remaining contents through a food mill, using the disc with the smallest holes, into another flameproof casserole. Place the casserole over me-dium heat, taste for salt and pepper, and when the broth reaches a boil, add the *spaghetti* and reserved lobster meat. Stir very well and cook the pasta for 9 to 12 minutes depending on the brand. Transfer the soup to a warmed tureen and cover. Let the soup rest 2 minutes before serving.

NOTE:
If the especially juicy fresh tomatoes grown for making sauce in Italy are available, they are best. But other types of fresh tomatoes, even very ripe, are not juicy enough.

PASTA ALLA MARINARA ALLA TRAPANESE

PASTA ALLA *MARINARA*, TRAPANI STYLE

F R O M   S I C I L Y

SERVES 4 TO 6

Also from Sicily is this dish from Trapani which combines shrimp with canned tuna. It is a rather quick dish in which the shrimp are parboiled and cooked for just a few minutes with the tuna in the tomatoes. As in the previous recipe, no wine is added. Both of these recent dishes are successful and delicious.

Soak the shrimp in a bowl of cold water for 30 minutes with 1 teaspoon of coarse salt. Bring a small saucepan of cold water to boil over medium heat; add coarse salt. Drain and rinse the shrimp, then add them to the pan. Cover and cook until tender, about 2 to 3 minutes depending on the size of the shrimp. Drain, shell, and devein the cooked shrimp leaving them whole.

Meanwhile, finely chop parsley and garlic together on a board. If fresh tomatoes are used, cut them into 1-inch pieces. Pass fresh or canned tomatoes through a food mill, using the disc with the smallest holes, into a crockery or glass bowl. Bring a large pot of cold water to a boil.

Heat the oil in a large skillet over low heat; add the parsley and garlic, and sauté for 5 minutes. Add the puréed tomatoes to the garlic and parsley, and sauté for 5 minutes more. Add the shrimp and tuna, mix very well, and season with salt and pepper. Cook for 10 minutes, stirring every so often with a wooden spoon.

When the water in the pot reaches a boil, add coarse salt to taste, then add the pasta and cook until al dente, for 9 to 12 minutes depending on the brand. Drain the pasta and add to the skillet, mix very well for 30 seconds, then transfer to a warmed serving dish and serve, sprinkled with parsley.

VARIATION
Boil 1 pound of mussels in salted water for 2 minutes. Drain, discard those that do not open, and remove the others from their shells. Add the mussels to the tomato sauce along with the shrimp and tuna.

1 pound small or medium-sized shrimp, unshelled
Coarse-grained salt
10 large sprigs Italian parsley, leaves only
2 medium-sized cloves garlic, peeled
12 ounces ripe, fresh tomatoes; or 12 ounces canned tomatoes, preferably imported Italian, drained
½ cup olive oil
1 (6½-ounce) can tuna packed in olive oil, drained
Salt and freshly ground black pepper
1 pound dried *vermicelli* or thick *spaghetti*, preferably imported Italian

TO COOK THE PASTA:
Coarse-grained salt

TO SERVE:
10 large sprigs Italian parsley, leaves only

VERMICELLI AI GRANCHI
PASTA WITH CRAB MEAT

FROM APULIA

SERVES 4 TO 6

4 large cloves garlic, peeled
½ cup olive oil
2½ pounds very ripe, fresh tomatoes; or 2½ pounds canned tomatoes, preferably imported Italian, drained
Salt and freshly ground black pepper
1 teaspoon hot red pepper flakes
½ pound lump crab meat
1 pound dried *vermicelli* or *spaghetti*, preferably imported Italian

TO COOK THE PASTA:
Coarse-grained salt

TO SERVE:
30 large sprigs Italian parsley, leaves only

Crab meat is used with pasta in Adriatic localities, where the crabs are particularly good. Since crab is sweet, often the white wine is omitted and, as in this recipe from Apulia, a little hot pepper is used to spice it up. The crab is often simmered in the tomatoes rather than separately in water in order to maximize the flavor of the sauce before extracting the meat.

Coarsely chop the garlic on a board. Place the oil in a medium-sized heavy casserole over medium heat. Add the chopped garlic and sauté for 5 minutes. If fresh tomatoes are used, cut them into pieces. Pass the fresh or canned tomatoes through a food mill, using the disc with the smallest holes, into a bowl. Add the tomatoes to the casserole; season to taste with salt and pepper, and add the red pepper flakes. Simmer for 25 minutes, stirring every so often with a wooden spoon.

Meanwhile, bring a large pot of cold water to a boil. Add coarse salt to taste, then add the pasta and cook until al dente, for 9 to 12 minutes depending on the brand. When the tomato sauce is ready, add the crab meat and simmer for 5 minutes more. Coarsely chop the parsley. Drain the pasta and transfer to a large, warmed serving platter; pour the sauce over and toss very well. Sprinkle the parsley over, toss again, and serve immediately.

SPAGHETTI E GAMBERI
SPAGHETTI WITH SHRIMP

FROM MARSALA
(SICILY)

SERVES 6 TO 8

1 pound medium-sized shrimp, unshelled
Coarse-grained salt
1 medium-sized red onion, peeled
1 large clove garlic, peeled
½ cup olive oil

*Pasta with shrimp alone does not have a long tradition in Italy. One can only ponder why this combination was avoided for such a long time; the few recipes that do exist now are from the last fifty years. Why did they use shrimp in combination with other seafood, but not alone? Food for thought! The **Spaghetti** with Shrimp from Marsala in Sicily here emphasizes the sweetness of Sicilian cooking by the addition of onion and of course, since it is a recent recipe, tomatoes. The shrimp are shelled raw and cooked briefly at the end before the sauce is mixed with the pasta.*

Soak the shrimp in a bowl of cold water with coarse salt for 30 minutes. Finely chop the onion and garlic together on a board. Heat the oil in a large skillet over medium heat, and when the oil is warm, add the chopped onion and garlic; sauté for 5 minutes. Meanwhile, pass the tomatoes through a food mill, using the disc with the smallest holes, into a small bowl. Add the tomatoes to the skillet, season with salt and pepper, and simmer for 15 minutes.

Drain the shrimp, rinse very well under cold running water, and shell and devein them. Bring a large pot of cold water to a boil, add coarse salt to taste, then add the pasta and cook for 8 to 11 minutes depending on the brand; that is, 1 minute less than normal for al dente. Meanwhile, add the shelled shrimp to the tomato sauce, cover the skillet, and cook for 2 minutes more. Taste for salt and pepper. Finely chop the parsley on a board and add it to the skillet. By that time the shrimp should be almost cooked.

Drain the pasta, add it to the skillet, and sauté for 2 minutes, mixing very well with a wooden spoon. Transfer to a large, warmed serving dish and serve immediately.

1½ pounds ripe, fresh tomatoes; or 1½ pounds canned tomatoes, preferably imported Italian, drained and chopped
Salt and freshly ground black pepper
1 pound dried *spaghetti*, preferably imported Italian
15 large sprigs Italian parsley, leaves only

TO COOK THE PASTA:
Coarse-grained salt

RECIPE APPENDIX
Pasta and Fish Dishes in Other Bugialli Books

SPAGHETTI ALL'ACCIUGATA (*Spaghetti* with Anchovy Sauce) *FA* p. 159
CHIOCCIOLE CON SALSA DI TONNO (Shells with Tuna Sauce) *FA* p. 160
SPAGHETTI DI SCHEGGINO (*Spaghetti* with Trout-Black Truffle Sauce) *CT* p. 140
MINESTRA DI LASAGNE CON LUCCIO (*Lasagne* with Pike) *CT* p. 161
SPAGHETTI CON PASSATO DI PESCE ALLA GENOVESE (Genoese Fish Sauce with *Spaghetti*) *CT* p. 184
PASTA CON LE SARDE (Pasta with Fresh Sardines) *CT* p. 189
SPAGHETTI CON CAVIALE DI TONNO (*Spaghetti* with Fresh Fish Roe) *CT* p. 186
SPAGHETTI ALL'ARAGOSTA (*Spaghetti* with Lobster) *CT* p. 186
SPAGHETTI NERI (*Spaghetti* with the Ink of the Squid) *CT* p. 187
INSALATA DI PASTA I (Pasta Salad with Peppers and Anchovies) *CT* p. 196
INSALATA DI PASTA II (Pasta Salad with Tuna) *CT* p. 197
INSALATA DI PASTA III (Pasta Salad with Swordfish) *CT* p. 197
TRIANGOLI DI PESCE (Pasta Triangles Stuffed with Fish) *FI* p. 101
PASTA CON TONNO FRESCO (Pasta with Marinated Tuna) *FI* p. 112
SPAGHETTI DELLA PINA (*Spaghetti* Pina Style) *FI* p. 113

FA   The Fine Art of Italian Cooking
CT   Giuliano Bugialli's Classic Techniques of Italian Cooking
FI   Giuliano Bugialli's Foods of Italy

Pappardelle sulla pecora

PASTA WITH

CHAPTER 4

MEAT AND GAME

MEAT SAUCES

Each region and city has its classic meat sauces. Among the most famous are those from Bologna, Naples, Florence, Lucca, Abruzzi, Apulia, and Sicily. We include all these examples.

The famous Bolognese *ragù* is one of several meat sauces of its area and is the most popular one. Its distinctive features are the sautéing of the meat together with the aromatic chopped vegetables, the omission of garlic among these vegetables, the combination of snipped, chopped, or ground beef and pork for the meat, the frequent usc of white rather than red wine, and especially, the inclusion of heavy cream. We choose this one of the several Bolognese versions of meat sauce, and would like to point out as well that the ones from Bologna differ slightly from those made in neighboring Romagna. (I should like to remind once again that pasta with meat sauce is not automatically *alla bolognese*. Only those pastas specifically using a Bolognese meat sauce are such; the many employing such sauces from other regions would never be considered *alla bolognese*.)

This Bolognese *ragù* is employed to dress the paprika pasta on page 292 as well as the *Tagliatelle al ragù alla bolognese*. The pasta used in Bologna is generally rolled thicker than my Tuscan-derived basic recipe, it uses a greater proportion of eggs to pasta, and because it omits the touch of olive oil, it is generally less soft and is therefore more appropriate to this richer sauce.

It is the celebrated *ragù alla napoletana* that has created the legend of the sauce which cooks slowly for hours and hours. One hears stories about Neapolitan grandmothers who cooked the sauce over the lowest of flames for innumerable hours, even twenty-four. And lost in the mists of this legend is the fact that we are dealing here with a meat sauce, and particularly with a cut of meat—rump—which requires and benefits from a long cooking time. I have heard the legend of the long cooking time incorrectly applied to tomato sauces, a practice that produces rather dubious results. The recipe that follows takes a longish period but remains under three hours. In that time, the rump meat emerges succulent and tender, and the sauce is rich with the meat essence. The meat itself, tied like a salami, is served as a second dish at the same or, more often at another meal, is served hot, dressed with its *ragù*, or sliced cold and served with some other, piquant sauce.

The simple Tuscan meat sauce so popular in central Italy uses only snipped (or chopped or ground) beef for the meat and includes the aromatic vegetables (carrot, onion, celery, garlic, parsley, lemon peel, but no leek), red wine, and a small amount of dried porcini, and the tomato is reinforced with a little tomato paste (see Recipe Appendix).

The meat sauce from Lucca in Tuscany, *tocco di carne*, is almost identical with the sauce just described, except that it is lightly flavored with clove and has nutmeg in the sauce itself. It also employs a higher percentage of tomatoes. *Tocco di*—"touch of"—is a linguistic usage for a sauce that Lucca shares with nearby Liguria. The pasta served with this dressing in Lucca is usually fresh rather than dried.

Pasta alla boscaiola, from its name invoking the woods, clearly stresses wild mushrooms. It is a sauce with just a little lean meat, sometimes veal rather than beef, and a few chicken livers. But it is the mushrooms, added in larger quantity than in other meat sauces, which gives greatest impact to the sauce. Some black Greek olives underline the mushrooms and chicken liver flavors. In Italy, where wild mushrooms are part of everyone's diet, this sauce has an important place all over the country.

The *sugo di manzo* used with *tagliatelle* in Livorno and with boiled *lasagne* in Genoa (see Recipe Appendix) extracts the essence of the beef by cooking it slowly for five hours. The meat is then removed and the sauce is passed through a mill and reduced to a rich denseness. With no garlic in the aromatic vegetables, the sauce is flavored with *pancetta* and cloves. The veal sauce from Livorno is used for their version of *Penne strascicate* (see Recipe Appendix). Dried porcini, *pancetta*, and clove flavor the veal shoulder and chicken drumstick cooked in wine, tomato paste, and broth. The technique is clearly related to that of the *sugo di manzo*, since the meats are simmered again for five hours, passed through a mill, and reduced.

The remarkable pork of the Siena area is the basis for the meat sauce of nearby Montalcino, served with their unique *pinci*. Three kinds of pork—ground fresh, sausages, and *pancetta*—are combined with a little chicken breast and cooked in tomatoes and the incomparable Brunello wine, then sprinkled with the Siennese sheep's cheese, pecorino (see Recipe Appendix).

FROM BOLOGNA

SERVES 6 TO 8

TAGLIATELLE AL RAGÙ ALLA BOLOGNESE
TAGLIATELLE WITH BOLOGNESE *RAGÙ* MEAT SAUCE

FOR THE SAUCE:
**Ragù alla bolognese
(page 292)**

FOR THE PASTA:
**4 cups unbleached all-
   purpose flour
5 extra-large eggs
Pinch of salt**

TO COOK THE PASTA:
Coarse-grained salt

TO SERVE:
**4 tablespoons (2 ounces)
   sweet butter
½ cup freshly grated
   Parmigiano cheese**

Prepare sauce according to directions on page 292.

Make the pasta with the ingredients and quantities listed and following instructions on page 14. Stretch layer to ¹⁄₁₆ inch thick—on the pasta machine take to next to last notch. Cut into *tagliatelle* (see page 33).

Bring a large pot of cold water to a boil. When the water reaches a boil, add coarse salt, then add the pasta and cook for 1 to 3 minutes, depending on the dryness. Meanwhile, place the butter in a warmed serving dish and put over the boiling water to melt the butter.

When ready, drain the pasta, transfer to the prepared platter, mix very well with the melted butter, then pour the sauce all over. Mix and serve immediately. Pass cheese at the table.

FROM LUCCA
(TUSCANY)

SERVES 6 TO 8

MACCHERONI SPIANATI AL TOCCO DI CARNE
FLAT *MACCHERONI* WITH LUCCHESE MEAT SAUCE

FOR THE SAUCE:
**1 pound boneless beef
   sirloin, in 1 piece
2 Italian sweet sausages
   without fennel seeds; or
   6 ounces ground pork
4 ounces *prosciutto*, in 1
   piece
1 large carrot, scraped
1 medium-sized red onion,
   peeled
1 medium-sized leek (or 1
   additional medium-sized
   red onion), cleaned**

Prepare the sauce. Use a scissors to snip the meat into tiny pieces. Remove the skins from the sausages and cut the prosciutto into very small pieces. Finely chop the carrot, onion, leek, garlic, parsley, celery, and lemon rind together on a board.

Place the oil and butter in a heavy, medium-sized saucepan over medium heat. When the butter is completely melted, add the *prosciutto* and sauté for 2 minutes. Put in the chopped vegetables and sauté for 15 minutes, stirring occasionally with a wooden spoon. Add the beef and sausages, and sauté for 10 minutes more. Pour in the wine, add the clove, and let the wine evaporate, cooking for 15 minutes.

Meanwhile, if fresh tomatoes are used, cut them into pieces. Pass fresh or canned tomatoes through a food mill, using the disc with smallest holes, into a crockery or glass bowl. Remove the clove from the sauce and discard. Add the tomatoes; season to taste with salt, pepper, and nutmeg; and simmer, covered, for 2 hours, adding the broth as needed, but keep the sauce thick, not soupy.

As the sauce cooks, prepare the pasta with the ingredients and quantities listed, following the directions on page 14. Stretch layer to a little less than 1/16 inch thick—on the pasta machine take to the notch just before the last one. Use a scalloped pastry wheel to cut the sheet of pasta into 2½-inch squares, and let squares rest on cotton dish towels until needed.

When the sauce is ready, bring a large quantity of cold water to a boil, add coarse salt to taste, then add the pasta; cook the pasta from 1 to 3 minutes depending on dryness. Drain the pasta, transfer to a warmed serving dish with the butter, and mix well. Start adding the sauce, a ladleful at a time, while tossing the pasta gently but thoroughly. Serve hot, sprinkling the cheese over each serving.

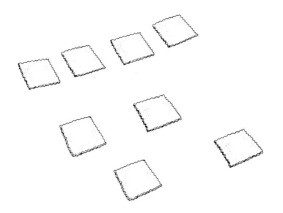

1 large clove garlic, peeled
10 large sprigs Italian parsley, leaves only
1 large stalk celery
1 small piece lemon rind
¼ cup olive oil
6 tablespoons (3 ounces) sweet butter
1 cup dry red wine
1 whole clove
1½ pounds ripe, fresh tomatoes; or 1½ pounds canned tomatoes, preferably imported Italian, drained
Salt and freshly ground black pepper
Pinch of freshly grated nutmeg
2 cups hot chicken or beef broth, preferably homemade

FOR THE PASTA:
3 cups unbleached all-purpose flour
4 extra-large eggs
Pinch of salt

TO COOK THE PASTA:
Coarse-grained salt

TO SERVE:
2 tablespoons (1 ounce) sweet butter
8 tablespoons freshly grated Parmigiano cheese

FROM NAPLES

SERVES 4 TO 6

VERMICELLI CON RAGÙ ALLA NAPOLETANA

PASTA WITH NEAPOLITAN MEAT SAUCE

FOR THE MEAT:
2 pounds boneless beef rump roast
4 ounces *pancetta* or *prosciutto*
10 large sprigs Italian parsley, leaves only
Freshly ground black pepper

FOR THE SAUCE:
4 ounces *pancetta* or *prosciutto*
2 medium-sized red onions, peeled
1 large clove garlic, peeled
8 tablespoons lard or olive oil
1½ cups dry red wine
6 ounces tomato paste, preferably imported Italian
4 cups lukewarm water
Salt and freshly ground black pepper

FOR THE PASTA:
1 pound *spaghetti* or *vermicelli*, preferably imported Italian

TO COOK THE PASTA:
Coarse-grained salt

Roll and tie the meat like a salami (see page 155). Cut into small pieces, then finely chop the *pancetta* or *prosciutto* with the parsley together on a board; transfer mixture to a plate, season with pepper, and mix very well. Lard the meat on all sides with the chopped ingredients and set aside.

To make the sauce, finely chop or grind the *pancetta* or *prosciutto*, onions, and garlic all together, and place in a heavy medium-sized casserole; add the lard or oil, and place the casserole over low heat. When the lard is melted or the oil is hot, put in the meat and then sauté for 20 minutes, turning the meat over twice. Add the wine and let it evaporate for 30 minutes. Add the tomato paste and 2 cups of lukewarm water, cover, and simmer for 1 hour. Season with salt and pepper, add 2 more cups of lukewarm water, and simmer for 1 hour more. The meat should be completely cooked and tender. Transfer the meat to a platter. Continue to simmer the sauce, uncovered, for 1½ hours more, stirring every so often with a wooden spoon and tasting for salt and pepper; it should reduce to about 2 cups.

Cook the pasta in a large quantity of salted water for 9 to 12 minutes depending on the brand. Dress the pasta with the sauce—about 2 cups sauce to 1 pound of pasta.

NOTE:
The meat can be eaten hot as a main dish at the same meal or can be reserved for another meal, sliced and served with some of the same sauce. It is particularly good eaten cold, sliced thin and accompanied by some piquant sauce.

In Naples, and Campania in general, pasta is eaten very al dente, cooked as much as 2 minutes less than for normal al dente.

PASTA ALLA BOSCAIOLA

PASTA WITH MUSHROOM-MEAT SAUCE

Soak the mushrooms in a bowl of lukewarm water for 30 minutes. Finely chop the carrots, garlic, celery, parsley, and onion all together on a board. Place the oil and butter in a medium-sized flameproof casserole over medium heat. When the butter is melted, add the chopped ingredients and sauté for 10 minutes, stirring every so often with a wooden spoon.

Use a scissors to snip the meat into tiny pieces, add it to the casserole, and cook for 10 minutes. Clean the mushrooms, making sure no sand remains attached to the stems, and add them to the casserole; sauté for 10 minutes more. Add the wine and let it evaporate for 15 minutes. Season with salt and pepper, stir very well and reduce the heat to low.

If using fresh tomatoes, cut them into pieces. Pass fresh or canned tomatoes through a food mill, using the disc with smallest holes, into a bowl; add to the casserole and simmer for 30 minutes, stirring every so often with a wooden spoon. Put in ½ cup of the broth, cover the casserole, and cook for 15 minutes more. Add the remaining broth and cook for another 15 minutes. Taste for salt and pepper, and reduce the sauce for 10 minutes more, uncovered.

Bring a large pot of cold water to a boil. Add coarse salt to taste, then add the pasta and cook until al dente for 9 to 12 minutes depending on the brand. Meanwhile, cut the chicken livers into fourths, add them to the sauce, and 3 minutes later, put in the whole olives, cooking for 5 minutes more, stirring and tasting for salt and pepper. Drain the pasta, transfer to a warmed bowl, pour the sauce over, mix very well, and serve immediately.

FROM ALL OVER ITALY

SERVES 4 TO 6

2 ounces dried porcini mushrooms
2 medium-sized carrots, scraped
2 small cloves garlic, peeled
2 medium-sized stalks celery, scraped
15 large sprigs Italian parsley, leaves only
1 medium-sized red onion, peeled
4 tablespoons olive oil
2 tablespoons (1 ounce) sweet buttter
4 ounces boneless veal shoulder or lean beef, in 1 piece
1 cup dry red wine
Salt and freshly ground black pepper
1 pound ripe, fresh tomatoes, or 1 pound canned tomatoes, preferably imported Italian, drained
1 cup meat or chicken broth, preferably homemade
5 chicken livers
4 ounces black Greek olives
1 pound dried *penne rigate* or *rigatoni*, preferably imported Italian

TO COOK THE PASTA:
Coarse-grained salt

ORECCHIETTE O LASAGNETTE ALLA MACELLARA
PASTA WITH A SAUCE OF MIXED MEATS

The wonderful sauce in this first recipe, of mixed meats, pork, beef, veal, and lamb, is used throughout the southern Adriatic side of Italy, Abruzzi and Apulia. Only onions among the aromatic vegetables and herbs are used; the sauce is also flavored with cloves and hot red pepper flakes, as popular in Abruzzi as in Calabria. The meat is cooked in olive oil, tomatoes, and red wine—and no broth. This meatiest of sauces requires a sturdy pasta; and indeed, it is traditionally wedded to pasta, dried or fresh made with the coarser semolina flour. In the fresh pasta dough, the semolina is mixed in with the all-purpose flour. This complex of meat flavors should not he obscured by adding grated cheese when serving.

FOR THE MEAT SAUCE:
½ **pound boneless pork, in 1 piece**
½ **pound boneless beef, in 1 piece**
½ **pound boneless veal, in 1 piece**
½ **pound boneless lamb, in 1 piece**
2 large red onions, peeled
½ **cup olive oil**
2 cups dry red wine
1½ pounds ripe, fresh tomatoes; or 1½ pounds canned tomatoes, preferably imported Italian, drained
Salt and freshly ground black pepper
½ **teaspoon hot red pepper flakes**
2 whole cloves

FOR THE PASTA:
2 pounds dried *orecchiette* or *lasagnette*, preferably imported Italian
or
2 cups semolina flour
4 cups unbleached all-purpose flour
Water
Large pinch of salt

TO COOK THE PASTA:
Coarse-grained salt

Use a meat grinder to coarsely grind all the meats together. Finely chop the onions on a board. Heat the oil in a large, heavy casserole over low heat; when the oil is warm, add the onions and sauté for 10 minutes. Put in the ground meat, raise heat to medium, and sauté for 15 minutes, stirring every so often with a wooden spoon. Add 1 cup of the wine, mix well, and simmer for 15 minutes more. If using fresh tomatoes, cut them into 1-inch cubes. Pass fresh or canned tomatoes through a food mill, using the disc with smallest holes, into a crockery or glass bowl. Season purée with salt and pepper to taste and add the red pepper flakes. Add the tomatoes to the sauce and cook, covered, for 30 minutes.

If using fresh pasta, prepare it with the ingredients listed, following the directions on page 14 and shape into *orecchiette* (see page 29), or for *lasagnette*, stretch layer to ¹⁄₁₆ inch, on the hand pasta machine, take to the notch before last. Then see *Trenette* (page 230), but cut both sides with the scalloped pastry wheel into 2-inch-wide strips, still using ingredients listed here. Set aside until ready to use.

Add the remaining cup of wine to the saucepan, taste for salt and pepper, and add the cloves. Cover again and cook for 30 minutes more, stirring sauce every so often with a wooden spoon. Remove the lid and let the sauce reduce over medium heat for 15 minutes.

Meanwhile, bring a large quantity of cold water to a boil, add coarse salt, then add the pasta. If using dried pasta, cook it for 9 to 12 minutes depending on the brand; if homemade, from 4 to 9 minutes depending on dryness. Drain the pasta. Transfer it to

a large bowl, pour the sauce over, then mix very well. Transfer onto a large warmed serving dish and serve immediately.

VARIATION

The meats can be snipped into tiny pieces with scissors instead of
being ground.

NOTE:

Orecchiette are mainly used in Apulia, *lasagnette* in Abruzzi.

PENNE STRASCICATE ALLA LUCCHESE

STIR-SAUTÉED *PENNE*, LUCCA STYLE

*This meat sauce from Lucca departs from the ones previously pre-
sented, since it relies completely upon sausage. The pork in the
Lucca and Siena area is sensationally good. The sausages are
cooked, flavored with sage and rosemary, and only garlic is combined with them in the oil and butter. Tomatoes are added, as is
heavy cream. Pork and cream are a favored combination in nearby
Emilia, while Lucca shares the tradition from there and from Liguria with its central Tuscan heritage. The cream in this recipe is
used in place of the more normal Tuscan wine.*

Remove the skins from the sausages and cut links into 1-inch
pieces. Finely chop the sage, rosemary, and garlic on a board.
Place the oil and butter in a deep, medium-sized saucepan over
medium heat; when the butter is melted, add the chopped ingredients along with the sausage pieces. Sauté for 10 minutes, mixing
every so often with a wooden spoon. If using fresh tomatoes, cut
them into pieces. Pass fresh or canned tomatoes through a food
mill, using the disc with smallest holes, into a bowl. Add the tomatoes to the saucepan and simmer for 30 minutes, stirring every
so often. Taste for salt and pepper.

Bring a large stockpot of cold water to a boil, add coarse salt to
taste, then add the pasta and cook for 8 to 11 minutes depending
on the brand, that is, 1 minute less than for normal al dente; the
pasta is to continue cooking with the sauce, and so should be quite
firm. Drain the pasta and add it to the saucepan, letting the pasta
sauté directly in the sauce while continuously stirring with a
wooden spoon and adding the cream ¼ cup at a time. Sauté until
the liquid is completely absorbed by the pasta, about 4 minutes.
Remove pan from the stove, transfer pasta onto a warmed platter,
and serve hot.

**F R O M   L U C C A
(T U S C A N Y)**

SERVES 4 TO 6

**6 sweet sausages without
    fennel seeds; or 1½
    pounds ground pork**
**4 large sage leaves, fresh
    or preserved in salt**
**1 scant tablespoon
    rosemary leaves, fresh,
    preserved in salt, or
    dried and blanched**
**1 medium-sized clove
    garlic, peeled**
⅓ cup olive oil
**2 tablespoons (1 ounce)
    sweet butter**
**1½ pounds ripe, fresh
    tomatoes; or 1½ pounds
    canned tomatoes,
    preferably imported
    Italian, drained**
**Salt and freshly ground
    black pepper**
**1 pound dried *penne*,
    preferably imported
    Italian**
½ cup heavy cream

TO COOK THE PASTA:
Coarse-grained salt

ANELLINI AL FORNO

BAKED PASTA RINGS, SICILIAN STYLE

FOR THE MEAT SAUCE:

1 medium-sized red onion, peeled
2 large cloves garlic, peeled
2 ounces *pancetta*, sliced thick, then cut into tiny pieces
¼ cup olive oil
4 ounces ground pork
4 ounces ground beef
½ cup dry red wine
2 tablespoons tomato paste
2 pounds ripe, fresh tomatoes; or 2 pounds canned tomatoes, preferably imported Italian, drained
Salt and freshly ground black pepper
4 large basil leaves, fresh or preserved in salt
10 large sprigs Italian parsley, leaves only
1 bay leaf
2 cups lukewarm chicken or beef broth; preferably homemade

FOR THE PEAS:

1 small red onion, peeled
10 large sprigs Italian parsley, leaves only
1 small clove garlic, peeled
¼ cup olive oil
3½ pounds fresh tiny peas, shelled; or 2½ pounds fresh large peas (see Note)
1½ cups lukewarm chicken or beef broth, preferably homemade

*This Sicilian meat sauce employs a mixture of pork and beef, plus pancetta flavoring. For aromatic vegetables there are only onions and garlic, but there is also an array of herbs—basil, parsley, and bay leaves, even this last generally available fresh on the island. A little wine and tomato paste are combined with lots of tomatoes. A favorite use of this sauce is in the baked pasta dish, **Anellini al forno**: little pasta rings baked with the meat sauce and fresh peas cooked in olive oil, garlic, onion, and parsley with only enough broth to cook them (no water). Another flavor is added with the lusty caciocavallo cheese, grated. These baked pasta dishes, sometimes layered, were once very popular, indeed. They are made less now, with the tendency toward shorter cooking times and the search for increased lightness in cooking. Some, such as this almost signature Sicilian dish, are so good, however, that they continue to be cherished.*

Prepare the sauce. Finely chop the onion, garlic, and pancetta all together on a board. Heat the oil in a medium-sized saucepan or heavy pot over medium heat. When the oil is warm, add the chopped ingredients and sauté for 5 minutes. Add the pork and beef, mix well, and cook for 5 minutes more. Add the wine and tomato paste, and let the wine evaporate for 10 minutes more. If using fresh tomatoes, cut them into pieces. Pass the fresh or canned tomatoes through a food mill, using the disc with smallest holes, into a crockery or glass bowl. Add the tomatoes to the saucepan, season with salt and pepper, and simmer for another 15 minutes. Finely chop the basil and parsley together on a board and add to the saucepan along with the whole bay leaf and broth. Cover and simmer for 40 minutes, then discard the bay leaf.

Meanwhile, prepare the peas. Finely chop the onion and set aside. Then chop the parsley together with the garlic. Place a medium-sized skillet with the oil over low heat, and when the oil is warm, add the chopped onion. Sauté for 2 minutes, then add the peas and sauté for another 2 minutes. Add the chopped parsley and garlic and 1 cup of the broth. Season with salt and pepper, cover, and cook for 10 to 20 minutes, depending on the tenderness of the peas, adding more broth as needed. Let the peas cool, about 30 minutes.

Bring a large pot of cold water to a boil, add coarse salt to taste, then add the pasta and cook until al dente, for 9 to 12 minutes depending on the brand. Drain the pasta and place it in a large bowl with half the sauce (about 4 cups). Mix well and let rest until the sauce is absorbed by the pasta and has cooled, about 1 hour. Meanwhile, reduce the remaining sauce over medium heat until it measures about 2 cups.

Preheat the oven to 375 degrees. Coarsely grate the caciocavallo cheese, then with 1 ounce of butter heavily coat a 3-quart deep, glass or other baking dish and coat it with bread crumbs. With one-fourth of the pasta, make a layer in the prepared dish. Arrange one-third of the peas over this, using a slotted spoon to avoid adding any liquid. Then use one-fourth of the remaining meat sauce, finally sprinkling one-third of the cheese over. Repeat this procedure with 2 more layers of pasta. Add the fourth pasta layer and top with the remaining meat sauce only. Arrange the bits of butter on top and bake for 35 minutes. Remove from oven, let rest for a few minutes, then serve.

NOTE:
Other than during the Spring, when small, fresh peas are in season, a cook has two options in making this and other recipes based on peas:

1. Use the large fresh peas available out of season, but first shell and boil them with a clove or two of garlic, peeled but left whole, and a pinch of coarse salt for about 13 minutes. Then they can be sautéed for the same cooking time as the smaller ones.

2. Use the excellent petit pois or "tiny tender" peas sold frozen in 10-ounce packages. Do not defrost or precook them. Sauté them for the same cooking time as small fresh ones. (This is one of the very few frozen products I sometimes use, because the result is totally without compromise.)

Salt and freshly ground black pepper

FOR THE PASTA:
1 pound dried *anellini*, preferably imported Italian

TO COOK THE PASTA:
Coarse-grained salt

TO BAKE:
4 ounces caciocavallo cheese
4 tablespoons (2 ounces) sweet butter, half cut into small bits
6 tablespoons unseasoned bread crumbs

FROM
EMILIA-ROMAGNA

SERVES 4 TO 6

FOR THE SAUCE:
**1 medium-sized red onion,
peeled
8 tablespoons (4 ounces)
sweet butter
4 Italian sweet sausages
without fennel seeds; or
12 ounces coarsely
ground pork
1 cup dry white wine
Salt and freshly ground
black pepper
1 bay leaf
1 pound very ripe, fresh
tomatoes; or 1 pound
canned tomatoes,
preferably imported
Italian, drained**

FOR THE PASTA:
**1 pound dried *gramigna*
or fresh *gramigna* (made
with 3 cups unbleached
all-purpose flour, 4
extra-large eggs, pinch
of salt)**

TO COOK THE PASTA:
Coarse-grained salt

TO SERVE:
**4 to 6 heaping tablespoons
freshly grated
Parmigiano cheese**

GRAMIGNA AL SUGO DI SALSICCE

GRAMIGNA WITH SAUSAGE-FLAVORED SAUCE

*This recipe in contrast to the version from Lucca is for a sauce of sausages from Emilia-Romagna that uses white wine and no cream; but in place, it contains much butter, with the oil omitted altogether. Emilia-Romagna has almost no olive oil, so it is understandable if the natives overvalue the little there is. But the bottom line is that dishes from this area simply do not call for it. (In contrast, Lucca has a soft and mild oil that is among the best that exist, especially if you can obtain it from a small local vineyard.) This wonderful butter-wine tomato sauce used with **gramigna** pasta is sweetly flavored with onion and bay leaf.*

Prepare the sauce. Finely chop the onion on a board. Place the butter in a heavy saucepan over medium heat. When the butter is completely melted, add the chopped onion and sauté for 10 minutes, stirring every so often with a wooden spoon. Meanwhile, remove the skins from the sausages and break the meat into pieces; add the sausages or pork to the pan and sauté for 10 minutes more. Pour in the wine, salt and pepper to taste, and the bay leaf, and let the wine evaporate for 10 minutes. If using fresh tomatoes, cut them into pieces. Pass fresh or canned tomatoes through a food mill, using the disc with smallest holes, into small bowl, then add to the meat mixture and simmer, covered, for 20 minutes, stirring every so often.

Bring a large quantity of cold water to a boil, add coarse salt to taste, then add the pasta and if dried cook for 9 to 12 minutes depending on the brand; if fresh, for 1 to 3 minutes depending on the dryness. Reheat the sauce. When ready, drain the pasta and transfer it to a large, warmed serving dish. Pour the sauce over, toss very well, and serve. Sprinkle a heaping tablespoon of Parmigiano over each portion.

NOTE:
To prepare fresh *gramigna*, prepare *spaghetti* with ingredients and quantities listed (see above), following instructions on page 14. Stretch pasta to about ⅛ inch thick—on the pasta machine take to several notches before last—then cut into *spaghetti* (see page 57). Finally cut *spaghetti* into 3-inch pieces.

BUCATINI ALLA MATRICIANA *OR* ALL'AMATRICIANA

PASTA, AMATRICE STYLE

1 medium-sized red onion, peeled
8 ounces *pancetta* or *prosciutto*, in 1 piece
3 tablespoons olive oil
1½ pounds very ripe, fresh tomatoes; or 1½ pounds canned tomatoes, preferably imported Italian, drained
½ teaspoon hot red pepper flakes
Salt and freshly ground black pepper
1 pound dried *bucatini*, *vermicelli*, or *spaghetti*, preferably imported Italian

TO COOK THE PASTA:
Coarse-grained salt

TO SERVE:
½ cup freshly grated pecorino romano or Parmigiano cheese

*The famous **all'amatriciana** treatment, which originates in Amatrice, near Rome, uses abundant **pancetta** or **prosciutto** as the meat. It is a simple and highly spiced preparation with black pepper and hot red pepper flakes. The dish is related to **pasta alla carbonara**, except that tomatoes replace the eggs; and as in that treatment, **all'amatriciana** employs grated cheese, though not as abundantly as the other. This is certainly among the most popular recipes, for its simplicity and excellence, so don't mess it up by adding extraneous ingredients or by trying to be original. Its classic simplicity is its strength. The substantial **bucatini**, with the hole down the middle, is the preferred pasta where this preparation originates.*

Coarsely chop the onion. Cut the *pancetta* or *prosciutto* into cubes less than ½ inch thick. Place the oil and pancetta in a medium-sized saucepan over low heat and sauté for 15 minutes, or until all the fat has been rendered out and the meat is very crisp. If fresh tomatoes are used, cut them into pieces. Pass the canned or fresh tomatoes through a food mill, using the disc with the smallest holes, into a crockery or glass bowl. Use a slotted spoon to transfer the meat to a plate and set it aside until needed. Add the onion to the saucepan and sauté for 5 minutes, then add the tomatoes along with the red pepper flakes and salt and black pepper to taste. Simmer for 20 minutes, stirring every so often with a wooden spoon.

Bring a large pot of cold water to a boil, add coarse salt to taste, then add the pasta and cook until al dente, for 9 to 12 minutes depending on the brand. Transfer the sauce to a large skillet set over low heat. Drain the pasta, and add it to the skillet. Raise the heat, and add the reserved meat; sauté for 30 seconds. Remove the skillet from the heat, add the cheese, mix very well, and transfer the pasta to a warmed serving platter. Serve immediately.

NOTE:
In Italy, the cured meat used for this dish is pork cheek *(guanciala)*, not easily available elsewhere, rather than *pancetta* or *prosciutto*. The dish is a rare example of the combination of cheese and hot red pepper.

MEAT FILLINGS

Three recipes follow in which meat is assigned principally to a stuffing. In the interesting *Tortelli*, Prato Style, the stuffing is potatoes flavored with ground beef, eggs, and Parmigiano. They are dressed simply with butter and more cheese.

The large Stuffed Pasta Roll from Calabria is filled with beef, sausages, and salami cubes as well as hard-boiled eggs. Sausages with fennel seeds, to be avoided in northern and central Italian recipes, are in order for a dish from this region. The poached pasta roll is dressed only with the juices left from sautéing the stuffing, and it is sprinkled with pecorino or Parmigiano cheese.

Prosciutto, beef, and chicken breast are in the stuffing for the *Cannelloni di carne ai funghi* from Lucca, along with the porcini mushrooms reflected in the name. The mushroom sauce itself contains a fourth meat: sausage. The *cannelloni* are baked with this sauce and a *balsamella*.

In addition to these recipes, the *tortelli* from Casentino are stuffed primarily with sausage and dressed with sage-flavored butter and Parmigiano. *Prosciutto* is used as the primary meat in several recipes: the stuffing for Bolognese *tortellini* contains *prosciutto*, *mortadella* (the famous sausage which gave rise to the familiar bologna), and veal marrow. And two Parma recipes naturally stress the celebrated *prosciutto* of the area, both in the sauce: *Tagliatelle* with Creamed *Prosciutto* Sauce, and *Anolini* with *Prosciutto* Sauce—the latter containing *prosciutto* and veal brains in the stuffing. Another recipe containing *prosciutto* and veal brains is that found in the notebooks of the great Michelangelo Buonarotti. Also employed in this complex stuffing are veal shoulder and chicken breast. As is usual with such meat combinations, the dressing is simple butter, sage, and grated Parmigiano. (See Recipe Appendix for sources of these recipes.)

Based on *pancetta* alone, the famous *Spaghetti alla carbonara* from Rome mixes eggs and cheese with the meat to produce another wonderful, basic combination that should not be toyed with. Only garlic and more abundant cheese should be tried in the variations. Of course, smoked bacon should never be substituted in this dish, since the *pancetta* itself must dominate (see Recipe Appendix).

Tortelli or Mezzelune di Prato presented in a pastry drum in the courtyard of a Renaissance palace in Florence. The formality of the presentation is appropriate to this very aristocratic and formal cortile, also echoed in the classic table setting.

FROM TUSCANY

SERVES 8

TORTELLI O MEZZELUNE ALLA PRATESE

TORTELLI, OR HALF-MOON *TORTELLI* PRATO STYLE

FOR THE STUFFING:

**12 ounces potatoes (not
new potatoes)**
Coarse-grained salt
5 tablespoons olive oil
1 bay leaf
¼ pound lean ground beef
**Salt and freshly ground
black pepper**
**1 medium-sized clove
garlic, peeled**
**10 large sprigs Italian
parsley, leaves only**
1 extra-large egg
**½ cup freshly grated
Parmigiano cheese**
Freshly grated nutmeg

FOR THE PASTA:

**4 cups unbleached all-
purpose flour**
4 extra-large eggs
**4 teaspoons olive or
vegetable oil**
Pinch of salt

FOR THE SAUCE:

**16 tablespoons (8 ounces)
sweet butter**
**1 cup grated Parmigiano
cheese**
**Freshly ground black
pepper**

TO COOK THE PASTA:
Coarse-grained salt

Prepare the stuffing. Place cold water in a medium-sized saucepan with the unpeeled potatoes and coarse salt to taste. Set the saucepan over medium heat and cook potatoes until soft, for 30 to 40 minutes depending on size. Remove the potatoes, immediately peel them, then pass them through a potato ricer into a crockery or glass bowl. Let stand until cold, about 30 minutes.

Put a small saucepan with the oil over medium heat. When the oil is warm, add the bay leaf and ground meat. Sauté for about 5 minutes, then taste for salt and pepper. Discard the bay leaf, and put the meat and juices in the bowl with the potatoes. Let rest until cool, about 5 minutes.

Finely chop the garlic and coarsely chop the parsley on a board. When the meat is cool, add the egg, Parmigiano, and chopped garlic and parsley. Taste for salt and pepper, and add a pinch of nutmeg. Mix well with a wooden spoon, cover the bowl, and refrigerate until needed.

Prepare pasta, using the ingredients and quantities listed, according to the directions on page 14. Stretch to less than ¹⁄₁₆ inch; on the pasta machine take to the last notch. Make 1½-inch square *tortello* (see page 113), using ½ tablespoon of filling for each *tortello*. Let the *tortelli* rest on cotton towels until needed. If using half-moon shape, follow directions on page 113, using 3-inch-in-diameter scalloped cookie cutter.

Bring a large pot of cold water to a boil, and put a large serving dish with the butter on it over the pot so that the better melts as the water heats. When the water reaches a boil and the butter is melted, remove the serving dish. Add coarse salt to the water, then add the *tortelli*, quickly but gently. Cook for 30 seconds to 2 minutes depending on the dryness of the pasta. When cooked, remove with a strainer-skimmer and arrange half in a layer on the prepared serving dish. Sprinkle over half the Parmigiano and some black pepper. Use the remaining *tortelli* to make a second layer and sprinkle with the remaining Parmigiano and more black pepper. Serve immediately.

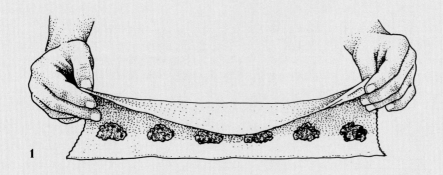

TORTELLI

1. *If you wish to prepare half-moon* **tortelli (mezzelune),** *place the line of dots of filling down the center of the pasta layer, then fold the sheet lengthwise in half. Press down around the dots of filling.*

2. *Prepare* **mezzalune** *by placing only half of a round* **ravioli** *cutter over the area containing the filling. For* **mezzalune,** *as for all types of* **tortelli,** *press the edges all around between two fingers to be sure they are completely sealed.*

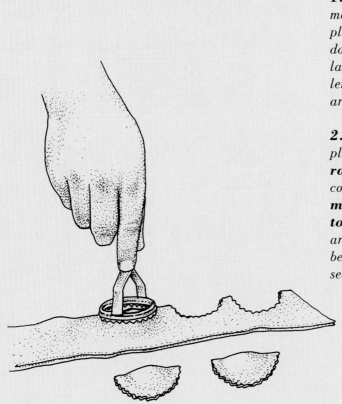

SCHIAFFETTONI ALLA CALABRESE

STUFFED PASTA ROLL, CALABRIAN STYLE

FROM CALABRIA

SERVES 8 TO 10

TO COOK THE PASTA:
Coarse-grained salt
2 tablespoons vegetable or olive oil

FOR THE PASTA:
2 cups unbleached all-purpose flour
3 extra-large eggs
Pinch of salt

FOR THE STUFFING:
2½ pounds ground beef
4 Italian sweet sausages with fennel seeds (about 1 pound), skinned
8 ounces Genoa salami, in 1 slice
¼ cup olive oil
6 tablespoons tomato paste
Salt and freshly ground black pepper
4 cups lukewarm chicken or beef broth, preferably homemade
4 extra-large eggs, hard-boiled

FOR THE POACHING BROTH:
1 medium-sized red onion, peeled
1 large stalk celery
1 medium-sized carrot, scraped
1 large clove garlic, peeled
Coarse-grained salt
5 large sprigs Italian parsley

TO SERVE:
½ cup freshly grated pecorino sardo or Parmigiano cheese

Bring a large pot of cold water to a boil, then add coarse salt to taste. Put a bowl of cold water with the oil next to the boiling water and dampen 4 cotton dish towels with cold water.

Prepare the pasta with the ingredients and quantities listed, following instructions on page 14. Divide the dough into 2 pieces. Using a rolling pin, roll out the pieces of dough into 2 rectangular sheets of pasta, ⅟₁₆ inch thick, following directions on page 16.

When the sheets of pasta are ready, cook them one at a time in the boiling water for 1 minute each, then carefully—to avoid making holes—use a large strainer-skimmer to transfer the pasta to the bowl of cold water. When the pasta is cool, spread it on a damp towel and let it stand until needed, covered with another damp towel.

Prepare the stuffing. Place the ground beef in a bowl, then the skinned sausages. Finely chop the salami on a board and add it to the other meats; mix well with a wooden spoon. Heat the oil in a saucepan over medium heat, and when the oil is warm, add the meat. Sauté for 4 minutes, continuously mixing with a wooden spoon then add the tomato paste and season with salt and pepper. Pour in ½ cup of the broth. Cook for 5 minutes, then add the remaining broth. Taste again for salt and pepper and cook 5 minutes longer. Remove the pan from the heat and, using a slotted spoon, remove the solids to a crockery or glass bowl, leaving the juices in the pan. Let the cooked meat cool, covered, for 30 minutes, then coarsely chop the hard-boiled eggs and add them to the meat. Mix gently but thoroughly, and taste for salt and pepper, keeping in mind that some of the saltiness will dissipate when the stuffed pasta is poached in boiling water.

Prepare the poaching broth. Place a large fish poacher filled with cold water over medium heat. Cut the vegetables into large pieces. When the water reaches a boil, add coarse salt to taste, the vegetables, and the parsley. Simmer for 30 minutes.

Remove the top towel from the pasta, and with a spatula, spread the stuffing over both sheets, leaving only a 1-inch edge all around. Roll up the *schiaffettoni* by taking one of the short sides in both hands and folding it over about 1 inch of the filling. Then pick up the edge of the towel on which it is resting with both hands. As you lift the edge of the towel a little higher, the pasta sheets will continue to roll up like a jelly roll. Repeat the procedure with the other pasta sheet. Move each roll onto a dry dish towel and wrap the towel all around, then tie like a salami (see drawings). Place

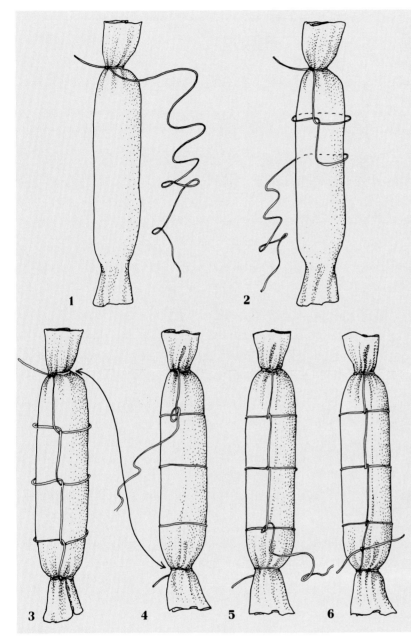

HOW TO TIE "LIKE A SALAMI"

1. *Knot string at one end, leaving only enough string on one side to pull over.*

2. *Bring the long end of the string down about 2 inches and hold the string in place with a finger. With the other hand, pull the string under and around again to the point where the string has been held by your finger. Pass the end of the string over, then under. Remove your finger, hold the short end of the string with one hand and pull other end tight with the other hand.*

3. *Repeat procedure until you reach the other end.*

4. and 5. *Reverse the "salami" and as the end of the string intersects with each ring of string wrapped around the "salami," pull under and over, fastening in the same way as was done on the other side.*

6. *After the last intersection, tie a knot using the two ends of the string.*

the pasta rolls in the boiling water and simmer, covered, for 30 minutes.

While the rolls are cooking, place the juices left from the stuffing in the pan over medium heat and reduce until the pasta is ready; you should have about 2 cups. Remove the pasta rolls from the water, unwrap them on a board, and cut into 1-inch slices. Arrange the slices on a large serving platter, pour the sauce over, and sprinkle with the cheese. Serve immediately.

FROM LUCCA
(TUSCANY)

MAKES ABOUT 12

FOR THE PASTA:
2 cups unbleached all-purpose flour
2 extra-large eggs
2 teaspoons olive or vegetable oil
Pinch of salt

TO COOK THE PASTA:
Coarse-grained salt
2 tablespoons olive or vegetable oil

FOR THE STUFFING:
½ ounce dried porcini mushrooms
4 cups lukewarm milk
4 ounces *prosciutto*, in 1 piece
8 ounces lean beef, in 1 piece
1 whole chicken breast, skinned and boned
1 small red onion, peeled
1 medium-sized stalk celery
1 large carrot, scraped
1 large clove garlic, peeled
10 large sprigs Italian parsley, leaves only
10 tablespoons (5 ounces) sweet butter
¼ cup olive oil
1 cup dry red wine
3 tablespoons tomato paste
1 cup beef broth, preferably homemade
½ cup unbleached all-purpose flour
Salt and freshly ground black pepper

CANNELLONI DI CARNE AI FUNGHI
CANNELLONI WITH WILD MUSHROOM STUFFING AND SAUCE

Prepare the pasta with the ingredients and quantities listed, according to the instructions on page 14. Stretch sheet to less than ¹⁄₁₆ inch thick; on the pasta machine, take to the last notch and out into squares (see page 158). Preboil the squares in a large amount of salted boiling water for two seconds. Transfer the pasta to a large bowl of cold water to which the oil has been added. Cool the pasta in the water, then let the precooked squares rest between dampened cotton dish towels until needed.

Prepare the stuffing. Soak the porcini in the lukewarm milk for 30 minutes. Using a meat grinder, coarsely grind the prosciutto, beef, and chicken together. Finely chop the onion, celery, carrot, garlic, and parsley on a board. Melt 2 tablespoons of the butter with the olive oil in a deep saucepan over medium heat, and when the butter is completely melted, add the chopped vegetables and sauté for 5 minutes. Add the ground meats and sauté for 5 minutes more. Drain the mushrooms, saving the soaking milk. (Be sure that no sand remains attached to the mushrooms.) Add mushrooms to saucepan, pour in the wine, and let wine evaporate for 15 minutes. Meanwhile, pass the mushroom soaking milk through several layers of paper towels to remove all sand.

Add the tomato paste to the saucepan and gradually start adding the broth, ¼ cup at a time, until all is incorporated and the stuffing is cooked and quite thick. Set aside.

Prepare a *balsamella* to be incorporated later into the stuffing, using the remaining 8 tablespoons of butter, the flour, and the strained mushroom milk. Follow the basic recipe on page 92 and add enough water to the milk to make 4 cups of liquid. Season with salt and pepper. Transfer this *balsamella* to a crockery or glass bowl, press a piece of buttered waxed paper over the surface, and let stand until cool.

Prepare a second *balsamella*, for the topping, using the ingredients and quantities listed. Transfer it to a second crockery or glass bowl, press a piece of buttered waxed paper over, and also let stand until cool.

Prepare the mushroom sauce. Soak the mushrooms in the lukewarm water for 30 minutes. Remove the skins from the sausages and finely chop the meat with the onion, garlic, and parsley on a board. Heat the oil and 3 tablespoons of the butter in a saucepan over low heat. When the butter is melted, add the chopped ingredients and sauté for 15 minutes. Then add the tomato paste and ½ cup of the broth; cook for 15 minutes more. Meanwhile, drain the mushrooms, saving the soaking water. (Be sure that no sand remains attached to the stems.) Pass the mushroom water through several layers of paper towels to strain out the sand. Add the mushrooms to pan along with the remaining broth. Taste for salt and pepper, lower heat, and cook for 1 hour more, adding the strained mushroom water near the end. Using a fork, incorporate the remaining tablespoon of butter with the flour on a small plate and add it by bits to the sauce. Stir very well and cook for 10 minutes more.

Preheat the oven to 375 degrees. Butter 2 glass or other oven-proof 13½- x 8¾-inch baking dishes. Combine the first *balsamella* (made with the mushroom milk) and the stuffing together in a large bowl; mix very well with a wooden spoon.

If using the black truffle, chop it very fine and add it to the stuffing at this point.

To stuff the *cannelloni*, place a square of pasta on a wooden board and spread about 4 heaping tablespoons of the stuffing along one of the jagged edges. Then roll it up, starting at the same edge and ending with the other jagged edge on top. Repeat until all the *cannelloni* are rolled up. Then place them seam side up in the baking dishes. Pour the balsamella topping over and bake for 25 minutes. Meanwhile, reheat the mushroom sauce. When the *cannelloni* are ready, serve at once, spooning some of the mushroom sauce over each portion.

FOR THE MUSHROOM SAUCE:
4 ounces dried porcini mushrooms
3 cups lukewarm water
3 Italian sweet sausages without fennel seeds; or 12 ounces ground pork
1 small red onion, peeled
1 large clove garlic, peeled
20 large sprigs Italian parsley, leaves only
¼ cup olive oil
4 tablespoons (2 ounces) sweet butter
3 tablespoons tomato paste
1 cup lukewarm chicken or beef broth, preferably homemade
Salt and freshly ground black pepper
1 tablespoon unbleached all-purpose flour
1 black truffle, fresh or canned (about 2 ounces) (optional)

FOR THE *BALSAMELLA* TOPPING:
4 tablespoons (2 ounces) sweet butter
¼ cup unbleached all-purpose flour
2½ cups milk
Salt and freshly ground black pepper
Freshly grated nutmeg

CANNELLONI

1. With a pastry cutter, cut the layer of pasta into pieces about 6 inches long. Let the pieces dry for a few minutes.

2. Once the pasta has been precooked in salted boiling water, then cooled in cold water with oil and transferred onto wet towels, spread stuffing along one of the jagged edges.

3. Then roll, starting at the edge containing the stuffing and

4. ending with the other jagged edge on top. **Cannelloni** *are baked, seam up.*

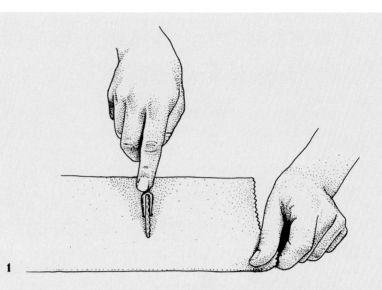

1

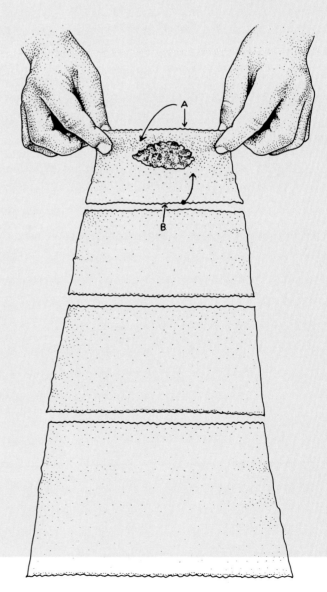

2

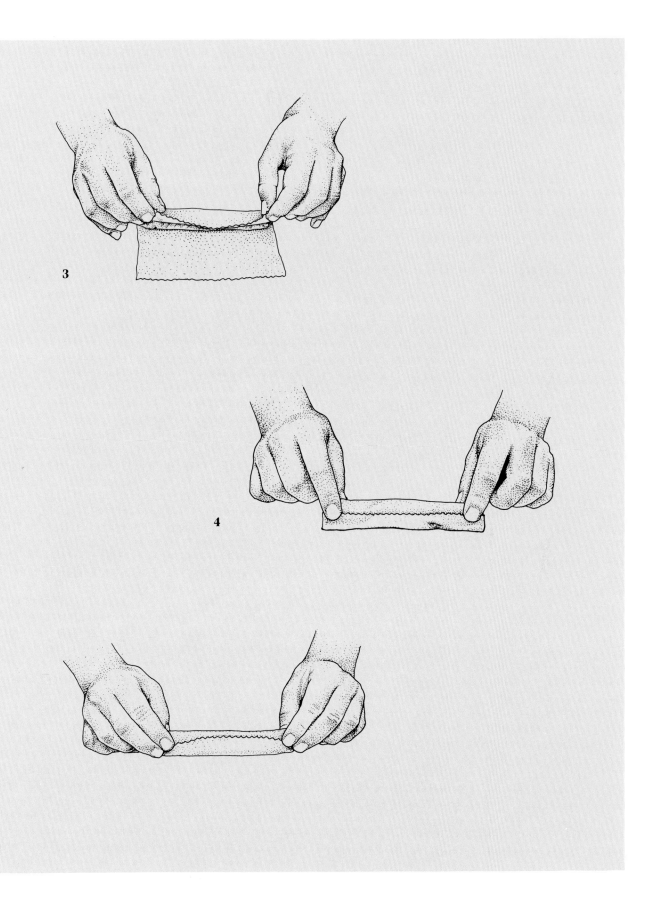

3

4

LASAGNE FOR CARNIVAL

The well-known and very popular *Lasagne imbottite*, using the long *lasagne* strips alternating layers of pasta with manifold ingredients such as Neapolitan *ragù*, tiny meat balls, sausage pieces, slices of mozzarella and hard-boiled egg, ricotta, and grated Parmigiano is Naples' version of the elaborate baked pasta made for the festivities of Carnival time. Such festival dishes once had a special meaning and were really made just at one time of year. Not only Carnival but each holiday season and even each saint's day had its special dishes that were for just such an occasion, and they varied among the different regions and towns. But now one finds *Lasagne imbottite* on menus all over and at most times of year, since the special meaning of such dishes has faded.

The *Lasagne imbottite* from neighboring Calabria is different. The fresh pasta is made with rougher semolina flour, whereas the Neapolitan is made with normal all-purpose flour; the little meat balls are made with pork rather than beef; the grated cheese is more likely to be pecorino; there is a simpler tomato sauce rather than the Neapolitan *ragù*; and along with the mozzarella, ricotta, and hard-boiled eggs is a special vegetable stuffing including dried porcini, artichokes, peas, and aromatic vegetables flavored with bay. A grand dish indeed to celebrate Carnival, it is called in dialect form by the name, *Sagne chine*. Unfortunately, there are nonauthentic versions of the dish circulating that must be avoided. Inexplicably, one recent recipe for this dish calls for ginger, which is unknown in post-Renaissance Italian cooking and would be particularly out of place in Calabria, where hot spices are preferred over sweet ones. A little thought solves the mystery. Medieval Italian cooking, related to that of ancient Rome, used many oriental spices brought in by the Venetian and Genoese traders, but these spices disappeared with the Renaissance. If one who has an imperfect knowledge of Italian looks up *zenzero* in the dictionary, it will say "ginger" because the strict Italian language academy keeps the classical meanings of words even more than the French academy. But *zenzero* in modern times has come to mean hot red pepper (though *peperoncino* is the "correct" word for hot red pepper) which came to Europe from the New World about the time ginger stopped being used there.

Our third type of *Lasagne imbottite* is a fascinating Abruzzese transformation of the dish in which *crespelle* (crêpes) are used instead of pasta for the layering. The result is a timballo of *crespelle* with manifold ingredients much related to the Neapolitan and Calabrian versions. The little meat balls are made of pork with Parmigiano and egg; there is a sauce of chicken gizzards cooked in white wine and bay leaf; a chicken breast is cut into small cubes; unsmoked scamorza cheese is used instead of mozzarella; and a simple tomato sauce is flavored with butter.

LASAGNE DI CARNEVALE (LASAGNE IMBOTTITE)

NEAPOLITAN "STUFFED" LASAGNE FOR CARNIVAL

The sauce can be prepared as much as several days in advance. Prepare the pasta with the ingredients and quantities listed, according to the instructions on page 14. Stretch layer to less than 1/16 inch; on the pasta machine take to the last notch. Cut the pasta for Neapolitan "long" *lasagne*—not into squares, but into strips 12 inches long and 3 inches wide. Preboil the strips in a large amount of salted boiling water for two seconds. Transfer the pasta to a large bowl of cold water to which the oil has been added. Cool the pasta in the water, then let it rest on dampened cotton dish towels until needed.

Prepare the *polpettine*, the little meat balls for the stuffing. Finely chop the garlic and parsley together on a board. Place the ground beef in a crockery or glass bowl, add the chopped ingredients, Parmigiano, eggs, and salt and pepper to taste; mix all the ingredients, then shape *polpettine* the size of a hazelnut, using 1/2 tablespoon of stuffing for each one. Heat the vegetable oil and the 1/4 cup olive oil in a deep-fat fryer until hot (375 degrees). Lightly flour the meat balls and fry until golden all over, about 1 minute. Transfer to a platter lined with paper towels to drain excess fat; let stand until needed.

Cut the sausages into 1-inch pieces and sauté in a skillet with the lard or olive oil over medium heat for 5 minutes. Transfer them, without their juices, to a platter. Cut the mozzarella and hard-boiled eggs into thin slices.

Butter a 13½- x 8¾-inch glass baking dish and preheat the oven to 375 degrees. Make a layer of pasta on the bottom of the baking dish and cover with some of the meat balls, sausages, and mozzarella and egg slices. Crumble some ricotta over all, then sprinkle Parmigiano on and spread some sauce over. Repeat with more layers of pasta and other ingredients. The top layer should be sauce and Parmigiano only. Bake for 25 minutes. Remove from oven, let stand for a few minutes, then serve.

NOTE:
In Naples and Campania, lard, rather than olive oil, would traditionally be used to sauté the sausages, and fry the *polpettine*.

FROM NAPLES

SERVES 8 TO 10

2 cups *Ragù alla napoletana* (page 142)

FOR THE PASTA:
3 cups unbleached all-purpose flour
3 extra-large eggs
1/4 cups lukewarm water
Pinch of salt

TO COOK THE PASTA:
Coarse-grained salt
2 tablespoons olive or vegetable oil

FOR THE *POLPETTINE*:
1 large clove garlic, peeled
10 large sprigs Italian parsley, leaves only
1 pound ground beef
1/4 cup freshly grated Parmigiano cheese
2 extra-large eggs
Salt and freshly ground black pepper
1 quart vegetable oil (see Note)
1/4 cup olive oil (see Note)
1 cup unbleached all-purpose flour

TO BAKE:
6 Italian sweet sausages (about 1½ pounds)
4 tablespoons lard or olive oil
8 ounces mozzarella cheese
4 extra-large eggs, hard-boiled
15 ounces ricotta
3/4 cup freshly grated Parmigiano cheese

FROM CALABRIA

SERVES 8 TO 10

SAGNE CHINE O LASAGNE IMBOTTITE
CALABRIAN "STUFFED" LASAGNE FOR CARNIVAL

FOR THE PASTA:
4 cups semolina flour
1¾ cups cold water
Pinch of salt

TO COOK THE PASTA:
Coarse-grained salt
2 tablespoons olive or
   vegetable oil

FOR THE VEGETABLE
STUFFING:
1 ounce dried porcini
   mushrooms
2 cups lukewarm water
4 medium-sized artichokes
Juice of 1 lemon
1 medium-sized stalk
   celery
1 medium-sized red onion,
   peeled
1 medium-sized carrot,
   scraped
½ cup olive oil
1 pound shelled peas
1 bay leaf
Salt and freshly ground
   black pepper
1 cup lukewarm chicken
   or beef broth, preferably
   homemade, as needed

FOR THE MEAT BALLS:
1 pound ground pork
¼ cup grated pecorino
   romano sardo or
   pecorino romano cheese
Salt and freshly ground
   black pepper
2 extra-large eggs
2 cups vegetable oil
¼ cup olive oil
1 cup unbleached all-
   purpose flour

If using fresh pasta, prepare the dough first, using the ingredients and quantities listed, and according to the instructions on page 14. Stretch to less than ¹⁄₁₆ inch; on pasta machine take to last notch. Cut into squares for *lasagne*. Preboil the squares in a large amount of salted boiling water for two seconds. Transfer the pasta to a large bowl of cold water to which the oil has been added. Cool the pasta in the water, then let them rest on dampened cotton dish towels until needed.

Soak the porcini in the lukewarm water for 30 minutes. Clean the artichokes (see page 67), cut them into eighths, and set them aside in a bowl of cold water with the lemon juice.

Finely chop the celery, onion, and carrot on a board. Put the oil in a medium-sized flameproof casserole and set it over medium heat; when the oil is warm, add the chopped ingredients and sauté until the onion is translucent and soft but not browned, about 5 minutes. Drain the artichokes and add them to the casserole along with the peas and bay leaf. Season with salt and pepper, and sauté for 2 minutes. Drain the mushrooms, making sure that no sand remains attached to the stems; reserve the mushroom water. Add the mushrooms to casserole and mix well. Strain the mushroom water by passing it through several layers of paper towels. Add ¼ cup of this water to the casserole, cover, and cook, adding more mushroom water or lukewarm broth as needed until the vegetables are cooked, for 30 to 45 minutes, depending on their size and tenderness. (Do not add excess liquid to the vegetables—just enough to braise gently.) Remove the vegetables to a crockery or glass bowl, discarding the bay leaf, and let cool for 30 minutes.

Prepare the meat balls. Place the ground meat in a crockery or glass bowl, add the cheese, salt and pepper to taste, and eggs. Mix well with a wooden spoon, then form small balls, using ¼ tablespoon of the mixture for each. Heat the vegetable and olive oils in a deep-fat fryer over medium heat. When the oil is hot (about 375 degrees), lightly flour the meat balls and fry them until lightly golden all over, about 30 seconds. Transfer them, using a strainer-skimmer or slotted spoon, onto a serving platter lined with paper towels to absorb excess fat; let stand until needed.

Prepare the tomato sauce. If fresh tomatoes are used, cut them into small pieces. Put fresh or canned tomatoes in a medium-sized flameproof casserole with the oil and basil, and place casserole over medium heat. Cook for 25 minutes, then season with salt and pepper. Pass the sauce through a food mill, using the disc with smallest holes, into a second pot. Reduce the sauce over low heat for 10 minutes more.

Assemble the *lasagne*. Preheat the oven to 375 degrees. Shell the hard-boiled eggs and cut them into eighths. Cut the ricotta (in Italy ricotta is quite solid and may be sliced) or mozzarella into small pieces (if the ricotta is too moist, separate it into small pieces). Oil a 13½- x 8¾-inch glass baking dish and make a layer of the pasta on the bottom of the dish, then place over it some of all the different preparations: vegetables, meat balls, tomato sauce, ricotta or mozzarella, and grated sardo cheese in that order. Continue alternating layers of pasta and stuffing. The top layer should have abundant tomato sauce and some grated cheese only. Bake for 30 minutes, then remove from oven, let cool for a few minutes, and serve.

FOR THE TOMATO SAUCE:

3 pounds ripe, fresh tomatoes; or 3 pounds canned tomatoes, preferably imported Italian, drained

4 tablespoons olive oil

4 large basil leaves, fresh or preserved in salt

Salt and freshly ground black pepper to taste

TO BAKE:

4 extra-large eggs, hard-boiled

12 ounces ricotta or mozzarella cheese

1 cup freshly grated pecorino romano sardo or pecorino romano cheese

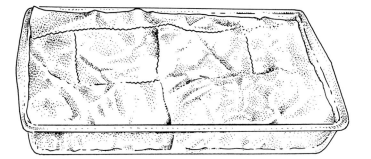

FROM ABRUZZI

SERVES 8 TO 10

FOR THE *CRESPELLE:*
**1 cup unbleached all-
  purpose flour
4 extra-large eggs
1¼ cups cold milk
Pinch of salt
3 tablespoons (1½ ounces)
  sweet butter or olive oil**

FOR THE PORK BALLS:
**8 ounces ground pork
1 cup freshly grated
  Parmigiano cheese
1 extra-large egg
Salt and freshly ground
  black pepper
Freshly grated nutmeg
2 cups vegetable oil
¼ cup olive oil**

FOR THE GIZZARD
SAUCE:
**6 ounces chicken gizzards
4 tablespoons (2 ounces)
  sweet butter
¼ cup olive oil
1 bay leaf
1 cup dry white wine
Salt and freshly ground
  black pepper
1 cup lukewarm chicken
  or beef broth, preferably
  homemade**

FOR THE CHICKEN
BREAST:
**1 whole chicken breast,
  skin removed
¼ cup olive oil
Salt and freshly ground
  black pepper**

SCRIPELLE ALL'ABRUZZESE (CRESPELLE ALL'ABRUZZESE)
TIMBALLO OF STUFFED CRÊPES FOR CARNIVAL

Prepare the *crespelle,* or *scripelle,* first. Sift the flour, then put it in a crockery or glass bowl and make a well in it. Place the eggs in the well and start incorporating some of the flour from the edges of the well into the eggs. When all the flour is incorporated and a thick batter is formed, start adding the cold milk, continuously stirring with a wooden spoon. When all the milk is incorporated, add salt, mix again, then cover the bowl and put it in a cool place to rest for at least 1 hour, to allow the gluten in the flour to relax.

When ready, use 3½ tablespoons of the batter to prepare each *crespella,* in an 8-inch crêpe pan. Grease the pan each time with oil or melted butter, and cook on both sides until lightly golden. This amount of batter will yield 15 *crespelle.* Stack one on top of the other on a dish, cover, and let stand until needed.

Prepare the meat stuffings. For the pork balls, mix the ground pork with the Parmigiano in a crockery or glass bowl. Add the egg, salt and pepper, and nutmeg to taste. Stir well, then prepare small meat balls, using ½ tablespoon of the mixture for each. Let all the meat balls rest on a board while you heat the combination of vegetable and olive oil in a deep-fat fryer over medium heat. When the oil is hot (375 degrees), add the balls a few at a time, and fry until lightly golden all over, about 30 seconds, then transfer to a dish until needed.

Clean the chicken gizzards very well under cold running water, removing any fat still attached. Place a medium-sized flameproof casserole with the butter and olive oil over medium heat. When the butter is melted, add the gizzards along with the bay leaf, and sauté for 10 minutes. Add the wine and let it evaporate for 15 minutes. Season to taste with salt and pepper, then add the broth, cover, and cook for 20 minutes. Discard the bay leaf. Drain and finely chop the gizzards on a board, then put them back into the casserole to reduce, uncovered, over low heat for 20 minutes, stirring every so often with a wooden spoon. Transfer to a crockery or glass bowl to rest for 1 hour or until cool.

Cut the chicken breast in half. Place a medium-sized skillet with the oil over medium heat. When the oil is warm, add the chicken to pan and sauté for 3 minutes on each side, season to taste with salt and pepper; the breast should remain somewhat undercooked. Transfer chicken to a board, discarding the juices from the pan. Cut the chicken into pieces half the size of the meat balls, and set aside.

Prepare the tomato sauce. If using fresh tomatoes, cut them into pieces. Put fresh or canned tomatoes in a saucepan with the butter over medium heat and cook for 35 minutes; stir every so often with a wooden spoon, and season to taste with salt and pepper. Pass the tomatoes through a food mill, using the disc with smallest holes, into a second saucepan, then reduce over low heat for 15 minutes more. Transfer the sauce to a crockery or glass bowl and let stand until cool (about 30 minutes).

Preheat the oven to 375 degrees. Assemble the dish. Use 1 tablespoon of the butter to heavily butter an 11-inch round cake pan or the bottom and sides of a springform pan with the butter. Lay out 1 *crespella* in the pan and on it place modest amounts of pork balls, chicken breast, gizzard sauce, tomato sauce, Parmigiano, and scamorza. Gauge the amount carefully, remembering that the ingredients have to be divided evenly among 14 of the 15 *crespelle*. Top with some bits of the butter, saving 1 tablespoon for the top. Cover the pan with aluminum foil and bake for 35 minutes. (If using a springform pan, wrap the whole form in aluminum foil so the juices do not leak out.) Remove the pan from oven, let rest for 2 minutes before uncovering, then unmold onto a large serving platter. Serve, slicing the timballo like a pie.

FOR THE TOMATO SAUCE:

2 pounds ripe, fresh tomatoes; or 2 pounds canned tomatoes, preferably imported, drained

2 tablespoons (1 ounce) sweet butter

Salt and freshly ground black pepper

TO BAKE:

5 tablespoons (2½ ounces) sweet butter, 4 cut into small bits

1 cup freshly grated Parmigiano cheese

4 ounces unsmoked scamorza cheese, thinly sliced; or 4 ounces additional freshly grated Parmigiano cheese

CRESPELLE (CRÊPES)

1. *Quickly swirl the batter around until the bottom of the pan is covered.*

2. *Once the batter sets, shake the pan vigorously to detach* **crespella** *from pan.*

3. *Shake the* **crespella** *onto the edge of the pan so you can either*

4. *flip it, by giving the pan a short abrupt movement forward then up, when the* **crespella** *should turn in the air,*

5. *or leaving pan on the stove, hold the* **crespella** *and quickly turn it over.*

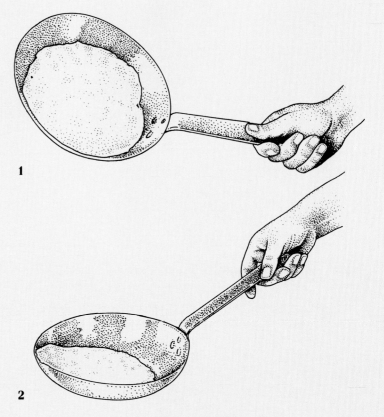

1

2

3

4

5

CHICKEN AND DUCK

Chicken is occasionally an ingredient used to flavor a sauce, but there do not seem to be chicken sauces analogous to meat, duck, or rabbit sauces. Occasionally one finds the combination of pasta and a chicken dish such as a stew; or this striking first recipe in which the separately baked chicken pieces are added to the bell pepper sauce for the pasta. It is an unusual example of a *piatto unico*, or combination of first and second course.

There are two classic recipes in which duck meat is used in the sauce itself. One is from Arezzo, the other from Parma. They are really quite different, and unfortunately some recipes combine elements of both. In the Arezzo recipe the duck liver is added at the end, a crucial difference; cold water rather than wine and broth is added to the tomatoes, and leeks are added to the aromatic vegetables. Two often mistaken elements are adding cloves, which is more typical of Bologna than Parma or Arezzo, and employing Grano Padano when Parmigiano would certainly be used in either place. The pasta in both places is made without oil and with an extra egg because of the richness of the sauce. Sage is used in Parma, not in Arezzo.

A third dish is the *Lasagne* with Duck, also from Arezzo. In this spectacular recipe, it is only the essence of the duck, cooked at length in the sauce and combined with the duck liver added at the end, which ends up in the sauce. The meat is reserved for a later use (see Recipe Appendix).

PAPPARDELLE AI PEPERONI

PAPPARDELLE WITH CHICKEN IN SWEET PEPPER SAUCE

FROM LUCANIA

SERVES 6

1 chicken, about 3½ pounds

FOR THE MARINADE:
3 large lemons
20 large sprigs Italian parsley, leaves only
2 medium-sized cloves garlic, peeled
½ cup olive oil
Salt and freshly ground black pepper

FOR THE PASTA:
3 cups unbleached all-purpose flour
4 extra-large eggs
Pinch of salt
                or
1 pound dried wide egg pasta, such as *pappardelle*, preferably imported Italian

FOR THE SAUCE:
3 red bell peppers
½ cup dry white wine
Salt and freshly ground black pepper

TO COOK THE PASTA:
Coarse-grained salt

TO SERVE:
15 large sprigs Italian parsley, leaves only, coarsely chopped

Clean and wash the chicken well, and cut it into 12 pieces. Place chicken in a crockery or glass bowl, squeeze the lemons, and add their juice to the bowl. Coarsley chop the parsley and finely chop the garlic; add them to the bowl along with the oil. Sprinkle with salt and pepper to taste. Mix all the ingredients with a wooden spoon, and let the chicken marinate for 1 hour, turning the pieces several times.

Prepare the fresh pasta with the ingredients and quantities listed, according to the instructions on page 14. Stretch pasta to ¹⁄₁₆ inch; on the pasta machine take to next to last notch. To cut into *pappardelle* follow directions for *trenette* (page 230) but cut both sides with the scalloped pastry wheel into 2-inch-wide strips.

Preheat the oven to 400 degrees. Prepare the sauce. Clean the peppers, removing stems, pulp, and seeds, then cut them into 1-inch strips. Place in a bowl of cold water for 30 minutes.

Use a tongs to transfer the chicken pieces, with parsley and garlic clinging to them, from the bowl to a 13½- x 8¾-inch glass baking dish. Reserve the marinade and bake the chicken for 35 minutes. While the chicken bakes, transfer the marinade to a large saucepan and place over medium heat. When it is hot, drain the peppers and add them to the pan. Sauté for 10 minutes, then cover and cook sauce for 15 minutes more. Add the wine and let it evaporate, uncovered, for 5 minutes. Pass the sauce including peppers through a food mill into a bowl, and then return the purée to the pan; simmer, uncovered, for 3 minutes, and taste for salt and pepper.

Bring a large pot of cold water to a boil, then add coarse salt to taste. Remove the baking dish from oven and transfer the chicken pieces to a large serving dish, forming a ring of pieces around the edge of the dish. Cover with foil to keep the chicken warm. Add the liquid from the baking dish to the puréed peppers and mix well with a wooden spoon.

Cook the *pappardelle* in the boiling salted water for 30 seconds to 1 minute depending on dryness. Drain and place the pasta in the pan with the sauce, tossing very well. Remove the foil from the serving dish and arrange the pasta in the center. Sprinkle the parsley over and serve immediately.

PAPPARDELLE SULL'ANITRA

PAPPARDELLE WITH DUCK

FROM AREZZO
(TUSCANY)

SERVES 8 TO 10

Prepare the pasta with the ingredients and quantities listed, following instructions on page 14. Stretch the sheets of pasta to a thickness of ¹⁄₁₆ inch; on the pasta machine, take to next to last notch. To cut into *pappardelle* follow directions for *trenette* (see page 230) but cut both sides with the scalloped pastry wheel into 2-inch-wide strips. Let the pasta rest on cotton towels until needed.

Prepare the sauce. Clean and wash the duck very well in cold water. Set the liver aside until later. Discard all the excess fat in the cavity. Place the leeks, celery, carrots, and onion in a bowl of cold water and let them soak for 30 minutes, then drain the vegetables and finely chop all together on a board. Cut the *prosciutto* or *pancetta* into cubes less than ¼ inch thick. Place the oil in a large, heavy casserole over medium heat; when the oil is warm, add the duck and sauté, turning all over, for 5 minutes. Add the chopped vegetables and *prosciutto* or *pancetta*, mix very well, and sauté for 5 minutes more.

Pass the tomatoes and juice through a food mill, using the disc with the smallest holes, into a bowl. Add to the casserole, mix very well with a wooden spoon, and cook for 5 minutes more. Season with salt, pepper, and nutmeg. Add 2 cups of the cold water, cover, and simmer for 1 hour, turning the duck every so often. Add the remaining water and keep cooking, uncovered, for at least 1 hour more.

Remove the casserole from the heat and transfer the duck to a chopping board. Remove the meat from the duck, discarding bones and skin. Cut the larger pieces of meat into ½-inch pieces. Coarsely chop the liver. Return the meat and liver to the casserole, set over medium heat, and reduce liquid for 15 minutes more, stirring every so often with a wooden spoon. Taste for salt and pepper.

Meanwhile, bring a large pot of cold water to a boil. Preheat the oven to 375 degrees. When the water reaches a boil, add coarse salt to taste, then add the pasta and cook for 1 to 3 minutes, depending on dryness. As the pasta cooks, use 1 tablespoon of the butter to heavily coat a 13½- x 8¾-inch glass baking dish. Place the remaining butter in a large bowl. Drain the pasta, add it to the bowl with the butter, mix very well, then add the sauce and the Parmigiano and mix again. Transfer to the baking dish and bake for 10 minutes. Remove from the oven, let rest for 1 minute, then serve directly from the baking dish. No extra cheese should be added.

FOR THE PASTA:
4 cups unbleached all-purpose flour
5 extra-large eggs
Pinch of salt

FOR THE SAUCE:
1 duck, Long Island-type (about 5 pounds), with its liver
3 medium-sized leeks, cleaned
3 medium-sized stalks celery
4 medium-sized carrots, scraped
1 large red onion, peeled
4 ounces *prosciutto* or *pancetta*, in 1 piece
½ cup olive oil
2 pounds canned tomatoes, preferably imported Italian, undrained
Salt and freshly ground black pepper
Pinch of freshly grated nutmeg
4 cups cold water

TO COOK THE PASTA:
Coarse-grained salt

TO BAKE:
6 tablespoons (3 ounces) sweet butter
½ cup freshly grated Parmigiano cheese

FROM PARMA

SERVES 6 TO 8

PASTA ALL'ANITRA ALLA PARMIGIANA
PASTA WITH DUCK SAUCE, PARMA STYLE

FROM PARMA

SERVES 6 TO 8

FOR THE SAUCE:
1 **Long Island-type duck (about 5 pounds)**
1 **medium-sized red onion, peeled**
4 **ounces *prosciutto*, in 1 piece**
6 **tablespoons (3 ounces) sweet butter**
2 **tablespoons olive oil**
3 **medium-sized cloves garlic, peeled but left whole**
5 **large sage leaves, fresh or preserved in salt**
1 **cup dry white wine**
½ **pound ripe, fresh tomatoes; or ½ pound canned tomatoes, preferably imported Italian, drained**
Salt and freshly ground black pepper
1 **to 2 cups lukewarm chicken or beef broth, preferably homemade**

FOR THE PASTA:
4 **cups unbleached all-purpose flour**
5 **extra-large eggs**
Pinch of salt

TO COOK THE PASTA:
Coarse-grained salt

TO SERVE:
4 **tablespoons (2 ounces) sweet butter**
½ **cup freshly grated Parmigiano cheese**

Make the sauce. Clean the duck very well, discarding the extra fat from the cavity and the liver. Dry duck with paper towels and cut into 3-inch pieces. A poultry shears is good for this.

Finely chop the onion on a board and cut the *prosciutto* into cubes less than ½ inch thick. Put the butter and oil in a heavy casserole over medium heat. When the butter is melted, add the onion, *prosciutto*, the garlic, and the sage leaves, left whole. Lightly sauté for 15 minutes, stirring every so often with a wooden spoon, then remove and discard the garlic and sage. Add the duck pieces and sauté until lightly golden all over, about 15 minutes. Then add the wine and let it evaporate for 15 minutes more. Meanwhile, if using fresh tomatoes cut them into small pieces. Pass the fresh or canned tomatoes through a food mill, using the disc with smallest holes, into a small bowl. Add the tomato purée to the saucepan and season to taste with salt and pepper. Cook for 45 minutes, turning the meat several times and adding the broth as needed. By that time the duck should be soft and the sauce thick and homogeneous.

Prepare the pasta with the ingredients and quantities listed, following the instructions on page 14. Stretch the sheet of pasta to about ¹⁄₁₆ inch thick; on the hand pasta machine take to the notch before last. Use a scalloped pastry wheel to cut the sheet into 2-inch squares and place squares on cotton towels until needed.

Bring a large pot of cold water to a boil, and place a large serving dish with the butter over the boiling water to melt. When the sauce is ready, and the water is boiling, remove the serving dish. Add coarse salt to the water, then add the pasta and cook for 1 to 3 minutes depending on dryness. Drain the pasta, transfer to the dish with the melted butter, toss very well, add the duck sauce, mix well, and arrange the duck pieces all over. Sprinkle with the Parmigiano and serve immediately.

GAME STUFFINGS AND SAUCES

Squab meat is popular for stuffing pasta, as in *Tortelli* Stuffed with Squab (see Recipe Appendix) as well as the wonderful little *tortellini* eaten in broth, a recipe for which follows. They may also be made with the *cappelletti* shape. Squab meat is used in the sauce itself in Squab with *Macaroni* in a Pastry Drum (see Recipe Appendix).

Two recipes for pasta with rabbit sauce follow, one from Umbria and the other from Tuscany. They share ingredients: both use the rabbit liver, and after cooking the rabbit itself in the sauce to extract its essence, both call for it to be removed and used for another meal. The main difference in flavoring—and it is significant—is that the Tuscan version stresses rosemary and sage, and the Umbrian one parsley and black olives.

One of the most characteristic of all Tuscan dishes is *Pappardelle sulla lepre*, made with a sauce of hare, its dark meat imparting a rich game flavor to the sauce. Many game sauces originate in Tuscany but have spread to other places, and what is fundamentally the same sauce can also be made with wild boar, when available.

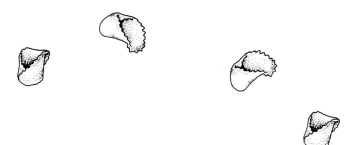

FROM TUSCANY

SERVES 6 TO 8

PAPPARDELLE SULLA PECORA
PAPPARDELLE WITH LAMB SAUCE

FOR THE SAUCE:
1 **medium-sized red onion,
    peeled**
1 **large stalk celery**
1 **medium-sized carrot,
    scraped**
½ **pound coarsely ground
    lamb**
4 **tablespoons olive oil**
½ **pound boneless lamb,
    cut into ½-inch cubes**
1 **medium-sized sprig fresh
    thyme, or 1 tablespoon
    dried**
1 **medium-sized sprig fresh
    rosemary, or 1
    tablespoon dried and
    blanched**
1 **cup dry white wine**
1½ **pounds ripe, fresh
    tomatoes; or 1½ pounds
    canned tomatoes,
    preferably imported
    Italian, drained**
**Salt and freshly ground
    black pepper**
1 **cup lukewarm chicken
    or beef broth, preferably
    homemade**

FOR THE PASTA:
3 **cups unbleached all-
    purpose flour**
4 **extra-large eggs**
Pinch of salt

TO COOK THE PASTA:
Coarse grained salt

*The lamb sauce of Abruzzi, used with fresh pasta cut with the "gui-tar," is made with true lamb (see Recipe Appendix), but the Tuscan dish—made not so much in Prato as in the area between that town and Florence, called Campi—uses meat from an animal a year old, called there not lamb but "sheep," or **pecora**. (In Italy lamb is not likely to be more than twelve weeks old.) But the long-cooked **pecora** is a specialty of Campi, and indeed in our days it is one of the few places in Italy where it can still be found. In earlier times, lamb, sheep, and mutton (**montone**) all had their separate reper-tories, but both **pecora** and **montone** dishes are extremely rare now. The lamb usually available suits this dish rather well; it is much older than the twelve-week-old "baby" lamb, though younger than the **pecora** used in Campi. Campi, Prato, and Florence were all once the center of the Western European wool industry; indeed, Florence's original fortunes were made in that trade, and only later in banking.*

Prepare the sauce. Finely chop the onion, celery, and carrot all together on a board, then mix with the ground lamb in a small bowl. Place the oil in a deep saucepan over low heat; when the oil is warm, add the contents of the bowl and sauté for 5 minutes. Add the lamb cubes and the thyme and rosemary if you are using fresh sprigs. If you are using dried thyme and rosemary, tie them in a piece of cheesecloth and reserve for later use. Sauté for 5 minutes more, then pour in the wine and let it evaporate for 5 minutes. If using fresh tomatoes, cut them into small pieces. Pass fresh or canned tomatoes through a food mill, using the disc with smallest holes, into a small bowl. Add the tomatoes to the saucepan and season with salt and pepper to taste. Cook for 15 minutes, then add the broth. If you are using dried thyme and rosemary, submerge the cheesecloth bag of herbs into the sauce at this point. Simmer the sauce for 1 hour over low heat, stirring every so often with a wooden spoon.

As the sauce cooks, prepare the pasta with the ingredients and quantities listed, following the directions on page 14. Stretch layer to about ¹⁄₁₆ inch; on the hand pasta machine, to the next to last setting. To cut into *pappardelle* follow directions for *trenette* (see page 230) but cut both sides with the scalloped pastry wheel into 2-inch-wide strips and set on cotton towels until needed.

When the sauce is ready, discard the sprigs of thyme and rose-mary or the cheesecloth bag and transfer the sauce to a large skillet over low heat. Place a large pot of cold water over medium heat; when the water reaches a boil, add coarse salt to taste, then add the pasta, and cook 1 to 3 minutes, depending on the dryness. Drain the pasta, transfer it to a large bowl, add the butter, and toss very well. Transfer the pasta to the skillet, mix very well, then arrange on a warmed serving dish. Sprinkle with cheese and serve immediately.

TO SERVE:
8 tablespoons (4 ounces) sweet butter, cut into small pieces
½ cup freshly grated Parmigiano cheese

TORTELLINI O CAPPELLETTI DI PICCIONE

TORTELLINI OR *CAPPELLETTI* STUFFED WITH SQUAB

FROM MANTUA (LOMBARDY)

SERVES 8 TO 10

Clean and wash the squab very well. Place the cold water in a small, deep saucepan over medium heat, and when the water reaches a boil, add coarse salt to taste, the bay leaf, and the clove. When the water returns to a boil, add the squab and simmer for 45 minutes. Transfer squab to a chopping board and bone it. Discard the bones and the water; reserve the meat and skin. Finely chop the prosciutto, squab meat, and squab skin together on a board, then transfer to a crockery or glass bowl. Add the egg and Parmigiano, and season with salt, pepper, and nutmeg. Mix well with a wooden spoon and refrigerate, covered, until needed.

Prepare the pasta with the ingredients and quantities listed, according to the instructions on page 14. Stretch to less than 1/16 inch thick; on the pasta machine, take to last notch. Prepare the *tortellini* or *cappelletti* (see page 174 or 175) using ¼ teaspoon of stuffing for each *tortellino* or *cappelletto*. Let the pasta rest on floured cotton dish towels until needed. When ready, heat the broth in a medium-sized pot over medium heat. When the broth reaches a boil, add the *tortellini* or *cappelletti* and cook for 1 to 3 minutes depending on dryness. Serve in warmed bowls, along with some broth and sprinkle each serving with Parmigiano.

FOR THE STUFFING:
1 squab (about ½ pound)
About 1 quart cold water
Coarse-grained salt
1 bay leaf
1 whole clove
3 ounces *prosciutto*, in 1 piece
1 extra-large egg
¼ cup freshly grated Parmigiano cheese
Salt and freshly ground black pepper
Large pinch freshly grated nutmeg

FOR THE PASTA:
3 cups unbleached all-purpose flour
4 extra-large eggs
Pinch of salt

TO SERVE:
2½ quarts defatted chicken or beef broth, preferably homemade
½ cup freshly grated Parmigiano cheese

TORTELLINI

1. As the pasta is prepared, immediately cut it into discs using a cookie cutter without jagged edges, the diameter appropriate to the size for the individual recipe. Place an amount of filling appropriate to the recipe in the center.

1

2. Moisten the edges slightly with water or egg whites then double over one side of the pasta disc, but not all the way to the other edge; leave a little border arc of the pasta undoubled.

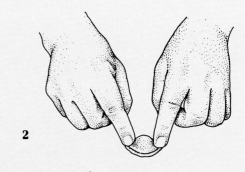

2

3. Wrap the half-moon around your index or little finger, depending on size, the top of the finger reaching only to the top of the filled section.

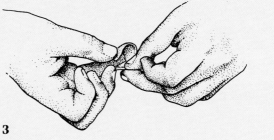

3

4. With your thumb, connect the two edges of the half-moon.

4

5. Take the pasta overlapping your fingers and curl it outward.

6. The finished **tortellino.**

5

6

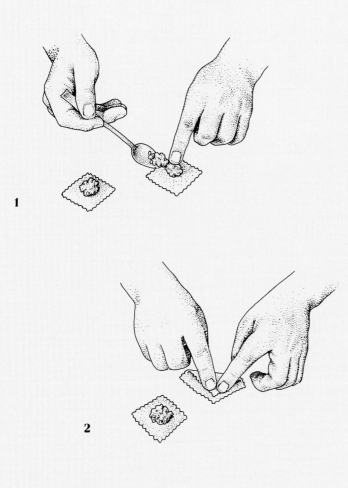

CAPPELLETTI

1. *With a pastry cutter, with scalloped or non-scalloped edge, cut the layer of pasta into squares of appropriate size for the individual recipe. Place the appropriate amount of filling in the center of each square.*

2. *Moisten the edges with water or egg whites. Pick up one corner and draw it to the opposite corner, but not all the way to the edge. Leave a border undoubled.*

3. *Wrap the now triangular-shaped pasta around your index finger, the top of the finger reaching only to the top of the filled section.*

4. *With your thumb, connect the two edges of the pasta triangle and curl the overlap of pasta outward. The result should resemble the little hat which gives* **cappelletti** *their name.*

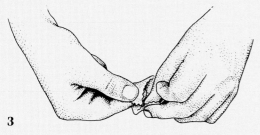

175

PAPPARDELLE SUL CONIGLIO

PASTA WITH RABBIT SAUCE

FOR THE SAUCE:
**1 small rabbit with liver
(about 2 pounds)
8 ounces *pancetta* or
prosciutto, in 1 piece
2 medium-sized carrots,
scraped
1 small red onion, peeled
3 medium-sized stalks
celery
1 medium-sized clove
garlic, peeled
1 tablespoon rosemary
leaves, fresh or
preserved in salt or dried
and blanched
3 large sage leaves, fresh
or preserved in salt
½ cup olive oil
1 cup dry red wine
2 tablespoons tomato paste
2 cups lukewarm beef or
chicken broth,
preferably homemade
Salt and freshly ground
black pepper**

FOR THE PASTA:
**3 cups unbleached all-
purpose flour
4 extra-large eggs
Pinch of salt**
or
**1 pound dried
pappardelle, preferably
imported Italian**

TO COOK THE PASTA:
Coarse-grained salt

Prepare the sauce. Wash the rabbit very well; set the liver aside until later. Cut the rabbit into 3 pieces and pat dry with paper towels. Place a large skillet over medium heat; when it is hot, add the rabbit pieces without oil, cover, and sauté for 4 minutes. Discard the juices that emerge, since their flavor is very gamey. Remove skillet from the heat, wash the rabbit again, and pat dry with paper towels.

Mince the *pancetta* or *prosciutto*; finely chop the carrots, onion, celery, garlic, rosemary, and sage all together on a board. Heat the oil over medium heat in a large flameproof casserole. When the oil is warm, add the rabbit and sauté for 5 minutes on each side. Pour in the wine and let it evaporate for 10 minutes. Add the chopped ingredients along with the pancetta or prosciutto and sauté for 15 minutes more. Dissolve the tomato paste in 1 cup of the broth and add it to casserole; season to taste with salt and pepper, cover, and simmer for 25 minutes, stirring every so often with a wooden spoon. Add the second cup of broth and cook, uncovered, for 20 minutes more, or until the rabbit is very tender. Remove the rabbit and save it for another meal. Taste the sauce for salt and pepper. Finely chop the rabbit liver on a board, add it to casserole, mix well, and cook for 5 minutes.

During the last stages of cooking the sauce, you will have time to prepare the pasta with the ingredients and quantities listed and following the directions on page 14. Stretch sheets to ¹⁄₁₆ inch thick. To cut the pasta into *pappardelle* follow directions for *trenette* (see page 230) but cut both sides with the scalloped pastry wheel into 2-inch-wide strips and let rest on cotton dish towels until needed.

Bring a large pot of cold water to a boil, add coarse salt to taste, then add the pasta. If fresh pasta, cook 1 to 3 minutes depending on dryness; if dried, for 9 to 12 minutes depending on the brand. Drain the pasta and transfer it to a large, warmed serving platter; pour the sauce over, toss well, and serve.

TAGLIATELLE ALLA FRANTOIANA
TAGLIATELLE IN RABBIT SAUCE WITH OLIVES

Clean the rabbit very well and rinse it under cold running water. Place a large flameproof casserole over medium heat (with no oil or other fat), put in the rabbit, cover, and sauté for 3 minutes on each side to drain out the gamey white liquid. Remove the rabbit and rinse again in cold water.

Cut the *pancetta* into small pieces. Place the butter and oil in a medium-sized flameproof casserole over medium heat. When the butter is melted, add the *pancetta* and sauté until lightly golden, about 5 minutes.

Finely chop the onion, carrots, celery, parsley, and garlic all together on a board. When *pancetta* is ready, add the chopped ingredients and sauté for 2 minutes. Put in the whole rabbit and cook for 15 minutes, stirring all the vegetables constantly and turning the rabbit 3 or 4 times. Add the wine and evaporate for 5 minutes, then season with salt and pepper. Dissolve the tomato paste in the broth, and pour 1 cup of the mixture into the casserole. Cover and cook for 1 hour, adding the remaining broth, ½ cup at a time, each time stirring the sauce. Turn the rabbit 4 or 5 more times while cooking.

Prepare the pasta with the ingredients and quantities listed above, following the directions on page 14. Make pasta sheet a little thicker than usual, about ¹⁄₁₆ inch thick, and cut into *tagliatelle* (see page 33), to accompany this full-bodied sauce. Set aside to rest on cotton towels until needed.

When the sauce is ready, taste again for salt and pepper and lift out the cooked rabbit, reserving it for a later use, at this or another meal. Finely chop the raw rabbit liver on a board.

When ready to serve, put a large pot of cold water over medium heat. When the water reaches a boil, place a large serving dish containing the butter over the pot to melt it. Reheat the sauce and mix in the chopped up liver and the chopped olives. Add coarse salt to the boiling water, then add the pasta and cook for 1 to 3 minutes, depending on the dryness. Drain pasta, transfer to the prepared serving platter, mix well, add all the sauce, mix again, sprinkle the parsley and whole olives over, and serve immediately.

FOR THE SAUCE:

1 small rabbit (about 4 pounds), liver reserved

4 ounces *pancetta* or *prosciutto*

2 tablespoons (1 ounce) sweet butter

½ cup olive oil

1 small red onion, peeled

3 medium-sized carrots, scraped

2 medium-sized stalks celery

10 large sprigs Italian parsley, leaves only

1 medium-sized clove garlic, peeled

1 cup dry red wine

Salt and freshly ground black pepper

4 tablespoons tomato paste

2½ cups beef broth, preferably homemade

20 black Greek olives, packed in brine, pitted and finely chopped

FOR THE PASTA:

4 cups unbleached all-purpose flour

5 extra-large eggs

Pinch of salt

TO COOK THE PASTA:

Coarse-grained salt

TO SERVE:

4 tablespoons (2 ounces) sweet butter

10 large sprigs Italian parsley, leaves only, coarsely chopped

10 black Greek olives, pitted but left whole

FROM FRIULI

SERVES 8 TO 10

PASTA SUL CERVO

PASTA WITH VENISON SAUCE

FOR THE MARINADE:
**2 medium-sized red
  onions, peeled**
3 large stalks celery
**3 medium-sized carrots,
  scraped**
3 cups dry red wine
3 bay leaves
3 whole cloves
**1 large clove garlic, peeled
  but left whole**
**2 pounds boneless venison
  steak**

FOR THE SAUCE:
**¼ cup unbleached all-
  purpose flour**
¼ cup olive oil
2 cups dry red wine
**Salt and freshly ground
  black pepper**
4 tablespoons tomato paste
**3 cups lukewarm chicken
  or beef broth, preferably
  homemade**

FOR THE PASTA:
**1½ pounds dried
  pappardelle, preferably
  imported Italian**

TO COOK THE PASTA:
Coarse-grained salt

TO SERVE:
**8 to 10 tablespoons freshly
  grated aged latteria or
  Parmigiano cheese
  (optional)**

Venison meat from a variety of deer types is used in Italy, especially in the hilly and mountainous regions of the Apennines and Alps. In Friuli, a venison sauce is made from the meat marinated in wine, spices, and aromatic vegetables and mixed with broth, a little tomato, and the chopped marinade vegetables. This fragrant red wine sauce is usually served with a dried pasta and pieces of the meat itself.

Cut the onions into quarters and the celery and carrots into large pieces; place them with the wine, bay leaves, cloves, garlic, and venison steak in a large crockery or glass bowl. Cover and marinate in the refrigerator for 24 hours, turning the meat twice.

Remove the meat and vegetables. Discard the wine, bay leaves, and cloves. Lightly flour the steaks on both sides. Place the oil in a heavy, medium-sized casserole and set over medium heat. When the oil is warm, add the meat and sauté for 5 minutes on each side. Meanwhile, finely chop the marinated vegetables on a board, then add them to the casserole and sauté for 15 minutes. Add 1 cup of the fresh wine and cook again for 15 minutes, then add the second cup of wine to cook once again for 15 minutes. Add salt and pepper to taste. Dissolve the tomato paste in 1 cup of the broth, add it to the casserole, cover, and simmer for 3 hours, adding the remaining broth as needed and stirring every so often with a wooden spoon. The meat should become very tender and the sauce creamy and quite thick. Taste again for salt and pepper and cook for 2 minutes more, uncovered.

Bring a large pot of cold water to a boil, add coarse salt to taste, then add the pasta and cook until al dente, for 9 to 12 minutes depending on the brand. Meanwhile, place some of the liquid from the sauce on a large warmed serving platter. Drain the pasta and transfer it to the warmed platter. Pour the remaining sauce and meat over, toss very well, and serve immediately. Pass the cheese, if using, at the table.

RECIPE APPENDIX

Pasta with Meat in Other Bugialli Books

TAGLIATELLE AL SUGO DI CARNE (*Tagliatelle* with Meat Sauce) *FA* p. 146

TORTELLINI AL SUGO DI CARNE (*Tortellini* in Meat Sauce) *FA* p. 177

LASAGNE AL FORNO (Baked *Lasagne*, Northern Italian Style) *FA* p. 189

CANNELLONI CON CARNE (*Cannelloni* with Meat) *FA* p. 178

PINCI DI MONTALCINO (*Pinci*, Montalcino Style) *CT* p. 147

TAGLIATELLE AL SUGO DI MANZO (*Tagliatelle* with Beef Sauce) *CT* p. 132

LASAGNE ALLA GENOVESE (Boiled *Lasagne* with Beef Sauce) *CT* p. 160

PASTICCIO DI PASTA (Baked Pasta Mold) *CT* p. 193

PENNE STRASCICATE ALLA FIORENTINA (*Penne* Stir-Sautéed in Meat Sauce) *CT* p. 192

PENNE STRASCICATE AL SUGO DI VITELLA (*Penne* Stir-Sautéed in Veal Sauce) *CT* p. 191

TORTELLONI ALLA CASENTINESE (Large *Tortelli*, Casentino Style) *CT* p. 168

TAGLIATELLE CON DADI DI PROSCIUTTO (*Tagliatelle* with Creamed *Prosciutto* Sauce) *FI* p. 86

PASTICCIO DI TORTELLINI OR CAPPELLETTI ALLA BOLOGNESE (Baked *Tortellini*) *CT* p. 177

ANOLINI AL RAGÙ DI PROSCIUTTO (*Anolini* with *Prosciutto* Sauce) *FI* p. 98

SPAGHETTI ALLA CARBONARA (*Spaghetti* with Egg-*Pancetta* Sauce) *FA* p. 155

TIMBALLO DI MEZZELUNE (*Timballo* of Half-Moon Pasta) *FI* p. 104

TORTELLI DI MICHELANGELO (*Tortelli* of Michelangelo Buonarotti) *CT* p. 167

PENNE TRIPPATE (*Penne* with Tripe Sauce) *CT* p. 191

CANNELLONI CON LINGUA SALMISTRATA (*Cannelloni* Stuffed with Tongue and Chicken) *CT* p. 158

TAGLIATELLE CON CIBREO (Fresh *Tagliatelle* with Cibreo Sauce) *FA* p. 148

TAGLIATELLE AL SUGO DI FEGATINI (Fresh *Tagliatelle* with Chicken Liver Sauce) *FA* p. 149

SPAGHETTI AL SUGO DI "CIPOLLE" (*Spaghetti* with Chicken Gizzard Sauce) *FA* p. 157

TORTELLINI ALLA PANNA (*Tortellini* in Butter and Cream Sauce) *FA* p. 176

TIMBALLO DI TORTELLINI (*Tortellini* in a Pastry Drum) *FA* p. 212

CANNELLONI ALLA SORPRESA (Green *Cannelloni* Stuffed with *Tortelli alla panna*) *FA* p. 187

LASAGNE ALL' ANITRA ALL' ARETINA (*Lasagne* with Duck, Arezzo Style) *FA* p. 195

TAGLIATELLE CON SUGO DI OCA CONSERVATO (*Tagliatelle* with Sauce of Preserved Goose) *CT* p. 134

TIMBALLO DI PICCIONE (Squab with *Macaroni* in a Pastry Drum) *FA* p. 206

TORTELLI DI PICCIONE (*Tortelli* Stuffed with Squab) *CT* p. 169

TORTELLI AL CONIGLIO (*Tortelli* in Rabbit Sauce) *FA* p. 172

PAPPARDELLE ALLO SPEZZATONI DI CONIGLIO (*Pappardelle* with Stewed Rabbit Sauce) *CT* p. 150

PAPPARDELLE SULLA LEPRE (*Pappardelle* with Hare Sauce) *FA* p. 151

MACCHERONI ALLA CHITARRA (*Maccheroni* Cut with the "Guitar" in Lamb Sauce) *CT* p. 144

FA   *The Fine Art of Italian Cooking*
CT   *Giuliano Bugialli's Classic Techniques of Italian Cooking*
FI   *Giuliano Bugialli's Foods of Italy*

Corzetti stampati: These beautifully patterned discs of pasta, stamped like a coin, may be made of several types of flour, producing a variety of color and taste.

FRESH

REGIONAL PASTAS

ach region of Italy and many of its cities and towns have one or more trademark
pastas. These pastas are made only in that place and are thus savoured in their
native habitat. I include here some of the most famous dishes, arranged by
region. My choice necessarily must be somewhat limited and includes some notable ones
that are not well known and some better known ones that I feel have not been
represented authentically enough. We begin with Piedmont, with its various *agnolotti*
and its bread crumb pasta.

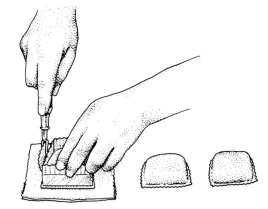

PIEDMONT

Agnelotti, spelled in this older manner, appeared in the early Piedmont cookbook of 1798. It is interesting to see them in this early form, closer to their origins, in order to clarify the essentials behind the many stuffings that now exist. At this earlier time, dishes were divided between those without meat, called *di magro*, which were served on fasting days, and those with meat, called *di grasso*. *(Magro* and *grasso* are also used as adjectives to denote "thin" and "fat.")

The more common version then was *di magro*, usually made with spinach along with butter, cream, cheese, eggs, and—to bind it together—"mollica," the crumb of the bread. On non-fasting days, the meat used was breast of veal, boiled to make the veal broth in which the *agnelotti* were eaten, sprinkled with additional cheese. Since broth was generally made with some kind of meat then, the *di magro* versions were eaten with butter and grated cheese.

One might speculate that the earliest versions of the butter and cheese dressing came about in just this manner, because the pasta, especially stuffed pasta, could not be eaten with a broth. On the other hand, in the fourteenth century, Boccaccio has his ladies in the Calandrino story of the Decameron dressing pasta *cooked in broth* with butter and abundant cheese. Butter seems to have become popular in medieval times, and not to have come from the Roman world, so in Boccaccio's time it may have still been a new sensation. But this butter and cheese dressing would have remained on as a necessary one for fasting days, especially in areas like Piedmont, which produce no olive oil.

Under *Classic Agnolotti*, we discuss the general categories of ingredients used. Some vegetables remain in all versions as a reminder of the origins of the dish, but the types of meat have multiplied in their variations. Roasted meats, often mixed and left over from a feast of *arrosto misto*, are preferred, especially because the juices left over may be used as a dressing. A combination of beef and pork are most often used, but both veal and chicken are also sometimes used.

A unique adaptation is the large *tortelli* in the recipe of *Agnolotti alla piemontese*, in which a little ring of rice and sauce contains an inner stuffing of meat and aromatic vegetables. The dressing is the usual butter and cheese.

It is worth noting that the original *agnelotti* used pasta made with only the whites of eggs.

FROM PIEDMONT

SERVES 6 TO 8

AGNELOTTI ALL' ITALIANA (DI MAGRO) (1798)

ANTIQUE *AGNOLOTTI* WITH VEGETABLE STUFFING

FOR THE STUFFING:
1½ pounds fresh spinach, large stems removed
Coarse-grained salt
2 slices white bread, crusts removed
1 cup cold milk
4 tablespoons (2 ounces) sweet butter
Salt and freshly ground black pepper
Freshly grated nutmeg
½ cup heavy cream
1 extra-large egg
1 extra-large egg yolk
1 cup freshly grated Parmigiano cheese

FOR THE PASTA:
3 cups unbleached all-purpose flour
4 extra-large egg whites
½ cup lukewarm water
Pinch of salt

TO COOK THE PASTA:
Coarse-grained salt

TO SERVE:
8 tablespoons (4 ounces) sweet butter
1 cup freshly grated Parmigiano cheese
Freshly grated black pepper

Prepare the stuffing. Clean the spinach and let it rest in a bowl of cold water for 30 minutes. Bring a large pot of cold water to a boil, add coarse salt to taste, drain the spinach, add it to the pot, and cook for 10 minutes. Meanwhile, soak the bread in the milk. Drain the spinach, cool it under cold running water, squeeze very well, and chop it fine on a board.

Place the butter in a medium-sized skillet over medium heat, and when it is melted, add the spinach. Squeeze the milk out of the bread and add it to the skillet. Season to taste with salt, pepper, and nutmeg; sauté for 2 minutes, mixing with a wooden spoon to incorporate the bread into the spinach. Start adding the cream, a little at a time, continuously mixing; when the cream is all added, sauté for 1 minute more. Transfer the mixture to a crockery or glass bowl and rest until completely cool, 30 minutes. Add egg, egg yolk, and Parmigiano; mix well and refrigerate, covered, until needed.

Prepare the pasta with the ingredients and quantities listed, following the directions on page 14. Let the ball of dough rest for 30 minutes, wrapped in a cotton dish towel and covered tightly with a bowl. When pasta is ready, stretch the dough to less than ¹⁄₁₆ inch thick—on the pasta machine take to the finest setting. Prepare *agnolotti*, using the method for *tortelli* or *ravioli* on page 113. Use ½ tablespoon of stuffing for each *agnolotto* and cut the stuffed pasta into 2½-inch squares. Let *agnolotti* rest on floured cotton dish towels until needed, turning them over once or twice.

Bring a large pot of cold water to a boil. Place the butter for the sauce on a large serving platter as a lid. When the water reaches a boil and the butter is melted, remove the platter from the pot, add coarse salt to taste, then add the *agnolotti* and cook for 6 to 9 minutes, depending on the dryness. Use a strainer-skimmer to transfer the cooked *agnolotti* to the platter. Make a layer of pasta, then another of butter; sprinkle on cheese and abundant black pepper. Repeat until all the pasta is on the platter, the top layer of melted butter, cheese, and pepper. Serve hot.

NOTE:
Pasta made with egg whites only requires a longer cooking time than whole-egg pasta. *Agnelotti* is the old spelling for *agnolotti*.

AGNELOTTI ALL'ITALIANA (DI GRASSO)

ANTIQUE *AGNOLOTTI* WITH MEAT STUFFING

*The **di grasso** meat stuffing may be substituted, using the following ingredients and cooking them in the veal broth made with the veal shoulder that yields the meat for the stuffing. The **agnelotti** are eaten together with the broth, sprinkled with additional grated cheese.*

Prepare the broth. Place a stockpot containing the meat, cold water, and coarse salt on a low flame. When the water reaches a boil, add carrots, celery, onion, and parsley, all whole, and simmer very slowly, half covered, for 3 hours. While simmering, spoon off any foam or impurities that come to the surface.

Remove meat from stockpot, reserving it for the stuffing, and strain broth through a colander into a large non-metal bowl. Allow broth to cool completely, about 1 hour, then place bowl, covered, in the refrigerator for at least 1 hour. Then remove all fat from surface.

To prepare the stuffing and fill the *agnelotti*, follow the instructions for the recipe on the preceding page, except delete the bread and add the chopped veal to the spinach in the skillet.

To serve, bring broth to a simmer, cook *agnelotti* 6 to 9 minutes, depending on dryness. Sprinkle each serving of *agnelotti* and broth with additional cheese.

FOR THE BROTH:
2 pounds breast of veal
15 cups cold water
Coarse-grained salt
2 medium-sized carrots
2 celery stalks
1 medium-sized red onion, peeled
15 sprigs Italian parsley

FOR THE STUFFING:
1 pound fresh spinach, large stems removed
Coarse-grained salt
½ pound of the boiled breast of veal from the broth, finely chopped
4 tablespoons (2 ounces) sweet butter
Salt and freshly ground black pepper to taste
Freshly grated nutmeg to taste
½ cup heavy cream
1 extra-large egg
1 extra-large egg yolk
1 cup freshly grated Parmigiano cheese

FOR THE PASTA:
3 cups unbleached all-purpose flour
4 extra-large egg whites
½ cup lukewarm water
Pinch of salt

TO COOK THE PASTA:
Veal broth (see above)

TO SERVE:
1 cup freshly grated Parmigiano cheese

FROM PIEDMONT

SERVES 8

AGNOLOTTI ALLA PIEMONTESE

GIANT SQUARE *AGNOLOTTI*

**FOR THE MEAT
STUFFING:**

**4 ounces *prosciutto*, in 1
    piece**
**6 tablespoons (3 ounces)
    sweet butter**
2 tablespoons olive oil
**1 medium-sized carrot,
    scraped**
1 large white onion, peeled
1 large stalk celery
**10 large sprigs Italian
    parsley, leaves only**
**1 pound boneless veal
    shoulder, in 1 piece**
1 cup dry white wine
1 tablespoon tomato paste
**Salt and freshly ground
    black pepper**
**Pinch of freshly grated
    nutmeg**
**1 cup beef broth,
    preferably homemade**

**FOR THE RICE
STUFFING:**

**1 medium-sized white
    onion, peeled**
**5 tablespoons (2½ ounces)
    sweet butter**
1 tablespoon olive oil
**1 cup rice, preferably
    Italian Arborio**
**3 cups beef broth,
    preferably homemade,
    heated to boiling**
**Salt and freshly ground
    black pepper**
**5 tablespoons freshly
    grated Parmigiano
    cheese**

Cut the *prosciutto* into tiny pieces. Heat the butter and oil in a saucepan over medium heat; when the butter is completely melted, add the *prosciutto*, lower the heat, and cook for 5 minutes. Meanwhile, finely chop the carrot, onion, celery, and parsley together on a board. Add to the pan and sauté for 2 minutes more. Add the veal and sauté on all sides for 2 minutes. Pour in the wine and let it evaporate for 5 minutes. Then add the tomato paste; salt, pepper, and nutmeg to taste; and ½ cup of the broth. Keep adding broth while veal cooks until tender, about 20 minutes. Remove saucepan from the heat and, using a slotted spoon, transfer all the solid ingredients to a bowl. Reserve the cooking juices in the saucepan. With a meat grinder, coarsely grind everything back into the saucepan. Return pan to medium heat, taste for salt and pepper, and cook until the mixture is quite thick, about 5 minutes longer. Transfer stuffing to a crockery or glass bowl to cool for 1 hour.

Prepare the rice stuffing. Preheat the oven to 375 degrees. Finely chop the onion on a board, then heat the butter and oil in a medium-sized flameproof casserole over medium heat. When the butter is completely melted, add the rice and sauté for 4 minutes. Add the boiling broth to the rice, season with salt and pepper, and stir very well. Cover the casserole and bake in the oven for 20 minutes. Remove from oven, transfer rice to a crockery or glass bowl, and cool for 1 hour. When the meat and rice stuffings are both cool, incorporate one-third of the meat stuffing and all the Parmigiano into the rice stuffing, mixing thoroughly with a wooden spoon.

Prepare the pasta with the ingredients and quantities listed, following the directions on page 14. Stretch the pasta to less than ¹⁄₁₆ inch thick, on the pasta machine take to the last setting. Place a jagged-edged cookie cutter with 4-inch sides on the sheet of pasta. With a pastry bag, make a narrow border of rice all along the inside edge of the cookie cutter (see drawing). Fit a tablespoon of the meat stuffing inside the rice border. Carefully remove the cookie cutter. Repeat the procedure for the remaining *agnolotti*, then fit a similar sheet of pasta over the prepared rice squares. Replace the cookie cutter, this time upside down (the top part is wider), and cut all around the cookie cutter with a pastry wheel. Seal the edges together well and let squares rest on floured cotton dish towels until needed.

Bring a large pot of cold water to a boil. Meanwhile, melt the butter on a large serving platter and place platter over the pot of

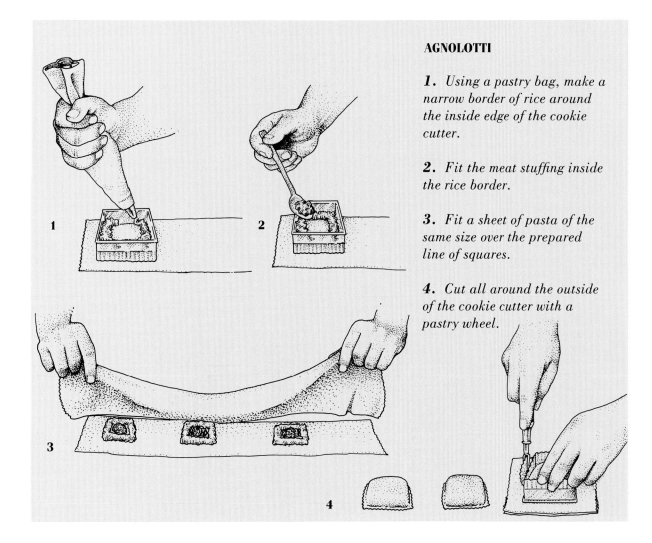

AGNOLOTTI

1. *Using a pastry bag, make a narrow border of rice around the inside edge of the cookie cutter.*

2. *Fit the meat stuffing inside the rice border.*

3. *Fit a sheet of pasta of the same size over the prepared line of squares.*

4. *Cut all around the outside of the cookie cutter with a pastry wheel.*

water as a lid. When the water reaches a boil, remove platter and add coarse salt. Put in the giant *agnolotti* one at a time, and cook each for 1 to 3 minutes, depending on the dryness. With a slotted spoon, transfer the giant *agnolotti* to the warmed platter and spoon some of the butter over, then sprinkle with Parmigiano. When all the *agnolotti* are on the platter, serve immediately. If using the truffle, shave a few slices over each serving.

FOR THE PASTA:
4 cups unbleached all-purpose flour
5 extra-large eggs
Pinch of salt

TO COOK THE PASTA:
Coarse-grained salt

TO SERVE:
12 tablespoons (6 ounces) sweet butter
½ cup freshly grated Parmigiano cheese
1 small white truffle (optional)

FROM PIEDMONT

SERVES 6 TO 8

AGNOLOTTI (AGNELOTTI OR AGNOLLOTTI)

CLASSIC *AGNOLOTTI*

FOR THE STUFFING:

1¾ **pounds endive (about 3 bunches)**
Coarse-grained salt
8 **tablespoons (4 ounces) sweet butter**
Salt and freshly ground black pepper
2 **bay leaves**
1 **large clove garlic, peeled**

Many variations on the stuffing may be substituted, but keep in mind that there must be both vegetables and meat and that modern normal-sized **agnolotti** *are* **always** *sautéed in butter after they are boiled. See the variations listed below; any combination is possible.*

Prepare the stuffing. Bring a large pot of cold water to a boil over medium heat. Clean the endive, removing the large stems and washing the leaves well. When the water reaches a boil, add coarse salt to taste, then add the endive and cook for 25 minutes. Drain,

cool under cold running water, and squeeze very well to remove as much water as possible. Finely chop the endive.

Place a large skillet with 4 tablespoons of the butter over medium heat; when the butter is melted, add the chopped endive, season with salt and pepper, and sauté, stirring with a wooden spoon for 2 minutes. Transfer to a crockery or glass bowl and cool for 30 minutes.

Place a small saucepan with the remaining butter over medium heat. When the butter is melted, add the bay leaves and garlic, and sauté for 1 minute. Add the ground beef and pork, season with salt and pepper, and sauté for 5 minutes more, stirring every so often with a wooden spoon. Discard the garlic and bay leaves, and transfer the meat with the juices to a crockery or glass bowl; let rest until cool, about 30 minutes. Combine the contents of the 2 bowls, add the eggs and Parmigiano, and mix well. Taste for salt and pepper and season to taste with nutmeg.

Prepare the pasta with the ingredients and quantities listed, following the directions on page 14. Stretch the sheet of pasta to less than 1/16 inch thick, on a pasta machine take to the finest setting. Prepare 2-inch square *tortelli (agnolotti)*, with 1 tablespoon of stuffing for each following the directions on page 113. Let the *agnolotti* rest on floured cotton dish towels until needed.

Bring a large quantity of cold water to a boil, add coarse salt to taste, then add the *agnolotti* and cook for 6 to 9 minutes depending on dryness. Meanwhile, melt the butter for the sauce in a large skillet over low heat. As the *agnolotti* are cooked, transfer them to the skillet and sauté gently for 1 minute more. Arrange on a warmed serving platter and serve with cheese and abundant black pepper.

6 ounces ground beef
6 ounces ground pork
3 extra-large eggs
½ cup freshly grated Parmigiano cheese
Freshly grated nutmeg

FOR THE PASTA:
3 cups unbleached all-purpose flour
4 extra-large eggs
Pinch of salt

TO COOK THE PASTA:
Coarse-grained salt

FOR THE SAUCE:
8 tablespoons (4 ounces) sweet butter
¾ cup freshly grated Parmigiano cheese
Freshly ground black pepper

VARIATIONS
1. Spinach or Swiss chard can be used instead of endive.
2. Beef, veal, or pork that is boiled, braised, or stewed can be used in place of the sautéed beef and pork.
3. *Prosciutto*, boiled ham, or *pancetta* can be added.
4. Brains or sweetbreads can be added.
5. White truffles can be used in season, but shaved over the *agnolotti* when served. In Piedmont this is the usual style.

Display of fresh pasta with other food in *Piazze delle erbe*, one of Mantua's loveliest squares. This is the locale of the early morning vegetable market, transformed for lunch and dinner into a center of restaurants and bars.

FROM PIEDMONT

SERVES 8

PISAREI E FASO

PASTA AND BEANS, MONFERRATO STYLE

FOR THE BEANS:
1 cup dried *borlotti* or
  cranberry beans
3 quarts cold water
2 tablespoons olive oil
2 ounces *pancetta* or
  prosciutto, in 1 piece
2 teaspoons coarse-grained
  salt

FOR THE SAUCE:
1 medium-sized red onion,
  peeled
2 medium-sized stalks
  celery
1 medium-sized carrot,
  scraped
10 large sprigs Italian
  parsley, leaves only
1 small clove garlic, peeled
5 large basil leaves, fresh
  or preserved in salt
2 pounds ripe, fresh
  tomatoes; or 2 pounds
  canned tomatoes,
  preferably imported
  Italian, drained
4 ounces *pancetta* or
  prosciutto, in 1 piece
¼ cup olive oil
Salt and freshly ground
  black pepper

FOR THE PASTA:
½ cup unseasoned bread
  crumbs, preferably
  homemade, uniformly
  finely ground
3½ cups unbleached all-
  purpose flour
½ cup lukewarm water
Pinch of salt

Pisarei e faso is not a soup but is the combination of a special pasta made with bread crumbs and a sauce containing beans. The beans are first simmered with olive oil and **pancetta** *and are then combined with the tomato sauce, which is made with aromatic vegetables and* **pancetta**. *The pasta combines finely ground bread crumbs with the flour and some water, no eggs. This ancient preparation survives in the locale of Monferrato and interestingly in Piacenza, in the extreme north of Emilia-Romagna. It is curious that the dish survives in two places that are not very close together and apparently nowhere else.*

Soak the beans overnight in a bowl of cold water. The next morning, drain the beans, rinse them under cold running water, and put them in a saucepan with the cold water, oil, *pancetta* or *prosciutto*, and coarse salt. Cover the pan and place over medium heat. Simmer until the beans are cooked but still firm, for 1 to 2 hours, depending on their dryness. Leave beans in the pan, covered, until needed.

Meanwhile, prepare the sauce. Coarsely chop the onion, celery, carrot, parsley, garlic, and basil together on a board. If using fresh tomatoes, cut them into pieces. Pass fresh or canned tomatoes through a food mill, using the disc with the smallest holes, into a crockery or glass bowl. Cut the *pancetta* or *prosciutto* into less than ½-inch cubes. Place a medium-sized saucepan with the oil over medium heat, and when the oil is warm, add the chopped ingredients, tomatoes, and *pancetta* or *prosciutto*. Cover and simmer for about 2 hours, stirring every so often with a wooden spoon. When the sauce is almost ready, taste for salt and pepper. Let sauce stand, covered, until needed.

Prepare the *pisarei*. Soak the bread crumbs in a small bowl of lukewarm water for 15 minutes. Use a very fine strainer to drain the bread crumbs very well, and discard the water. Following the directions on page 14, prepare the pasta with the flour, lukewarm water, salt, and bread crumbs, placing the bread crumbs in the well with the water and salt. Knead the dough until it is very elastic. Cut into several pieces and use your hands to stretch each piece into a long cord less than ½ inch thick. Cut the cord into pieces of less than ½ inch, then use your thumb or a small knife to curl them up into tiny shells (see drawings). Let the *pisarei* stand on a lightly floured towel until needed.

Bring a large quantity of cold water to a boil, add coarse salt to

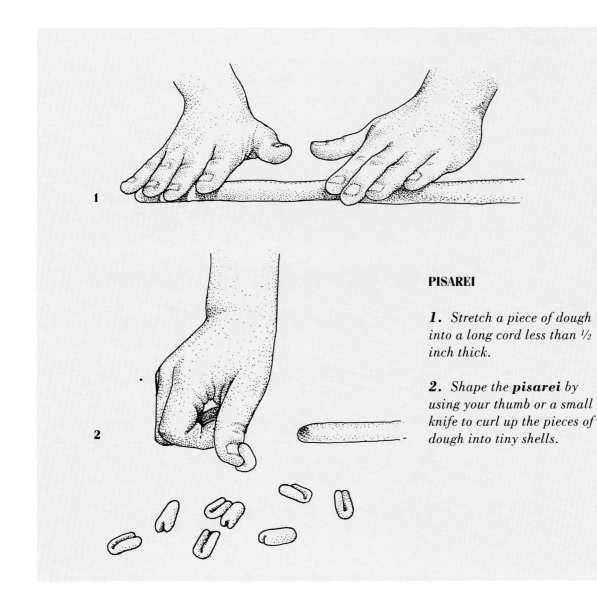

PISAREI

1. Stretch a piece of dough into a long cord less than ½ inch thick.

*2. Shape the **pisarei** by using your thumb or a small knife to curl up the pieces of dough into tiny shells.*

taste, then add the pasta. Stir with a wooden spoon and cook for 1 to 3 minutes, depending on dryness. Meanwhile, drain the beans, discarding the *pancetta* or *prosciutto*, and transfer along with the hot sauce to a large saucepan. Drain the *pisarei* and add to the saucepan. Place the saucepan over medium heat for 1 minute, mixing well to allow pasta to absorb some sauce. If using grated Parmigiano, sprinkle a tablespoon of cheese over each portion, then serve.

NOTE:
Pisarei are somewhere between pasta and *gnocchi*, and are therefore not as tender as pasta.

TO COOK THE PASTA:
Coarse-grained salt

TO SERVE:
8 tablespoons freshly grated Parmigiano cheese (optional)

FROM TRENTINO-ALTO/ADIGE

SERVES 6 TO 8

FOR THE STUFFING:
**2½ pounds fresh spinach,
 large stems removed
Coarse-grained salt
Salt and freshly ground
 black pepper
1 tablespoon caraway seeds**

FOR THE PASTA:
**3 cups rye flour
2 extra-large eggs
2 tablespoons (1 ounce)
 sweet butter, at room
 temperature
¼ cup cold milk
Salt**

TO COOK THE PASTA:
**6 quarts chicken or beef
 broth, preferably
 homemade**

FOR THE SAUCE:
**16 tablespoons (8 ounces)
 sweet butter
6 tablespoons unseasoned
 bread crumbs,
 preferably homemade
Salt and freshly ground
 black pepper**

TURTELN ALTO ADIGE
RYE FLOUR *TORTELLI*

Turteln uses a pasta made with rye flour—which contrary to what many think is even lighter than wheat flour—combined with eggs and butter. The most popular stuffing is made of spinach flavored with ground caraway seeds. It is most important that the whole seeds be pulverized with a mortar and pestle, a tiring job because they are quite hard. Since part of the powdered caraway should be spread over one side of the layer of pasta, it would be quite unsuccessful to attempt this with whole seeds. And the flavor of the ground caraway is different, softer, and more aromatic.

I have chosen the version in which the turteln are boiled in broth and served with bread crumbs browned in butter. In the fried version they are cooked in lard, which makes them a bit heavier though delicious. They are served completely without any dressing, not even the lemon juice commonly used with fried dishes. The boiled version is also known as Krapfen, a name once associated with Bomboloni pastries in other parts of Italy. Alto Adige is a bilingual area, using German as well as Italian.

*Other classic stuffings are sauerkraut sautéed in butter with onions (sauerkraut is preferred to plain cabbage), ricotta flavored with chives (**erba cipollina**), or ricotta with sautéed onions, marjoram, and parsley. Marjoram would not be used in a stuffing that employs caraway seeds, but is typical here.*

Prepare the stuffing. Soak the spinach in a bowl of cold water for 30 minutes. Bring a large pot of cold water to a boil, add coarse salt to taste, then drain the spinach, add it to the pot, and cook for 10 minutes. Drain and cool spinach under cold running water, squeeze it very well, and finely chop on a board. Place the spinach in a crockery or glass bowl, season with salt and pepper, mix well, and refrigerate, covered, until needed. Finely grind the caraway seeds in a marble mortar; this will take a little time.

Prepare the pasta with the ingredients and quantities listed, following the directions on page 14, placing the butter in the well of the flour together with the other ingredients. Stretch the sheet of pasta to less than 1/16 inch thick, on a pasta machine take to the last setting. Cut the sheet into strips 12 inches long and about 6 inches wide.

Sprinkle half the strips with the powdered caraway. Place tablespoons of spinach 6 inches apart down the center of a pasta strip. Cover the strip with another strip, without caraway. Press down between mounds of filling. Use a pastry wheel with scalloped edges to cut into 3-inch *tortelli* squares. Press the edges together. Continue to make until pasta and filling are used up. Rest the *tortelli* on cotton dish towels until needed.

Bring the broth to a boil in a large pot over medium heat. Meanwhile, warm a large serving platter. Place the butter in a small saucepan over low heat. When the butter is melted, add the bread crumbs and sauté until golden, about 1 minute. Season with salt and abundant black pepper. When the broth reaches a boil, add the *tortelli* and cook for 1 to 3 minutes, depending on dryness. With a strainer-skimmer, transfer the cooked *tortelli* to the warmed platter and spoon some of the melted butter and bread crumbs over. Continue to alternate layers of *tortelli* with butter and bread crumbs, making the top layer of butter and bread crumbs; top with some black pepper and serve immediately.

VARIATIONS
Here are some other stuffings for *turteln*.

1 medium-sized white onion, peeled and coarsely chopped
4 tablespoons (2 ounces) sweet butter
12 ounces sauerkraut
Salt and freshly ground black pepper
1 tablespoon dried whole caraway seeds

Sauté the onion in the butter. Coarsely chop the sauerkraut and add it to the sautéed onion. Season with salt, pepper, and caraway seeds.

1 ½ pounds whole milk ricotta
20 chive leaves, coarsely chopped
Salt and freshly ground black pepper
1 tablespoon dried whole caraway seeds

Drain the ricotta, mix it with the chives and season with salt, pepper, and caraway seeds.

1 medium-sized white onion, peeled and coarsely chopped
4 tablespoons (2 ounces) sweet butter
15 ounces whole milk ricotta, drained
15 sprigs Italian parsley, leaves only, coarsely chopped
Salt and freshly ground black pepper
1 tablespoon marjoram

Sauté the onion in butter, let cool, and then mix with the ricotta and parsley. Season with salt, pepper, and marjoram.

LOMBARDY

The two main pastas that employ buckwheat flour survive in Lombardy. Buckwheat is grown in the highlands and other areas such as the hilly and mountainous parts of Friuli where buckwheat once was used much more than now, and that usage even spilled over into neighboring Veneto. The special treatment of buckwheat flour, its liquid absorption, lack of gluten, and so forth, are discussed later on. We begin with *sciatt*, from the mountainous Valtellina region of northern Lombardy. *Sciatt* sometimes appears as a pasta, but is really most often found as batter enveloping bits of cheese and fried. In this form, it is really used as an appetizer rather than as a *primo piatto*.

Two versions of the batter follow. In one a cup of cold water is added to the flours, along with an optional egg. In the other, sometimes called *chiscioi*, beer is the liquid, producing a crisp and luscious result. The beer batter is best when allowed to rest overnight before frying. Both of these employ a little baking soda and grappa (or *aquavit* or vodka as a substitute).

In the pasta version, additional flour is added to the water and egg to make the consistency of a dough rather than a batter—no more than 2 tablespoons of white flour should be added to all the buckwheat and requires truly expert handling to work it. Perhaps for this reason the dough version has all but disappeared in favor of the batter. It is much easier to work this dough if additional white flour is added for its gluten, and this compromise has been adopted in recent years, using ⅓ white flour to ⅔ buckwheat. This is really no longer the original dish.

The layer of dough is used to make *ravioli* with any of the stuffings, which are then fried, lard being the really authentic shortening. The cheese called for may be either a type of local fresh *formaggio di casera* or a *bitto*, which may be aged. Since these local cheeses are difficult to obtain, a good melting cheese from a nearby area may be substituted, fontina being perhaps the closest and easiest to find.

Sciatt is often accompanied by a type of horseradish called *ramolaz neri*, which is grated and combined with olive oil to make a sauce or is eaten whole. Any grated horseradish may be substituted to produce a very similar result.

The dialect word *sciatt* means "frog," referring to the shape produced by the batter version, which is therefore probably the original method. There is also a dough form of *chiscioi*, made with half white flour and half buckwheat, cut into pieces and then shaped as discs. The discs are then generally boiled together with potatoes and salt and served with fresh cheese and grated Parmigiano. This is really a bridge between the pasta version of *sciatt* and Valtellina's other and more famous buckwheat pasta, *pizzoccheri*.

The famous philologist Devoto traces the word from *pinzochero*, meaning "bigot," but possibly implying "provincial" or "rustic." Again, the original dish used very little white flour with the buckwheat, but in modern times, with the reduction of skill and patience in making pasta, the proportion has increased to one third. Because buckwheat is not a real cereal like wheat, its flour lacks the gluten to easily hold together the dough, and so it takes very great skill to make a sheet of pasta with it. The sheet will still emerge thicker than normal, from $\frac{1}{16}$ to under $\frac{1}{8}$ of an inch, but anything thicker than that would make it more like cookie thickness than pasta.

Buckwheat flour takes a little less liquid than ordinary flour. A cup of white flour absorbs an egg plus a little liquid, roughly $\frac{1}{3}$ cup of liquid in all. A little more normal flour will be absorbed by water than egg, and still more buckwheat flour by the same amount. For the cup and a half of the mixed flours I use, a little over half a cup of liquid should do, in this case 1 egg plus 5 tablespoons ($\frac{1}{4}$ cup plus 1 tablespoon) of milk. It would be good to keep these general measurements in mind when making pasta with eggs and pasta with water or other liquid.

This most classic version includes several vegetables, cooked one after the other in the same water, which is finally used to cook the pasta. I recommend Asiago cheese as a substitute for the bitto here, because there is general agreement in the sources that a leaner cheese should be used, leaving out fontina.

The *cappellacci* from Cremona feature the cooked unripe marinated fruit called *mostarda*, mixed together with the squash in the filling. No Amaretti would be used in this version, and the spiciness of the black pepper contrasts with the sweetness of the fruit, as preferred in these survivors of the Renaissance. Here, as in other such stuffings, it is not pumpkin that is used but squash, developed by the Italians from the New World originals of butternut and acorn.

The *casonsei* of Brescia differ from those of Bergamo in that they are stuffed a bit differently and aren't flavored with sage, but they retain the horseshoe shape generally. See the discussion about the ones from Bergamo, which also explains the probable origin of the name from *cascio*, meaning cheese, with which they are most often dressed. I retain the *mollica* in the stuffing rather than bread crumbs, as it is the older version as well as appropriate since the dish is not particularly light.

Very special are the stuffed tiny squares, or *quadrucci*, served in broth. The stuffing of sweetbreads, ham, eggs, and cheese, held together by *mollica*, adds a rich touch to the broth. Dumplings in broth or dumplings covered with pasta in broth were once the most common type of first course, before pasta with sauce became so popular in the mid-nineteenth century.

Venetian *bigoli* spread to nearby Lombardy. The most common Venetian sauce, with salted sardines or anchovies, was transformed in Lombardy into one of fresh sardines. It is for this reason that the Sicilians sometimes add to their *Pasta alle sarde* the phrase *alla milanese*, that is, in the style of Milan.

SCIATT

BUCKWHEAT "PASTA"

Put the two flours in a crockery or glass bowl and with a wooden spoon mix them together very well. Make a well, and if using the egg, put it in and start incorporating some of the flour. Then add the water and salt and keep mixing until a homogeneous batter is formed. If making the second version, use the beer instead of the egg and water. Add the grappa. Mix well and let the batter rest, covered, in a cool place, the first batter for 2 hours, the beer batter overnight. When the batter is ready, cut the cheese into ½-inch cubes.

Heat the oil in a deep-fat fryer over medium heat. When the oil is hot (400 degrees), add the baking soda to the batter, mix well, put in the cheese cubes and mix again. Take about 1½ tablespoons of the batter with one cheese cube in a small ladle and pour it into the hot oil. The batter should be surrounding and covering the cube of cheese and should puff up when it hits the hot oil. When the outside is uniformly crusty, transfer it with a strainer-skimmer to a serving dish that is lined with paper towels to absorb any excess fat. When all the *sciatt* are on the dish, remove the paper towels and serve hot, accompanied by the horseradish sauce made of grated horseradish *(ramolaz neri)* mixed with olive oil.

**F R O M
V A L T E L L I N A
(L O M B A R D Y)**

SERVES 6 TO 8

FOR THE BATTER:
First version
1 cup buckwheat flour
2 tablespoons unbleached all-purpose flour
1 extra-large egg
1 cup cold water (and a little more if not using an egg)
Pinch of salt
1 tablespoon grappa (or *aquavit* or vodka)
6 ounces bitto or fontina cheese
1 quart vegetable oil
¼ teaspoon baking soda

FOR THE BATTER:
Second version *(chiscioi)*
1 cup buckwheat flour
4 tablespoons unbleached all-purpose flour
1½ cups beer
Pinch of salt
1 tablespoon grappa (or *aquavit* or vodka)
6 ounces bitto or fontina cheese
1 quart vegetable oil
¼ teaspoon baking soda

FROM LOMBARDY

SERVES 6 TO 8

PIZZOCCHERI DELLA VALTELLINA

BUCKWHEAT PASTA FROM VALTELLINA

FOR THE VEGETABLES:
1 pound savoy cabbage,
**   cleaned and large stems**
**   removed**
12 ounces string beans,
**   cleaned**
2 medium-sized potatoes
**   (not new potatoes)**
Coarse-grained salt

FOR THE PASTA:
1 cup buckwheat flour
½ cup unbleached all-
**   purpose flour**
1 extra-large egg
5 tablespoons cold milk
Pinch of salt
                or
½ pound dried
**   *pizzoccheri*, preferably**
**   imported Italian**

TO COOK THE PASTA:
Coarse-grained salt

FOR THE SAUCE:
12 tablespoons (6 ounces)
**   sweet butter**
15 large sage leaves, fresh
**   or preserved in salt**
4 large cloves garlic,
**   peeled and left whole**
Salt and freshly ground
**   black pepper**
¾ cup grated aged bitto
**   cheese from Valtellina or**
**   aged Asiago cheese**

Cut the cabbage into 1-inch strips and put in a bowl of cold water. Place the string beans in a second bowl of cold water. Cut the potatoes into 1-inch cubes and put them in a third bowl with cold water. Bring a large stockpot of cold water to a boil, add coarse salt to taste, then add the potatoes and cook for about 10 minutes; the potatoes should remain very firm, since they are to be cooked again. Use a strainer-skimmer to transfer the potatoes to a crockery bowl and cover with a wet towel. Drain the string beans and cook in the potato water for about 12 minutes or less, depending on their size, and also leaving them still very firm. Place the beans over the potatoes in the same bowl. Cook the cabbage in the same water for about 6 minutes, making sure that it does not become soft. With a strainer-skimmer, spoon the cabbage over the beans and cover again with the towel, letting vegetables stand until needed. Reserve the cooking water.

Prepare the pasta. Make the dough using the ingredients and quantities listed, mixing the flours together and placing the egg, salt, and milk in the well of the flour at the same time. (See page 14 for directions.) Knead the dough much longer than a usual wheat dough, about 15 minutes. By hand or with a pasta machine, stretch the dough to a thickness of less than ⅛ inch (with a hand machine, to the next to last setting). Cut the sheet of pasta into pieces about 2½ x ¾ inches, and let rest on cotton dish towels or paper towels for at least 1 hour before cooking. Buckwheat flour lacks the gluten of wheat flour, so it requires a longer kneading and resting time.

Bring a large pot of cold water to a boil. Warm a large serving dish by placing it over the water as it boils. Meanwhile, melt the butter in a small, heavy saucepan over low heat. When the butter melts, put in the sage leaves and garlic, and saute for 1 minute, adding salt and abundant pepper.

When the water reaches a boil, add coarse salt to taste, then add the cooked vegetables. When the water returns to a boil, put in the pasta and cook until al dente, 3 to 5 minutes for fresh pasta, according to dryness, or 9 to 12 minutes for dried pasta depending on brand.

Place some of the cheese and some of the melted butter in the warmed dish. Drain the pasta and vegetables, and arrange in a layer over the sauce. Repeat this procedure with butter-cheese layers and the vegetable-pasta layers, adding more black pepper. Continue until all ingredients are used up. Gently mix the pasta and vegetables with the butter and the by-now melted cheese, and serve immediately with more freshly ground black pepper.

VARIATIONS FOR PASTA

1. The pasta can be prepared with equal amounts of buckwheat flour and unbleached all-purpose flour, with the egg omitted and the amount of cold or lukewarm milk increased by several tablespoons.

2. The pasta can be prepared with equal amounts of buckwheat flour and unbleached all-purpose flour, cold or lukewarm water instead of milk, with or without egg.

VARIATIONS FOR COOKING

1. Cabbage and potatoes are present in all versions, but the string beans can be omitted and other vegetables added, such as sliced carrots and/or spinach and/or Swiss chard, cut into strips.

2. Cook the vegetables beginning with the ones requiring the longest cooking time and adding the others, timing it so that they all finish together. Meanwhile, cook the pasta so it is ready at the same time.

3. Fresh bitto cheese from the Valtellina can be used, but it should be thinly sliced instead of grated, placed over the different layers of pasta and vegetables, and the whole dish baked for a few minutes at the end.

4. Vegetables can be boiled at first, then sautéed a little with butter. Once the pasta is cooked, the pasta and vegetables should be mixed together and dressed with a sauce prepared with onions, garlic, or both, sautéed in butter and sprinkled with grated cheese.

Pizzoccheri: The famous buckwheat pasta from hilly Valtellina in northern Lombardy combines especially well with a variety of vegetables.

FROM LOMBARDY

SERVES 6 TO 8

MARUBINI

STUFFED PASTA FROM CREMONA

FOR THE STUFFING:
**1 cup freshly grated
Parmigiano cheese
Scant ½ cup unseasoned
bread crumbs,
preferably homemade
1 extra-large egg
2 extra-large egg yolks
4 tablespoons (2 ounces)
sweet butter, at room
temperature
15 large sprigs Italian
parsley, leaves only
Salt and freshly ground
black pepper
Freshly grated nutmeg**

FOR THE PASTA:
**3 cups unbleached all-
purpose flour
4 extra-large eggs
Pinch of salt**

TO COOK THE PASTA:
Coarse-grained salt

TO SERVE:
**8 tablespoons (4 ounces)
sweet butter
½ cup freshly grated
Parmigiano cheese**

*The really old traditional version of **marubini**, Cremona's signature stuffed pasta, was made **di magro**, without meat. The basis was **mollica**, the crumb of the bread, with beef marrow. Eggs, grated Parmigiano, and herbs and spices enriched the flavor. In modern times, there has been a tendency to lighten the dish by substituting bread crumbs for the **mollica**.*

There also exists a less classic meat version, much more recent, made with three kinds of braised meat and calves brains, which is usually eaten without broth, in a dressing of butter and Parmigiano.

*The older **di magro** may be eaten either with this dressing, as we have it, or in a wonderful unique broth used primarily in the Cremona area and called **tre brodi**, meaning "three broths." It is made from three different meats—veal, chicken, and beef or pork.*

Prepare the stuffing. Place the Parmigiano, bread crumbs, egg and egg yolks, and butter in a medium-sized crockery or glass bowl; mix well with a wooden spoon. Coarsely chop the parsley, add it to the bowl, and season to taste with salt, pepper, and nutmeg. Mix again until all the ingredients are well amalgamated. Cover bowl with aluminum foil and refrigerate until needed.

Prepare the pasta with the ingredients and quantities listed, following directions on page 14. Stretch the sheet of pasta to the finest setting on the pasta machine. Prepare the *marubini* as you would *tortelli* (page 113), using a round, scalloped cutter not wider than 2 inches and placing a heaping teaspoon of the stuffing in each pasta circle. Let the *marubini* rest on cotton dish towels until needed.

Bring a large pot of cold water to a boil, add coarse salt to taste, then add the pasta and cook for 1 to 3 minutes depending on dryness. Meanwhile, melt the butter in a double boiler. Use a strainer-skimmer to transfer the *marubini* to a warmed platter. Pour some of the melted butter over the layer of *marubini*, then sprinkle on some cheese. Continue to make layers of *marubini* until all are on the platter. Top the last layer of pasta with the remaining butter and cheese. Serve immediately.

**The attractive round *marubini*
from Cremona, home of the
famous violin makers Stradivarius
and Guarnieri.**

**FROM CREMONA
(LOMBARDY)**

SERVES 4 TO 6

FOR THE STUFFING:
**1 medium-sized butternut
    squash
⅓ cup unseasoned bread
    crumbs, preferably
    homemade
1 extra-large egg yolk
Salt and freshly ground
    black pepper
6 ounces *mostarda di
    Cremona* (see Note),
    drained and finely
    chopped**

FOR THE PASTA:
**2 cups unbleached all-
    purpose flour
3 extra-large eggs
Pinch of salt**

TO COOK THE PASTA:
Coarse-grained salt

TO SERVE:
**8 tablespoons (4 ounces)
    sweet butter
¾ cups freshly grated
    Parmigiano cheese**

CAPPELLACCI CON LA MOSTARDA
CAPPELLACCI WITH *MOSTARDA* STUFFING

Preheat the oven to 375 degrees. Prepare the stuffing. Bake the squash on a jelly-roll pan for 1 hour. Remove from the oven and cool for 30 minutes. Remove the peel, seeds, and filaments from the squash, then pass the pulp through a food mill, using the disc with medium-sized holes, into a crockery or glass bowl. Measure out 1 cup of the puréed pulp for the stuffing, put it in a crockery or glass bowl, and add the bread crumbs, and egg yolk. Season to taste with salt and pepper, add the *mostarda di Cremona*, and mix well with a wooden spoon. Cover and place in the refrigerator until needed.

Prepare the pasta with the ingredients and quantities listed, following the instructions on page 14. Stretch the sheet of pasta to less than 1/16 inch thick, on the pasta machine take to last notch. Make *cappellacci* shaped like *ravioli*, 3 inches square, using 1 heaping teaspoon of the stuffing for each. Let them rest on cotton dish towels or paper towels for at least 15 minutes, turning them over at least once.

Bring a large pot of cold water to a boil, add coarse salt to taste, then add the *cappellacci* and cook for 1 to 3 minutes depending on dryness. Meanwhile, melt the butter in a double boiler and warm a large serving platter. Use a strainer-skimmer to transfer the pasta to the warmed platter. Make a layer of *cappellacci*, pour some of the melted butter over, and sprinkle on some of the cheese. Make another layer of the remaining pasta, butter, and cheese.

NOTE:
Mostarda di Cremona is cooked unripe fruit that has been marinated in a syrup flavored with yellow mustard seeds. It is available commercially in jars, sometimes labeled "mustard fruits." It may also be made at home following the recipe in *Classic Techniques of Italian Cooking*.

CASONSEI DI BRESCIA

STUFFED PASTA FROM BRESCIA

Prepare the stuffing. Remove the skins from the sausages and put the meat or the ground pork into a crockery or glass bowl. Soak the bread in the milk for 10 minutes, then squeeze it dry and add to bowl with the meat. Put in the Parmigiano, season to taste with salt and pepper, and mix well, combining the meat thoroughly with the other ingredients. Cover the bowl and refrigerate until needed.

Prepare the pasta with the ingredients and quantities listed following the directions on page 14. Stretch the sheet of pasta to less than 1/16 inch thick, on the pasta machine take to the last notch. Prepare *casonsei* (page 219) and let rest on cotton dish towels until needed.

Bring a large pot of cold water to a boil. Meanwhile, place the butter on a serving dish and melt it by placing the dish over the pot as a lid. When the water reaches a boil, remove the dish, add coarse salt to taste, then add the *casonsei* and cook for 1 to 3 minutes depending on dryness. Use a strainer-skimmer to transfer the *casonsei* to the serving dish and spoon some of the butter over each layer, also sprinkling each with some cheese. Serve hot.

FOR THE STUFFING:
5 Italian sweet sausages, without fennel seeds, or 1¼ pounds ground pork
4 slices white bread, crusts removed
1 cup cold milk
½ cup freshly grated Parmigiano cheese
Salt and freshly ground black pepper

FOR THE PASTA:
4 cups unbleached all-purpose flour
5 extra-large eggs
Pinch of salt

TO COOK THE PASTA:
Coarse-grained salt

TO SERVE:
12 tablespoons (6 ounces) sweet butter
1 cup freshly grated Parmigiano cheese

FROM LOMBARDY

SERVES 6 TO 8

FOR THE STUFFING:
2 slices white bread, crusts
    removed
1 cup cold milk
4 ounces veal sweetbreads
Coarse-grained salt
2 ounces boiled ham
½ cup freshly grated
    Parmigiano cheese
1 to 2 extra-large eggs
2 extra-large egg yolks
Salt and freshly ground
    black pepper
Large pinch of freshly
    grated nutmeg

FOR THE PASTA:
3 cups unbleached all-
    purpose flour
4 extra-large eggs
Pinch of salt

PLUS:
2 quarts chicken or beef
    broth, preferably
    homemade

TO SERVE:
Freshly grated Parmigiano
    cheese

Quadrucci Ripieni

STUFFED TINY PASTA SQUARES

Prepare the stuffing. Soak the bread in the milk for 30 minutes. Place a medium-sized saucepan with cold water over medium heat, and when the water reaches a boil, add coarse salt, then add the sweetbreads and simmer for 5 minutes. Drain sweetbreads and cool under cold running water. Remove and discard all the membrane around the sweetbreads. Finely chop the sweetbreads together with the boiled ham on a board and place in a crockery or glass bowl. Add the cheese. Squeeze the milk out of the bread and add to the bowl. Put in 1 egg and the egg yolks; season to taste with salt, pepper, and nutmeg; and mix everything with a wooden spoon. If the stuffing is too dense, add an additional egg. Cover the bowl and refrigerate until needed.

Prepare the pasta with the ingredients and quantities listed, following the directions on page 14. Stretch the sheet of pasta to less than 1/16 inch thick, on the pasta machine take to the finest setting. Use a metal spatula to evenly spread out a very thin layer of stuffing over half the pasta layer, like one page of an open book. Cut in half and fit the other half layer over the stuffing. Gently press all over to attach the 2 layers together. With a scalloped pastry wheel, cut the stuffed pasta into 1-inch squares, then transfer these *quadrucci* onto floured cotton dish towels and let them rest until needed.

Place the broth over medium heat, and when it reaches a boil, add the *quadrucci* and cook for 1 to 3 minutes depending on dryness. Serve with a sprinkling of Parmigiano.

BIGOLI CON SARDELLE

PASTA WITH FRESH SARDINES

FROM LOMBARDY

SERVES 4 TO 6

Clean the sardines following the instructions on page 118; you should have about ½ pound. Place the sardines in a bowl of cold water with ½ tablespoon coarse salt; let stand until needed.

Bring a large pot of cold water to a boil. Meanwhile, place a medium-sized saucepan with the oil over medium heat, and when the oil is warm, add the garlic and sauté until golden brown all over, about 5 minutes. Discard the garlic and remove the pan from heat.

Drain and rinse the sardines under cold running water. Add the sardines to the pan with the oil. Using a fork, mash the sardines into the oil as they cook. Season with salt and pepper, and place the pan over low heat for 2 minutes.

When the water reaches a boil, add coarse salt to taste, then add the pasta and cook until al dente, for 9 to 12 minutes depending on the brand. Coarsely chop the parsley on a board. Drain the pasta and transfer to a large, warmed serving platter; pour the sauce over, sprinkle on the parsley, toss very well, and serve immediately.

1 pound fresh sardines
Coarse-grained salt
1 pound dried white *bigoli*
 or *spaghetti*, preferably
 imported Italian
¾ cup olive oil
1 large clove garlic, peeled
 but left whole
Salt and freshly ground
 black pepper

TO SERVE:
15 large sprigs Italian
 parsley, leaves only

TO COOK THE PASTA:
Coarse-grained salt

VARIATIONS

1. Mash 4 ounces, drained, of tuna packed in olive oil into the oil with the sardines.

2. Omit the parsley from either of the above.

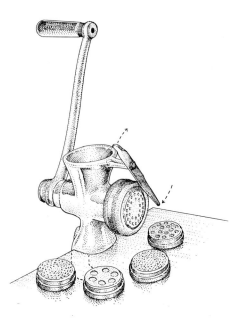

An early hand extrusion machine, with different discs to prepare different shapes of pasta. This gentle hand machine still allowed for hand kneading, still using the true dough for fresh pasta. Modern electrical machines require a totally different kind of dough and we must recognize that as a result such pasta is different from traditional fresh pasta.

VENETO

Bigoli is the sole traditional pasta of the Veneto. Other pastas used there are borrowed from other regions. Until recently, every Venetian home had a hand *torchio* machine called *bigolo* permanently attached to the kitchen table (see drawing of my old *bigolo* and photo), and the making of good *bigoli* was a test of domestic art. This pasta is made longer than other pasta nowadays, but we must remember that until dried pastas began being sold primarily in boxes, *spaghetti* and other forms were made longer than they usually are now; *bigoli* have simply retained the older tradition. Passed through a *bigolo*, the pasta has a very thin hole through its length, like southern Italian *bucatini* or *perciatelli*. But commercially dried *bigoli* are made like *spaghetti* now, too, and this form has even been adopted by some for the fresh pasta if the *bigolo* is not available.

Originally, dark *bigoli* probably were made using buckwheat flour, since that grain was once plentiful in the Tre Veneti. (Today, the region is more commonly known as Friuli-Venezia Giulia.) But earlier in this century the Italian government began to require that certified commercial pasta be made only from durum wheat flour, and soon even in the home whole-wheat flour came to replace the buckwheat.

Bigoli were made with eggs, butter, and milk added to the flour. When the Venetians said *bigoli* "in sauce," they referred to their most popular, classic dressing, using anchovies or sardines preserved in salt with olive oil and onion. Venice had to keep a store of preserved foods on hand in the event its islands were cut off from the mainland

An antique *Bigolo*, the original machine to prepare *bigoli*, a fixture of every Venetian kitchen during Venice's days of glory.

during a siege. Naturally, most of its fresh food came from the mainland territories it ruled, extending almost from Milan all the way down to Dalmatia on what is now the Yugoslav coast. Sardines preserved in salt are no longer as available as anchovies. As mentioned elsewhere, when the mainland neighboring Milanese adapted the dish, they employed fresh sardines.

As mentioned, the recipe for *Bigoli scuri in salsa* employs the whole wheat flour now typically used, but also included is the old version, *Bigoli scuri con grano saraceno*, using buckwheat flour. Since this flour usually comes from Friuli, this version is still made there, but not often.

Another classic version is *Bigoli all' anitra* (*bigoli* cooked in duck broth) and dressed with the liver and giblets sautéed with rosemary and sage in olive oil. The broth may be defatted and saved if you wish, but since the Venetians preferred the flavor imparted by the fat, they usually discarded the broth after the cooking. Naturally, the duck itself may be used at another time.

As traditionally Venetian as it is possible to be is *Bigoli con sugo di oca conservato*, the dish that combines *bigoli* with another standby, the *confit* of preserved goose, which was once so traditional in the cucina of the "queen of the Adriatic." Venice once so dominated that region that it is far more likely that the confit went from Venice to Toulouse than the other way around. The Venetians, however, came to debone the meat before preserving it.

A unique dish, *Tagliatelle* with Sauce of Preserved Goose, uses the old Venetian boneless *confit* of goose (goose with the goose fat in which it has been preserved) to dress the pasta. The flavor of the goose, seasoned from three to six months, is unlike anything else and should be tried at least once in everyone's life—though when tried, once is not enough (see Recipe Appendix).

The large red crab of the Adriatic is one of the most delicious types of crab and is used in many dishes, among them a combination with *bigoli*, *Bigoli con granzeola*. Crab meat is so popular now that the dish may be made even with *spaghetti* if *bigoli* are unavailable.

The two versions of *casonsei* from Bergamo, like the one from Brescia, have meat stuffings. There is a version with vegetable stuffing from Cortina d'ampezzo.

The first Bergamesque version of *casonsei* uses beef in the stuffing, cold water instead of the extra egg in the pasta, and simply butter, Parmigiano, and sage in the dressing. The second version, like the Brescia version, is stuffed with pork, usually sausage, has the egg-rich pasta like the Brescia version, but adds abundant *pancetta* to the butter, sage, and cheese of the dressing. In both versions, I have opted for the lighter, more modern bread crumbs instead of *mollica*.

Pierrot, who is the Bergamo mask of the commedia dell'arte, could not have retained his sad face had he eaten one of these versions. And the moonlight-crazed Pierrot of Schoenberg's *Pierrot Lunaire* would certainly have been calmed by them.

***Bigoli con granzeola*: The luscious crabs of the Adriatic combine beautifully with this traditional Venetian pasta.**

BIGOLI SCURI IN SALSA
WHOLE-WHEAT *BIGOLI*, VENETIAN STYLE

FOR THE PASTA:
3 cups whole-wheat flour
3 extra-large eggs
2 tablespoons (1 ounce) sweet butter, at room temperature
2 tablespoons cold milk
Pinch of salt
or
1½ pounds dried *bigoli scuri*, preferably imported Italian

FOR THE SAUCE:
1 large white or red onion, peeled
Scant cup olive oil
Freshly ground black pepper
8 anchovies preserved in salt; or 16 anchovy fillets packed in olive oil (not in vegetable oil or brine), drained

TO COOK THE PASTA:
Coarse-grained salt

Bigoli Scuri in salsa, the most traditional sauce for *bigoli,* surrounded by a Venetian carnival mask and the world famous glass from Murano, one of Venice's islands. The equally famous Venetian lace of Burano sits under the plate.

Prepare the pasta with the ingredients and quantities listed, following the directions on page 14, placing the butter in the well of flour with the other ingredients. Stretch sheet to about ⅛ inch thick, on the pasta machine take to several notches before last. Prepare *spaghetti* (see page 57), but cut them about 15 or 16 inches long; this length is characteristic of the pasta. Let rest on cotton towels until needed.

As the *bigoli* are drying prepare the sauce. Cut the onion into paper-thin slices. Place a very small saucepan with the oil over medium heat. When the oil is lukewarm, add the onion slices—the olive oil should be barely covering the onion. Season with pepper and sauté, without raising the heat, for at least 45 minutes, stirring every so often with a wooden spoon. By that time, the onion should be almost dissolved. (The slow sautéing of onions and other vegetables into the perfect *soffritto* is a special Venetian art.) When finished, remove the saucepan from the heat and set aside, covered.

Meanwhile, bring a large pot of cold water to a boil, adding very little or no coarse salt (the anchovies will add their salt to the sauce). Add the pasta and cook fresh pasta for 1 to 3 minutes depending on dryness; if using dried pasta, cook for 9 to 12 minutes depending on the brand. As the pasta cooks, clean the anchovies under cold running water if you are using whole ones, removing bones and excess salt. Add anchovy fillets to the sautéed onion. The onion should still be very hot; use a fork to dissolve the fillets and incorporate them into the other ingredients. Drain the pasta, transfer to a large, warmed serving platter, pour the sauce over, toss very well and serve immediately.

VARIATIONS
1. Sometimes 10 sprigs of Italian parsley, leaves only coarsely chopped, are added to the sauce before pouring it over the pasta.

2. A half cup of white dry wine can be added to the onion when it is half cooked, along with a pinch of ground cinnamon.

3. Onion and anchovies are finely chopped together and sautéed in the oil for the same length of time, with or without wine and with or without parsley.

4. Two cloves of garlic can be substituted for the onion; they should be peeled and coarsely chopped.

5. With any of the above variations or the original recipe, 2 tablespoons of white wine vinegar can be added at the end and allowed to evaporate for 2 minutes.

FROM VENETO
AND FRIULI

SERVES 4 TO 6

FOR THE PASTA:
1½ cups unbleached all-purpose flour
1½ cups buckwheat flour
3 extra-large eggs
2 tablespoons (1 ounce) sweet butter, at room temperature
6 tablespoons cold milk
Pinch of salt

FOR THE SAUCE:
¾ cup olive oil
5 whole anchovies preserved in salt; or 10 anchovy fillets packed in oil (not in vegetable oil or brine), drained
Freshly ground black pepper

TO COOK THE PASTA:
Coarse-grained salt

BIGOLI SCURI CON GRANO SARACENO
BIGOLI WITH BUCKWHEAT FLOUR

Prepare the pasta. Mix the flours, then prepare the pasta with the ingredients and quantities listed, following the instructions on page 14, placing the butter and milk in the well of flour with the other ingredients. Stretch sheet to about ⅛ inch thick, on the pasta machine take to several notches before last. Cut into *spaghetti* (see page 57) and let rest on cotton towels until needed.

Bring a large pot of cold water to a boil, add coarse salt to taste, then add the pasta and cook for 1 to 3 minutes depending on dryness.

If using whole anchovies, clean them under cold running water, removing bones and excess salt. As the pasta cooks, place a small saucepan with the oil over medium heat; when the oil is hot, remove the pan from heat and add the anchovy fillets. Using a fork, mash them into the oil. Season with black pepper.

Drain the pasta, transfer to a large, warmed serving platter, pour the sauce over, toss very well, and serve immediately.

VARIATIONS
1. 20 sprigs Italian parsley, leaves only, coarsely chopped, can be sprinkled over the pasta before serving.

2. 1 large clove of garlic, peeled and left whole, can be sautéed with the oil, then discarded before adding the anchovies. Serve with or without parsley.

BIGOLI ALL'ANITRA

BIGOLI COOKED IN DUCK BROTH

Clean and wash the duck very well, saving the liver and all the giblets for later use, discarding the extra fat from the cavity. Place a large stockpot with the duck, the cold water, and the vegetables over medium heat. When the water reaches a boil, add coarse salt to taste. Simmer, uncovered, until the duck is completely cooked, about 1½ hours.

Prepare the pasta with the ingredients and quantities listed, following the directions on page 14, placing the butter and milk in the well of flour with the other ingredients. Stretch sheet to about ⅛ inch thick; on the pasta machine, take to several notches before the last. Cut into *spaghetti* (see page 57), but make them about 15 or 16 inches long. Let the *bigoli* rest on cotton towels until needed.

When the duck is cooked, transfer it to a chopping board. Remove the meat from the bones; discard the carcass and skin. (Note: The boiled duck meat is very good and may be served as a second course following the pasta, perhaps accompanied with a green sauce, but it is not part of the pasta course. It would be more typical to serve the duck at a different dinner.)

Use a thick strainer to strain the duck broth, but do not remove any of the fat. Place the strained broth back in a stockpot and put the pot over medium heat. Meanwhile, prepare the sauce. Finely chop the reserved liver and giblets with the rosemary and sage all together on a board. Place a medium-sized saucepan with the chopped ingredients and the ¾ cup of olive oil over medium heat, and sauté for 10 minutes. Season with salt and pepper, then add a cup of the duck broth and simmer for 30 minutes more.

When the broth in the stockpot reaches a boil, add the pasta and cook fresh pasta for 1 to 3 minutes depending on dryness; or cook 9 to 12 minutes for dried pasta depending on the brand. Drain the pasta; transfer to a large, warmed serving platter, pour the sauce over, toss very well, and serve immediately. No cheese should be added.

FOR THE BROTH:
1 **Long Island duck (about 5 pounds), with liver and giblets**
4 **quarts cold water**
2 **medium-sized stalks celery, cleaned and cut into large pieces**
1 **large red onion, peeled and cut into large pieces**
2 **medium-sized carrots, scraped and cut into large pieces**
Coarse-grained salt

FOR THE PASTA:
3 **cups unbleached all-purpose flour**
3 **extra-large eggs**
2 **tablespoons (1 ounce) sweet butter, at room temperature**
2 **tablespoons cold milk**
Pinch of salt
or
1½ **pounds dried *bigoli bianchi* or *spaghetti*, preferably imported Italian**

FOR THE SAUCE:
2 **tablespoons fresh rosemary leaves**
15 **large fresh sage leaves**
¾ **cup olive oil**
Salt and freshly ground black pepper

BIGOLI CON SUGO DI OCA CONSERVATO

BIGOLI WITH PRESERVED GOOSE

FOR THE GOOSE *CONFIT* (*OCA IN PIGNATTO*):
1 goose, about 8 pounds
3 large cloves garlic, peeled
2 to 3 sprigs fresh rosemary, or 1 heaping tablespoon rosemary leaves preserved in salt
2 cups olive oil
Salt and freshly ground black pepper
6 or 7 bay leaves

FOR THE PASTA:
3 cups unbleached all-purpose flour
3 extra-large eggs
2 tablespoons (1 ounce) sweet butter, at room temperature
2 tablespoons cold milk
Pinch of salt
or
1½ pounds dried *bigoli* or *spaghetti*, preferably imported Italian

TO COOK THE PASTA:
Coarse-grained salt

FOR THE SAUCE:
6 tablespoons (3 ounces) sweet butter
16 large sage leaves, fresh or preserved in salt
Salt and freshly ground black pepper

For this, you will need to prepare the preserved goose several months before. You will need a large airtight masonry jar or crock.

Prepare the *confit*. Clean and wash the goose very well and dry with paper towels. Do not remove any fat from the goose. Cut the garlic into small pieces. Place the goose in a large, flameproof casserole and add the garlic and rosemary. Pour 1 cup of oil over the goose and sprinkle with salt and pepper to taste. Cover the casserole and put it over low heat. Cook very slowly for about 2½ hours, turning the goose once. Remove the goose from the casserole and place on a chopping board. Let the fat in the casserole cool for about 10 minutes, then put 1 ladleful into a masonry jar. Reserve the rest.

With a knife, remove the skin from the breast of the goose. Detach half the breast from the bone in a single piece. Set it aside on a plate until needed. Repeat the procedure with the other breast and the rest of the goose, until all the meat is removed from the bones and is on the plate. Discard the skin. When the fat in the jar has cooled enough to solidify (about 1 hour), place a layer of meat over it. Then pour over enough fat to completely cover the meat; this layer of fat from the casserole should still be slightly liquified but cool enough not to melt the fat below. After the second layer of fat has solidified, continue making layers of fat and meat until they are all used. However, do not add another layer of meat until the previous layer of fat is solidified. As the fat cools, each layer takes less time to solidify. The top layer should be of fat. Place the bay leaves over the last layer of fat, and then pour over the remaining cup of olive oil. Close the jar tightly and keep it this way, preferably in the refrigerator, for at least 3 months.

When ready to use the preserved goose, prepare the pasta with the ingredients and quantities listed, following the directions on page 14. Stretch sheet to about ⅛ inch thick; on the pasta machine, take to several notches before last. Prepare *spaghetti* (see page 57) but cut them about 15 or 16 inches long for characteristic *bigoli*. Let rest on floured cotton dish towels until ready to cook.

Prepare the sauce. Using tongs, remove half the goose meat, trying not to have a lot of fat clinging to the meat. Coarsely chop the meat on a board. Place the butter in a heavy, medium-sized skillet over low heat, and when the butter is melted, add the chopped meat and the sage leaves. Sauté for 5 minutes, mixing with a wooden spoon; season with salt and pepper.

Bring a large pot of cold water to a boil, add coarse salt to taste, then add the pasta and cook for 1 to 3 minutes depending on dryness for fresh pasta, and for 8 to 12 minutes depending on the brand for dried pasta. Drain the pasta; transfer to a large, warmed serving platter, add the sauce, toss very well, and serve.

Bigoli con Granzeola

SPAGHETTI WITH CRAB MEAT

Prepare the pasta with the ingredients and quantities listed, following the directions on page 14, placing the butter and milk in the well of flour with the other ingredients. Stretch sheet to about ⅛ inch thick; on the pasta machine, take to several notches before the last. Prepare *bigoli* like *spaghetti*, following the instructions on page 57, but cut them about 15 to 16 inches long. Let the *bigoli* rest on cotton towels until needed.

Prepare the crab sauce. Place a large pot with the cold water over medium heat. When the water reaches a boil, add coarse salt to taste, then place the crab meat in a small strainer and submerge the strainer in the boiling water for 4 minutes. Remove the strainer, transfer the crab meat to a bowl, and reserve the boiling water. Add the oil and salt and pepper to taste to the crab meat; set aside until needed.

Add enough additional cold water to the crab-boiling water to cook the pasta. When the water reaches a boil, add more coarse salt to taste, then add the pasta. Cook fresh pasta for 1 to 3 minutes depending on dryness. If dried pasta is used instead, cook it for 9 to 12 minutes depending on the brand. Meanwhile, coarsely chop the parsley and garlic together on a board. Place a small saucepan with the oil over medium heat. When the oil is warm, add the chopped ingredients and sauté for 2 minutes. Season with salt and pepper. When the pasta is ready, drain and transfer it to a large, warmed serving platter. Add the crab meat with its juices and the sautéed parsley with the oil, toss very well, and serve immediately.

FOR THE PASTA;
3 cups unbleached all-purpose flour
3 extra-large eggs
2 tablespoons (1 ounce) sweet butter, at room temperature
2 tablespoons cold milk
Pinch of salt
or
1½ pounds dried *bigoli bianchi* or *spaghetti*, preferably imported Italian

FOR THE CRAB SAUCE:
2 quarts cold water
Coarse-grained salt
¾ pound boiled crab meat
4 tablespoons olive oil
Salt and freshly ground black pepper

TO COOK THE PASTA:
Coarse-grained salt

FOR THE PARSLEY SAUCE:
30 large sprigs Italian parsley, leaves only
4 medium-sized cloves garlic, peeled
8 tablespoons olive oil
Salt and freshly ground black pepper

FROM BERGAMO
IN VENETO

SERVES 8

CASONSEI ALLA BERGAMASCA I
STUFFED PASTA, BERGAMO STYLE, FIRST VERSION

FOR THE STUFFING:
1 pound ground beef
**4 tablespoons (2 ounces)
sweet butter, at room
temperature**
**Salt and freshly ground
black pepper**
**20 large sprigs Italian
parsley, leaves only**
**2 medium-sized cloves
garlic, peeled**
**¼ cup unseasoned bread
crumbs, preferably
homemade**
**¼ cup freshly grated
Parmigiano cheese**

FOR THE PASTA:
**4 cups unbleached all-
purpose flour**
4 extra-large eggs
4 teaspoons cold water
Pinch of salt

FOR THE SAUCE:
**12 tablespoons (6 ounces)
sweet butter**
**20 large sage leaves, fresh
or preserved in salt**
**1 cup freshly grated
Parmigiano cheese**
**Freshly ground black
pepper**

TO COOK THE PASTA:
Coarse-grained salt

Prepare the stuffing. Combine the beef and butter in a crockery or glass bowl, mix very well, and season to taste with salt and pepper. Transfer to a skillet and place over medium heat. Sauté for 5 minutes, mixing constantly with a wooden spoon, then transfer the sautéed meat to a clean crockery or glass bowl and let rest until cool, 30 minutes. Coarsely chop the parsley and finely chop the garlic on a board, then add them to the bowl along with the bread crumbs and Parmigiano. Taste for salt and pepper, and mix all the ingredients well. Cover bowl and refrigerate until needed.

Prepare the pasta with the ingredients and quantities listed, following the directions on page 14. Roll the pasta to a thickness of less than ¹⁄₁₆ inch, on the hand pasta machine take to the finest setting, and roll the dough into sheets.

Sometimes *casonsei* are shaped like round *tortelli*, but the classic shape is obtained by cutting the pasta into 3- x 2-inch rectangles (see drawing). To form, use 1 tablespoon of stuffing for each. Arrange the stuffing lengthwise along the 3-inch side; fold in half, covering the stuffing; and seal the 3 open sides by pressing them firmly together. Finally, twist the stuffed pasta into a horseshoe shape. Let the *casonsei* rest on floured cotton dish towels for 30 minutes before using.

Prepare the sauce. Melt the butter in a double boiler, then add the sage leaves; cover the pan and let rest for 30 minutes before using.

Bring a large stockpot of cold water to a boil. Add coarse salt to taste, then add the *casonsei* and cook for 30 seconds to 2 minutes depending on dryness. Use a strainer-skimmer to transfer them to a warmed platter, arranging the pasta in layers. Pour some of the sage butter and some Parmigiano over each layer. Serve immediately with 2 or 3 twists of black pepper on each serving.

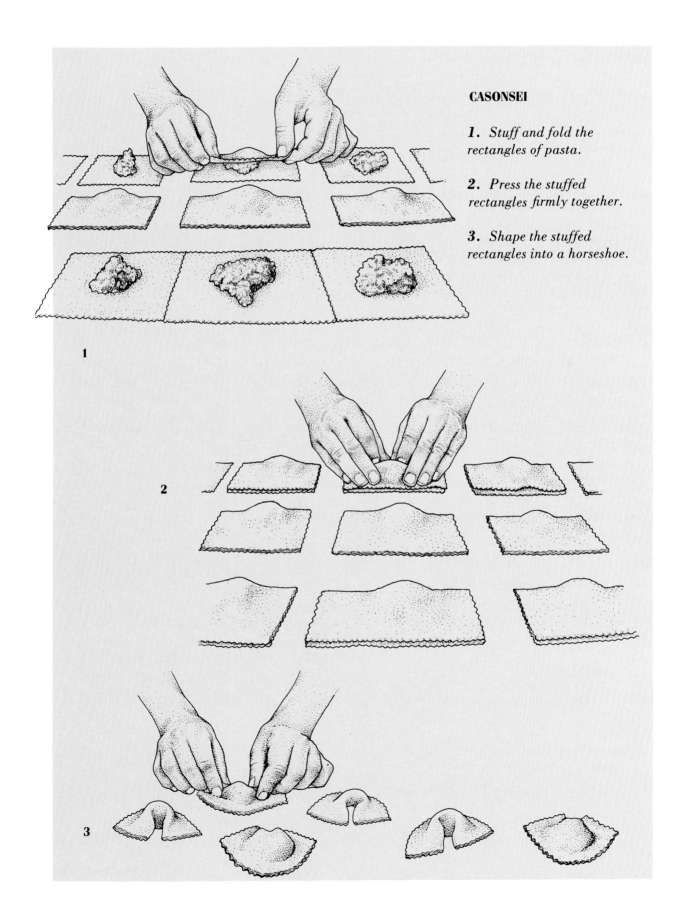

CASONSEI

1. *Stuff and fold the rectangles of pasta.*

2. *Press the stuffed rectangles firmly together.*

3. *Shape the stuffed rectangles into a horseshoe.*

1

2

3

CASONSEI ALLA BERGAMASCA II
STUFFED PASTA, BERGAMO STYLE, SECOND VERSION

FOR THE STUFFING:
**3 Italian sweet sausages
without fennel seeds,
skinned; or ½ pound
coarsely ground pork
4 tablespoons (2 ounces)
sweet butter, at room
temperature
1 cup freshly grated
Parmigiano cheese
2 extra-large eggs
Pinch of freshly grated
nutmeg
2 tablespoons unseasoned
bread crumbs,
preferably homemade
Salt and freshly ground
black pepper**

FOR THE PASTA:
**4 cups unbleached all-
purpose flour
5 extra-large eggs
Pinch of salt**

TO COOK THE PASTA:
Coarse-grained salt

FOR THE SAUCE:
**8 tablespoons (4 ounces)
sweet butter
6 ounces *pancetta* or
prosciutto, in one piece,
then cut into less than
½-inch cubes
20 sage leaves, fresh or
preserved in salt**

TO SERVE:
**1 cup freshly grated
Parmigiano cheese**

Prepare the stuffing. Combine the sausage or pork and butter in a crockery or glass bowl, and mix very well. Transfer to a skillet and place over medium heat. Sauté for 5 minutes, mixing constantly with a wooden spoon, then transfer the sautéed meat to a clean crockery or glass bowl and let rest until cool, 30 minutes. Add the Parmigiano, eggs, nutmeg, and bread crumbs. Taste for salt and pepper, and mix all the ingredients well. Cover bowl and refrigerate until needed.

Prepare the pasta with the ingredients and quantities listed, following the directions on page 14. Roll the pasta to a thickness of less than 1/16 inch, on the hand pasta machine take to the finest setting, and roll the dough into sheets.

Sometimes *casonsei* are shaped like round *tortelli*, but the classic shape is obtained by cutting the pasta into 3- x 2-inch rectangles (see drawing). To form, use 1 tablespoon of stuffing for each. Arrange the stuffing lengthwise along the 3-inch side; fold in half, covering the stuffing; and seal the 3 open sides by pressing them firmly together. Finally, twist the stuffed pasta into a horseshoe shape. Let the *casonsei* rest on floured cotton dish towels for 30 minutes before using.

Prepare the sauce. Melt the butter in a double boiler, add the *pancetta*, and lightly sauté it, then add the sage leaves and sauté for 1 minute more. Cover the pan and let rest for 30 minutes before using.

Bring a large stockpot of cold water to a boil. Add coarse salt to taste, then add the *casonsei* and cook for 30 seconds to 2 minutes depending on dryness. Use a strainer-skimmer to transfer them to a warmed platter, arranging the pasta in layers. Pour some of the sage butter and some Parmigiano over each layer. Serve immediately with 2 or 3 twists of black pepper on each serving.

FRIULI-VENEZIA GIULIA

Friuli-Venezia Giulia province has several pasta dishes that are not found elsewhere. *Ofelle* use a pasta that contains potato mixed with the flour. Once potatoes arrived in Europe from the New World, they were adapted to a variety of purposes. Potato flour is useful as a lighter thickener than wheat flour; potatoes also ferment very slowly and so make a slow-rising dough, used for some types of flat breads, pizzas, and so on. And in Trieste, as in areas beyond the Alps, they are used in the pasta for various types of *ravioli*. *Ofelle* incorporate an egg and one teaspoon of baking soda to help with the rising. Stuffed with spinach, beef, and pork, they make a wonderful stuffed pasta dressed with the simple butter and Parmigiano of northern Italy.

The plum-filled *gnocchi* also use a potato dough, incorporating a little semolina and all-purpose flour. The fruit filling may be fresh or dried plums, with a little sugar. The butter dressing is made with bread crumbs, cinnamon, and a little more sugar. In Friuli, the dish is not considered a sweet or dessert dish, but rather a typical first course, indeed a very popular one.

The large half-moon pasta of Friuli, *cialzons*, is somewhat related to *casoncelli*, but is distinguished by the great variety of fresh herbs in the stuffing along with the meat. Here we have together sage, parsley, basil, marjoram, and mint. Though they are usually dressed with butter and Parmigiano, they are cooked first in broth rather than water.

The unique very, very fine pasta used for the *lasagne* with poppy seeds is made primarily with egg yolks and only one whole egg; thus it may be rolled super-fine. Between the pasta squares we have the poppy seeds with butter and sugar. Again, in Trieste, this is not considered a dessert but a first course.

FROM TRIESTE

SERVES 8

OFELLE ALLA TRIESTINA
STUFFED POTATO PASTA

FOR THE PASTA:
2 pounds potatoes (not new potatoes)
5 quarts cold water
Coarse-grained salt
2 cups plus ½ cup unbleached all-purpose flour
1 extra-large egg
2 teaspoons salt
1 teaspoon baking soda

FOR THE STUFFING:
1 pound fresh spinach, stems removed and rinsed several times
Coarse-grained salt
1 medium-sized red onion, peeled
4 tablespoons (2 ounces) sweet butter
1 tablespoon olive oil
2 Italian sweet sausages made without fennel seeds; or 6 ounces ground pork
2 ounces ground beef
Salt and freshly ground black pepper

TO COOK THE PASTA:
Coarse-grained salt

TO SERVE:
16 tablespoons (8 ounces) sweet butter
1½ cups freshly grated Parmigiano cheese
Freshly ground black pepper

Prepare the pasta. Place a large pot with the cold water over medium heat. Meanwhile, peel the potatoes and cut them into 2-inch cubes. When the water reaches a boil, add coarse salt to taste, then place a large colander with the potatoes over the boiling water. Be sure that the water is not touching the potatoes. Cover the colander with a large piece of aluminum foil so the steam does not escape, and let the potatoes steam for 30 minutes. Then pass the cooked potatoes through a potato-ricer into a crockery or glass bowl, and let stand until cool, about 30 minutes.

Make the stuffing. Place a large pot of cold water over medium heat, and when the water reaches a boil, add coarse salt, then the spinach, and boil for 10 minutes. Drain the spinach, cool it under cold running water, and squeeze very well. Finely chop the onion on a board. Place the butter and oil in a small saucepan over medium heat, and when the butter is completely dissolved, add the onion and sauté for 5 minutes, stirring with a wooden spoon every so often. Remove the skins from the sausages. Add the ground beef and the sausages or ground pork to the onion. Sauté for 3 minutes more, stirring with a wooden spoon to amalgamate the ingredients. Add the spinach, taste for salt and pepper, and cook until all the juices are incorporated, about 10 minutes longer, continuously stirring with a wooden spoon. Transfer the stuffing to a crockery bowl and let rest until cool, about 30 minutes.

Place the cooled potatoes in a mound on a board and make a well. Arrange the 2 cups of flour all around the potatoes, then put the egg, salt, and baking soda in the well. Use a fork to mix the ingredients in the well. Start incorporating the potatoes, then add the flour; use your hands to finish incorporating the flour. Knead the ball of dough for 2 minutes, then wrap in a cotton dish towel and let rest for 10 minutes in a cool place.

Spread the remaining flour all over the board and, using a rolling pin, roll out the ball of dough to a thickness of ¹⁄₁₆ inch, about 6 inches wide. Starting 1 inch from the top and side edges, begin a horizontal row of 1-tablespoon portions of filling, each 3 inches from its neighbor (see drawings). Carefully lift the bottom end of the sheet of dough and fold it over the row of filling. (The width of the doubled sheet should be about 3 inches.) Quickly press down around each filling. Using a scalloped-edge pastry wheel, cut through the dough every 3 inches to form squares. Pinch the edges together with 2 fingers all around. Repeat the procedure until all the dough and filling is used. Transfer the finished *ofelle* onto a floured cotton dish towel and let stand until needed.

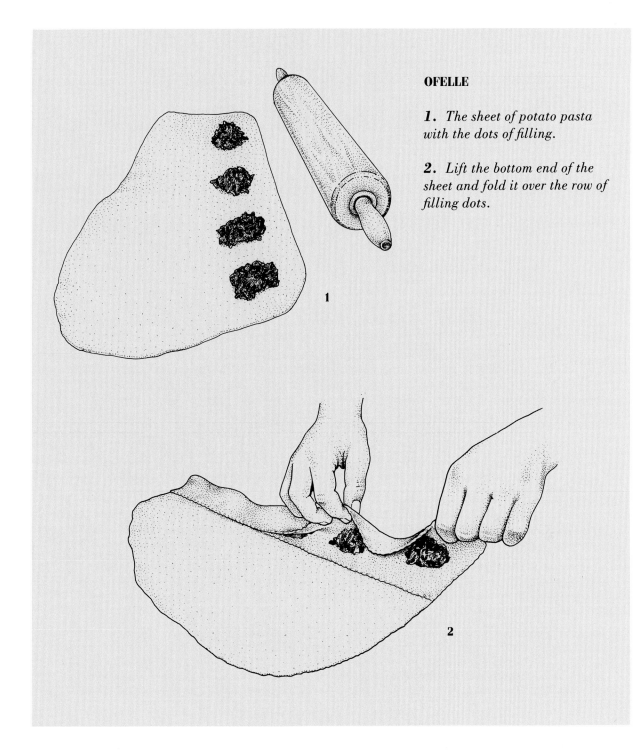

OFELLE

1. *The sheet of potato pasta with the dots of filling.*

2. *Lift the bottom end of the sheet and fold it over the row of filling dots.*

1

2

Place a large stockpot of cold water over medium heat. Put a large, deep serving dish containing the butter over it as a lid. When the water reaches a boil, add coarse salt to taste, then, one by one, add the *ofelle*. Cook for 10 to 12 minutes. Use a strainer-skimmer to transfer the pasta to the serving dish with the melted butter. Sprinkle the cheese over and serve immediately with a twist of pepper on each serving.

FROM TRIESTE

SERVES 4 TO 6

FOR THE PASTA:
**1 ¾ cups unbleached all-
purpose flour
5 extra-large egg yolks
1 extra-large egg
Pinch of salt**

TO COOK THE PASTA:
Coarse-grained salt

FOR THE SAUCE:
**8 tablespoons (4 ounces)
sweet butter
1 heaping tablespoon
granulated sugar
1 heaping tablespoon
poppy seeds**

LASAGNE FINISSIME CON SEMI DI PAPAVERO

FINE *LASAGNE* WITH POPPY SEEDS

Prepare the pasta with the ingredients and quantities listed, following the directions on page 14. When the ball of dough is formed, wrap it in a cotton dish towel dampened with cold water and let rest in a cool place or on the bottom shelf of the refrigerator for 24 hours. Save the unincorporated flour—you will need it when stretching the dough.

Spread the unused flour on a board, unwrap the dough, and knead until very elastic and smooth, about 1 minute. Stretch the sheet of pasta less than ¹⁄₁₆ inch thick—on the pasta machine take to the finest setting—and cut into 5-inch squares. Let the squares rest on cotton dish towels for at least 30 minutes before cooking.

Bring a large pot of cold water to a boil and add coarse salt—a little more than usual because of the sweetness of the sauce. Put the butter, sugar, and poppy seeds in a small saucepan and place the pan over low heat. When the water returns to a boil, add the pasta and cook for 2 to 5 minutes depending on dryness. Use a strainer-skimmer to transfer the cooked pasta squares to a warmed serving platter, adding 2 tablespoons of the melted butter and poppy seeds every 3 or 4 pasta squares. Serve very hot.

NOTE:
In Friuli, this is eaten as a first course *(primo piatto)*. It may be used as a dessert, in which case ½ cup of warmed honey is added to the butter–sugar mixture with the poppy seeds.

FROM FRIULI

SERVES 6 TO 8

FOR THE STUFFING:
**2 slices white bread, crusts
removed
1 cup lukewarm chicken
or beef broth, preferably
homemade**

CIALZONS

LARGE HALF-MOON PASTA STUFFED WITH MEAT AND MANY HERBS

Prepare the stuffing. Soak the bread in the broth for 30 minutes. Place the butter in a heavy, medium-sized saucepan over low heat, and when the butter is completely melted, add the meat and sauté for 2 minutes, stirring several times with a wooden spoon. Meanwhile, finely chop the sage, parsley, basil, marjoram, and mint all together on a board. Add the herbs to the pan, mix very well, and cook for 10 minutes more, seasoning with salt and pepper. Transfer the meat mixture to a crockery or glass bowl. Squeeze the broth from the bread, then add the bread to the bowl and incorporate it into the meat. Let rest until cool—about 30 minutes. When cool, season with nutmeg, then add the eggs and Parmigiano, mix well, and refrigerate, covered, until needed.

Prepare the pasta with the ingredients and quantities listed, following the directions on page 14. Let the ball of dough rest for 30 minutes, wrapped in a cotton dish towel and tightly covered by a bowl.

Stretch the layer of pasta to less than $\frac{1}{16}$ inch thick, on the pasta machine take to the finest setting. Use a 4-inch round cookie or biscuit cutter with a scalloped edge to cut the pasta into discs. Place a scant tablespoon of stuffing on one side of each disc, leaving a little border of pasta, then fold the other half over. Seal the edges very well and transfer the prepared *cialzons* onto floured cotton dish towels to rest until needed.

Place a large pot with the broth over medium heat, and put a large serving platter with the butter over the pot as a lid. When the broth reaches a boil and the butter is melted, remove the platter, add the pasta to the pot and cook for 9 to 12 minutes. Use a strainer-skimmer to transfer the cooked *cialzons* onto the platter, spooning some of the butter over each layer. Sprinkle some cheese and grind some black pepper over each layer. The last layer should also be topped with butter, cheese, and pepper. Serve hot.

6 tablespoons (3 ounces) sweet butter
1 pound ground beef
5 large sage leaves, fresh or preserved in salt
10 large sprigs Italian parsley, leaves only
6 large basil leaves, fresh or preserved in salt
1 tablespoon fresh marjoram leaves
1 heaping tablespoon fresh mint leaves
Salt and freshly ground black pepper
Pinch of freshly grated nutmeg
2 extra-large eggs
½ cup freshly grated Parmigiano cheese

FOR THE PASTA:
1½ cups unbleached all-purpose flour
½ cup very fine semolina flour
4 extra-large eggs
Pinch of salt

TO COOK THE PASTA:
5 quarts chicken or beef broth, preferably homemade

FOR THE SAUCE:
8 tablespoons (4 ounces) sweet butter, cut in pieces
¾ cup freshly grated Parmigiano cheese
Freshly ground black pepper

SERVES 6 TO 8

FOR THE *GNOCCHI*:
**1 pound potatoes (not new
  potatoes)**
Coarse-grained salt
**32 fresh Italian prune
  plums or pitted dried
  prunes**
**4 teaspoons granulated
  sugar**
2 extra-large eggs
Pinch of salt
**1 tablespoon (½ ounce)
  sweet butter, at room
  temperature**
**1 tablespoon semolina
  flour**
**¾ cup to 1 cup unbleached
  all-purpose flour**

TO COOK THE *GNOCCHI*:
Coarse-grained salt

FOR THE SAUCE:
**12 tablespoons (6 ounces)
  sweet butter**
**4 tablespoons unseasoned
  bread crumbs**
**2 large pinches ground
  cinnamon**
**1½ tablespoons granulated
  sugar**

GNOCCHI DI SUSINE

PLUM-FILLED *GNOCCHI*

Boil the potatoes in a medium-sized saucepan with the salted water until very soft, about 45 minutes, depending on size. Peel the potatoes and pass them through a potato ricer, using the disc with smallest holes, onto a board. Arrange potatoes in a mound, make a well, and let rest until cool, about 20 minutes.

Prepare the plums. If using fresh, pit them by cutting open on one side and pulling out pit. If using dried, poke them open. Put ⅛ teaspoon of sugar in the hole left by the pit, close again, and let stand until needed.

Put the eggs, salt, butter, and semolina flour in the potato well and use a fork to mix the ingredients. Then use your hands to knead the dough, incorporating about ½ cup of the all-purpose flour. Cut the dough into 4 pieces and, using your fingers and a little flour, roll each piece into a cord about 1 inch thick. Cut each cord into 8 pieces and, with your fingers, press each piece into a disc less than ½ inch thick. Place a plum in the center of each disc and wrap it up with the dough. When all the plums are ready, bring a very wide pot full of cold water to a boil. Add coarse salt to taste, then add the plums and simmer for 2 minutes. Meanwhile, put a large skillet with the butter over medium heat, and when the butter is completely melted, add the bread crumbs, cinnamon, and sugar. Transfer the *gnocchi* to the skillet and sauté for 30 seconds until they are coated with the butter mixture. Serve from the skillet, pouring some of the sauce over each serving.

LIGURIA

Liguria, with its chief city Genoa, has a variety of pastas that are its own. *Trenette*, the pasta made without eggs and the classic recipient of the pesto sauce, are also traditionally paired with the famous artichoke sauce. *Trenette* are also made with a combination of whole-wheat and white flour, but in this case a single egg is usually added. Since the Genoese are legendary for their frugality, it gives rise to comment in other parts of Italy when they hear that the recipe uses only one egg. But here we can be sure that the single egg is appropriate for gastronomic rather than economic reasons. *Trenette avvantaggiate con fagiolini* combines stringbeans, preferably the small young ones as used in Italy, with the pasta and another, slightly different but still Ligurian version of pesto.

Troffiette, also generally eaten with pesto, are twisted into a corkscrew shape. They may be made with white or whole-wheat flour, or even with a little chestnut flour mixed into the white.

Corzetti stampati, named after the old Genoese money pieces, are stamped on both sides like a coin. The old wooden stamps, made in two pieces of beechwood, have a cutter at the end of one and the two images to be impressed on the pasta. Traditionally the stamps were highly personal, using a family coat of arms on one side, and perhaps a ship or some other image of Genoa's maritime glory on the other. The old families often have them as heirlooms, but unfortunately few continue to make the pasta. I have made a real attempt to revive this great traditional dish and have had some stamps hand-carved by an old Ligurian who remembers how they were once made. They must of course be hand-carved. (One locale in Emilia-Romagna, Bedonia, also makes this shape as *crosetti.*)

Corzetti stampati may be made with white, whole-wheat, or chestnut flour and may be dressed with a simple sauce of fresh marjoram and pine nuts in good Ligurian olive oil or with a traditional veal sauce. It is also fun and authentic to serve a combination of *corzetti* made with three different flours, so you have three different colors or shades of pasta, and of course three somewhat different tastes.

Also called *corzetti* are the figure-8 shapes made by pushing the little ball of pasta down with both thumbs simultaneously. These are traditionally served with the Genoese Mushroom Sauce. The older version is made with a fine semolina flour, the more modern but still authentic second version is made with all-purpose flour.

The Genoese often use *lasagne* simply boiled and dressed with an intense sauce. They use a more normal dough for the *lasagne* squares. The special eggless pasta using white wine for the liquid instead of water is a special feature of the *Fazzoletti di seta*, called "silk handerchiefs." (Also called *Mandilli de sêa*.) They are so called because after being boiled, these delicate pasta squares are dropped on the plate like a handkerchief rather than flattened out and sauced; the silky texture of the pasta also accounts for the name.

Ravioli stuffed with fish have become a standard feature of "nuova cucina" and "nouvelle cuisine," but there is a perfectly traditional version from Liguria with the stuffing containing both fish and cooked greens. The greens used are escarole and watercress, not often encountered in stuffings. Tomatoes, butter, garlic, and marjoram form the basis of the sauce for these wonderful *Zembi d'arzillo*.

The most characteristic Ligurian stuffed pasta, however, is the *ravioli*-like *pansoti*. The fresh local cheese called "prescinséua" which binds the filling can be substituted by ricotta and the unique mixture of wild field greens called "pregoggión" by swiss chard and watercress. These are not unauthentic substitutions, and in any case these greens in their wild form are present in the mixture. Undoubtedly, the stuffing cannot be reproduced exactly outside the specific localities, which are Rapallo, Camogli and others, rather than Genoa itself. The grated cheese, marjoram, and nutmeg are always used. The dressing is a version of the celebrated and ancient Ligurian sauce that combines walnuts with garlic, cream, butter, oil and marjoram thickened with *mollica*. Traditionally, of course, this sauce, like the more familiar pesto made with basil, was pounded to a paste in a mortar and pestle.

NOTE:
Troffiette and *troffie* could be spelled with one or two *f*'s. *Troffiette* are not small *troffie* but rather Ligurian *gnocchi*.

TRENETTE AVVANTAGGIATE CON FAGIOLINI

WHOLE-WHEAT *TRENETTE* WITH STRING BEANS

Prepare the pasta. Mix the 2 flours together and prepare the pasta according to the instructions on page 14. Stretch the sheet of pasta to a thickness of 1/16 inch—on the pasta machine, take to the next to the last setting—and cut it into *trenette* (see page 230). Let the pasta rest on cotton towels until needed.

Place the beans in a bowl of cold water to soak for 30 minutes. Meanwhile, prepare the pesto. If using a mortar and pestle, place the parsley, basil, pine nuts, and garlic in the mortar and grind until very smooth. Transfer to a crockery or glass bowl; add the cheese, butter, salt, and pepper, and mix with a wooden spoon until all the ingredients are well incorporated. Add the olive oil a few drops at a time, as if preparing mayonnaise, continously mixing in a rotating motion until all the olive oil is incorporated. Taste for salt and pepper. If using a food processor, put in all the ingredients except the olive oil and, using the metal blade, grind until the texture is very creamy. With the blade still rotating, add the olive oil through the funnel, a very small amount at a time until all the oil is amalgamated. Add salt and pepper to taste, and transfer the pesto to a crockery or glass bowl; refrigerate, covered, until needed.

Bring a large pot of cold water to a boil, and add coarse-grained salt to taste. Drain the beans and add to the pot.

The cooking time of the beans will vary greatly, depending on their thickness and freshness, from 5 to 10 minutes. They should retain their shape but be tender enough to match the tenderness of the fresh pasta; crisp, half-cooked beans rarely work in combination with other ingredients in Italian cooking, and this is particularly true in this dish.

The pasta should be added to the beans so that both finish cooking at the same time. The cooking time of fresh *trenette* also varies, from 1 to 3 minutes depending on dryness. Ascertain how long before the beans are finished the pasta should be added in order for both to finish cooking at the same time.

As the pasta cooks, take 1/4 cup of the boiling pasta water and mix it into the pesto. Spread out half the sauce on a large, warmed serving platter. Drain the pasta and beans, and place them over the sauce. Pour the remaining sauce over, toss gently but very well, and serve immediately. No extra cheese should be added to the individual servings.

* When *trenette*, usually eggless, are made with whole-wheat flour, one egg is added.

FOR THE PASTA:
2¼ cups unbleached all-purpose flour
2¼ cups whole-wheat flour
1 extra-large egg *
1 cup cold water
Pinch of salt

PLUS:
1 pound string beans, cleaned and left whole
Coarse-grained salt

FOR THE PESTO:
15 large sprigs Italian parsley, leaves only
25 large fresh basil leaves
5 tablespoons pine nuts (*pignolis*)
2 large cloves garlic, peeled
¾ cup freshly grated Parmigiano cheese; or ½ cup freshly grated Parmigiano and ¼ cup freshly grated pecorino sardo
4 tablespoons (2 ounces) sweet butter, at room temperature
Salt and freshly ground black pepper
½ cup olive oil

TO COOK THE PASTA:
Coarse-grained salt

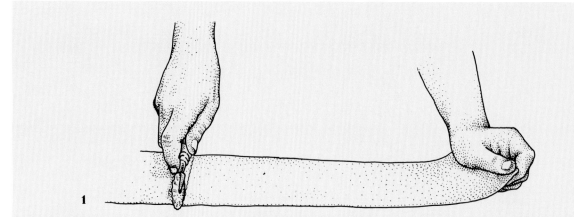

TRENETTE

1. *Cut the layer of pasta with a pastry cutter into pieces about 15 inches long.*

2. *Use the pastry cutter to cut into ½-inch-wide scalloped strips for one side, and*

3. *for the other, use a knife for a straight side.*

3

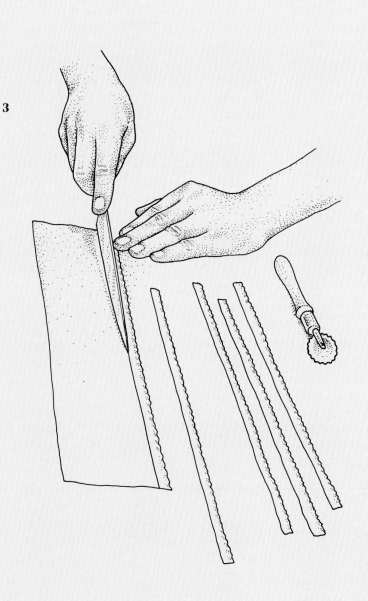

FROM LIGURIA

SERVES 4 TO 6

FOR THE PASTA:
**2 cups unbleached all-
   purpose flour
¾ cup boiling water
Pinch of salt**

FOR THE SAUCE:
**1½ cups olive oil
12 whole walnuts, shelled
2 tablespoons pine nuts
   (*pignolis*)
4 cups loosely packed
   fresh basil leaves
3 heaping tablespoons
   boiled and chopped
   spinach
3 medium-sized cloves
   garlic, peeled
4 ounces freshly grated
   Parmigiano cheese
4 ounces freshly grated
   sardo or romano cheese;
   or additional freshly
   grated Parmigiano
   cheese
Salt and freshly ground
   black pepper to taste**

TO COOK THE PASTA:
Coarse-grained salt

TO SERVE:
**Freshly grated Parmigiano
   cheese**

TROFFIETTE

GENOESE CORKSCREW PASTA

Prepare the pasta with the ingredients and quantities listed, following the instructions on page 14, and knead the dough for 15 minutes, incorporating the flour a little at a time. Detach pieces of dough the size of a chick-pea, roll them to finger-length cords between your palms, then flatten the cord a little with your finger tips. Let dry for 30 seconds, then, holding onto both ends, make several twists in the cords (see drawing). Let pasta rest on floured cotton dish towels until needed. Prepare pesto sauce with ingredients and quantities listed, using a blender or food processor, following directions on page 229, but adding ½ cup of the oil at the beginning.

Bring a large quantity of cold water to a boil, add coarse salt to taste, then add the pasta and cook for 9 to 12 minutes depending on dryness (like dried rather than fresh pasta). Add 2 tablespoons of the boiling water from the pasta pot to the pesto sauce, and mix well. Drain the pasta, add the sauce, mix well, and serve, sprinkled with Parmigiano.

VARIATIONS

1. Whole-wheat flour can be used instead of all-purpose flour in the pasta.

2. The pasta can be made with 2 cups less 3 tablespoons all-purpose flour, and 3 tablespoons of chestnut flour as a substitute.

3. Green pasta can be used, made with 2½ cups unbleached all-purpose flour, 1 tablespoon boiled, chopped spinach, ¾ cup boiling water, and a pinch of salt.

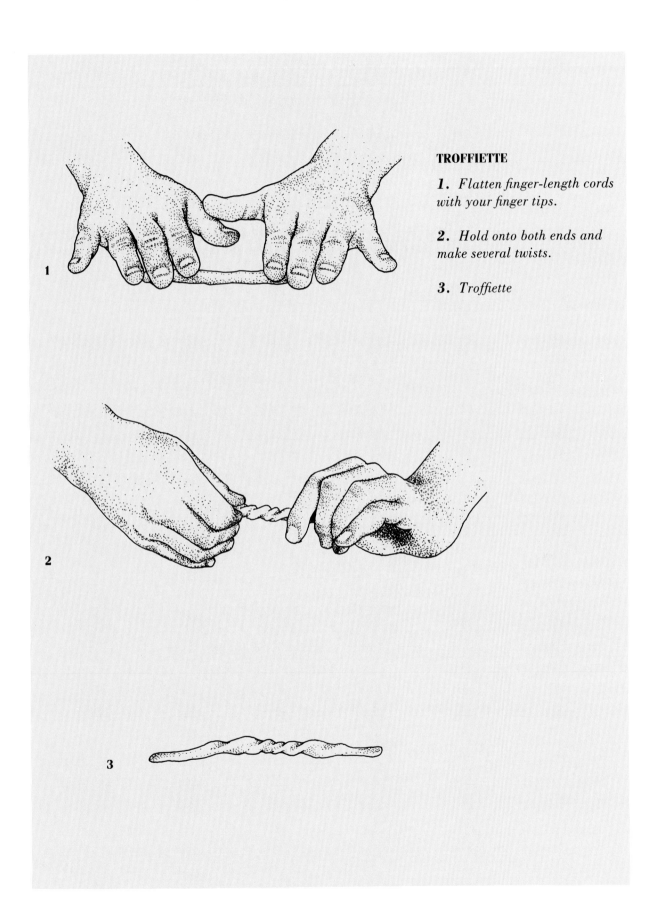

TROFFIETTE

1. *Flatten finger-length cords with your finger tips.*

2. *Hold onto both ends and make several twists.*

3. *Troffiette*

CORZETTI STAMPATI ALLA MAGGIORANA

"STAMPED" LIGURIAN PASTA

FOR THE PASTA:
**3½ cups unbleached all-
purpose flour
1 cup cold water
1 extra-large egg
Pinch of salt**

FOR THE SAUCE:
**12 tablespoons (6 ounces)
sweet butter
3 teaspoons dried
marjoram
6 tablespoons pine nuts
(pignolis)
Salt and freshly ground
black pepper**

TO COOK THE PASTA:
Coarse-grained salt

VARIATIONS

WHOLE-WHEAT
CORZETTI
**2½ cups unbleached all-
purpose flour
1 cup whole-wheat flour
1 cup cold water
1 extra-large egg
Pinch of salt**

CHESTNUT-FLOUR
CORZETTI
**3 cups unbleached all-
purpose flour
1 cup fresh chestnut flour
(imported from Italy or
France)
1 cup cold water
1 extra-large egg
Pinch of salt**

Prepare the pasta with the ingredients and quantities listed, following the instructions on page 14. Stretch the sheet of pasta a little thicker than usual, ¹⁄₁₆ inch, on the pasta machine take to the next to last setting. *Corzetti* stamps are in 2 pieces. The bottom piece serves two functions. Its bottom side is like a cookie cutter, the top side is carved to produce an image. The top piece has a handle and its bottom produces a second image. Cut the pasta layer into discs using the cutter of the stamp and let them rest for several minutes on cotton towels. Discard pasta remnants.

Place a disc between the 2 carved images and press, producing a disc with different images on each side. Continue until all discs are stamped, lightly flouring the 2 carved sides each time. Let the *corzetti* rest on cotton towels at least 1 hour before using, otherwise the printed design will disappear in the boiling water.

Bring a large pot of cold water to a boil, add coarse salt to taste, then add the pasta and cook for 3 to 5 minutes depending on dryness. Don't overcook. This type of pasta is different from other fresh pastas, since once it is cooked it retains some kind of "bite" and is not completely soft and tender.

As the pasta cooks, place the butter, marjoram, and pine nuts in a small saucepan over medium heat and sauté for 3 minutes, stirring very often with a wooden spoon. Season to taste with salt and pepper.

Drain the pasta, transfer to a warmed serving dish, pour over the sauce and more freshly ground black pepper, toss gently but very well, and serve immediately.

Make the pasta with the ingredients listed for either variation and cut and stamp as indicated for the main recipe.

NOTE:
It is traditional to prepare all three types together, cook in the sauce stockpot, and serve with the marjoram sauce.

CORZETTI STAMPATI CON SUGO DI VITELLA

STAMPED *CORZETTI* WITH VEAL SAUCE

FROM LIGURIA

SERVES 6 TO 8

Prepare the pasta, following the directions on page 234.

Prepare the sauce. Soak the mushrooms in a bowl of lukewarm water for 1 hour. Meanwhile, cut the onion into quarters and the carrots into 2-inch pieces; place in a bowl of cold water to soak for 30 minutes. Drain.

Place the olive oil, butter, veal, and onion and carrots in a medium-sized heavy saucepan over medium heat. Sauté for 15 minutes without mixing or stirring. Sprinkle the flour over, mix very well with a wooden spoon and cook for 1 minute more. Add the wine, raise the heat to high, and let it evaporate for 5 minutes. Season to taste with salt and pepper. If using fresh tomatoes, cut them into 1-inch pieces. Add fresh or canned tomatoes to the saucepan, mix, and cook for 5 minutes more. Drain the mushrooms and clean them very well, removing any sand attached to the stems. Add the mushroom pieces as they are to the saucepan along with the broth. Cover and simmer for 1½ hours, stirring every so often with a wooden spoon.

Remove the meat and undissolved bits of meat and reserve for another use; using a food mill with the disc with the smallest holes, pass the contents of the saucepan into a second pan. Place the sauce over medium heat, taste for salt and pepper, and reduce for 10 minutes more; at that time the sauce will be ready to be used immediately. If you wish to use it later, let it cool completely, then transfer to a crockery or glass bowl, cover, and refrigerate until needed.

Bring a large pot of cold water to a boil, add coarse salt to taste, then add the pasta. Cook the *corzetti* for 3 to 5 minutes depending on dryness. Drain the pasta, transfer to a warmed serving dish, pour over the sauce, toss gently, and serve immediately.

VARIATION
A similar sauce can be prepared by substituting the same amount of beef (chuck) for the veal.

FOR THE PASTA:
3½ cups unbleached all-purpose flour
1 cup cold water
1 extra-large egg
Pinch of salt

FOR THE SAUCE:
2 ounces dried porcini mushrooms
1 large red onion, peeled
4 medium-sized carrots, scraped
1 tablespoon olive oil
6 tablespoons (3 ounces) sweet butter
1 pound boneless veal, any cut, untrimmed, in 1 piece
2 tablespoons unbleached all-purpose flour
1 cup dry white wine
Salt and freshly ground black pepper
1 pound very ripe, fresh tomatoes; or 1 pound canned tomatoes, preferably imported Italian, drained
1 quart lukewarm chicken or beef broth, preferably homemade

TO COOK THE PASTA:
Coarse-grained salt

CORZETTI ALLA POLCEVERASCA CON TOCCO DI FUNGHI

FIGURE-8 *CORZETTI* (2 VERSIONS) WITH GENOESE MUSHROOM SAUCE

FOR THE ORIGINAL,
AUTHENTIC PASTA:
**2½ cups fine semolina
    flour
1 extra-large egg
3 extra-large egg yolks
¼ cup lukewarm water
Pinch of salt**

FOR A MODERN,
LIGHTER PASTA:
**3 cups unbleached all-
    purpose flour
4 extra-large eggs
Pinch of salt**

FOR THE SAUCE:
**1 ounce dried porcini
    mushrooms
2 cups lukewarm water
1 medium-sized red onion,
    peeled
1 large clove garlic, peeled
15 large sprigs Italian
    parsley, leaves only
4 tablespoons (2 ounces)
    sweet butter
4 tablespoons olive oil
1 pound ripe, fresh
    tomatoes; or 1 pound
    canned tomatoes,
    preferably imported
    Italian, drained
1 tablespoon tomato paste
Salt and freshly ground
    black pepper**

TO COOK THE PASTA:
Coarse-grained salt

Prepare either dough with the set of ingredients listed for it, following directions on page 14. If you are making the semolina version, wrap the dough in a cotton dish towel and let it rest for 1 hour, covered with a bowl. If using all-purpose flour, make the figure-8s immediately, without letting the pasta rest.

Prepare the *corzetti*. Detach pieces of dough the size of chick-peas. Form solid figure-8s by pressing the "chick-pea" down with both thumbs, then stretching the middle a little by pulling the thumbs in opposite directions. Let the prepared *corzetti* rest on floured dish towels until needed.

Meanwhile prepare the sauce. Soak the mushrooms in the lukewarm water for 30 minutes. Drain, saving the soaking water, and clean the mushrooms very well, being sure that no sand remains attached to the stems. Pass the mushroom water through several layers of paper towels to strain out remaining sand. Finely chop the mushrooms, onion, garlic, and parsley all together on a board. Place the butter and oil in a medium-sized skillet over medium heat, and when the butter is completely melted, add the chopped ingredients and sauté for 15 minutes. If using fresh tomatoes, cut them into pieces. Pass fresh or canned tomatoes through a food mill, using the disc with the smallest holes, into a second bowl. Add tomatoes and tomato paste to the skillet, season to taste with salt and pepper, and cook for 25 minutes more. Add the strained mushroom water, cover, and simmer for 1 hour, stirring every so often with a wooden spoon.

Bring a large pot of cold water to a boil, add coarse salt to taste, then add the pasta. Cook the *corzetti* made with semolina for 9 to 12 minutes depending on dryness; the others take 5 to 8 minutes. Drain the pasta, put it in the skillet with the sauce, sauté for 30 seconds, then transfer to a large, warmed serving platter and serve.

FAZZOLETTI DI SETA

PASTA SQUARES WITH PESTO SAUCE ("SILK
HANDKERCHIEFS")

FROM LIGURIA

SERVES 6 TO 8

Prepare the pasta with the ingredients and quantities listed, following the directions on page 14, placing the wine in the well of the
flour with salt. Stretch the sheet of pasta to less than ⅟₁₆ inch; on
the pasta machine take to the finest setting and cut it into squares,
as for *lasagne*. Let the pasta rest on cotton dish towels until you
need it, turning the squares once or twice to avoid sticking.

Prepare the pesto with a mortar and pestle or food processor.
Grind the basil and garlic finely, then place them in a crockery or
glass bowl. Add the butter, oil, and cheese, and mix the ingredients
with a wooden spoon. Season to taste with salt and pepper, cover
the bowl with aluminum foil, and refrigerate until needed.

Bring a large pot of cold water to a boil, add coarse salt to taste,
then add the pasta a few squares at a time. Cook for 1 to 3 minutes
depending on dryness, then use a strainer-skimmer to transfer the
squares from the pot to the individual dishes, dropping the squares
on the plate so they assume the form of a dropped handkerchief.
While the pasta is cooking, remove the pesto from the refrigerator
and add ¼ cup of the boiling pasta water, mixing very well with a
wooden spoon. Each portion consists of 4 to 5 pasta squares, with
2 or 3 tablespoons of the pesto and 1 tablespoon of cheese sprinkled
on top.

FOR THE PASTA:
**3½ cups unbleached all-
purpose flour**
1 cup dry white wine
Pinch of salt

FOR THE PESTO:
**3 cups fresh basil leaves
(about 2 ounces)**
**5 medium-sized cloves
garlic, peeled**
**8 tablespoons (4 ounces)
sweet butter**
½ cup olive oil
**3 ounces freshly grated
pecorino romano or
Parmigiano cheese**
**Salt and freshly ground
black pepper**

TO COOK THE PASTA:
Coarse-grained salt

TO SERVE:
**6 to 8 tablespoons freshly
grated pecorino romano
or Parmigiano cheese**

Fazzoletti di seta: the boiled pasta squares, with wine in the delicate dough, are dropped on the plate to resemble a fallen handkerchief.

FROM LIGURIA

SERVES 6 TO 8

PANSOTI O PANSOOTI ALLE NOCI

STUFFED GENOESE PASTA

FOR THE STUFFING:
1 pound Swiss chard,
  cleaned and large stems
  removed
4 ounces watercress, large
  stems removed
Coarse-grained salt
8 ounces whole-milk
  ricotta
¾ cups freshly grated
  Parmigiano cheese
2 extra-large eggs
20 fresh marjoram leaves,
  or 1 teaspoon dried
Salt and freshly ground
  black pepper
Pinch of freshly grated
  nutmeg

FOR THE PASTA:
4 cups unbleached all-
  purpose flour
1 extra-large egg
¼ cup dry white wine
¾ cup cold water
Pinch of salt

Put the Swiss chard and watercress in a bowl of cold water and let them soak for 30 minutes. Meanwhile, bring a large pot of cold water to a boil, then add coarse salt to taste. Drain the vegetables, add them to the boiling water, and cook for 10 minutes. Drain and cool the greens under cold running water; squeeze them very well. Finely chop the greens on a board and transfer to a large crockery or glass bowl. Add the ricotta, Parmigiano, eggs, and marjoram. Season with salt, pepper, and nutmeg. Mix all the ingredients together with a wooden spoon, then cover bowl and refrigerate until needed.

Prepare the pasta with the ingredients and quantities listed, following the instructions on page 14. Stretch the layer of pasta to less than 1/16 inch thick, on the pasta machine to the finest setting. Cut the layer into 5- or 6-inch squares, and divide each square diagonally into 2 triangles (see drawings). Put a scant tablespoon of stuffing in the center of each triangle, fold the triangle in half, and seal on the 2 open sides. (Sometimes 2 of the ends are then brought together and attached.) Let the *pansoti* rest on cotton dish towels for at least 30 minutes before cooking them.

Prepare the sauce. Soak the bread in a small bowl with the milk for 10 minutes. Use a mortar and pestle or food processor to finely grind the walnuts, garlic, and marjoram all together, then place them in a crockery or glass bowl. Squeeze the milk from the bread and add the bread to the bowl along with the Parmigiano. Mix all the ingredients together well. Season with salt and pepper,

PANSOTTI

1. *The squares divided into triangles.*

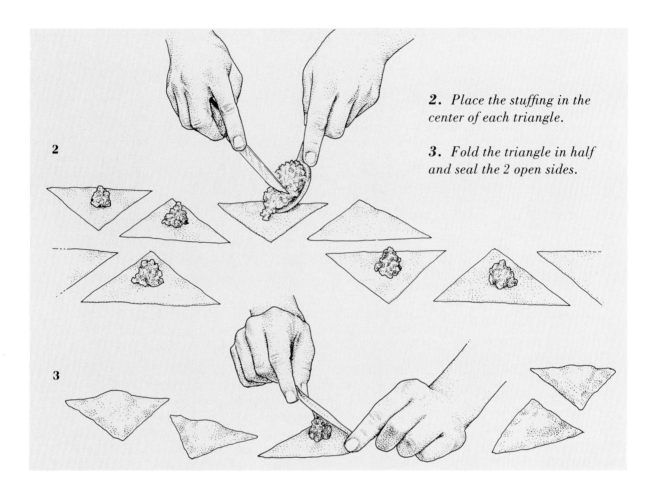

2. *Place the stuffing in the center of each triangle.*

3. *Fold the triangle in half and seal the 2 open sides.*

then start adding the cream, butter, and olive oil, constantly mixing with a wooden spoon until all the ingredients are well amalgamated and the sauce is smooth. Cover the bowl and refrigerate until needed.

Bring a large pot of cold water to a boil, add coarse salt to taste, then add the *pansoti* and cook for 1 to 3 minutes depending on dryness. Remove sauce from refrigerator, add 2 tablespoons of the boiling pasta water, and mix very well. Use a strainer-skimmer to transfer the *pansoti* to a warmed serving dish. Make a layer, pour some of the sauce over, then put on more layers of pasta, then sauce. Serve very hot.

FOR THE SAUCE:
3 slices white bread, crusts removed
1 cup cold milk
8 ounces walnuts, shelled
1 large clove garlic, peeled
20 fresh marjoram leaves, or 1 teaspoon dried
½ cup freshly grated Parmigiano cheese
Salt and freshly ground black pepper
1 cup heavy cream
2 tablespoons (1 ounce) sweet butter
4 tablespoons olive oil

TO COOK THE PASTA:
Coarse-grained salt

ZEMBI D'ARZILLO (RAVIOLI DI PESCE)

RAVIOLI STUFFED WITH FISH

FOR THE VEGETABLE
STUFFING:
¾ **pound escarole, dark**
   outer leaves removed
4 **ounces watercress, large**
   stems removed
Coarse-grained salt
10 **large sprigs Italian**
   parsley, leaves only
1 **medium-sized clove**
   garlic, peeled
½ **tablespoon fresh**
   marjoram leaves, or 1
   teaspoon dried

FOR THE FISH
STUFFING:
¾ **pound fish fillets, a**
   mixture of 2 or 3 of the
   following: sea bass,
   porgy, grouper, red
   snapper
Coarse-grained salt
1 **large lemon**
1½ **quarts cold water**
½ **cup dry white wine**
2 **tablespoons olive oil**
2 **tablespoons (1 ounce)**
   sweet butter
Salt and freshly ground
   black pepper
½ **cup freshly grated**
   Parmigiano cheese
1 **extra-large egg**
2 **extra-large egg yolks**

FOR THE PASTA:
4 **cups unbleached all-**
   purpose flour
2 **extra-large eggs**
1 **cup lukewarm water**
Pinch of salt

Prepare the vegetable stuffing. Soak the escarole and watercress in a bowl of cold water for 30 minutes. Bring a large pot of cold water to a boil, and add coarse salt to taste. Drain the vegetables, add them to the pot, and cook for 10 minutes. Drain again and cool under cold running water; squeeze the vegetables very dry. Finely chop the cooked vegetables together with the parsley, garlic, and marjoram on a board; let stand until needed.

Prepare the fish stuffing. Put fish in a bowl of cold water with a little salt, and the lemon cut in half and squeezed, for half an hour. Place a medium-sized saucepan with the cold water and the wine over medium heat. When the water reaches a boil, drain fish, wash it under cold running water, and add it to the pan. Lower heat, and simmer for 5 minutes. Remove fish, taking care to remove all bones; finely chop the fish on a board.

Place a medium-sized skillet with the olive oil and butter over medium heat; when the butter is completely melted, add the vegetable stuffing and the fish. Sauté, stirring constantly for 2 minutes and mixing the two together. Season to taste with salt and pepper. Transfer to a crockery or glass bowl and let stand for 30 minutes until cool. Add the cheese, egg, and egg yolks, then taste for salt and pepper, cover, and refrigerate until needed.

Prepare the pasta with the ingredients and quantities listed, following the directions on page 14. Stretch sheet to less than 1/16 inch thick; on the pasta machine, take to the last setting. Prepare 2-inch square *tortelli* and put ½ tablespoon stuffing on each (see page 113). Let pasta rest on cotton dish towels until needed.

Prepare the sauce. Place a medium-sized saucepan with the tomatoes (if using fresh, cut them into pieces) and the garlic over medium heat. Cook for 20 minutes, then pass through a food mill, using the disc with the smallest holes, into a crockery or glass bowl. Melt the butter in a medium-sized saucepan over low heat, and when the butter is melted, add the tomatoes, taste for salt and pepper, and simmer for 10 minutes more.

Meanwhile, bring a large pot of cold water to a boil, add coarse salt to taste, then add the *tortelli* and cook for 1 to 3 minutes depending on dryness. When ready, add the marjoram to the tomato sauce and ladle some of the sauce onto a large, warmed serving platter. Use a strainer-skimmer to transfer the *tortelli* from the boiling water to the prepared platter, and ladle more tomato sauce over each layer of pasta. Serve hot.

FOR THE SAUCE:

3 pounds ripe, fresh tomatoes; or 3 pounds canned tomatoes, preferably imported Italian, drained

2 medium-sized cloves garlic, peeled

8 tablespoons (4 ounces) sweet butter

Salt and freshly ground black pepper

4 tablespoons fresh marjoram leaves, or 2 teaspoons dried

TO COOK THE PASTA:
Coarse-grained salt

EMILIA-ROMAGNA, TUSCANY

Many of the egg pastas that originated in Central Italian Tuscany and Emilia-Romagna—such as *lasagne alla ferrarese*, *tagliatelle*, *tortellini*, and *tortelli*—have spread throughout Italy and are no longer considered specifically regional. Surviving early cookbook manuscripts suggest, suprisingly, that these pastas moved from Tuscany to Emilia-Romagna and not the other way around. But these areas do retain certain regional specialties such as *Pinci di Montalcino* and *Tortelli di zucca* (see Recipe Appendix) and the ones that follow.

The most celebrated *tortelli* with a tail, *Turtei cu la cua*, come from Piacenza and are stuffed not with meat, but with mascarpone cheese combined with ricotta and spinach, bound with Parmigiano, and egg yolks and egg. The twisting of the two ends of overlapping pasta to make the "tails" is reminiscent of the way some hard candies are wrapped (see page 246). They are dressed with either a butter–basil or tomato–basil sauce.

The *cappellacci* from Ferrara are stuffed with squash, like the *Tortelli di zucca* from nearby Modena. These stuffings are often approximated abroad with the use of pumpkin (sweet potato is an inappropriate substitution here). The squash used in Mantua and Ferrara is a large version of either butternut or acorn squash, widely available, so there

really is no need for a substitution. All these squashes originated in the New World and were taken to Italy, probably in the sixteenth century.

The most typical fresh *garganelli* are made with grated cheese in the pasta itself. These ridged, twisted short pasta work well with two characteristic dressings, one with a sweetish sauce made with boiled ham, *prosciutto cotto* (rather than the more common *prosciutto crudo*), butter, cream, and nutmeg; the other with the bacon-like smoked *pancetta*, in place of the more usual unsmoked version. The lightly smoked meat is combined with tomatoes, butter, and oil. Both are from Emilia-Romagna, as is this regional pasta.

The form of *cappelli* in the shape of a three-cornered hat, very popular in Tuscany a generation or two ago, have all but disappeared there, though they are said to be still used in parts of certain other northern regions. The way my family used to make them is described below, and I would be most grateful if the dish were revived. The stuffing with the pork meat is flavored with bay leaf and clove, *mollica*, eggs, and cheese. The Tuscan type of sauce we used was tomato flavored with sage, garlic, and olive oil. The pasta used was the basic Tuscan egg pasta with some oil in it. When we made it with a vegetable stuffing, artichokes formed its base, as can be seen from the variation included here.

Turtei cu la cua, the famous pasta from Emilia Romagna, is twisted to resemble a wrapped candy.

FROM PIACENZA
(EMILIA-
ROMAGNA)

SERVES 8

FOR THE STUFFING:
**2 pounds fresh spinach,
large stems removed**
Coarse-grained salt
¼ pound ricotta
**½ pound mascarpone
cheese or ¼ pound
ricotta blended with 1
cup heavy cream**
**½ cup freshly grated
Parmigiano cheese**
1 extra-large egg
3 extra-large egg yolks
**Salt and freshly ground
black pepper**
**Pinch of freshly grated
nutmeg**

TURTEI CU LA CUA
TORTELLI WITH A TAIL

Prepare the stuffing. Clean the spinach well, then soak in a bowl of cold water for 30 minutes. Bring a large pot of cold water to a boil. Add the coarse salt, then add the spinach and boil for 10 minutes. Drain the spinach and cool it under cold running water. When cool, squeeze spinach dry, finely chop on a board, and transfer to a glass or crockery bowl. Add the ricotta, mascarpone, Parmigiano, and egg and egg yolks to the bowl; mix all the ingredients with a wooden spoon. Season with salt, pepper, and nutmeg, and mix again to blend all the ingredients very well. Cover the bowl and refrigerate until needed.

Prepare the pasta with the ingredients and amounts listed, following the directions on page 14. Stretch the sheet of pasta to less than ¹⁄₁₆ inch thick, on the pasta machine take to the last notch. Cut into 4½- x 5½-inch rectangles, using a scalloped pastry wheel. Place 1 heaping tablespoon of the stuffing in the middle of each rectangle, fold the left third of the pasta over, then the right third. Holding the top and bottom of the pasta, twist one end to the left and the other to the right to make a shape resembling a

TURTEI CU LA CUA

1. Twist the ends of the stuffed pasta. Turn one end toward you,

2. the other end away from you. Be careful not to press the two layers of pasta too tightly together.

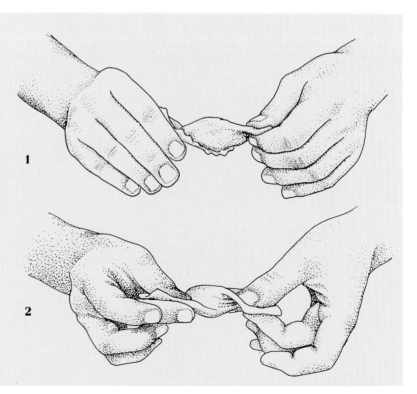

wrapped candy (see drawings). Let *turtei* rest on a floured wooden surface or cotton towel, being sure that they do not touch and stick together. If prepared in advance, turn them over once or twice.

Bring a large pot of cold water to a boil over medium heat. Place a large serving dish with the butter for the sauce on the pot as a lid. When the water reaches a boil, add coarse salt to taste, then add 5 to 10 *turtei* (depending on the size of the pot) and cook for 1 to 2 minutes depending on dryness. Use a strainer-skimmer to transfer the cooked pasta to the serving dish with the butter. Sprinkle some cheese over this first layer. Repeat the same procedure until all the *turtei* are cooked. On top of the last layer of pasta and Parmigiano, sprinkle the basil leaves and serve immediately.

If using the tomato sauce, heat the oil in a small saucepan over medium heat. When warm, add the garlic and sauté for 3 minutes. Discard the garlic, then add the tomatoes, cover, and cook for 20 minutes. Pass the contents of the saucepan through a food mill, using the disc with the smallest holes, into a different pan. Add salt and pepper to taste, and reduce over medium heat for 15 minutes more. Melt the butter and cook the pasta as for the main recipe, pouring the sauce on the top layer of pasta, then covering with Parmigiano and basil leaves.

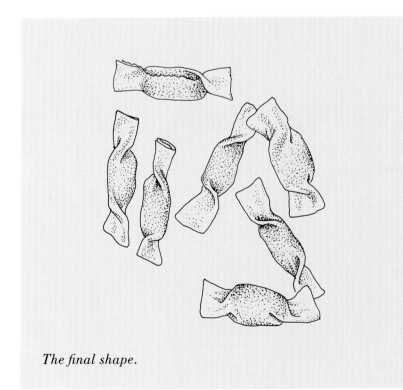

The final shape.

FOR THE PASTA:
3 cups unbleached all-purpose flour
4 extra-large eggs
Pinch of salt

FOR THE SAUCE:
8 ounces (16 tablespoons) sweet butter
1 cup freshly grated Parmigiano cheese
10 large fresh basil leaves

TO COOK THE PASTA:
Coarse-grained salt

VARIATION: *TURTEI* WITH TOMATO SAUCE

3 tablespoons olive oil
1 medium-sized clove garlic, peeled and left whole
2 pounds ripe, fresh tomatoes, cut in pieces; or 2 pounds canned tomatoes, preferably imported Italian, drained
Salt and freshly ground black pepper
4 ounces (8 tablespoons) sweet butter
1 cup freshly grated Parmigiano cheese
10 large fresh basil leaves

FROM EMILIA-
ROMAGNA

SERVES 6

FOR THE PASTA:
**½ cup freshly grated
  Parmigiano cheese**
**2 cups unbleached all-
  purpose flour**
3 extra-large eggs
Pinch of salt

FOR THE SAUCE:
**4 ounces boiled ham, in 1
  piece**
**6 tablespoons (3 ounces)
  sweet butter**
1 cup heavy cream
**Salt and freshly ground
  black pepper**
Freshly grated nutmeg
**1 cup fresh Parmigiano
  cheese**

TO COOK THE PASTA:
Coarse-grained salt

GARGANELLI AL PROSCIUTTO

GARGANELLI IN HAM SAUCE

Sift the cheese to be sure there are no lumps. Prepare the pasta with the ingredients and quantities listed, following the directions on page 14. Place the Parmigiano in the well with the other ingredients. When the ball of dough is formed, wrap it in a cotton dish towel and let it rest for 30 minutes in a cool place covered with a bowl. When ready, stretch the pasta to a very thin sheet, less than ¹⁄₁₆ inch thick, by hand or machine. Cut the sheet of pasta into 1½-inch squares, and prepare *garganelli* (see drawing).

Prepare the sauce. Cut the ham into pieces smaller than ½ inch. Place the butter in a large skillet over low heat; when the butter is melted, add the ham and sauté for 5 minutes, stirring every so often with a wooden spoon. Keep warm.

Bring a large pot of cold water to a boil, add coarse salt to taste, then add the pasta and cook for 1 to 3 minutes depending on dryness. Drain the pasta, add it to the skillet with the ham, and start adding the cream, a very small quantity at a time, constantly mixing with a wooden spoon. Season to taste with salt, pepper, and nutmeg, and when all the cream is incorporated (about 1 minute), sprinkle the cheese over, mix, and transfer immediately to a warmed platter and serve.

VARIATIONS

1. A pinch of grated nutmeg can be added to the dough along with the grated cheese.

2. Though the classic *garganelli* are made with Parmigiano in the dough, the pasta also exists in a form without cheese. Mix 2½ cups unbleached all-purpose flour, 3 extra-large eggs, 2 teaspoons cold water, and a pinch of salt.

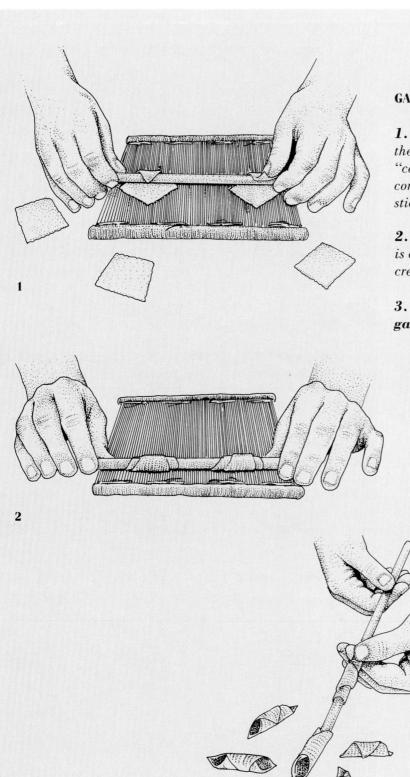

GARGANELLI

1. Place the pasta squares on the **pettine**, the traditional "comb" and, starting from one corner, wrap them around a stick.

2. Roll up the square until it is closed along the **pettine** to create ridged pattern.

3. Slip the finished **garganelli** off the stick.

1

2

3

FROM EMILIA-
ROMAGNA

SERVES 4 TO 6

½ **pound smoked**
pancetta; **or ½ pound**
bacon (not too smoky;
see Note), sliced
3 **tablespoons olive oil**
4 **tablespoons (2 ounces)**
sweet butter
1 **pound ripe, fresh**
tomatoes; or 1 pound
canned tomatoes,
preferably imported
Italian, drained
Salt and freshly ground
black pepper
1 **pound dried** *garganelli*,
preferably imported
from Italy or fresh
garganelli **(see page**
249)

TO COOK THE PASTA:
Coarse-grained salt

GARGANELLI CON PANCETTA AFFUMICATA

GARGANELLI WITH SMOKED *PANCETTA*

Cut the smoked *pancetta* or bacon into ½-inch pieces. Place a medium-sized skillet with the oil and butter over low heat. When the butter is completely melted, add the *pancetta* or bacon and sauté for 15 minutes, stirring every so often with a wooden spoon. Meanwhile, bring a large pot of cold water to a boil.

If using fresh tomatoes, cut them into pieces. Pass fresh or canned tomatoes through a food mill, using the disc with the smallest holes, into a crockery or glass bowl. Add tomatoes to the skillet with salt and pepper to taste, and simmer for 15 minutes more.

When the water reaches a boil, add the pasta and cook for 8 to 11 minutes depending on the brand; that is, 1 minute less than for normal al dente. Drain the pasta, add it to the skillet, raise the heat, and sauté for 1 minute. Transfer to a warmed platter and serve immediately. If fresh pasta is used, cook it from 30 seconds to 2½ minutes, depending on the dryness, then follow recipe as for dried pasta.

VARIATION
½ pound peas, shelled, parboiled in water, can be added to the tomatoes 5 minutes before they finish simmering.

NOTE:
Smoked *pancetta* is not widely available outside Italy, but bacon is just about the same thing and substitutes well.

CAPPELLACCI DI ZUCCA

CAPPELLACCI WITH SQUASH STUFFING

FROM FERRARA

SERVES 4 TO 6

Preheat the oven to 375 degrees. Prepare the stuffing. Bake the squash on a jelly-roll pan for 1 hour. Remove from the oven and cool for 30 minutes. Remove the peel, seeds, and filaments from the squash, then pass the pulp through a food mill, using the disc with medium-sized holes, into a crockery or glass bowl. Measure out 1 cup of the puréed pulp for the stuffing, put it in a crockery or glass bowl, and add the bread crumbs, egg and egg yolk, and Parmigiano. Season to taste with salt, pepper, and nutmeg, and mix well with a wooden spoon. Cover and place in the refrigerator until needed.

Prepare the pasta with the ingredients and quantities listed, following the instructions on page 14. Stretch the sheet of pasta to less than 1/16 inch thick, on the pasta machine take to last notch. Make *cappellacci* shaped like *ravioli*, 3 inches square, using 1 heaping teaspoon of the stuffing for each. Let them rest on cotton dish towels or paper towels for at least 15 minutes, turning them over at least once.

Bring a large pot of cold water to a boil, add coarse salt to taste, then add the *cappellacci* and cook for 1 to 3 minutes depending on dryness. Meanwhile, melt the butter in a double boiler and warm a large serving platter. Use a strainer-skimmer to transfer the pasta to the warmed platter. Make a layer of *cappellacci*, pour some of the melted butter over, and sprinkle on some of the cheese. Make another layer of the remaining pasta, butter, and cheese. Serve with a twist of black pepper.

FOR THE STUFFING:
1 medium-sized butternut squash
1/3 cup unseasoned bread crumbs, preferably homemade
1 extra-large egg
1 extra-large egg yolk
2/3 cup freshly grated Parmigiano cheese
Salt and freshly ground black pepper
Freshly grated nutmeg

FOR THE PASTA:
2 cups unbleached all-purpose flour
3 extra-large eggs
Pinch of salt

TO COOK THE PASTA:
Coarse-grained salt

TO SERVE:
8 tablespoons (4 ounces) sweet butter
3/4 cup freshly grated Parmigiano cheese
Freshly ground black pepper

FROM TUSCANY

SERVES 6 TO 8

CAPPELLI DEL PRETE (NICCHI)

"THREE-CORNERED HATS"

FOR THE STUFFING:

4 tablespoons (2 ounces) sweet butter
1 pound ground pork
2 bay leaves
2 whole cloves
Salt and freshly ground black pepper
3 extra-large eggs
2 slices white bread, crusts removed
¼ cup freshly grated Parmigiano cheese
Freshly grated nutmeg

FOR THE SAUCE:

2 pounds ripe, fresh tomatoes; or 2 pounds canned tomatoes, preferably imported Italian, drained
5 large sage leaves, fresh or preserved in salt
1 medium-sized clove garlic, peeled and left whole
¼ cup olive oil
Salt and freshly ground black pepper

FOR THE PASTA:

3 cups unbleached all-purpose flour
3 extra-large eggs
3 tablespoons olive or vegetable oil
Pinch of salt

TO COOK THE PASTA:

Coarse-grained salt

TO SERVE:

Freshly grated Parmigiano cheese (optional)

Begin the stuffing. Melt the butter in a small saucepan over low heat, then add the pork, bay leaves, and cloves. Sauté for 10 minutes, mixing with a wooden spoon; season to taste with salt and pepper. Remove from the stove, transfer to a crockery or glass bowl, and set aside until cool, about 30 minutes.

Break the eggs in a crockery or glass bowl and lightly beat them with a fork. Crumble the bread into the eggs to soak for 30 minutes.

Begin the sauce. If using fresh tomatoes, cut them into pieces. Put fresh or canned tomatoes in a medium-sized flameproof casserole with the sage, garlic, and oil, and simmer over medium heat for 45 minutes.

Finish the stuffing. Discard the bay leaves and cloves, and transfer the meat and all the juices to the bowl with the eggs. Season with salt, pepper, and nutmeg to taste, and thoroughly mix the ingredients with a wooden spoon. Cover the bowl and refrigerate until needed.

Prepare the pasta with the ingredients and quantities listed, following the directions on page 14. Stretch the sheet of pasta to less than 1/16 inch thick, on the hand pasta machine take to the finest setting. Cut dough into 4 pieces and stretch one sheet of dough at a time, so the rest does not dry out while you are filling and shaping the *nicchi*. Cut each sheet of pasta into a 6-inch square, then use a knife to cut each diagonally into 2 triangles (see drawings). Place 1 heaping tablespoon of stuffing in the center of each triangle, then fold the longer side in half, pressing the edges together very well to seal them. Holding the top point between the right hand thumb and index finger, with the other hand lift the point of the free side to meet the others 1 inch from the top. Seal both sides to close the triangle completely. The resultant shape resembles an old "tricorno," or three-cornered hat, with the top end able to flop over like a feather. Let the *nicchi* rest on cotton towels until needed.

Finish the sauce. Pass the contents of the casserole through a food mill, using the disc with the smallest holes, into a crockery or glass bowl. Transfer back to the casserole, taste for salt and pepper, and reduce over medium heat for 15 minutes more.

Bring a large quantity of cold water to a boil, add coarse salt to taste, then add the *nicchi* carefully, one by one, and cook for 8 to 12 minutes depending on dryness.* Meanwhile, pour some of the sauce onto a warmed platter. When the pasta is ready, transfer to the platter with a strainer-skimmer, being careful to let all the

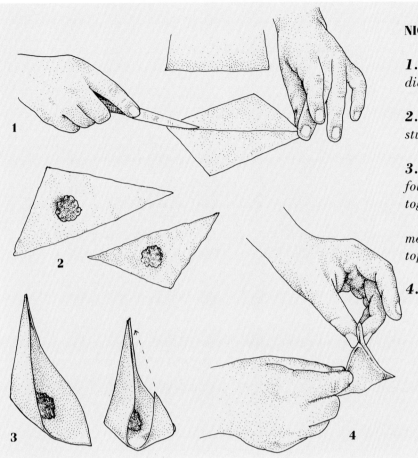

NICCHI

1. *Cut the pasta squares diagonally into triangles.*

2. *The triangles with the stuffing in the center.*

3. *a) The longer sides are folded in half and pressed together.*

b) Lift the shorter side to meet the other 1 inch from the top.

4. *Seal all the sides well.*

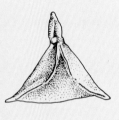

water drain off. Serve hot with the remaining sauce served on the side, with or without cheese.

For the artichoke stuffing, clean the artichokes according to the directions on page 67, and cut them into eighths. Place them in a bowl of cold water with the lemon halves, and let rest for 30 minutes. Heat the oil in a medium-sized flameproof casserole over low heat; when the oil is warm, drain the artichokes and add to casserole. Sauté for 5 minutes, then add some of the broth, cover, and cook for 15 minutes. Season with salt and pepper, and keep adding broth as needed until the artichokes are cooked. Use a strainer-skimmer to transfer the artichokes to a crockery or glass bowl and set aside until cool, about 30 minutes. Coarsely chop the artichokes on a board, transfer to a crockery or glass bowl, add the eggs and Parmigiano, then taste for salt and pepper and mix very well. Use a heaping tablespoon of the stuffing for each of the *nicchi*.

VARIATION

ARTICHOKE STUFFING
3 large artichokes
1 large lemon, cut in half
4 tablespoons olive oil
Salt and freshly ground black pepper
1 cup lukewarm chicken or beef broth, preferably homemade
3 extra-large eggs
¼ cup freshly grated Parmigiano cheese

* The long cooking time is necessary because of the thickness produced when several ends of pasta are pressed together in the many corners.

UMBRIA

Hilly Umbria has maintained some of its traditional pastas more than some other, less rustic regions. Long, thick *ciriole*, sometimes called *umbrici*, are made with semolina mixed with white flour and do not include eggs. (None of the following Umbrian specialties are made with eggs.) *Ciriole* are as thick as the *bucatini* of the South, but do not have holes through the center. Umbrians like a tomato sauce spiced with hot red pepper, which appears here in the version from Terni.

Umbrici may also be hand-rolled and are made by using the same technique as the *Pinci* of Montalcino. In the version here, in a basil-flavored tomato sauce and ricotta, they are probably rolled a little thinner than those in the *ciriole* recipe. Even with this sauce, hot red pepper is an option.

Stringozzi are rolled thick before cutting, sometimes giving a square shape to the width of the string-like pasta. They are typical of the Spoleto area, but share with other Umbrian specialties the spicy sauce and the combination with ricotta, usually homemade in these areas. A special feature of this Spoleto recipe is the rosemary flavoring.

CIRIOLE ALLA TERNANA

PASTA FROM TERNI

FROM TERNI
(UMBRIA)

SERVES 6

Prepare the pasta. Mix the semolina flour with ½ cup of the all-purpose flour, then prepare the dough following the instructions on page 14, kneading for at least 15 minutes. Wrap the dough in a cheesecloth and let rest for 30 minutes covered by a bowl. Spread out the remaining ¼ cup of flour on a board and, using a rolling pin, stretch the pasta dough into a sheet a little more than ⅛ inch thick and about 18 inches long. Let the sheet of pasta rest until a thin film forms, then cut *taglierini*, using a cutter (see page 34) or by hand. The result should resemble a thicker and longer *spaghetti*. These are *ciriole*. Let the pasta rest on cotton dish towels until needed.

Prepare the sauce. Cut the garlic into small pieces, then place the oil in a medium-sized flameproof casserole over low heat. When the oil is warm, add the garlic and sauté until lightly golden, about 5 minutes. Meanwhile, if using fresh tomatoes, blanch them in salted boiling water, remove seeds, and cut flesh into fourths or eighths—"filleto." If using canned tomatoes, pass them through a food mill, using the disc with smallest holes, into a crockery or glass bowl. Add tomatoes to the casserole and season with salt, pepper, and the red pepper flakes. Simmer for 35 minutes, stirring every so often with a wooden spoon.

Bring a large pot of cold water to a boil, add coarse salt to taste, then add the pasta and cook for 1 to 3 minutes depending on dryness. Drain the pasta, transfer to a warmed serving dish, pour the sauce over, mix well, and serve immediately.

FOR THE PASTA:
1¾ cups semolina flour
¾ cup unbleached all-purpose flour
1 cup lukewarm water
Pinch of salt

FOR THE SAUCE:
2 large cloves garlic, peeled
¼ cup olive oil
1½ pounds ripe, fresh tomatoes; or 1½ pounds canned tomatoes, preferably imported Italian, drained
Salt and freshly ground black pepper
½ teaspoon hot red pepper flakes

TO COOK THE PASTA:
Coarse-grained salt

FROM UMBRIA

SERVES 4 TO 6

FOR THE PASTA:
3 cups unbleached all-purpose flour
1 cup cold water
1 tablespoon olive oil or vegetable oil
Pinch of salt
        or
1 pound dried *spaghetti*, preferably imported Italian

FOR THE SAUCE:
2 medium-sized cloves garlic, peeled and left whole
4 tablespoons olive oil
1½ pounds ripe, fresh tomatoes; or 1½ pounds canned tomatoes, preferably imported Italian, drained
6 large basil leaves, fresh or preserved in salt
Salt and freshly ground black pepper
½ teaspoon hot red pepper flakes (optional)

TO COOK THE PASTA:
Coarse-grained salt

TO SERVE:
15 ounces ricotta, preferably homemade (page 348) or commercial
Freshly ground black pepper

UMBRICI CON POMODORO E RICOTTA
UMBRIAN *PINCI* WITH RICOTTA AND TOMATO SAUCE

Prepare the pasta with the ingredients and quantities listed, following the directions on page 14. Prepare *umbrici (pinci)* (see drawings), and let pasta rest on cotton dish towels until needed.

Prepare the sauce. Place a medium-sized flameproof casserole over medium heat. Add the garlic, olive oil, tomatoes, and basil; simmer for 30 minutes, stirring every so often with a wooden spoon. Pass the contents of the casserole through a food mill, using the disc with the smallest holes, into a crockery or glass bowl. Return the sauce to the casserole and simmer over low heat for 15 minutes, seasoning to taste with salt and pepper. If using red pepper flakes, add them at this point.

Bring a large pot of cold water to a boil, add coarse salt to taste, then add the pasta and cook for 1 to 3 minutes depending on dryness. As the pasta cooks, arrange the ricotta in a flat layer over the surface of a large serving platter. Drain the pasta, arrange it over the ricotta, then pour the tomato sauce over everything and mix well. Serve with several twists of black pepper.

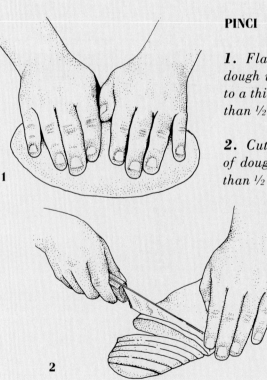

PINCI

1. *Flatten the ball of dough with both hands to a thickness of less than ½ inch.*

2. *Cut the thick layer of dough into strips less than ½ inch wide.*

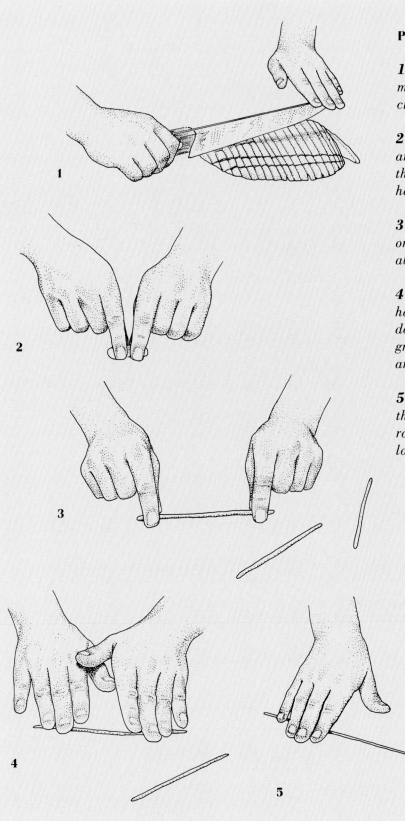

PINCI

1. *Cut across the pasta, making the strips into small cubes.*

2. *Take an individual cube, and, holding it between the thumbs and first fingers of both hands, pinch the cube*

3. *so that it extends sideways only, into a non-rounded strip about 3 inches long.*

4. *With the 4 fingers of both hands, lightly roll the strip of dough, moving both hands gradually apart from the center and*

5. *to the sides. Keep repeating this motion until the strip is rounded and about 9 inches long.*

STRINGOZZI AL POMODORO

STRINGOZZI WITH SPICY TOMATO SAUCE

FOR THE PASTA:
3 cups unbleached all-purpose flour
1 cup cold water
1 tablespoon olive oil or vegetable oil
Pinch of salt

FOR THE SAUCE:
2 pounds ripe fresh tomatoes; or 2 pounds canned tomatoes, preferably imported Italian, drained.
2 large cloves garlic, peeled
1 heaping teaspoon rosemary leaves—fresh, preserved in salt, or dried and blanched
¼ cup olive oil
Salt and freshly ground black pepper
½ teaspoon hot red pepper flakes

TO COOK THE PASTA:
Coarse-grained salt

TO SERVE:
15 ounces ricotta
¼ cup olive oil
¼ cup freshly grated pecorino romano cheese

Prepare the pasta with the ingredients and quantities listed above, following instructions on page 14, prepare *pinci* (see page 256) and let rest on cotton dish towels until needed.

Prepare the sauce. If using fresh tomatoes, cut them into large pieces. Place fresh or canned tomatoes in a medium-sized saucepan. Finely chop garlic and rosemary together, add them to the pan along with the oil, and place the pan over medium heat for half an hour, stirring every so often with a wooden spoon. Pass the contents of the pan through a food mill, using the disc with the smallest holes, into a crockery or glass bowl. Return the passed tomatoes to pan, add salt, pepper, and the red pepper flakes, and let simmer for 15 minutes more.

Bring a large pot of cold water to a boil and reheat the sauce over low heat. Place the ricotta in a crockery or glass bowl, season with salt and pepper, then start adding the oil and cheese little by little, constantly mixing with a wooden spoon, until all the oil and cheese are integrated.

When the water reaches a boil, add coarse-grained salt to taste, then the pasta, and cook it from 1 to 3 minutes depending on the dryness. Combine the tomato sauce with the ricotta mixture. Drain pasta, transfer it to a large serving dish, and add the sauce and mix very well, putting in a little of the pasta water if the sauce is too thick. Season with more freshly ground black pepper and serve.

ABRUZZI

Throughout Abruzzi, the regional pasta is cut with the "guitar." For the sauce, the lamb is cut into sizable cubes, and red wine, onion, rosemary, and *pancetta* are used (see Recipe Appendix for a reference to another version). The hot red pepper so typical of the region is also used in the sauce. (See page 261 for the technique of making the *maccheroni* and cutting it with the "guitar.")

The *scripelle* or *crespelle* used for the stuffed *lasagne* made during Carnival time in the Abruzzi version are also used simply, rolled up with a Parmigiano stuffing and eaten in a rich broth. More Parmigiano may be sprinkled over.

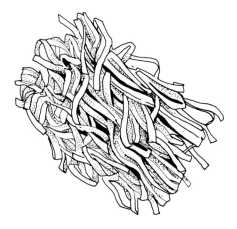

FROM ABRUZZI

SERVES 6 TO 8

MACCHERONI ALLA CHITARRA SULL'AGNELLO

MACCHERONI CUT WITH THE "GUITAR," WITH LAMB CUBES AND *PANCETTA* SAUCE

FOR THE SAUCE:

1½ pounds boneless lamb
   shoulder
1 medium-sized red onion,
   peeled
1 teaspoon rosemary
   leaves, fresh, preserved
   in salt, or dried and
   blanched
4 ounces *pancetta* or
   prosciutto, in 1 piece
¼ cup olive oil
½ cup dry red wine
2 tablespoons tomato paste
2 cups lukewarm chicken
   or beef broth, preferably
   homemade
Salt and freshly ground
   black pepper
½ teaspoon hot red pepper
   flakes

FOR THE PASTA:

4 cups unbleached all-
   purpose flour
5 extra-large eggs
Pinch of salt

TO COOK THE PASTA:

Coarse-grained salt

TO SERVE:

¾ cup freshly grated
   pecorino or Parmigiano
   cheese

Cut the lamb into 1-inch cubes. Finely chop the onion and rose-mary together on a board. Cut the *pancetta* or *prosciutto* into ½-inch cubes. Place a heavy, medium-sized flameproof casserole, preferably of terra-cotta or enamel, with the olive oil over low heat. When the oil is warm, add the chopped ingredients and the *pancetta* or *prosciutto*. Sauté for 10 minutes, then add the lamb, mix well, and cook for 5 minutes more. Pour in the wine and let it evaporate for 5 minutes. Dissolve the tomato paste in 1 cup of the broth and add to the casserole. Season to taste with salt, pepper, and the red pepper flakes; simmer, covered, for 1 hour, stirring every so often with a wooden spoon. Add the remaining cup of broth, and simmer, still covered, for 1 hour more. Remove the lid, taste for salt and pepper, raise the heat and cook for 5 minutes more.

As the sauce is simmering, prepare the pasta with the ingredients and quantities listed, following the directions on page 14. Stretch layer to ⅛ inch thick; on the pasta machine take to several notches before last. Prepare the *maccheroni* cut with the "guitar" (see drawings), cutting the layer into pieces 2 inches shorter than the length of the guitar. Let the pasta rest on cotton dish towels until needed.

When the sauce is almost ready, bring a large quantity of cold water to a boil, add coarse salt to taste, then add the pasta and cook for 1 to 3 minutes depending on dryness. Meanwhile, warm a large serving platter and ladle half the sauce onto the platter. Drain the pasta, arrange it over the sauce, pour the remaining sauce over, and sprinkle on the cheese. Mix well and serve.

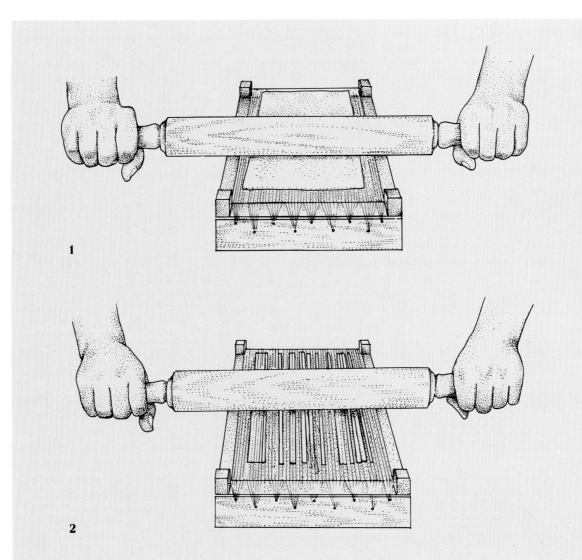

MACCHERONI ALLA CHITARRA

1. *Place a piece of pasta, about 12 inches long, on the guitar, leaving about 2 inches free on each end of the guitar. Roll back*

2. *and forth with a rolling pin.*

3. *"Play" the guitar, drawing your thumb across the string until all the loosened strips fall through onto the tray below.*

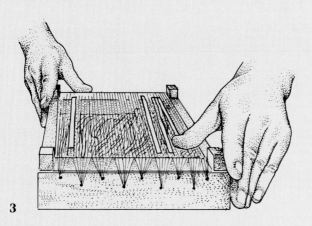

FROM ABRUZZI

SERVES 6 TO 8

SCRIPELLE 'MBUSSE (CRESPELLE IN BRODO)
CRÊPES IN BROTH

FOR THE BATTER:
½ cup unbleached all-
   purpose flour
2 extra-large eggs
½ cup plus 2 tablespoons
   cold milk
Pinch of salt
10 large sprigs Italian
   parsley, leaves only,
   finely chopped

TO COOK/STUFF THE
CRESPELLE:
2 tablespoons (1 ounce)
   sweet butter or olive oil
16 tablespoons freshly
   grated Parmigiano
   cheese

TO SERVE:
2 quarts defatted chicken
   or beef broth, preferably
   homemade
Freshly grated Parmigiano
   cheese

Prepare the *crespelle*. Use the ingredients listed, and follow the instructions on page 166. Add the parsley to the batter.

Use a 4-inch crêpe pan and less than 2 tablespoons of batter to form each *crespella*. As each is cooked, sprinkle over 1 teaspoon of Parmigiano, then roll it up and put it on a large serving dish. When all the *crespelle* are prepared, bring the broth to a boil over medium heat. Place 2 or 3 rolled-up *crespelle* in each soup bowl and pour 1 cup of broth over each portion.

VARIATIONS

1. The Parmigiano used for the stuffing can be incorporated directly into the batter instead of sprinkling it over the already cooked *crespelle*; increase milk to 1 cup.

2. A local, fresh pecorino cheese is sometimes used instead of grated Parmigiano in Abruzzi. It is spread over the *crespelle* before rolling. No grated cheese is then used at all.

NOTE:
Black pepper is absolutely not used in any authentic version of this batter.

SARDINIA

The pasta for the interesting Sardinian *ravioli*, *culingionis*, contains both semolina and white flours, but varies in the amount of semolina included. The one with the ricotta–mint stuffing uses equal amounts of each, while that for the eggplant stuffing uses only a tiny bit of semolina, though there is some in the stuffing itself. Saffron is added to both pastas as is a little water, cold in one case, lukewarm in the other. An unusual feature is that the first pasta uses mostly egg whites and only one whole egg. The other uses only egg yolks. And so we see there is infinite variety in the way pasta is traditionally made, and it is enlightening to ponder why the pasta is varied for each particular stuffing.

Fresh mint is an important feature of both Sardinian stuffings and it is used abundantly. The other special feature is the use of saffron, in both pastas and in some cases the stuffing itself. A light tomato sauce is favored for these pastas, with the addition of basil, which combines well with the flavor of mint.

Malloreddus, the Sardinian short pasta, is ridged with a little opening in the center. The technique for making them follows. Dried *malloreddus* are now widely exported and are easily available outside of Sardinia. As usual, saffron may be included in the dough itself and most of the flour is semolina with a little white flour added.

The favored tomato sauce for *malloreddus* combines onion, garlic, and abundant basil. An alternative sausage dressing combines bay leaves, garlic, basil, and some saffron in the sauce itself. Sausage made with fennel seeds is appropriate for this recipe.

The Sardinian version of the large wheels of pecorino romano type, often called sardo for short, is the right cheese for these dishes and is widely available.

CULINGIONIS *OR* CULURZONES *OR* CULURJONES

SARDINIAN *RAVIOLI*

FOR THE STUFFING:
15 ounces ricotta
4 extra-large egg yolks
30 large fresh mint leaves,
  torn into thirds
Salt and freshly ground
  black pepper
Generous pinch of ground
  saffron

FOR THE PASTA:
1½ cups finely ground
  semolina flour
1½ cups unbleached all-
  purpose flour
4 extra-large egg whites
1 extra-large egg
⅛ teaspoon ground saffron
¼ cup cold water
Pinch of salt
All-purpose flour for
  rolling out pasta

FOR THE SAUCE:
2 pounds ripe, fresh
  tomatoes
Coarse-grained salt
10 large sprigs Italian
  parsley, leaves only
2 large stalks celery
5 large basil leaves, fresh
  or preserved in salt
½ cup olive oil
Salt and freshly ground
  black pepper

TO COOK THE PASTA:
Coarse-grained salt

TO SERVE:
1 cup freshly grated
  pecorino sardo cheese

Prepare the stuffing. Place the ricotta in a cheesecloth square, and let it hang, draining very well to remove all excess water. Place the ricotta in a crockery or glass bowl, add the egg yolks, mint leaves, salt and pepper to taste, and saffron. Mix all the ingredients, then cover the bowl with aluminum foil and refrigerate until needed.

Prepare the pasta with the ingredients and quantities listed, following the directions on page 14. Wrap the dough in a cotton dish towel and let rest for 30 minutes in a cool place under a bowl or on the bottom shelf of the refrigerator.

Prepare the sauce. Blanch the tomatoes in salted boiling water, slip off skins, then cut them into fourths and seed them. Coarsely chop the parsley, celery, and basil on a board. Place the oil in a medium-sized saucepan over medium heat, and when the oil is warm, add the chopped ingredients and sauté for 10 minutes. Put in the tomatoes and salt and pepper to taste, cover, and cook for 15 minutes, stirring every so often with a wooden spoon. Let sauce stand, covered, until needed.

Use about ¼ cup of all-purpose flour to roll out the pasta until very thin, less than ¹⁄₁₆ inch thick, on the pasta machine take to the last notch. Prepare 2-inch *ravioli*, and fill each with 1 heaping teaspoon of stuffing (see page 113). Let the *culingionis* rest on cotton dish towels until needed, turning them several times while drying, to keep them from sticking.

Bring a large pot of cold water to a boil, add coarse salt to taste, then add the *ravioli* a few at a time, and cook for 1 to 3 minutes depending on dryness. Meanwhile, reheat the sauce and warm a serving dish. When the pasta is ready, use a strainer-skimmer to transfer to the warmed dish. Make a layer of the *culingionis*, sprinkle over some of the sauce and the cheese, and keep making layers of pasta with sauce and cheese until all is on the dish. Serve immediately.

Culingionis, the Sardinian stuffed pasta with authentic Sardinian shawl embroidered with gold and silver, worn on festive occasions. Note the hand-crafted rooster-shaped wine pitcher on the side.

CULINGIONIS DI MELANZANE

RAVIOLI STUFFED WITH EGGPLANT

FOR THE STUFFING:
**4 medium-sized eggplants
(2 pounds), cleaned and
peeled
Coarse-grained salt
3 cups vegetable oil
¼ cup olive oil
2 tablespoons very fine
semolina flour
2 extra-large eggs
2 extra-large egg yolks**

Begin the stuffing. Peel the eggplants, cut them into 1-inch cubes, place them on a large serving platter, and sprinkle with 2 table-spoons of coarse salt. Place a second platter on the eggplant as a weight and let rest for 30 minutes. Rinse the eggplant under cold running water to remove all the salt, and dry with paper towels. Place the vegetable and olive oils in a deep-fat fryer over medium heat. When the oil is hot (375 degrees), add the eggplant and fry until lightly golden all over, about 4 minutes. Transfer to a large serving platter lined with paper towels to drain excess oil; let rest until cool, about 30 minutes.

Begin the sauce. If using fresh tomatoes, cut them into pieces.

Place a heavy, medium-sized casserole over medium heat. Add the fresh or canned tomatoes, basil, and olive oil and simmer for 30 minutes.

Finish the stuffing. Transfer the eggplant to a crockery or glass bowl; add the semolina flour, eggs and egg yolks, cheese, and mint leaves. Mix very well and season with pepper only, since the cheese is salty. Cover the bowl and refrigerate until needed.

Prepare the pasta with the ingredients and quantities listed, following the directions on page 14, but placing the semolina flour in the flour well along with the egg yolks, the saffron dissolved in the water, and salt. Let the dough rest, wrapped in a cotton dish towel and tightly covered by a bowl, for 30 minutes.

Finish the sauce. Pass the tomatoes through a food mill, using the disc with smallest holes, into a second flameproof casserole and reduce over low heat for 5 minutes more, seasoning to taste with salt and pepper. Set aside.

Stretch the sheet of pasta to very thin, less than 1/16 inch thick, on a pasta machine take to the finest setting. Prepare *culingionis* (round *tortelli* or *ravioli*, page 113; see Note) with a 2-inch diameter. Use a heaping teaspoon of stuffing for each, placed in the center of the disc of pasta, and then fold the pasta over. Let *culingionis* rest on floured cotton dish towels until needed.

Bring a large pot of cold water to a boil, add coarse salt to taste, then add the *culingionis* and cook for 6 to 9 minutes depending on dryness (semolina requires a long cooking time). As the pasta cooks, reheat the sauce and then spoon some onto a large, warmed serving platter. Add some of the cooked *culingionis* and repeat the layers of sauce and pasta until all the *culingionis* are on the platter. Add a final layer of tomato sauce and serve hot, with just a teaspoon of cheese sprinkled over each serving.

NOTE:
Ravioli and *tortelli* can be either round or square.

1 cup grated pecorino romano or pecorino romano sardo cheese
40 large fresh mint leaves, torn into thirds
Freshly ground black pepper

FOR THE SAUCE:
3 pounds ripe, fresh tomatoes; or 3 pounds canned tomatoes, preferably imported Italian, drained
10 large basil leaves, fresh or preserved in salt
1/2 cup olive oil
Salt and freshly ground black pepper

FOR THE PASTA:
3 cups unbleached all-purpose flour
1/4 cup very fine semolina flour
3 extra-large egg yolks
Pinch of ground saffron, or threads ground with marble mortar and pestle, dissolved in 1 cup lukewarm water
Pinch of salt

TO COOK THE PASTA:
Coarse-grained salt

TO SERVE:
6 to 8 teaspoons freshly grated pecorino romano or pecorino romano sardo cheese

FROM SARDINIA

SERVES 6

2½ cups very fine semolina
   flour
½ cup unbleached all-
   purpose flour
Pinch of salt
Pinch of home-ground
   saffron (threads ground
   with marble mortar and
   pestle)
1 cup lukewarm water

HOMEMADE MALLOREDDUS

Place the semolina flour in a mound on a pasta board, make a well
in it, then place the all-purpose flour in the well. Dissolve the salt
and saffron in the lukewarm water, then pour the water into the
well of the flour. Prepare a ball of dough and knead it for 15 minutes, following the directions on page 14. Divide the dough into
several pieces and use your hands to roll out long cords about ½
inch in diameter. Cut the cords into pieces the size of chick-peas.
Use the special straw screen, the *cuiliri* (see drawing), to shape the
individual *malloreddus*, using the same technique as for making
gnocchi (see page 314). Let the *malloreddus* rest on floured cotton
dish towels until needed.

VARIATION
The saffron can be omitted. Also, 1 tablespoon of tomato paste or
boiled, finely chopped spinach can be substituted.

NOTE:
If you do not have a *cuilini*, you can shape the *malloreddus* with a
fork or hand cheese grater (see *gnocchi*).

MALLOREDDUS

1. *Roll out the
dough in a cord about
a half inch in
diameter (with some
of the pieces already
cut the size of a chick
pea).*

2. *Use the
traditional straw
screen to shape the
individual
malloreddus using
the thumb with the
same cursive "c"
motion as for shaping
gnocchi.*

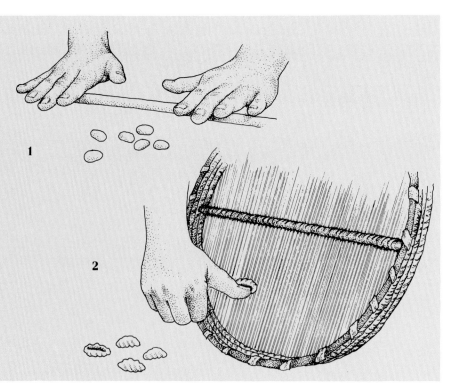

MALLOREDDUS CON SUGO DI POMODORO

MALLOREDDUS WITH SARDINIAN TOMATO SAUCE

Prepare the sauce. Finely chop the onion and garlic together on a board. Place the oil in a medium-sized saucepan over low heat, and when the oil is warm, add the chopped ingredients and sauté for 10 minutes. If using fresh tomatoes, cut them into pieces. Pass fresh or canned tomatoes through a food mill, using the disc with the smallest holes, into a crockery or glass bowl. Add the tomatoes and salt and pepper to taste, and simmer for 25 minutes, stirring every so often with a wooden spoon.

Bring a large pot of cold water to a boil, add coarse salt to taste, then add the pasta and cook dried pasta for 10 minutes or 6 to 10 minutes for homemade pasta, depending on dryness. Drain the pasta, transfer to the saucepan with the sauce, add the basil leaves torn into thirds, and let the sauce be absorbed by the *malloreddus*, simmering it over low heat for 1 minute more, stirring constantly. Serve with cheese.

VARIATION

Onion can be omitted, and 25 sprigs of Italian parsley leaves chopped together with the garlic can be added.

FOR THE SAUCE:
1 medium-sized white or red onion, peeled
1 medium-sized clove garlic, peeled
½ cup olive oil
1½ pounds ripe, fresh tomatoes; or 1½ pounds canned tomatoes, preferaby imported Italian, drained
Salt and freshly ground black pepper
20 large basil leaves, fresh or preserved in salt

FOR THE PASTA:
1 pound dried *malloreddus* or home-made *malloreddus* (page 268)

TO COOK THE PASTA:
Coarse-grained salt

TO SERVE:
Freshly grated pecorino romano sardo or pecorino romano cheese

Malloreddus alla
campidanese: White
and saffron colored
melloreddus with a rich
sausage sauce. Note
the flat Sardinian bread
on the side.

MALLOREDDUS ALLA CAMPIDANESE

SARDINIAN PASTA WITH SAUSAGES

1½ pounds ripe, fresh
   tomatoes
Coarse-grained salt
4 sweet Italian sausages
   with fennel seeds or
   without (about 1 pound)
½ cup olive oil
2 large cloves garlic,
   peeled but left whole
2 bay leaves
5 large basil leaves, fresh
   or preserved in salt
Pinch of ground saffron
Salt and freshly ground
   black pepper
1 pound dried
   malloreddus (containing
   some *malloreddus*
   prepared with saffron),
   preferably imported
   Italian

TO COOK THE PASTA:
Coarse-grained salt

TO SERVE:
¾ cup freshly grated
   pecorino sardo cheese

Blanch the tomatoes in boiling salted water, slip off the skins, then cut them into quarters and seed them. Cut the sausages into thirds. Place the oil in a heavy saucepan over low heat, and when the oil is warm, add the sausages and sauté until completely cooked, about 10 minutes. Use a slotted spoon to transfer the sausages to a bowl and cover with aluminum foil. Add the garlic to the pan and sauté for 4 minutes. Remove and discard the garlic, then add the tomatoes along with the bay leaves, basil, and saffron. Cook for 15 minutes, stirring every so often with a wooden spoon. Taste for salt and pepper.

Meanwhile, bring a large pot of cold water to a boil, add coarse salt to taste, then add the *malloreddus* and cook until still al dente, about 15 minutes depending on the brand. Drain the *malloreddus* and add to the saucepan, mixing very well and letting them incorporate all the sauce over low heat. Add the reserved sausages, mix well, and simmer for at least 2 or 3 minutes. Each portion consists of some *malloreddus*, sausage pieces, and a generous tablespoon of the cheese.

PUGLIA

Cavatelli (*cavatieddi* in dialect), along with *orecchiette*, the little "ear-shaped" pasta, are regional contributions of Puglia. Both are made with a combination of semolina and white flour and are also related in the way they are made, though the little dough pieces are shaped with the thumb in *orecchiette* and formed with a cursive movement like *gnocchi* or *malloreddus* for *cavatieddi*.

A very popular dish is the *cavatieddi* combined with cooked arugula, dressed with a tomato sauce containing onion, garlic, and olive oil, with grated pecorino sprinkled over. A number of greens eaten only in salad in most places are also cooked in Italy. Lettuce is a good example, forming the basis for a delicious soup. The cooked arugula is excellent and its peppery bitterness combines well with the substantial semolina pasta.

Stracnar, attractive pasta rectangles, which are patterned in herringbone with a suggestive antique board called a *cavarola*, are another contribution of Puglia. Again, some semolina is mixed in with the white flour, but the pasta is rich with egg. This is another of those great old pastas that must be made manually and is disappearing, but let us work to revive it. The Pugliese name is actually *stracenate*, while I have used the better-known name from Lucania, where it is also made. The sauce is made with halved cherry tomatoes (another Puglian speciality), anchovy, and little croutons, which probably represent the *midolla* or "marrow" of the name.

Troccoli are made fresh with a ridged rolling pin, which cuts them into a shape resembling *spaghetti*. This implement is called a *troccolo* and is native to the town of Foggia. The pasta is made with white flour and eggs, but no oil. The sauce combines a mixture of eggs and pecorino cheese grated with the separately cooked tomato, flavored with garlic and olive oil and, most special of all, abundant asparagus pieces.

Stracnar con la midolla:
The rich patterned
pasta surrounded by old
implements for making
pasta from Southern
Italy such as *cavarola,
troccolo*.

FROM APULIA

SERVES 4 TO 6

CAVATIEDDI CON LA RUCOLA
CAVATELLI WITH ARUGULA

FOR THE PASTA:
1½ cups unbleached all-
purpose flour
1 cup very fine semolina
flour
1 cup lukewarm water
Pinch of salt

FOR THE SAUCE:
1 large red onion, peeled
1 large clove garlic, peeled
½ cup olive oil
2 pounds ripe, fresh
tomatoes; or 2 pounds
canned tomatoes,
preferably imported
Italian, drained
Salt and freshly ground
black pepper

FOR THE ARUGULA:
1½ pounds arugula
(rocket), large stems
removed and leaves
washed

TO COOK THE PASTA:
Coarse-grained salt

TO SERVE:
¾ cup freshly grated
pecorino romano or
pecorino romano sardo
(optional)

Begin the pasta. Mix the flours, arrange in a mound, and make a well. Add the lukewarm water and salt, and prepare a ball of dough following the instructions on page 14. Keep kneading the dough for 10 minutes, then wrap it in a cotton dish towel and let it rest, covered with a bowl, for 30 minutes.

Prepare the sauce. Finely chop the onion and garlic together on a board. Put the olive oil in a medium-sized saucepan over medium heat. When the oil is warm, add the chopped ingredients and sauté for 10 minutes, stirring every so often with a wooden spoon. If using fresh tomatoes, cut them into pieces. Pass fresh or canned tomatoes through a food mill, using the disc with smallest holes, into a crockery or glass bowl and add them to the pan. Season with salt and pepper, and cook over medium heat for 20 minutes more, stirring every so often.

Finish the pasta. Take a small piece of dough and use your hands to roll out a cord not more than ½ inch thick; cut it into pieces the size of a chick-pea. Use a butter knife with a round tip to shape the individual *cavatelli*, making the same curling "c" motion as when preparing *gnocchi*, but doing it against a board instead of a grater (see page 313). Let the *cavatelli* rest on a floured cotton dish towel until needed.

Place the arugula in cold water to soak until needed. Bring a large pot of cold water to a boil, add coarse salt to taste, then add the pasta and cook for 9 to 12 minutes depending on dryness. After the pasta has been cooking for 5 minutes, drain the arugula, add it to the pot, and mix well. When the pasta is ready, drain the pasta and arugula together; transfer to a large, warmed serving platter, add the sauce, toss well, and serve, with or without cheese.

VARIATIONS
1. The garlic can be left whole, sautéed with the chopped onion, and discarded when the sauce is ready.
2. A large pinch of hot red pepper flakes can be added to the sauce together with the salt and pepper.

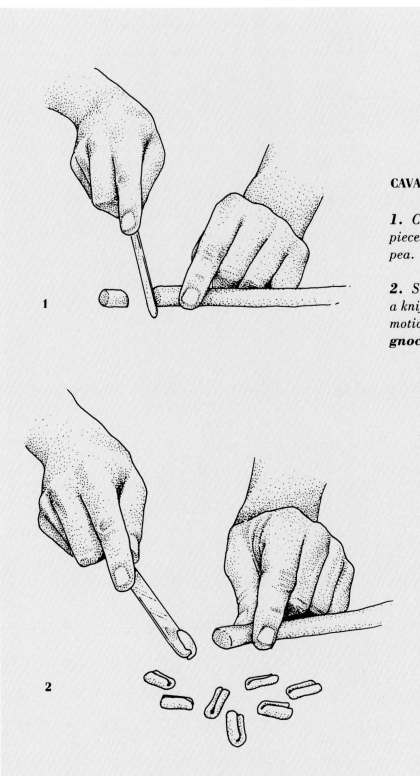

CAVATELLI

1. Cut the cord of dough into pieces about the size of a chick pea.

2. Shape the **cavatelli** using a knife in the same cursive "c" motion used for shaping **gnocchi**.

FROM APULIA

SERVES 6 TO 8

Stracnar con la Midolla

PATTERNED PASTA WITH CHERRY TOMATOES AND CROUTONS

FOR THE PASTA:
2 cups unbleached all-
   purpose flour
1 cup semolina flour
5 extra-large eggs
Pinch of salt

FOR THE SAUCE:
1 medium-sized red onion,
   peeled
1 large stalk celery
½ cup olive oil
3 whole anchovies in salt;
   or 6 anchovy fillets
   packed in oil, drained
1½ pounds cherry
   tomatoes, cut into halves
Salt and freshly ground
   black pepper

TO COOK THE PASTA:
Coarse-grained salt

FOR THE CROUTONS:
½ cup olive oil
1 slice white bread, crust
   removed, cut into very
   small pieces

Prepare the pasta with the ingredients and quantities listed, following the directions on page 14. Stretch the sheet of pasta to ¹⁄₁₆ inch, take to the notch before the last on the machine. Cut the pasta into pieces ¾ inch wide and 2¼ inches long. If possible, place the pasta pieces on the traditional little ridged pasta board called a *cavarola* to make the herringbone pattern, pressing the pasta down with your fingers to get the impression. In the absence of the *cavarola*, approximate the pattern by making the ridges with a fork in a herringbone arrangement (see page 274). Let the pasta pieces rest on cotton dish towels until needed.

Prepare the sauce. Finely chop the onion and celery together on a board. Heat the oil in a large skillet, and when the oil is warm, add the chopped ingredients and sauté for 5 minutes. Meanwhile, if using whole anchovies, clean them, removing bones and rinsing excess salt under cold water. Remove skillet from the heat, add the anchovy fillets, and, using a fork, mash them into the sautéed vegetables. Let the skillet rest off the heat for 10 minutes.

Bring a large pot of cold water to a boil, add coarse salt to taste, then add the pasta and cook for 1 to 3 minutes depending on dryness. As the pasta cooks, place the skillet over high heat and add the tomato halves. Season with salt and pepper, and set aside. Prepare the croutons. Place a small saucepan with the oil over high heat. When oil is warm, add the bread pieces and sauté until golden, about 3 minutes. Use a strainer-skimmer to transfer the sautéed bread to a dish lined with paper towels to drain excess oil.

When the pasta is ready, place skillet with the sauce over medium heat, then drain the pasta, add it to the skillet with the sauce, mix very well, then transfer to a warmed serving dish. Then sprinkle the bread pieces over the pasta and serve immediately.

TROCCOLI CON ASPARAGI

TROCCOLI WITH ASPARAGUS

Clean the asparagus and cut off the tough bottom ends. Cut the asparagus into 1½-inch pieces. Keep the tips and the other pieces separate, and put them into different bowls of cold water for 30 minutes.

Bring a large pot of cold water to a boil, add coarse salt, then add the stems of the asparagus. Cook for about 5 minutes, depending on the size of the asparagus, until almost cooked. Add the tips and cook for 3 minutes more. Using a strainer-skimmer, transfer the asparagus from the boiling water to a crockery or glass bowl, saving the water. Set the asparagus aside until needed.

Prepare pasta with ingredients and quantities listed, following directions on page 14. Stretch sheet to ⅛ inch thick; on the pasta machine take to several notches before last. The pasta sheet can be cut into *troccoli* either with the "guitar" (page 261) or with the ridged rolling pin called the *troccolo* (see photo page 274).

Prepare the tomato sauce. Heat the oil in a small saucepan over medium heat; when the oil is warm add the garlic and sauté for 2 minutes. If using fresh tomatoes, cut them into 1-inch pieces. Add fresh or canned tomatoes to the pan and simmer for 20 minutes, tasting for salt and black pepper. Mix the eggs with the cheese in a small bowl, stirring with a wooden spoon. Season with salt and pepper. Pass the cooked tomatoes through a food mill, using the disc with the smallest holes, into a second saucepan, then place pan over low heat and reduce for 5 minutes.

Bring the asparagus water back to a boil, add coarse salt then the pasta, and cook for 1 to 3 minutes if fresh pasta, for 9 to 12 minutes if dried. Meanwhile, mix the eggs with the cheese in a small bowl, stirring with a wooden spoon. Season with salt and pepper. Drain the pasta and put it on a large, warmed serving dish. Add the asparagus and the egg mixture. Toss very well to keep the eggs from curdling. Pour on the warm tomato sauce, mix very well, and serve immediately.

FOR THE ASPARAGUS:
1 pound fresh asparagus, preferably very thin; optimum would be wild asparagus
Coarse-grained salt

FOR THE TOMATO SAUCE:
¼ cup olive oil
2 medium-sized cloves garlic, peeled
1 pound very ripe, fresh tomatoes; or 1 pound canned tomatoes, preferably imported Italian, drained
Salt and freshly ground black pepper

FOR THE EGG SAUCE:
3 extra-large eggs
4 tablespoons freshly grated pecorino romano cheese
Salt and freshly ground black pepper

FOR THE PASTA:
2¼ cups unbleached all-purpose flour
3 extra-large eggs
Pinch of salt
                    or
1 pound dried *spaghetti*, preferably imported Italian

TO COOK THE PASTA:
Coarse-grained salt

SICILY

Among the native Sicilian fresh pastas are *crusetti*, or *rosette*. They are *cannelloni* that are closed at both ends, a highly unusual feature. The pasta is rich with egg yolk to which only a little water is added. The pasta squares are precooked and filled with a meat–zucchini–tomato stuffing. The *crusetti* are baked without *balsamella*, just half of the tomato sauce poured on top. They are typical of splendorous Monreale with its incredible Byzantine mosaics.

Pasta with a hole down the middle appear in the dried pasta form of *bucatini* and *perciatelli*. But they may be homemade with fresh pasta, and Sicily is probably the chief locus of this version. Shorter than the dried versions, these *maccheroni inferrettati* were once made with a special square implement, but for several generations now it has been more common to make them with knitting needles. The pasta, rolled into a thin rope, is cut into small pieces, then wrapped around the needle and pushed off. The tomato sauce dressing is flavored with oregano.

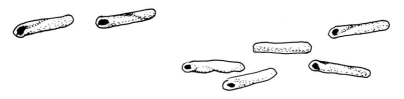

CRUSETTI O ROSETTE ALLA SICILIANA

SICILIAN CLOSED *CANNELLONI*

Prepare the sauce/stuffing. Finely chop the onion, celery, and parsley all together on a board. Place the oil in a medium-sized saucepan over medium heat. When the oil is warm, add the chopped ingredients and sauté for 10 minutes. If using fresh tomatoes, cut them into pieces. Pass fresh or canned tomatoes through a food mill, using the disc with smallest holes, into a crockery or glass bowl. Add the beef and sauté for 5 minutes on each side, then add the tomatoes and salt and pepper to taste. Simmer, covered, until the beef is fork-tender, about 20 minutes.

Transfer the cooked meat to a board and finely chop it. Reduce the sauce for 5 minutes more. Place the chopped meat in a crockery or glass bowl, add ½ cup of the sauce, mix well, cover the bowl, and set stuffing aside until needed.

Clean the zucchini and cut into thin slices—less than ½ inch thick. Heat the oils in a large skillet and when they are hot (about 375 degrees), put in the zucchini. Fry until golden on both sides, about 5 minutes, then use a strainer-skimmer to transfer the zucchini to the bowl of stuffing. Cover the bowl again and set aside. Preheat the oven to 375 degrees.

Prepare the pasta with the ingredients and quantities listed, following the directions on page 14. Stretch sheet to less than 1/16 inch thick—on the pasta machine, take to the last notch—and cut into squares. Preboil the squares in a large amount of salted boiling water for two seconds. Transfer the pasta to a large bowl of cold water to which the oil has been added. Cool the pasta, then place between wet cotton dish towels. When all the pasta squares are on the wet towels, add the cheese to the stuffing and gently mix all the ingredients. Use 2 tablespoons of olive oil to heavily grease a 13½- x 8¾-inch glass baking pan. Place a heaping tablespoon of the stuffing in the center of a pasta square, fold over the 2 scalloped sides, and gently press the ends closed. Put the prepared *crusetto* in the baking dish. Repeat procedure with more pasta squares until the bottom of the pan is completely covered. Pour half the reserved tomato sauce over the *crusetti*, then finish stuffing the remaining pasta squares. Make 1 or more additional layers and pour the remaining sauce over. Cover the baking dish with aluminum foil and bake for 35 minutes. Remove from oven, let rest for a few minutes, then remove foil and serve.

FOR THE SAUCE/
STUFFING:
1 large red onion, peeled
**3 medium-sized stalks
celery**
**20 large sprigs Italian
parsley, leaves only**
½ cup olive oil
**2 pound ripe, fresh
tomatoes; or 2 pounds
canned tomatoes,
preferably imported
Italian, drained**
**1 pound boneless beef
roast, such as top round
or sirloin, in 1 piece**
**Salt and freshly ground
black pepper**
**2 pounds small zucchini
(not miniature)**
1 quart vegetable oil
¼ cup olive oil
**3 tablespoons freshly
grated pecorino romano
or sardo cheese**

FOR THE PASTA:
**2 cups unbleached all-
purpose flour**
4 extra-large egg yolks
⅓ cup cold water
Pinch of salt

TO COOK THE PASTA:
Coarse-grained salt
**2 tablespoons vegetable or
olive oil**

PLUS:
**2 tablespoons olive oil to
grease the baking pan**

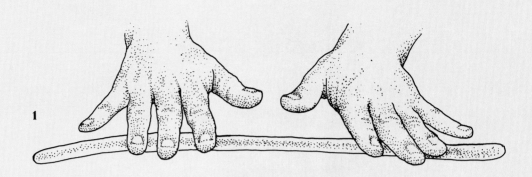

1

MACCHERONI INFERRETTATI

1. *Roll a piece of dough into a rope ½ inch thick.*

2. *Cut the rope into ½ inch pieces.*

3. *Place several ½ inch pieces under a ⅛-inch-thick knitting needle.*

4. *With both hands, give the needle a quick twirl so the pasta simultaneously flattens more*

5. *and wraps itself around the needle.*

6. *Push the pasta off the ends, so there remains a very narrow hole in the middle, giving you the **maccheroni inferrettati**.*

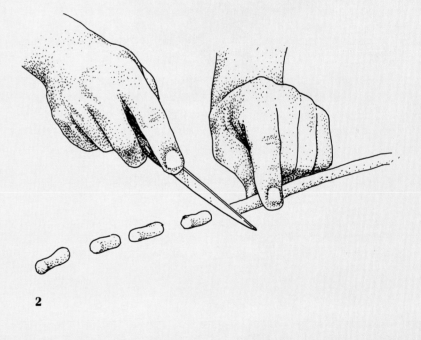

2

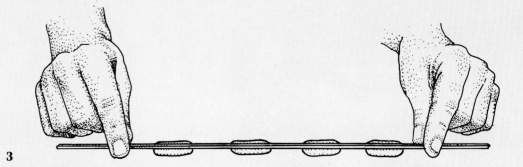

3

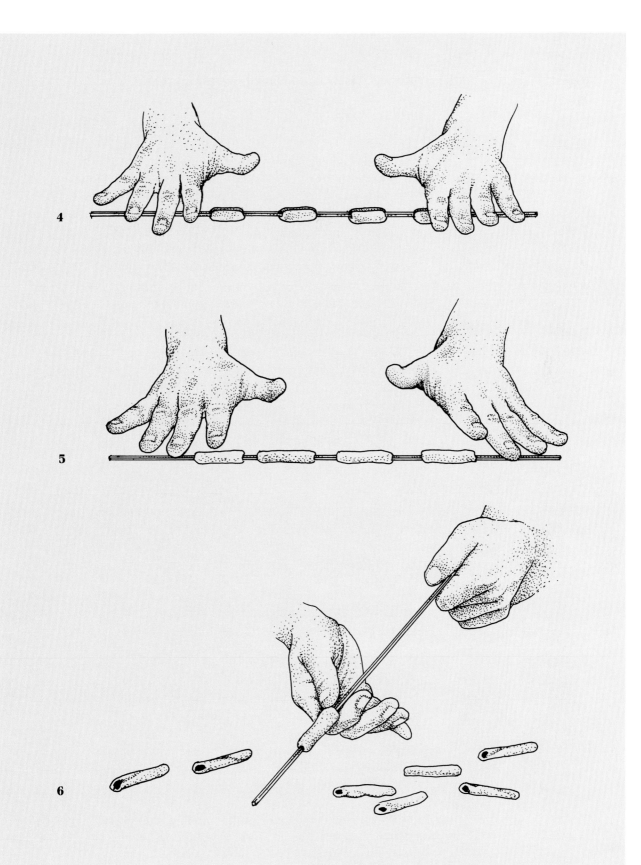

FROM SICILY

SERVES 6 TO 8

MACCHERONI INFERRETTATI

HOMEMADE SHORT *"BUCATINI"*

FOR THE SAUCE:
1 medium-sized red onion, peeled
2 large stalks celery
2 large cloves garlic, peeled
2 large carrots, scraped
20 large sprigs Italian parsley, leaves only
10 large basil leaves, fresh or preserved in salt
2 pounds ripe, fresh tomatoes; or 2 pounds canned tomatoes, preferably imported Italian, drained
5 tablespoons olive oil
Salt and freshly ground black pepper
1 heaping teaspoon dried oregano

FOR THE PASTA:
2 cups unbleached all-purpose flour
1 cup semolina flour
1¼ cups lukewarm water
Pinch of salt

TO COOK THE PASTA:
Coarse-grained salt

Prepare the sauce. Coarsely chop the onion, celery, garlic, carrots, parsley, and basil together on a board. If using fresh tomatoes, cut them into pieces. Place oil in a medium-sized, flameproof casserole, add the chopped ingredients and fresh or canned tomatoes, and put over medium heat. Cook, covered, for 30 minutes, stirring every so often with a wooden spoon. Pass the contents of the casserole through a food mill, using the disc with smallest holes, into a crockery or glass bowl. Then return the sauce to the casserole and cook over medium heat for 15 minutes more, adding salt and pepper to taste and the oregano.

Prepare the pasta with the ingredients and quantities listed, following the directions on page 14. Knead the ball of dough for 10 minutes, then wrap in a cotton dish towel and let rest for 30 minutes, covered with a bowl. After the dough has rested, cut the ball into 8 pieces. Take 1 piece and roll it into a long rope ½ inch thick. Detach ½-inch pieces from the rope and flatten them. Using a ⅛-inch thick knitting needle (see Note), place 2 or 3 pieces along the length of the needle, with spaces separating them; with both hands, give the needle a quick twirl so the pasta simultaneously flattens more and wraps itself around the needle. Push the pasta off the end, so there remains a very narrow hole through the middle, to create the *"bucatini."* The pasta pieces should be about 2½ inches long. Sometimes they do not close completely and the holes in some are more perceptible than in others, but these are not considered deficiencies. Remember, handmade things do not all come out exactly alike, and that is part of the charm. Let *maccheroni* dry for at least an hour before using so they will retain their shape when cooked.

Bring a large pot of cold water to a boil, add coarse salt to taste, then add the pasta and cook for 10 to 15 minutes depending on dryness. This longer cooking time is necessary because the pasta is rather thick and also because it contains semolina, which must cook thoroughly or the pasta will have a raw taste.

Meanwhile, reheat the sauce and when warm, place a ladleful on a warmed serving dish. Drain the pasta, transfer to the serving dish, ladle remaining sauce over, mix well, and serve.

NOTE:
The original square implement for making this pasta disappeared long ago and today even in Sicily a knitting needle has been the substitute for generations.

RECIPE APPENDIX

Special Regional Pastas in Other Bugialli Books

TAGLIATELLE CON SUGO DI OCA CONSERVATO (*Tagliatelle* with Sauce of Preserved Goose)
   CT p. 134

TRENETTE AL PESTO (*Trenette* with Basil Sauce) *FA* p. 153

TORTELLI DI ZUCCA ALLA MODENESE ("Pumpkin" *Tortelli*, Modena Style) *FA* p. 174

MACCHERONI ALLA CHITARRA (*Maccheroni* Cut with the Guitar in Lamb Sauce) *CT* p. 144

PINCI DI MONTALCINO (*Pinci* Montalcino Style) *CT* p. 147

TRENETTE CON SALSA DI CARCIOFI (*Trenette* with Artichoke Sauce) *CT* p. 149

ORECCHIETTE CON CIME DI RAPE (*Orecchiette* with Broccolirab) *CT* p. 153

ANOLINI AL RAGÙ DI PROSCIUTTO (*Anolini* with *Prosciutto* Sauce) *FI* p. 98

ORECCHIETTE CON CAVOLFIORE (*Orecchiette* with Cauliflower) *FI* p. 110

FA   *The Fine Art of Italian Cooking*
CT   *Giuliano Bugialli's Classic Techniques of Italian Cooking*
FI   *Giuliano Bugialli's Foods of Italy*

**The beautiful patterning
produced by the whole leaves of
Italian parsley.**

CHAPTER 6

FLAVORED PASTAS

FLAVORED PASTA

It is difficult to say when the idea first occurred to flavor or color pasta by adding ingredients—usually a vegetable or herb—to the dough itself; but several traditional colored or flavored pastas have been around for quite a while. The most popular, of course, is the green pasta created by adding chopped spinach to the dough. This classic method produces a beautifully flecked, irregular color, unlike the uniform green resulting from the commercial method in which green coloring is sometimes used. Made into *tagliatelle*, *taglierini*, and other long types, and combined with regular fresh pasta, this method produces the popular dish, *paglia e fieno*, Straw and Hay.

Red pasta colored with beets is the more common type in the north. Red pasta is sometimes combined with yellow and green pasta to make the three colors of the Italian flag; and the mixture is, in fact, referred as *tricolore*, or sometimes *arlecchino*, after harlequin, the Commedia dell'Arte character who wears a costume of such colors. Red pasta is also often colored with tomato, more specifically tomato paste. An example follows in the Red Pasta with Onion-Flavored Pésto, in which the sauce is a Sicilian basil pesto to which uncooked onion and fresh hot green pepper are added. *Tagliatelle alla pizzaiola* is an interesting example from the Veneto in which the full *pizzaiola* sauce is put into the well of the dough with the eggs. The lightly tomato-flavored pasta is then dressed with a simpler tomato sauce, melted butter and fresh basil.

Adding saffron to the pasta dough gives it not only a bright yellow color but also a different flavor and texture. Saffron *tagliatelle* may be dressed with an *ossobuco* sauce; it also appears here in the more elaborate and fancy Pasta Timballe with Braised Veal.

A unique recipe, *Lasagne* with Paprika Pasta, from a border area of Emilia-Romagna, gives food for speculation. Uniquely associated with Hungary, paprika was developed from chilies brought from the New World; trade in the powder continued with shippers from the Italian maritime cities. One wonders at which point paprika became the cheaper substitute for saffron in this small area. It is also possible that paprika entered through Hapsburg influence from adjoining Tuscan border areas, which were ruled by a Hapsburg dynasty after the Medici. But Tuscany itself does not have this paprika pasta, and so it is likely it entered through the Venetians or Genoese merchants at an earlier period. The pasta itself is remarkably good in its classic combination with the rich Bolognese *ragù*.

Pasta in forma: **The colorful saffron pasta makes an elegant receptacle for the veal-filled sauce.**

FROM SICILY

SERVES 6 TO 8

FOR THE PASTA:
**3½ cups unbleached all-
  purpose flour**
3 extra-large eggs
3 tablespoons tomato paste
Pinch of salt
4 twists black pepper

FOR THE SAUCE:
1 small red onion, peeled
**½ to 1 small, fresh green
  hot pepper, according to
  taste (jalapeño may be
  used), seeds and pulp
  removed**
**3 cups fresh basil leaves,
  loosely packed**
¾ cup olive oil
**Salt and freshly ground
  black pepper**

TO COOK THE PASTA:
Coarse-grained salt

PASTA ROSSA CON PESTO ALLA RAGUSANA

RED PASTA WITH ONION-FLAVORED PESTO

Prepare the pasta with the ingredients and quantities listed, following the directions on page 14, and placing the tomato paste in the well with the other ingredients. To cut the pasta into fresh *spaghetti* see page 57, and let rest on cotton dish towels until needed.

Prepare the sauce. Grind with mortar and pestle or finely chop the onion, hot pepper, and basil all together on a board. Transfer to a crockery or glass bowl and begin adding the oil, constantly stirring with a wooden spoon until the oil is completely incorporated. Season with salt and pepper, cover the bowl, and refrigerate until needed. (If using a blender or food processor, first finely grind the onion and pepper, then add the basil and oil, and grind again.)

Bring a large pot of cold water to a boil, add coarse salt to taste, then add the pasta and cook for 1 to 3 minutes depending on dryness. Drain the pasta; transfer to a large, warmed serving platter, add the sauce, mix well, and serve (without cheese).

NOTE:
The sauce can be prepared as much as a week in advance and kept in the refrigerator.

FROM LOMBARDY

SERVES 8 TO 10

**FOR THE SAFFRON
PASTA:**
**3 cups unbleached all-
  purpose flour**
4 extra-large eggs
½ teaspoon ground saffron
Pinch of salt

TO COOK THE PASTA:
Coarse-grained salt
**2 tablespoons olive or
  vegetable oil**

PASTA IN FORMA

PASTA TIMBALLE WITH BRAISED VEAL

Prepare the pasta with the ingredients and quantities listed, placing the saffron in the flour well along with the eggs and salt (see page 14). Stretch the pasta dough to ¹⁄₁₆ inch thick—on the pasta machine take to the notch before last—and cut into *tagliatelle* (see page 34). Then let rest on floured cotton dish towels for 30 minutes before cooking.

Bring a large pot of cold water to a boil, add coarse salt to taste, then add the pasta and partially cook it for 30 seconds to 1 minute depending on dryness. Undercook the pasta slightly—it will cook more when baked. Drain the pasta and place it in a bowl of cold water with the oil and let cool. Drain pasta and lay it out between dampened cotton dish towels to rest until needed.

Prepare the veal *spezzatino*. Finely chop the carrot, onion, celery, and *prosciutto* or *pancetta* all together on a board. Place the oil and butter in a heavy, medium-sized flameproof casserole over medium heat, and when the butter is melted, add the chopped ingredients and sauté for 5 minutes. Put in the veal, stir well, and sauté for 5 minutes more. Add the wine and let it evaporate for 5 minutes. Season with salt and pepper, then add the tomato paste and 1 cup of the broth. Simmer, covered, for 45 minutes, stirring every so often with a wooden spoon and adding more broth if needed.

As the *spezzatino* cooks, prepare the sauce. Melt the butter in a heavy, medium-sized saucepan over low heat. Coarsely chop the truffle on a board and add it to the melted butter. Add the flour, mix very well until it is all incorporated, then start adding 1 cup of the heavy cream, continuously stirring with a wooden spoon. Simmer for 5 minutes, then season with salt and pepper, and transfer the sauce to a crockery or glass bowl. Butter a piece of waxed paper, press it down over the sauce, and let rest until cool, about 30 minutes.

Preheat the oven to 375 degrees. Mix the cooled sauce with the egg yolks and Parmigiano, and taste for salt and pepper. Transfer to a large mixing bowl, add the pasta and the remaining ½ cup cream, and mix gently but thoroughly. With half the butter and all the bread crumbs, butter and line a 3-quart ring mold. Prepare a large baking dish for the water bath *(bagnomaria)* by placing several layers of paper towels in the pan along with a piece of lemon, and half-fill the pan with hot water. Fill the mold with pasta and sauce, dotting with bits of remaining butter throughout. Place mold in the prepared water bath and bake for 30 minutes. Remove the mold from the oven and let rest for 2 minutes. Meanwhile, reheat the veal *spezzatino*. Unmold the pasta onto a large, round serving platter. Spoon the veal pieces into the center of the ring and pour the veal sauce into a sauceboat. Serve each portion of pasta with several pieces of veal and a little sauce on the side.

FOR THE VEAL
SPEZZATINO STUFFING:
1 medium-sized carrot, scraped
1 medium-sized red onion, peeled
1 large stalk celery
4 ounces *prosciutto* or *pancetta*
¼ cup olive oil
2 tablespoons (1 ounce) sweet butter
2 pounds boneless veal shoulder, cut into 1-inch cubes
½ cup dry white wine
Salt and freshly ground black pepper
2 tablespoons tomato paste
1 to 2 cups lukewarm chicken or beef broth, preferably homemade

FOR THE SAUCE:
6 tablespoons (3 ounces) sweet butter
½ ounce fresh or canned black truffle
2 tablespoons unbleached all-purpose flour
2 cups heavy cream
Salt and freshly ground black pepper
4 extra-large egg yolks
½ cup freshly grated Parmigiano cheese

TO BAKE:
4 tablespoons (2 ounces) sweet butter
4 tablespoons unseasoned bread crumbs, preferably homemade

FROM
EMILIA-ROMAGNA

SERVES 8

FOR THE SAUCE (*RAGÙ
ALLA BOLOGNESE*):
1 medium-sized red onion,
    peeled
1 medium-sized carrot,
    scraped
1 large stalk celery
3 ounces *pancetta* or
    prosciutto, in 1 piece,
    then cut into cubes
6 ounces lean boneless
    beef, in cubes
6 ounces boneless pork, in
    cubes
4 tablespoons (¼ cup)
    sweet butter
2 tablespoons olive oil
1 pound ripe, fresh
    tomatoes; or 1 pound
    canned tomatoes,
    preferably imported
    Italian, drained
½ cup dry white wine
Salt and freshly ground
    black pepper
Pinch of freshly grated
    nutmeg
¾ cup lukewarm beef
    broth, preferably
    homemade
¾ cup heavy cream

FOR THE PASTA:
4 cups unbleached all-
    purpose flour
5 extra-large eggs
2 teaspoons sweet paprika
Pinch of salt

TO COOK THE PASTA:
Coarse-grained salt
2 tablespoons vegetable or
    olive oil

LASAGNE CON PAPRIKA
LASAGNE WITH PAPRIKA PASTA

Prepare the sauce. Finely chop the onion, carrot, and celery on a board. Coarsely grind the *pancetta* or *prosciutto*, beef, and pork all together in a meat grinder or mince with the knife. Heat the butter and oil in a heavy, flameproof casserole of terra-cotta, lined copper, or enameled iron over medium heat. When the oil mixture is warm, add the chopped vegetables and the ground meats, and sauté for 10 minutes, stirring every so often with a wooden spoon.

If using fresh tomatoes, cut into pieces. Pass fresh or canned tomatoes through a food mill, using the disc with smallest holes, into a crockery or glass bowl. Add the wine to the casserole and let it evaporate for 5 minutes. Add the strained tomatoes and simmer for 20 minutes. Season to taste with salt, pepper, and nutmeg, then add the broth, cover the casserole, and simmer for 45 minutes, stirring every so often with a wooden spoon. Add the cream, mix very well, lower the heat, and reduce for 20 minutes; for the last 5 minutes, remove the lid from the casserole. Remove the sauce from the heat and let rest until cool, about 1 hour.

Prepare the pasta with the ingredients and quantities listed, placing the paprika in the flour well with the eggs and salt (see page 14). Stretch the pasta dough to about 1/16 inch thick—on the pasta machine, take to the next to last notch. Cut the sheet into squares and place on cotton dish towels.

Precook the pasta squares in salted boiling water for 10 seconds after the water returns to a boil, then transfer to a large bowl of cold water with the vegetable oil added. When all the squares have been precooked, place them in a single layer on dampened cotton dish towels. Preheat the oven to 375 degrees.

To assemble the dish, use 1 tablespoon of the butter to heavily coat a 13½- x 8¾-inch glass baking dish. Fit in enough pasta squares to cover the bottom of the dish, but not the sides. Lightly cover this layer with about 5 tablespoons of the sauce, and sprinkle over some of the grated cheese. Keep alternating layers of pasta with sauce and cheese. The top layer should be of sauce and cheese; cut the remaining 3 tablespoons of butter into pats and spread out all over. Bake for 35 minutes. Remove dish from oven and let rest for 5 minutes before serving.

TO BAKE:
4 tablespoons (2 ounces) sweet butter
¾ cup freshly grated Parmigiano cheese

TAGLIATELLE ALLA PIZZAIOLA
PIZZAIOLA TAGLIATELLE WITH TOMATO SAUCE

FROM VENETO

SERVES 8

Begin the pasta. Make the pizzaiola flavoring by coarsely chopping the garlic on a board. Place the oil in a small saucepan over medium heat, and when the oil is warm, add the garlic and gently sauté for 3 minutes. Add the tomatoes, salt, black pepper, and oregano to the pan, mix, and simmer for 15 minutes.

Begin the sauce. Place the tomatoes in a large saucepan over medium heat and simmer for 30 minutes, stirring every so often.

When the *pizzaiola* flavoring for the pasta is cooked, pass it through a food mill, using the disc with smallest holes, into a second, small saucepan. Return the pan to medium heat and reduce for 10 minutes, then transfer to a crockery or glass bowl and set aside until cool, about 30 minutes. By that time the sauce should be very thick.

Finish the sauce. Pass the cooked tomatoes through a food mill, using the disc with smallest holes, into a second saucepan and return the pan to medium heat. Season with salt and pepper and reduce for 15 minutes, stirring every so often.

Prepare the pasta with the ingredients listed, placing the thick flavoring and eggs in the well of the flour mound, and following the technique for regular pasta (page 14). Cut into *tagliatelle* (see page 33).

Bring a large pot of cold water to a boil over medium heat. Place the butter in a large serving dish and put over the pot as a lid. Reheat the tomato sauce. When the water reaches a boil, add coarse salt, then add the *tagliatelle* and cook for 30 to 45 seconds depending on dryness. Ladle half the sauce onto the serving dish. Drain the pasta and add it to the dish. Pour the remaining tomato sauce over, sprinkle with the basil, toss gently but very well, and serve immediately.

FOR THE PASTA FLAVORING:
2 large cloves garlic, peeled
4 tablespoons olive oil
½ pound canned tomatoes, preferably imported Italian, drained
1 teaspoon salt
½ teaspoon freshly ground black pepper
1 teaspoon dried oregano

FOR THE PASTA:
3½ cups unbleached all-purpose flour
2 extra-large eggs

TO COOK THE PASTA:
Coarse-grained salt

FOR THE SAUCE:
1½ pounds ripe, fresh tomatoes; or 1½ pounds canned tomatoes, preferably imported Italian, drained
Salt and freshly ground black pepper

PLUS:
8 tablespoons (½ cup) sweet butter
10 large fresh basil leaves, torn into thirds

PURÉED VEGETABLE-FLAVORED

Certain puréed vegetables can be successfully added to pasta dough for both flavor and color. Those that work best of all are bell peppers, artichokes, green tomatoes (the red ones, of course, constitute a large category of their own), all producing various shades of green pasta.

Green pepper pasta served with a sauce made from red bell peppers is a combination made in heaven, and included here are two recipes using that combination. In the first and simpler version, the pasta is cut into *spaghetti*, which gives added thickness suitable for this texture. Garlic is puréed into the dough along with the peppers, and its flavor is repeated in the sauce. The red of the peppers is reinforced with some tomato in the sauce, and parsley is added. Black pepper flavors both the pasta and the sauce.

The more elaborate dish is the *lasagne* employing the same pasta and sauce, but layered also with *balsamella* and baked. It is interesting that the *spaghetti* is served with no grated cheese—only with additional fresh parsley scattered over—while the *lasagne* incorporates Parmigiano into the layers.

From the Veneto we have the pasta in which a thick, cooled artichoke purée is incorporated into the dough, and it is served with a sauce of only melted butter and sage, with Parmigiano grated over.

This may be the place in which to point out that a great deal of experimentation is now going on in adding ingredients to flavor pasta dough. These creations are not always very well thought out, nor are they based on much understanding of basic principles. If we are lucky, some few new ideas will emerge that are really valid. It is worthwhile to ponder why the flavors which have been successful do work, and to use that understanding in choosing some new possibilities.

FROM SOUTHERN ITALY

SERVES 8 TO 10

FOR THE PASTA:
2 medium-sized green bell peppers
2 medium-sized cloves garlic, peeled

LASAGNE DI PEPERONI

GREEN AND RED PEPPER *LASAGNE*

Prepare the pasta. Remove the stems, pulp, and seeds from the green peppers, and cut them into small pieces. Use a food processor or blender to finely grind the peppers and garlic together. Prepare the pasta with the ingredients listed, placing 5 ounces of the pepper-garlic mixture in the flour well together with the other ingredients following directions on page 14. Stretch the dough to a thickness of ¹⁄₁₆ inch, on the pasta machine, take to the next to last notch. (Do not try to stretch it thinner.) Cut the sheet into squares and place on cotton dish towels.

Precook the pasta squares in salted boiling water for 10 seconds after the water returns to a boil, then transfer to a large bowl of cold water with the vegetable oil added. Let precooked squares of pasta rest on cotton dish towels until needed.

Prepare the pepper-tomato sauce. Remove the stems, pulp, and seeds from the red peppers and cut them into small pieces. Coarsely chop the parsley. Place the oil in a heavy saucepan over medium heat; when the oil is warm, add the peppers and garlic and sauté for 5 minutes. If using fresh tomatoes, cut them into quarters. Add fresh or canned tomatoes to pan along with the chopped parsley. Cover and cook for 25 minutes stirring every so often with a wooden spoon and tasting for salt and pepper. Pass contents of pan through a food mill, using the disc with smallest holes, and return it to the saucepan to cook until the sauce is creamy and smooth, 15 minutes more. Taste again for salt and pepper, then transfer sauce to a crockery bowl to cool for 1 hour.

Make the *balsamella*. Melt the butter in a heavy, medium-sized saucepan over low heat. When the butter bubbles, mix in the flour. Remove from the heat for 15 seconds, then return to low heat and add the hot milk all at once, stirring until smooth. Bring to a boil, then reduce heat and simmer for 10 minutes, stirring constantly. Season with salt and pepper, and transfer to a large bowl. Press a sheet of buttered waxed paper onto the surface of the sauce to prevent a skin from forming. Cool to room temperature.

Preheat the oven to 375 degrees. To assemble the dish, butter a 13½- x 8¾-inch glass baking dish. Fit in enough squares of pasta to cover the bottom of the dish and to allow about 1 inch to hang over the edge all around (see page 126). Cover this bottom layer with one-third of the *balsamella* and sprinkle over one-third of the Parmigiano. Add another layer of pasta just to cover the *balsamella* and cheese, not to hang over. Cover this pasta with about 6 tablespoons of the cooled pepper-tomato sauce. Alternate pasta layers and sauce in the same way 3 more times. Over the next layer of pasta place another third of the *balsamella* and of the Parmigiano. Then make 4 more layers of pasta and sauce, using up all the remaining sauce. Over another layer of pasta spread the remaining *balsamella* and Parmigiano, covering these with a final layer of 3 squares of pasta. Pick up the ends of the bottom layer of pasta hanging over the edges of the baking dish and fold them in over the top layer of pasta squares. Bake for 25 minutes. The top layer should emerge lightly golden brown and crisp. Remove dish from oven and allow to cool for 5 minutes. Serve from the baking dish, slicing it with a knife and lifting out each portion with a spatula.

5¼ cups unbleached all-purpose flour
3 extra-large eggs
1 tablespoon olive or vegetable oil
Pinch of salt
4 or 5 twists black pepper

TO COOK THE PASTA:
2 tablespoons olive or vegetable oil

FOR THE PEPPER-TOMATO SAUCE:
2 medium-sized red bell peppers
15 large sprigs Italian parsley, leaves only
¾ cup olive oil
2 medium-sized cloves garlic, peeled
2 pounds ripe, fresh tomatoes; or 2 pounds canned tomatoes, preferably imported Italian, drained
Salt and freshly ground black pepper

FOR THE *BALSAMELLA*:
8 tablespoons (4 ounces) sweet butter
½ cup unbleached all-purpose flour
3½ cups milk
Salt and freshly ground black pepper

TO BAKE:
1 cup freshly grated Parmigiano cheese

SPAGHETTI DI PEPERONI

SWEET BELL PEPPER *SPAGHETTI*

Remove the stem, pulp, and seeds from the green pepper, then cut it into small pieces. Place the garlic and pepper in a blender or food processor and finely purée. Weigh out 3 ounces of the mixture, discarding the rest.

Prepare the pasta with the ingredients and quantities listed, placing the pepper-garlic mixture in the flour well together with the eggs, oil, salt, and pepper (see page 14). Stretch layer to about ⅛ inch thick—on the pasta machine take to several notches before last—then cut into *spaghetti* (see page 57) and let rest on cotton dish towels until needed.

Prepare the sauce. Remove the stem, pulp, and seeds from the red pepper and cut into small pieces. Coarsely chop the parsley together with the garlic on a board. If using fresh tomatoes, cut them into pieces. Heat the oil in a small saucepan over medium heat, and when it is warm, put in the pepper pieces and sauté for 5 minutes. Add the chopped ingredients along with the fresh or canned tomatoes. Cover the pan and cook for 30 minutes, stirring every so often with a wooden spoon. Taste for salt and pepper, then pass the contents of the pan through a food mill, using the disc with the smallest holes, and return the strained sauce to the pan. Cook for 15 minutes over medium heat, uncovered. By that time the sauce should be creamy and smooth.

Bring a large pot of cold water to a boil, add coarse salt to taste, then add the pasta and cook for 1 to 3 minutes, depending on dryness. Pour 1 ladleful of the sauce onto a warmed serving dish, drain the pasta, and arrange it over the sauce. Pour remaining sauce over the pasta, toss well, and serve immediately, sprinkling the chopped parsley on top.

Display of Bolognese pastas against the unique church of Santo Stefano in Bologna, a series of small churches from the 5th, 7th, and 11th centuries, perhaps Bologna's most impressive monument.

FROM SOUTHERN ITALY

SERVES 4 TO 6

FOR THE PASTA:
**1 medium-sized bell pepper
1 medium-sized clove garlic, peeled
2¾ cups unbleached all-purpose flour
2 extra-large eggs
2 teaspoons olive or vegetable oil
Pinch of salt
5 twists black pepper**

FOR THE SAUCE:
**1 large red bell pepper
5 large sprigs Italian parsley, leaves only
1 medium-sized clove garlic, peeled
1½ pounds ripe, fresh tomatoes; or 1½ pounds canned tomatoes, preferably imported Italian
¼ cup olive oil
Salt and freshly ground black pepper**

TO COOK THE PASTA:
Coarse-grained salt

TO SERVE:
15 large sprigs Italian parsley, leaves only, coarsely chopped

PASTA DI CARCIOFI

ARTICHOKE PASTA

Prepare the artichoke base. Place the artichokes in a bowl of cold water, squeeze the lemon halves and add, and let rest for 30 minutes. Meanwhile, coarsely chop the parsley and garlic together on a board. Clean the artichokes following the instructions on page 67, and cut them into eighths. Place the artichokes back in the water with the lemon until needed.

Place the oil in a heavy medium-sized casserole, preferably terra-cotta or enamel, over medium heat, and when the oil is warm, add the chopped ingredients and sauté for 2 minutes. Drain the artichokes, add them to the casserole, and sauté for 5 minutes more. Add the wine, raise the heat to high, and cook for 10 minutes. Season with salt and pepper, lower the heat, cover the casserole, and cook until the artichokes are very tender, about 15 minutes more, stirring every so often with a wooden spoon.

Pass the contents of the casserole through a food mill, using the disc with the smallest holes, into a second flameproof casserole. Place the puréed artichokes over low heat and cook for 2 or 3 minutes to let all the liquid evaporate, stirring constantly with a wooden spoon. Transfer the artichoke base to a crockery or glass bowl, and let rest until completely cold, about 1 hour.

Prepare the pasta with the ingredients and quantities listed, placing the artichoke purée in the well of the flour with the eggs and more salt and pepper to taste (see page 14). Make the sheet of pasta a little thicker than for usual *tagliatelle* (about ¹⁄₁₆ inch thick) —on the pasta machine take to the next to last notch. Cut into *tagliatelle* (see page 33), and let rest on cotton towels until needed.

Bring a large pot of cold water to a boil, add coarse salt to taste, then add the pasta and cook for 1 to 3 minutes depending on dryness. As the pasta cooks, place a small saucepan with the butter over medium heat, and when the butter is melted, put in the sage leaves and sauté for 1 minute. Season to taste with salt and pepper. Drain the pasta; transfer to a large, warmed, serving platter, pour the sauce over, and sprinkle with the cheese, if used; toss very well and serve.

FOR THE ARTICHOKE BASE:
3 large artichokes (yields almost 2 pounds cleaned)
1 large lemon, cut in half
15 large sprigs Italian parsley, leaves only
3 large cloves garlic, peeled
¼ cup olive oil
1 cup dry white wine
Salt and freshly ground black pepper

FOR THE PASTA:
5½ cups unbleached all-purpose flour
3 extra-large eggs
Salt and freshly ground black pepper

TO COOK THE PASTA:
Coarse-grained salt

FOR THE SAUCE:
12 tablespoons (6 ounces) sweet butter
15 large fresh sage leaves
Salt and freshly ground black pepper

TO SERVE:
¾ cup freshly grated Parmigiano cheese (optional)

Pasta and artichokes.

WILD MUSHROOM- AND TRUFFLE-FLAVORED

Dried wild mushroms, specifically porcini, easily impart their remarkable fragrance when soaked, puréed with garlic and parsley, and placed in pasta dough. The resulting pasta should be cooked in water to which has been added some of the mushroom soaking water to reinforce the flavor. Only melted butter and the special wild mint called *nipitella*, or *mentuccia*, are used to flavor the dish, but if the herb is unavailable, a clove of garlic can be used instead. Common mint is not a reasonable substitute.

Black truffle paste added to pasta dough produces a pasta with little black flecks. The pasta is best enhanced by butter, cream, nutmeg, and if you prefer, some grated Parmigiano. These simple *tagliatelle* are, however, a most rare dish because of the prized truffle flavoring.

FROM UMBRIA

SERVES 6

TAGLIATELLE AL TARTUFO

BLACK TRUFFLE *TAGLIATELLE* IN CREAM SAUCE

FOR THE PASTA:
3 cups unbleached all-purpose flour
3 extra-large eggs
3 teaspoons black truffle paste
3 teaspoons vegetable or olive oil
Pinch of salt

FOR THE SAUCE:
12 tablespoons (6 ounces) sweet butter
1 cup heavy cream
Salt and freshly grated black pepper
Freshly grated nutmeg
6 tablespoons freshly grated Parmigiano cheese (optional)

TO COOK THE PASTA:
Coarse-grained salt

Make the pasta, using the ingredients and quantities listed, following the instructions on page 14 and placing the truffle paste in the well of flour together with the other ingredients. Stretch the sheet of pasta to less than 1/16 inch thick—on the pasta machine take to the last setting. Cut into *tagliatelle* (see page 33). Let the pasta rest on cotton dish towels until needed.

Bring a large pot of cold water to a boil over medium heat. Place a flameproof casserole with the butter over the pot. When the water reaches a boil, lift off the casserole, add coarse salt to the water, then add the pasta and cook it for a few seconds to 30 seconds, depending on dryness. Meanwhile, place the casserole containing the butter over very low heat. Drain the pasta well and add it to the casserole, pour the cream over, toss very well, and season with salt, pepper, and nutmeg. When the cream is incorporated, transfer the pasta to a warmed serving platter and serve immediately. Parmigiano is optional.

SPAGHETTI AI FUNGHI

WILD MUSHROOM *SPAGHETTI*

Soak the mushrooms in a small crockery or glass bowl with the lukewarm water for 1 hour. Drain the mushrooms, saving the soaking water. Clean them very well, removing the sand attached to the stems. Clean the water by pouring it through a strainer lined with several layers of paper towels into a second bowl. Finely chop the mushrooms, garlic, and parsley on a board, transfer to a crockery or glass bowl, add the oil, and mix very well. (If using a food processor, grind all the ingredients together along with the oil, using the normal metal blade.) Place a small saucepan with the mushroom paste and 1 cup of the mushroom water over low heat. Season with abundant salt and pepper because none will be added later to the flour. Simmer for 30 minutes, stirring every so often with a wooden spoon. Remove pan from the heat and rest until completely cooled, about 1 hour.

Prepare the pasta with the ingredients and quantities listed, placing the mushroom base in the well of the flour with the other ingredients following directions on page 14. Stretch layer to about ⅛ inch thick; on the pasta machine, take to several notches before last. Prepare *spaghetti* following the instructions on page 57. Let the pasta rest on cotton towels until needed.

Coarsely chop the parsley on a board. Add the remaining mushroom water to a large pot of cold water and put it over medium heat. When the water reaches a boil, add coarse salt to taste, then add the pasta and cook for 1 to 3 minutes depending on dryness. As the pasta cooks, melt the butter over low heat, add the *nipitella* or *mentuccia* (wild mint) or garlic, and salt and pepper to taste; sauté until the pasta is ready. Drain the pasta and transfer to a large, warmed serving platter. If garlic has been used, discard it. Pour the sauce over and sprinkle on the parsley, toss very well, and serve. On each serving, add 1 or 2 twists of black pepper.

FOR THE MUSHROOM BASE:
1 ounce dried porcini mushrooms
5 cups lukewarm water
2 large cloves garlic, peeled
15 large sprigs Italian parsley, leaves only
5 tablespoons olive oil
Salt and freshly ground black pepper

FOR THE PASTA:
4 cups unbleached all-purpose flour
2 extra-large eggs

FOR THE SAUCE:
12 tablespoons (6 ounces) sweet butter
1 heaping tablespoon *nipitella* or *mentuccia* (wild mint); or 1 large clove garlic, peeled
Salt and freshly ground black pepper

TO COOK THE PASTA:
Coarse-grained salt

TO SERVE:
15 large sprigs Italian parsley, leaves only
Freshly ground black pepper

HERB-FLAVORED

The herbs preferred to flavor pasta are rosemary, as we see in the Chick-pea Pasta, and parsley or sage. In Sage Pasta, sage leaves are torn into tiny pieces and placed in the well with the eggs and black pepper. The cooked pasta is put on a bed of melted butter and grated Parmigiano, and the individual servings are sprinkled with additional Parmigiano and pepper. If the sage is fresh rather than dried or preserved in salt, a whole sage leaf is added to each serving.

Parsley Pasta, with whole leaves showing through sheets of dough and resembling a tapestry, is one of my proudest rediscoveries. My own enthusiasm for it when I introduced it several years ago has been met by that of many chefs, among them practitioners of "nouvelle cuisine," who love its striking visual appeal. See Parsley Pasta *Quadrucci in brodo* in the Recipe Appendix; the dough also contains some grated cheese in it, another unusual feature. See also photo page 287.

PASTA DI CECI AL ROSMARINO

CHICK-PEA PASTA

The Chick-pea Pasta is a combination of chick-pea flour and wheat flour. We saw in the previous chapter examples of other grain flours mixed with wheat, specifically rye and buckwheat flours. Dried chick-peas produce a fine flour, which of course needs the gluten of wheat to hold together in a pasta; but the chick-pea flavor dominates and mixes well with the flavors of rosemary and garlic, which are also chopped and placed in the well with the eggs. To not mask the chick-pea and rosemary flavors, a simple sauce of oil with **pancetta** *or* **prosciutto** *is generally matched to this pasta.*

Prepare the pasta. Finely chop the rosemary leaves and garlic together on a board. Transfer to a small crockery or glass bowl, add the oil, and mix very well. Make a mound of the all-purpose flour. Shape a well in the center and place the chopped mixture in the well along with the chick-pea flour, eggs, salt, and pepper. Combine the ingredients and knead well following directions on page 14. Immediately stretch the dough less than 1/16 inch thick—on the pasta machine take to the last setting. Cut into *tagliatelle* (see page 33).

Prepare the sauce. Cut the *pancetta* or *prosciutto* into cubes less than 1/2 inch thick. Place the oil and *pancetta* or *prosciutto* in a small saucepan over medium heat and sauté until meat is crisp, about 15 minutes. Set aside.

Bring a large pot of cold water to a boil. When the water reaches a boil, add coarse salt to taste, then add the pasta. Stir and cook the pasta for 40 seconds to 1 minute depending on dryness. Drain; transfer the pasta to a large, warmed serving platter, pour the sauce over, mix gently but very well, and serve immediately.

NOTE:

This pasta could be served even with a very light tomato sauce or just uncooked good olive oil.

Chick-pea flour is available at Italian (especially Sicilian) or Indian groceries; the Indian stores have both toasted and regular chick-pea flour, so be sure to get the regular.

Pasta de ceci al rosmarino **served in a typically patterned Sicilian dish.**

FOR THE PASTA:
2 tablespoons rosemary leaves, fresh or preserved in salt or dried and blanched
3 medium-sized cloves garlic, peeled
5 teaspoons olive oil
2¼ cups unbleached all-purpose flour
½ cup chick-pea flour (see Note)
3 extra-large eggs
1 teaspoon salt
10 twists black pepper

FOR THE SAUCE:
6 ounces *pancetta* or *prosciutto*, in 1 piece
6 tablespoons olive oil

TO COOK THE PASTA:
Coarse-grained salt

FROM CHIANTI
(TUSCANY)

SERVES 4 TO 6

PASTA ALLA SALVIA
SAGE PASTA

FOR THE PASTA:
2 cups unbleached all-purpose flour
3 extra-large eggs
Pinch of salt
½ teaspoon freshly ground black pepper
25 large sage leaves, fresh or preserved in salt, stems completely removed and leaves torn into small pieces

FOR THE SAUCE:
8 tablespoons (4 ounces) sweet butter
¼ cup freshly grated Parmigiano cheese

TO COOK THE PASTA:
Coarse-grained salt

TO SERVE:
4 to 6 tablespoons freshly grated Parmigiano cheese
Freshly ground black pepper
4 to 6 large fresh sage leaves

Prepare the pasta with the ingredients and quantities listed, placing the sage pieces in the flour well along with the eggs, salt, and pepper following directions on page 14. Stretch the pasta dough about ¹⁄₁₆ inch thick, on the pasta machine to the setting before the last. Cut into *tagliatelle* (see page 33) and let rest on a cotton dish towel until needed.

Bring a large pot of cold water to a boil over medium heat, and place a large serving dish with the butter over the pot in order to melt the butter. When the water reaches a boil and the butter is melted, remove dish, add coarse salt to the water, then add the pasta and cook for 1 to 3 minutes depending on dryness. Drain the pasta, transfer it to the prepared dish, sprinkle with the Parmigiano, mix well, and serve immediately. Over each portion, grind some black pepper, add 1 tablespoon grated Parmigiano, and place a whole fresh sage leaf on top.

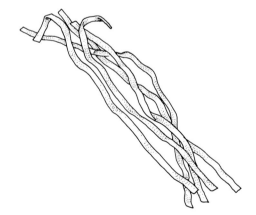

PEPPER-FLAVORED

Black pepper has been prized as flavoring for many centuries, and indeed at one time was the basis for great trading activities across the seas. In the Middle Ages and Renaissance, pepper sometimes formed the principal seasoning for a dish; so much pepper was used that its particular flavor as well as its spiciness became central. A few such dishes still survive in the Italian repertory, one of which is the fresh pasta that follows, made with abundant black pepper in the dough itself. A simple tomato sauce and fresh parsley are enough to dress it and allow the pepper to reign.

A very regional pasta is made in Pistoia, in Tuscany, which incorporates hot red pepper, dried and ground with mortar and pestle, into the dough itself (see Recipe Appendix). The dough is formed into *tagliatelle* and very simply dressed with olive oil and fresh parsley.

When I revived the old traditional chocolate pasta of Tuscany a few years ago, I was scarcely prepared for the notoriety and even popularity that it would achieve, especially among chefs in Europe and America who adapted it in their own ways. While this is their privilege, I still recommend the classic treatment that evolved over a long period in Tuscany, which appears in *Classic Techniques of Italian Cooking*, p. 136. The chocolate in it works only in the classic pairing with the Sweet and Spicy sauce given there. In a recent book, this pasta, incorrectly attributed to the author's "Sardinian grandmother" (the pasta is unknown in Sardinia), is given a new sauce of the author's invention.

FROM TUSCANY

SERVES 4 TO 6

PASTA CON PEPE NERO

BLACK PEPPER PASTA

FOR THE PASTA:
**3 cups unbleached all-
    purpose flour**
4 extra-large eggs
**1 tablespoon fresh,
    coarsely ground black
    pepper**
Pinch of salt

FOR THE SAUCE:
**1 pound ripe, fresh
    tomatoes; or 1 pound
    canned tomatoes,
    preferably imported
    Italian, drained**
**1 medium-sized clove
    garlic, peeled**
½ cup olive oil
**Salt and freshly ground
    black pepper**

TO COOK THE PASTA:
Coarse-grained salt

TO SERVE:
**25 large sprigs Italian
    parsley, leaves only**

Prepare the pepper pasta using the ingredients and quantities listed, placing the ground pepper in the flour well together with the eggs and salt (see page 14). Stretch the pasta dough to about ¹⁄₁₆ inch thick, to the next to the last notch on the pasta machine, and cut it into *tagliatelle* (see page 33). Let the *tagliatelle* rest on cotton towels until needed.

If using fresh tomatoes, cut them into pieces. Place fresh or canned tomatoes, garlic, and oil in a medum-sized saucepan, and cook over medium heat for 15 minutes. Taste for salt and pepper. Pass the contents of the pan through a food mill, using the disc with smallest holes, into a medium-sized crockery or glass bowl. Return the strained tomatoes to the saucepan and reduce the sauce over low heat for 5 minutes.

Bring a large pot of cold water to a boil, add coarse salt to taste, then add the pasta and cook for 1 to 3 minutes depending on dryness. When the pasta is ready, drain and transfer it to a warmed serving dish, pour the sauce over, and sprinkle with the parsley. Toss very well and serve immediately. No cheese should be served with this.

FIOCCHETTI AL POMODORO

"PINCHED" LEMON-FLAVORED PASTA

FROM UMBRIA

SERVES 4 TO 6

*The use of grated lemon in pasta, the Umbrian **fiocchetti**, works because the pasta is not cut into thin ribbons; it is thicker and cut into diamonds, pinched to almost resemble little bows. The lemon is combined with nutmeg in the pasta dough, and most important, the sauce of tomato or meat provides balancing flavor that does not allow any bitterness to emerge from the oil of the lemon.*

Grate the lemons to obtain 2 tablespoons grated peel, and put it in a small bowl. Add the nutmeg, eggs, and salt, and mix the ingredients with a fork. Prepare the pasta with the ingredients listed, placing the lemon mixture in the flour well (see page 14). Stretch the pasta dough to 1/16 inch, on the pasta machine take to next to last notch. Use a scalloped pastry wheel to cut the sheet into diamonds with 2-inch sides. Use your thumb and index finger to pinch each diamond into a bow, then transfer them onto a cotton dish towel to rest until needed.

Prepare the sauce. If using fresh tomatoes, cut them into pieces. Place fresh or canned tomatoes in a saucepan with the garlic, basil, and oil, and put the pan over medium heat to simmer for 15 minutes. Pass the contents of the pan through a food mill, using the disc with smallest holes, into a crockery bowl. Return the tomatoes to the pan and reduce over medium heat for 5 minutes; season with salt and pepper.

Bring a large pot of cold water to a boil, add coarse salt to taste, then add the pasta and cook for 1 to 3 minutes depending on dryness. Reheat the sauce and when pasta is ready, drain it, transfer to a large skillet, add the sauce, and incorporate it over medium heat for a few seconds. Transfer to a warmed serving dish and serve.

VARIATION
Instead of the tomato sauce, a meat sauce can be used.

FOR THE PASTA:
2 large lemons with thick skins
1/2 teaspoon freshly grated nutmeg
3 extra-large eggs
Pinch of salt
2 1/4 cups unbleached all-purpose flour

FOR THE SAUCE:
1 1/2 pounds ripe, fresh tomatoes; or 1 1/2 pounds canned tomatoes, preferably imported Italian, drained
2 medium-sized cloves garlic, peeled
5 large basil leaves, fresh or preserved in salt
1/4 cup olive oil
Salt and freshly ground black pepper

TO COOK THE PASTA:
Coarse-grained salt

F R O M   S I C I L Y

SERVES 8 TO 10

PASTA ALLA RICOTTA
RICOTTA PASTA

FOR THE PASTA:
20 ounces whole-milk ricotta
5½ cups unbleached all-purpose flour, approximately (see Note)
4 extra-large eggs
Pinch of salt
4 large pinches of freshly ground black pepper

FOR THE SAUCE:
12 ounces shelled walnuts
8 ounces freshly grated pecorino siciliano or pecorino romano cheese
8 tablespoons (4 ounces) sweet butter, at room temperature
Salt and freshly ground black pepper
1 cup olive oil

TO COOK THE PASTA:
Coarse-grained salt

This pasta has ricotta in the dough along with black pepper; the sauce is ground walnuts and grated sheep's cheese, with butter and oil. The unusual use of butter in this Sicilian dish comes from the connection with the ricotta flavor in the pasta. It is best to keep this pasta slightly thicker than usual because of its unique texture.

Prepare the pasta. Drain the ricotta very well to remove all the excess water. Prepare the pasta with the ingredients and quantities listed, following procedure on page 14, and placing the strained ricotta in the well with the eggs, salt, and pepper. Make the sheet of pasta a little thicker than for usual *tagliatelle* (about ¹⁄₁₆ inch thick)—on the pasta machine take to the notch before last. Cut into *tagliatelle* (see page 33) and let the prepared pasta rest on cotton towels for at least 30 minutes, being sure that the individual strips of pasta do not touch one another. This type of pasta requires a much longer drying time than usual before cooking, otherwise the strips will stick together in the pot.

Prepare the sauce. Finely chop the walnuts on a board or with a food processor and put in a crockery or glass bowl. Add the cheese and butter and, using a wooden spoon, mix all the ingredients. Season with salt and pepper, then start adding the oil, small amounts at a time, continuously mixing with a wooden spoon in a rotating motion until all the oil is incorporated and the ingredients very well amalgamated. (If the sauce seems too solid, add several tablespoons of the pasta water when tossing.) Cover the bowl and refrigerate until needed.

Bring a large pot of cold water to a boil, add coarse salt to taste, then add the pasta and cook for 1 minute to 3 minutes depending on dryness. Drain the pasta; transfer it to a large, warmed serving dish, spoon the sauce all over, toss gently but thoroughly, and serve with 2 twists of black pepper on each portion.

NOTE:
The amount of flour varies according to the dryness of the ricotta.

RECIPE APPENDIX

Flavored Pastas in Other Bugialli Books

PASTA VERDE (Green [Spinach] Pasta) *FA* p. 143

SFORMATO DI TAGLIATELLE VERDI (Green Pasta "Soufflé") *FA* p. 150

CANNELLONI VERDI DI RICOTTA (Green *Cannelloni* with Ricotta Filling) *FA* p. 186

LASAGNE VERDI ALLA NAPOLETANA (Green *Lasagne*, Neapolitan Style) *FI* p. 102

PASTA ROSSA (Red [Beet] Pasta) *FA* p. 144

SPAGHETTI ALLA PREMATURA (Green Tomato *Spaghetti*) *FI* p. 90

[Parsley Pasta] QUADRUCCI IN BRODO (*Quadrucci* in Broth) *FI* p. 92

TAGLIATELLE AL PEPERONCINO (Red Pepper *Tagliatelle*) *CT* p. 135

PASTA AL CIOCCOLATO IN DOLCE FORTE (Chocolate Pasta in Sweet and Spicy Sauce) *CT* p. 136

FA *The Fine Art of Italian Cooking*
CT *Giuliano Bugialli's Classic Techniques of Italian Cooking*
FI *Giuliano Bugialli's Foods of Italy*

CHAPTER 7

Passatelli coming through the potato ricer and dropping into the broth. See photo of the *passatelli* maker on page 321.

GNOCCHI, RAVIOLI NUDI, AND PASSATELLI

ORIGIN OF *GNOCCHI*

Gnocchi go back to the original *ravioli*, which were round in shape with no pasta covering. Gradually the variation, called "*ravioli* covered with pasta," displaced the original almost completely. However, during the Renaissance the most common first course was a spicy broth made with meat, fish, or fowl. The meat used was ground and made into *ravioli* without pasta and served in the broth. There was an enormous variety of these dumplings with their own broths, and some were taken to neighboring Austria, Germany, Hungary, and other countries. The Italian ancestry of these dishes has been forgotten, since they have disappeared in their place of origin. The best-known Italian survivors of that early period are the *ravioli nudi* (the "naked" in the name is an appellation from my own family, not the traditional name). These are very much alive in Florence to the present day, although only in family cooking, not served by restaurants.

While variations of *gnocchi* are made with semolina (in Rome) or with cornmeal, the overwhelming favorite in modern time is made with a potato base. These are popular, in slight variations, all over Italy—but the less flour used to hold them together, the lighter they are (see Recipe Appendix).

Potato *gnocchi* can also be flavored, and various ones are popular, especially in Tuscany. Recipes follow for two of the most interesting. The first is flavored with a dense tomato sauce in the potato mixture; the *gnocchi* are then dressed only with butter and cheese. The second type is made with dried porcini mushrooms. The mushroom flavor is enhanced by boiling the *gnocchi* in the mushroom soaking water. They are then dressed only with butter—the cheese option is not popular with Italians, who generally do not put grated cheese on anything flavored with wild mushrooms. (See the Note on the use of cheese, page 11).

Potato *gnocchi* are baked with cheese in Piedmont, a recipe originating in Cuneo. When the hot cheese melts and boils, it suggests to the Piemontesi, the frothing at the mouth of an animal, and so the dialect word *bava*, which means just that, was applied to this dish. There is often an earthy, not quite polite but humorous touch to such Italian names. This one is typical.

The Piedmont version of Naked *Ravioli* is, as one might expect, more complex, richer, and heavier than the Tuscan version. Chard is mixed with the spinach; and most typically, Gorgonzola cheese is incorporated along with the grated Parmigiano. Sage is added to the butter of the dressing.

From old Mantua, in Lombardy, we have dumplings of meat in the Renaissance manner. They are cooked in broth, but the broth is no longer eaten. These *Agnolotti ignudi* are then served with butter, cream, and mascarpone sauce and sprinkled with Parmigiano. Mantua retains its traditions from the time when, as we know from *Rigoletto* or from Shakespeare, it was an independent duchy. Another holdover from an earlier era is the inclusion of bread crumbs in the stuffing.

The Genoese *gnocchi*, or *troffie*, eaten with the traditional pesto, include *mollica* mixed with the potatoes. Of course, potatoes blend superbly with pesto.

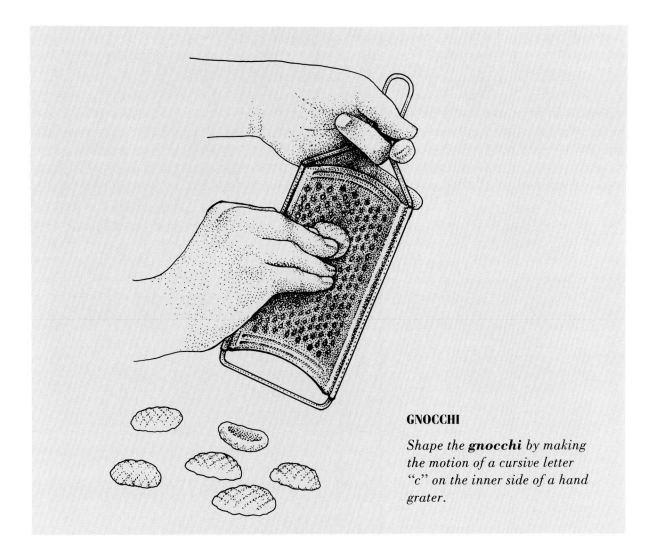

GNOCCHI

*Shape the **gnocchi** by making the motion of a cursive letter "c" on the inner side of a hand grater.*

FROM TUSCANY

SERVES 6

Gnocchi o Topini di Funghi

MUSHROOM *GNOCCHI*

FOR THE MUSHROOM
BASE:
**2 ounces dried porcini
mushrooms**
2 quarts lukewarm water
**1 medium-sized clove
garlic, peeled**
**15 large sprigs Italian
parsley, leaves only**
**2 tablespoons (1 ounce)
sweet butter**
3 tablespoons olive oil
½ cup dry red wine
**Salt and freshly ground
black pepper**
**½ tablespoon tomato paste,
preferably imported
Italian**

FOR THE *GNOCCHI*:
Coarse-grained salt
**1 pound potatoes (not new
potatoes)**
**1¾ cups unbleached, all-
purpose flour**
**Salt and freshly ground
black pepper**
Freshly grated nutmeg

TO COOK THE *GNOCCHI*:
Coarse-grained salt

TO SERVE:
**6 tablespoons (3 ounces)
sweet butter**
**15 large sprigs Italian
parsley, leaves only**
**6 tablespoons freshly
grated Parmigiano
cheese (optional)**

Soak the mushrooms in the lukewarm water for 30 minutes. Drain the mushrooms into a strainer lined with several layers of paper towels, saving the soaking water. Make sure that no sand remains attached to the stems, then finely chop the mushrooms and set aside.

Finely chop garlic and parsley on a board. Heat the butter and oil over medium heat in a heavy saucepan. When the butter is melted, add the chopped ingredients, sauté for 10 minutes, and then add the mushrooms. Sauté for 10 minutes longer, then add the wine and salt and pepper to taste. Let the wine evaporate over low heat for 10 minutes. Put in the tomato paste and cook for 15 minutes more, stirring every so often so that nothing sticks to the pan. Remove the pan from the heat and let rest for a few minutes. Use a food processor or blender to finely grind the contents, but do not completely purée. Transfer to a crockery or glass bowl and let cool completely.

Meanwhile bring a large pot of cold water to a boil and add coarse salt to taste. Peel the potatoes and put them in a colander or large strainer. Insert the colander in the pot of boiling water, but be sure the water level is low enough so that water does not touch the bottom of the colander. Place aluminum foil over the potatoes in the colander and steam for 45 minutes or until tender but not mushy.

Place the flour on a pasta board in a mound. Pass the potatoes through a potato ricer, using the disc with smallest holes, onto the flour. Make a well in the potatoes and put in the ground mushrooms. Add salt, pepper, and nutmeg to taste. Start incorporating the flour into the potato-mushroom mixture little by little until the dough is homogeneous and only a little of the flour remains. Cut the dough into several pieces, and with your hands, roll each piece into a long roll about 1 inch in diameter. Cut the rolls into ¾-inch-long pieces.

To shape the *gnocchi*, use the inside part of a convex hand cheese grater. Start by holding a piece of dough at the top of the grater with the index and middle finger of one hand. Lightly draw the piece of dough around in a motion that makes the letter "c" and let it drop. Continue this procedure until all the *gnocchi* are prepared (see page 313).

Add 2 cups of cold water to the reserved mushroom-soaking water and bring to a boil in a large pot, then add coarse salt to taste. Meanwhile, melt the butter on the serving dish by placing the dish over a second pot of boiling water. Gently drop the *gnocchi*

into the pot with the boiling mushroom water and stir gently with a wooden spoon to keep them from sticking. After a few seconds the *gnocchi* will rise to the surface of the water; Cook for 1 minute more. Then, using a strainer-skimmer, transfer the *gnocchi* to the prepared serving dish. Sprinkle the parsley over and serve immediately. Pass the grated Parmigiano cheese at the table if you choose.

Gnocchi o Topini di funghi e rossi: **The tan and red colors of the *gnocchi* are produced by wild mushrooms and by a tomato sauce base respectively.**

GNOCCHI O TOPINI ROSSI

SERVES 6

RED *GNOCCHI*

FOR THE TOMATO BASE:
¼ cup olive oil
1 large clove garlic, peeled but left whole
5 large sprigs Italian parsley, leaves only
¼ cup tomato paste
½ cup lukewarm chicken broth, preferably homemade
Salt and freshly ground black pepper

FOR THE *GNOCCHI*:
Coarse-grained salt
1 pound potatoes (not new potatoes)
2¼ cups unbleached all-purpose flour
Salt and freshly ground black pepper
Freshly grated nutmeg

TO COOK THE *GNOCCHI*:
Coarse-grained salt

TO SERVE:
6 tablespoons (3 ounces) sweet butter
6 tablespoons freshly grated Parmigiano cheese
15 large sprigs Italian parsley, leaves only

Make a tomato base that is to be incorporated into the potatoes. Heat the oil in a small, heavy saucepan over medium heat. When the oil is warm, add the garlic and sauté until golden, about 2 minutes. Finely chop the parsley on a board, then discard the garlic and add the parsley, tomato paste, and broth to the saucepan. Stir well and simmer over low heat until the sauce is thick, about 15 minutes; taste for salt and pepper.

Bring a large pot of cold water to a boil and add coarse salt to taste. Peel the potatoes and put them in a colander or large strainer. Insert the colander in the pot of boiling water, but be sure the water level is low enough so that water does not touch the bottom of the colander. Place aluminum foil over the potatoes in the colander and steam for 45 minutes or until tender but not mushy.

Place the flour on a pasta board in a mound. Pass the potatoes through a potato ricer, using the disc with smallest holes, onto the flour. Make a well in the potatoes and put in the tomato base. Add salt, pepper, and nutmeg to taste. Start incorporating the flour into the potato-tomato mixture little by little until the dough is homogeneous and only a little of the flour remains. Cut the dough into several pieces, and with your hands, roll each piece into a long roll about 1 inch in diameter. Cut the rolls into ¾-inch-long pieces.

To shape the *gnocchi*, use the inside part of a convex hand cheese grater. Start by holding a piece of dough at the top of the grater with the index and middle finger of one hand. Lightly draw the piece of dough around in a motion that makes the letter "c" and let it drop. Continue this procedure until all the *gnocchi* are prepared (see page 313).

Cook the *gnocchi* in boiling salted water and finish with butter, as with *Gnocchi di funghi*. Sprinkle with the cheese and parsley and serve.

GNOCCHI DI PATATE ALLA "BAVA"

GNOCCHI BAKED WITH MELTING CHEESE

FROM CUNEO (PIEDMONT)

SERVES 4 TO 6

Bring a large pot of cold water to a boil and add coarse salt to taste. Peel the potatoes and put them in a colander or large strainer. Insert the colander in the pot of boiling water, but be sure the water level is low enough so that water does not touch the bottom of the colander. Place aluminum foil over the potatoes in the colander and steam for 45 minutes or until tender but not mushy.

Heavily butter a 13½- x 8¾-inch glass baking dish and preheat the oven to 400 degrees.

Place the flour on a pasta board in a mound. Pass the potatoes through a potato ricer, using the disc with smallest holes, onto the flour. Make a well in the potatoes and put in the egg. Add salt to taste. Start incorporating the flour into the potato-egg mixture little by little until the dough is homogeneous and only a little of the flour remains. Cut the dough into several pieces, and with your hands, roll each piece into a long roll about 1 inch in diameter. Cut the rolls into ¾-inch-long pieces.

To shape the *gnocchi*, use the inside part of a convex hand cheese grater. Start by holding a piece of dough at the top of the grater with the index and middle finger of one hand. Lightly draw the piece of dough around in a motion that makes the letter "c" and let it drop. Continue this procedure until all the *gnocchi* are prepared (see page 313).

Bring a large pot of cold water to a boil, add coarse salt to taste, then add the *gnocchi*. When they rise to the surface, cook for 30 seconds more. Using a strainer-skimmer, transfer the *gnocchi* to the prepared baking dish. When they are all in the dish, arrange the bits of butter all over, then make a layer of the cheese slices on top. Bake for 5 minutes—just enough time for the cheese to melt and "froth." Remove from oven and serve hot.

FOR THE *GNOCCHI*:
Coarse-grained salt
¾ pound potatoes (not new potatoes)
Butter
1 cup unbleached all-purpose flour
1 extra-large egg
Salt

TO COOK THE *GNOCCHI*:
Coarse-grained salt

TO BAKE:
3 tablespoons (1½ ounces) butter, cut into small bits
3 ounces fontina Valdostana cheese, finely sliced

Ravioli Nudi con Gorgonzola

NAKED *RAVIOLI* WITH GORGONZOLA

FOR THE *RAVIOLI*:

1½ pounds fresh spinach, large stems removed

1½ pounds fresh Swiss chard, large stems removed

Coarse-grained salt

½ pound ricotta

½ pound Gorgonzola cheese, preferably sweet

5 extra-large egg yolks

3 cups freshly grated Parmigiano cheese

Salt and freshly ground black pepper

½ teaspoon freshly grated nutmeg

2 cups unbleached all-purpose flour

TO COOK THE *RAVIOLI*:

Coarse-grained salt

TO SERVE:

12 tablespoons (6 ounces) sweet butter

10 large fresh sage leaves, torn into thirds

Put the spinach and chard in a large bowl of cold water. Bring a large pot of cold water to a boil, add coarse salt to taste, then drain and add the vegetables and cook for 10 minutes. Drain again, rinse under cold running water, squeeze very dry, and finely chop on a board. Place the chopped vegetables in a bowl along with the ricotta, Gorgonzola, egg yolks, 2 cups of the Parmigiano, salt and pepper to taste, and nutmeg. Use a wooden spoon to mix all the ingredients, then taste again for salt and pepper.

Bring a large stockpot of cold water to a boil over medium heat. Spread the flour on a pasta board. Take a heaping tablespoon of the mixture from the bowl and roll it on the floured board into a small ball. Be sure the ball is uniformly compact, with no empty spaces inside; the outside should be uniformly floured. When the water reaches a boil, add coarse salt to taste, then gently drop the first ball in. When it rises to the top, let it cook for 30 seconds. Meanwhile, melt the butter by putting it on a large serving dish and placing the dish over a second pot of boiling water. Continue to form *ravioli*, rolling them on the flour, until the dough has been used up. Drop the *ravioli* into the salted boiling water, 5 or 6 at a time. The *ravioli* will rise to the surface; after an additional 30 seconds, use a strainer-skimmer to transfer them directly onto the serving dish containing the melted butter. They should be arranged in a single layer. When all the *ravioli* are on the dish, sprinkle with the remaining Parmigiano and the sage leaves. Serve immediately.

AGNOLOTTI O AGNELOTTI IGNUDI AL MASCARPONE

"NAKED" *AGNOLOTTI* IN *MASCARPONE* SAUCE

F R O M   M A N T U A

SERVES 8

Cut the *prosciutto* and *pancetta* into small pieces and remove the casing from the sausages. Using a meat grinder, grind together the *prosciutto*, *pancetta*, and sausages or pork. Place the ground meat in a crockery or glass bowl, add the butter and eggs, and mix very well with a wooden spoon until the butter is completely incorporated. Add the bread crumbs and Parmigiano, and season with salt and pepper. Cover the bowl and refrigerate for at least 1 hour before using.

When ready, bring the broth to a boil in a large pot over medium heat. Meanwhile, place a large skillet with the butter over low heat. When the broth reaches a boil, start shaping the stuffing into tiny meat balls; a heaping tablespoon of stuffing will be enough to prepare several. Make sure the meat balls are solid with no holes inside. Drop the balls into the boiling broth a few at a time, and as they rise to the top, transfer them with a slotted spoon to the skillet containing the butter. When all the *agnolotti* are cooked and in the skillet, add the *mascarpone* and heavy cream. Mix very well and simmer for 1 or 2 minutes, or until the *mascarpone* is completely dissolved. Season with salt, pepper, and nutmeg. Mix very well, then transfer to a warmed serving platter. Serve immediately, with some Parmigiano on the side.

FOR THE STUFFING:
4 ounces *prosciutto*, in 1 piece
4 ounces *pancetta*, in 1 piece
2 Italian sweet sausages, without fennel seeds; or 6 ounces boneless pork
4 tablespoons (2 ounces) sweet butter
4 extra-large eggs
About ¾ cup unseasoned bread crumbs, preferably homemade
5 tablespoons freshly grated Parmigiano cheese
Salt and freshly ground black pepper to taste

TO COOK THE *AGNOLOTTI*:
4 quarts chicken broth, preferably homemade

FOR THE SAUCE:
8 tablespoons (4 ounces) sweet butter
½ pound (8 ounces) *mascarpone*
½ cup heavy cream
Salt and freshly ground black pepper to taste
Pinch of freshly grated nutmeg

TO SERVE:
8 tablespoons freshly grated Parmigiano cheese

FROM LIGURIA

SERVES 4 TO 6

TROFFIE *OR* TROFIE

GENOESE *GNOCCHI*

FOR THE *TROFFIE:*
Coarse-grained salt
½ pound potatoes (not new
   potatoes)
2 slices good-quality white
   bread, crusts removed
1 cup cold milk
1 cup unbleached all-
   purpose flour
¼ cup freshly grated
   Parmigiano cheese
1 extra-large egg
Salt

TO COOK THE *TROFFIE:*
Coarse-grained salt

TO SERVE:
Genoese Pesto Sauce
   (page 232)

Bring a large pot of cold water to a boil and add coarse salt to taste. Peel the potatoes and put them in a colander or large strainer. Insert the colander in the pot of boiling water, but be sure the water level is low enough so that water does not touch the bottom of the colander. Place aluminum foil over the potatoes in the colander and steam for 45 minutes or until tender but not mushy.

Soak the bread in the cold milk for 30 minutes.

Place the flour on a pasta board in a mound. Pass the potatoes through a potato ricer, using the disc with smallest holes, onto the flour. Make a well in the potatoes. Mix the Parmigiano with the egg in a small bowl and season with salt. Squeeze the milk out of the bread, crumble up the bread, and add to the well along with the egg-cheese mixture, using a wooden spoon to mix thoroughly. Start incorporating the flour into the mixture little by little until the dough is homogeneous and only a little of the flour remains. Cut the dough into several pieces, and with your hands, roll each piece into a long roll about 1 inch in diameter. Cut the rolls into ¾-inch-long pieces.

To shape the *gnocchi*, use the inside part of a convex hand cheese grater. Start by holding a piece of dough at the top of the grater with the index and middle finger of one hand. Lightly draw the piece of dough around in a motion that makes the letter "c" and let it drop. Continue this procedure until all the *gnocchi* are prepared (see page 313).

Cook the *gnocchi* in boiling salted water, then dress with the Genoese Pesto Sauce. Serve hot.

A *passatelli* maker.

PASSATELLI

Passatelli are made by passing a stuffing mixture through the holes of a *passatelli* maker or potato ricer directly into boiling broth. In the broth, the *passatelli* congeal into tender strips which are then eaten with the broth. They are found throughout central Italy, with variations in the different regions. The basis is always bread crumbs, grated Parmigiano, and eggs. In Tuscany, a little spinach is added and grated lemon rind used for flavor.

In Romagna, butter and a little flour are added to the *passatelli*, but no spinach. And in the Marches, they use finely ground veal, with both spinach and butter. A little nutmeg rather than lemon peel flavors the mixture, and additional Parmigiano can be grated over each portion of broth.

Special *passatelli* makers are still available, but a potato ricer is usually used instead, with fine results. I do not recommend using a food mill, since the holes are too small to make really characteristic *passatelli*. There is nothing more soothing and warming than a delicious bowl of rich broth, made even more interesting by the *passatelli* floating in it.

PASSATELLI ALLA TOSCANA

PASSATELLI IN BROTH, TUSCAN STYLE

FROM TUSCANY

SERVES 6 TO 8

1 pound fresh spinach, large stems removed
Coarse-grained salt
4 ounces unseasoned bread crumbs, preferably homemade
6 ounces freshly grated Parmigiano cheese
4 extra-large eggs, at room temperature
1 large lemon with thick skin
Salt and freshly ground black pepper
3 quarts beef or chicken broth, preferably homemade

Clean the spinach and cook it in a large quantity of boiling water with coarse salt. Drain, rinse, and squeeze well to eliminate water. Finely chop the spinach, then weigh out exactly 3 ounces. If any extra, discard or save for another use.

Place the bread crumbs in a crockery or glass bowl along with the Parmigiano and eggs. Use a wooden spoon to mix ingredients very well. Grate the lemon and add it to the bowl. Taste for salt and pepper. Add the spinach to the bowl and mix very well. Cover the bowl with aluminum foil and refrigerate until needed, at least 30 minutes.

When ready, place the broth over medium heat. When it reaches a boil, use a *passatelli* maker or a potato ricer with the large-hole disc to pass the mixture directly into the boiling broth; the length of the *passatelli* should be not more than 4 inches. Cook for 1 minute, then serve immediately with the broth.

PASSATELLI ALLA ROMAGNOLA

PASSATELLI, ROMAGNA STYLE

FROM EMILIA-ROMAGNA

SERVES 4 TO 6

3 extra-large eggs
2 tablespoons (1 ounce) sweet butter, at room temperature
Grated peel of ½ large lemon with thick skin
8 tablespoons unseasoned bread crumbs, preferably homemade
8 tablespoons freshly grated Parmigiano cheese
1 tablespoon unbleached all-purpose flour
Salt and freshly ground black pepper
2 quarts beef or chicken broth, preferably homemade

Place the eggs in a crockery or glass bowl along with the butter, lemon peel, bread crumbs, and Parmigiano. Use a wooden spoon to mix ingredients well. Add the flour, season to taste with salt and pepper, mix again, cover bowl with aluminum foil, and refrigerate until needed, at least 30 minutes.

When ready to make the *passatelli*, place the broth over medium heat. When it reaches a boil, use a *passatelli* maker or potato ricer, using the disc with large holes, to pass the mixture directly into the boiling broth; the length of the *passatelli* should not be longer than 4 inches. Cook for 1 minute, then serve immediately, with the broth.

PASSATELLI DI CARNE ALLA MARCHIGIANA

MEAT *PASSATELLI*, MARCHES STYLE

FROM
THE MARCHES

SERVES 6 TO 8

Clean the spinach and cook it quickly in a large quantity of boiling water with coarse salt. Drain, rinse, and squeeze well of moisture. Finely chop the spinach, then weigh out exactly 3 ounces. If any extra, discard or save for another use.

Place the veal in a crockery or glass bowl along with the bread crumbs, Parmigiano, and spinach. With a wooden spoon, mix together very well. Add the butter, eggs, and salt, pepper, and nutmeg to taste; mix well again. Cover the bowl with aluminum foil and refrigerate until needed, for at least 30 minutes.

When ready to make the *passatelli*, place the broth over medium heat. When it reaches a boil, use a *passatelli* maker or a potato ricer using the disc with large holes, to pass the mixture directly into the boiling broth; the *passatelli* should not be more than 4 inches in length. Cook for 1½ minutes, then serve immediately with the broth. Serve with grated Parmigiano, if desired.

1 pound fresh spinach, large stems removed
Coarse-grained salt
¼ pound finely ground veal shoulder
4 tablespoons unseasoned bread crumbs, preferably homemade
6 tablespoons freshly grated Parmigiano cheese
2 tablespoons (1 ounce) sweet butter, at room temperature
2 extra-large eggs
Salt and freshly ground black pepper
Freshly grated nutmeg
3 quarts beef or chicken broth, preferably homemade
6 to 8 teaspoons freshly grated Parmigiano cheese (optional)

RECIPE APPENDIX

Gnocchi in Other Bugialli Books

TOPINI DI PATATE (Potato *Gnocchi*) ALLA FIORENTINA *FA* p. 232*
GNOCCHI DI SEMOLINO (Semolina *Gnocchi*) ALLA ROMANA *FA* p. 231
GNOCCHI DI PESCE (Fish *Gnocchi*) *FA* p. 226
RAVIOLI NUDI ALLA FIORENTINA (Naked *Ravioli*) *FA* p. 228
RAVIOLI NUDI DI PESCE (Naked Fish *Ravioli*) *FA* p. 228
RAVIOLI [*Gnocchi*] DI POLLO IN BRODO (Chicken *Ravioli* [*Gnocchi*] in Broth) *CT* p. 94
POLPETTINE DI SPINACI (Deep-fried Spinach Croquettes [*Gnocchi*]) *CT* p. 391

* GNOCCHI DI FARINA GIALLA (Cornmeal *Gnocchi*) *FA* p. 224, are not shaped into individual dumplings, so I do not include them as real *gnocchi*.

FA   *The Fine Art of Italian Cooking*
CT   *Giuliano Bugialli's Classic Techniques of Italian Cooking*

Minestra di farro against the Renaissance Medici walls of the old Tuscan town of Lucca.

COUSCOUS

AND OTHER GRAINS

Coarsely milled grain, usually of hard wheat, that is first rubbed with water, sometimes with oil, then steamed and eaten with a stew of meat or fish and vegetables, often including chick-peas, has become known in the English-speaking world as *couscous*. Assumed to be of North African, Berber origin, couscous is also found in other Mediterranean places. It is further assumed that couscous reached Sicily and other parts through Arab invasions from North Africa.

Knowing of couscous dishes in Sicily, Sardinia, and Leghorn in Tuscany (Livorno), I began to search for other such dishes throughout Italy. In the course of my travels, I came to seriously doubt the accepted theory about the origin and spread of couscous. Throughout Italy, in places untouched by a medieval Arab presence, I found the use of a hard wheat more coarsely ground than the usual Italian semolina. And this wheat is prepared with the same method of rubbing water into the coarse grain as is used for couscous. It appears in preparations of the following dishes, among others: *Manfregoli* (Tuscany), *Manfrigoli* (Romagna), *Fregoli* (Trentino), and *Fregula* (Sardinia).

In Sardinian recipes for *Fregula* (also spelled *"Firegoli"*) the grains are parboiled, then spread out. The recipe for *Fregula* included here incorporates water, egg yolks, and saffron into the grains, which enlarges them; they are then dried in the oven and finally boiled for the final preparation, like a pasta.

In Sardinian *Cascá*, a real couscous, the grain cooks—really steams—in a hermetically sealed terra-cotta pot.

I should like to suggest that all of these dishes are survivors of the Ancient Roman world. Egypt, North Africa, Sicily, and Tuscany were, at different times during the Roman epoch, the main sources of wheat. If couscous is of Berber origin, its use must have spread northward much earlier than during the Arab conquests. I suggest that the Berber origin itself be subjected to further verification.

For instance, looking into the 2,000-year-old cookbook fragment of the Roman

Apicius, we find in his chapter on *Pulse* a number of dishes that sound suspiciously like couscous. In *Pultes Iulianae*, the coarse wheat grain is cooked with water and oil, and a meat stew flavored with herbs and wine is gradually mixed in. There are three similar dishes described, including one using bread crumbs instead of grain. Bread crumbs are still used instead of wheat in couscous dishes, not only in modern North Africa but also in Leghorn in Italy. So there is no question here of Arabic influence. Coarsely ground barley as well as bread crumbs were used in *Pulse* dishes, and its use also survives in Italy as well as North Africa.

Couscous is made by Italian Jews and is assumed to be Sephardic, having traveled with the Arab-influenced Spanish Jews when they were expelled. But not all Italian Jews are Sephardic; some communities survive from Roman times. In Leghorn, the Jewish couscous is paralleled by the one made with bread crumbs by the rest of the population.

Spain was a great part of the Roman world, producing some of its important emperors. It would be interesting to try to verify surviving dishes in Spain and Portugal of a similar nature. In much later times, after the discovery of the Americas, we see Spanish influences on North African couscous. *Harissa*, the spicy sauce used there, is made from peppers brought back by the Spanish from the New World. Several of the squashes that are common vegetables in their stews made a similar trip. Couldn't the traffic have been both ways, even in ancient times?

Sicily, as the meeting place of European and North African cultures, is the most fascinating to examine for culinary survivors. Let us examine the differences between the North African and Sicilian pots used for cooking the grain. The Sicilian *cuscusera* is made of glazed or unglazed terra-cotta. The top section has quite large holes in the bottom, so large that the grain probably fell through without a typically secret Sicilian device not shared with outsiders—that the pot must be lined with bay or basil leaves, which flavor the grains as well as contain them. The top section rests on what is simply a terra-cotta stockpot. Strikingly, however, the Sicilians have a special terra-cotta lid because, unlike the North Africans, they always use a lid while steaming couscous. One further folkloristic touch is to cover the area where the upper and lower pots meet with a thick rope of dough made from a simple mixture of flour and water. This rope seals the escape route of steam, and sets the imagination reeling. It seems more ancient than the commonsense cloth method, and further suggests that in Sicily wheat was so plentiful it could be wasted, whereas in North Africa they had to be more frugal. Was this the original sealing method, with the cloth a later substitution? Did the steaming arrive in Sicily with the eleventh-century Arab occupiers, or was it already there in late Roman times when the island had such excess wheat that dried pasta was invented as a way of preserving it?

FROM SICILY

SERVES 6

Cuscusu

COUSCOUS, SICILIAN STYLE

*There are a number of traditional couscous dishes that survive in Sicily. This is the most popular one. It uses as its stew the **Ghiotta di pesce**, which also exists as an independent dish; some of the broth is added to the steaming water, and when reduced is reused as a sauce.*

FOR THE COUSCOUS:
1 pound couscous (not instant)
1 tablespoon salt
9 cups cold water

FOR THE FISH SOUP:
2½ pounds non-oily fish, 2 or 3 types cut into slices, with bone
Coarse-grained salt
1 large red onion, peeled
½ cup olive oil
1 pound canned tomatoes, preferably imported Italian, drained
4 large cloves garlic, peeled
20 large sprigs Italian parsley, leaves only
5 large fresh basil leaves, torn into thirds
1 cup dry white wine
4 tablespoons white wine vinegar
1 tablespoon tomato paste
Salt and freshly ground black pepper
2 generous pinches hot red pepper flakes

FOR THE STEAMER:
3½ cups unbleached all-purpose flour
1 cup cold water
15 large fresh or dried bay leaves; or large fresh basil leaves

Prepare the couscous. Spread out the grain on a large serving platter or cookie sheet. (In the Mediterranean there are special plates for this purpose; in Italy they are made of terra-cotta.) Dissolve the salt in a small bowl with 1 cup of the water. Sprinkle 2 teaspoons of the salted water on the grain, then use the fingers of one hand to rub some grains against the palm itself, using a rotating motion to incorporate the water evenly into the grain. Keep repeating this with additional teaspoons of salted water and grains until you have used up ¼ cup of water and the couscous is evenly wet all over. Spread the grain evenly over a cotton dish towel and let rest for 1 hour.

Prepare the fish soup. Soak the fish in a bowl of cold water with coarse salt for 30 minutes. Finely chop the onion on a board. Place the oil in a heavy, flameproof casserole over medium heat; when the oil is warm, add the onion, lower the heat, and sauté for 15 minutes, stirring every so often with a wooden spoon. Pass the tomatoes through a food mill, using the disc with the smallest holes. Finely chop the garlic and coarsely chop the parsley on a board. Add the tomatoes to the casserole, cover, and simmer for 25 minutes. Add the garlic, parsley, basil, white wine, vinegar, tomato paste, salt and pepper to taste, and red pepper flakes. Stir very well, cover again, and simmer for 15 minutes more.

Drain the fish and wash under cold running water. Add fish to the soup, cover, and cook for 10 minutes. When the fish is cooked, remove casserole from the heat and transfer two-thirds of the broth to the bottom part of a terra-cotta *cuscusera* or stockpot. Cover the casserole containing the remaining fish and set aside until needed.

Add the remaining 8 cups cold water to the soup in the bottom part of the *cuscusera* or stockpot, then put the top part of the *cuscusera* or a strainer over it. Using the flour and the cup of cold water, prepare a thick dough to seal the area connecting the 2 halves of the steamer. Roll this dough into a thick rope long enough to fit around the perimeter of the pot. Using the rope of dough, cover the circle where the top and bottom parts of the steamer (whether *cuscusera* or stockpot with strainer) meet to seal it. Place the steamer over medium heat, and when the broth-flavored water reaches a boil and the steam begins to rise through the holes of the strainer, cover the holes with the bay or basil leaves, and then add the couscous grain (see note). Cover tightly with the lid of the *cuscusera* (in contrast to some other Mediterraneans, Italians do cover the pot) with a lid or aluminum foil and steam for 30 minutes.

Spoon out the couscous onto a large platter (be sure leaves are still covering the holes) and start rubbing the grains between the palms of your hands, incorporating the remaining ¾ cup of salted water, little by little to separate any that have stuck together and to retain an even and uniform consistency of individual grains. Let the couscous cool for 15 minutes, then put the grain back into the leaf-lined steamer and cook for 20 minutes more. Reheat the fish, transfer the couscous onto a large warmed platter and discard the bay or basil leaves. Make a well in the grain and arrange the fish in the well. Pour the soup over and serve, adding some of the now reduced soup-flavored water from the steaming.

NOTE:
It is also convenient to spread a cheesecloth over the herbs to facilitate removing the steamed grains.

FROM SICILY

SERVES 4 TO 6

Couscus Nero

BLACK COUSCOUS

FOR THE SAUCE:
3 pounds cuttlefish (ink squid), uncleaned and with ink sacs
Coarse-grained salt
1 medium-sized red onion, peeled
5 large cloves garlic, peeled
30 large sprigs Italian parsley, leaves only
½ cup olive oil
1 cup dry white wine
6 cups lukewarm water
2 tablespoons tomato paste
Salt and freshly ground black pepper
½ teaspoon hot red pepper flakes

FOR THE COUSCOUS:
1 pound couscous (not instant)
1 tablespoon salt
1 cup cold water
8 cups fish broth (*fumetto*)

FOR THE STEAMER:
3½ cups unbleached all-purpose flour
1 cup water
10 large bay leaves

Here is the couscous with the sauce made from cuttlefish and their ink. This so-called black couscous is a traditional specialty of the nuns of a convent near Trapani. The sauce is the same as that used in Tuscany with pasta and in Venice with rice.

Sardinian couscous is characterized by an olive oil flavor in the grain and the skinning of the chick-peas before cooking. Removing the skins is not merely for aesthetic reasons; it produces a sweeter flavor. Though time consuming, it is worth trying at least once to taste the difference. The stew in Sardinia is always of chick-peas and vegetables only, and the meat is always an independently prepared dish, served together with the grain. Aside from the chicken used in this recipe, a number of Sardinian beef, lamb, and fish dishes are traditionally used.

Prepare the sauce. Clean the cuttlefish carefully, saving the sacs full of the ink and cutting the meat into strips about ¼ inch thick (see page 130). Place the strips in a bowl of cold water with a little coarse salt and let rest until needed.

Finely chop the onion with 3 cloves of the garlic and 15 sprigs of the parsley all together on a board. Place the oil in a heavy, flameproof casserole over medium heat, and when the oil is warm, add the chopped ingredients and sauté for 5 minutes. Finely chop the remaining 2 cloves of garlic and the 15 remaining sprigs of parsley together on a board; set aside. Drain and rinse the cuttlefish under cold running water. Add the chopped ingredients and the cuttlefish to the casserole, raise the heat, and sauté for 5 minutes longer. Add the wine and evaporate for 10 minutes.

Put the ink sacs in a very fine strainer and submerge the strainer in a bowl with 2 cups of the lukewarm water. Rub the sacs against the strainer, using a wooden spoon until all the ink is extracted from the membranes. Discard the membranes. Add the water with the ink to the casserole, together with the tomato paste, and simmer, covered, for 3½ hours, adding the remaining 4 cups of lukewarm water as needed; the mixture should be like a soup. Stir with a wooden spoon every so often; add salt and pepper to taste and the red pepper flakes when the cuttlefish is half cooked. (Cooking time here is for large cuttlefish. If they are smaller, they may become tender much sooner. Check every 30 minutes.)

Prepare the couscous. Spread out the grains on a large serving platter or cookie sheet. Dissolve the salt in a small bowl with the cold water. Sprinkle 2 teaspoons of the salted water on the grains, then use the fingers of one hand to rub the grains against the palm itself, using a rotating motion to incorporate the water evenly into the grains. Keep repeating this with additional teaspoons of the water until you have used ¼ cup. Spread the grains evenly on a cotton dish towel and let rest for 1 hour.

Place the fish broth in the bottom part of a *cuscusera* or a stockpot, then put the top part of the *cuscusera* or a strainer over it. Use the flour and water to prepare a thick dough to seal the area connecting the 2 parts of the steamer (see page 328). Line the bottom of the colander with 10 of the bay leaves (see note), then put in the couscous grains. Cover tightly with the lid of the *cuscusera* or with a piece of aluminum foil, and steam for 30 minutes.

Transfer the couscous to a large platter and rub the grains between the palms of your hands, incorporating the remaining ¾ cup of salted water, little by little and separating grains which have stuck together. There should be a uniform consistency of individual grains. Let the couscous cool for 15 minutes, then put the grains back into the steamer, cover, and cook for 20 minutes more.

Transfer the couscous to a large, warmed platter; discard the bay leaves, then make a large well in the center and place the fish with its sauce in the well. Serve immediately.

NOTE:
It is also convenient to spread a cheesecloth over the herbs to facilitate removing the steamed grains.

FROM LIVORNO
(TUSCANY)

SERVES 6

FOR THE CHICK-PEAS:
2 cups dried chick-peas
1 large red onion, peeled
10 cups cold water
Coarse-grained salt
**Freshly ground black
  pepper**

FOR THE COUSCOUS:
**¼ teaspoon ground saffron
  threads**
½ teaspoon salt
1 cup cold water
**1 pound couscous (not
  instant)**

FOR THE STEAMER:
**3½ cups unbleached all-
  purpose flour**
1 cup cold water

FOR THE SAUCE:
**3 medium-sized red
  onions, peeled**
**15 large sprigs Italian
  parsley, leaves only**
6 tablespoons olive oil
1 cup dry white wine
**3 cups lukewarm beef
  broth, preferably
  homemade**
**Salt and freshly ground
  black pepper**

FOR THE *POLPETTINE*:
**24 large leaves Boston
  lettuce**
Coarse-grained salt
**3 slices white bread, crusts
  removed**
**1 medium-sized clove
  garlic, peeled**

CUSCUS

COUSCOUS, LIVORNO STYLE

The Etruscans were once famous for the quality of their wheat, and perhaps this is connected with the survival of a variety of couscous-type dishes in Tuscany, especially among the Jewish communities, which tend to preserve old traditions. More interesting than the well-known Pitigliano version is this one from Livorno. The delicate little meat balls are wrapped in lettuce leaves rather than cabbage, and the more recent tomato sauce is avoided in favor of a wine-broth. Attesting to its antiquity is the addition of saffron to strongly season the grain.

Prepare the chick-peas. Soak them in a bowl of cold water overnight. The next morning, drain and then rinse the peas under cold running water. Put them in a heavy, medium-sized flameproof casserole with the whole onion and water. Place over medium heat and simmer until cooked and very soft, about 1 hour. Add coarse salt and pepper to taste, and simmer for 5 minutes more. Remove and discard the onion. Pass the contents of the casserole through a food mill, using the disc with smallest holes, into a small saucepan (see Note). Place the pan over medium heat, taste for salt and pepper, and simmer for 15 minutes, mixing every so often until a fairly thick sauce is formed. Cover the pan and set aside until needed.

Prepare the couscous. Dissolve the saffron and salt in the water. Follow the instructions on page 328, but incorporate the entire water mixture at the beginning, when the grain is first spread out. After the liquid is absorbed, do not transfer onto a cotton towel, but let rest on the serving platter for 1 hour. For the actual steaming, use just salted water. Seal the steamer with the dough. See page 328.

While the couscous grain is resting and later steaming, prepare the sauce and the *polpettine* (little wrapped meat balls). Begin with the sauce. Finely chop the onions and parsley together on a board. Heat the oil in a large skillet over medium heat, add the chopped ingredients and sauté for 10 minutes, then add the wine and let it evaporate for 10 minutes more. Put in the broth, taste for salt and pepper, and simmer for 1 hour, uncovered. Cover the skillet and set aside until needed.

For the *polpettine*, soak the lettuce leaves in cold water for 30 minutes. Bring a large pot of cold water to a boil and add coarse salt to taste. Have a bowl of cold water next to the pot of boiling water; line a cookie sheet with paper towels. Blanch each lettuce leaf for 40 seconds. Use a slotted spoon to quickly transfer it to the bowl of cold water for 1 minute, then onto the prepared towels; gently spread out the leaf. Repeat until all the leaves are blanched.

Soak the bread in a small bowl of cold water for 5 minutes. Finely chop the garlic and parsley on a board. Place the ground veal and beef in a crockery bowl, then add the chopped ingredients, olive oil, and salt and pepper to taste. Squeeze the water out of the bread and add the bread to the bowl. Mix very well with a wooden spoon until everything is well combined. Place 2 tablespoons of stuffing on each lettuce leaf, then wrap it up, being sure that the leaf completely encloses the meat. Place the *polpettine*, leaf ends facing down, in the skillet with the sauce. Cover the skillet and put it over low heat to simmer for 15 minutes.

When the couscous is ready, reheat the chick-pea purée, then spread the grain over a large, warmed serving platter. Pour the chick-pea purée on top to cover it, then arrange the *polpettine* with their sauce over everything. Serve immediately.

NOTE:
To pass easily through the holes, the bean purée needs liquid, so keep pouring the liquid from the pan back into the food mill until all the mixture has passed through.

15 large sprigs Italian parsley, leaves only
1 pound ground veal shoulder
1 pound ground beef
2 tablespoons olive oil
Salt and freshly ground black pepper

CASCÁ

COUSCOUS, SARDINIAN STYLE

FOR THE CHICK-PEAS:
2 cups dried chick-peas
**2 medium-sized cloves
garlic, peeled**
3 tablespoons olive oil
2 tablespoons tomato paste
**Salt and freshly ground
black pepper**

FOR THE COUSCOUS:
**1 pound couscous (not
instant)**
½ cup olive oil
½ teaspoon salt
¾ cup cold water

FOR THE STEAMER:
**3½ cups unbleached all-
purpose flour**
1 cup cold water

FOR THE VEGETABLES:
3 large artichokes
1 large lemon, cut in half
**1 pound carrots, scraped
and cut into quarters
lengthwise**
**3 large bulbs fennel,
cleaned and cut into
quarters**
**3 medium-sized red
onions, peeled and cut
into halves**
½ cup olive oil
**Salt and freshly ground
black pepper**

FOR THE CHICKEN:
½ cup olive oil
**1 chicken (about 3½
pounds), cleaned and cut
into 12 pieces**

Saffron was used in olden times in the Mediterranean as an omni-present condiment, like salt and pepper (pepper was then a luxury like saffron is today). Many surviving dishes in Italy were once made with saffron but are now usually prepared without it except in Sicily and Sardinia. (Sicilian pasta with fresh sardines is an example.) The pinches of saffron in this Sardinian chicken dish, as well as the large amount in the Livorno couscous, are survivors of an earlier era, as is Italian couscous itself.

Prepare the chick-peas. Soak them in a bowl with cold water over-night or until the skins are loosened. Drain and rinse under cold running water. Hold each chick-pea between the thumb and index finger, and pinch off the skin.

Finely chop the garlic on a board. Heat the oil in a heavy saucepan over medium heat and add the garlic and tomato paste. Sauté for 1 minute, then add the chick-peas, stir very well, and add enough cold water to cover completely. Simmer uncovered until the peas are cooked but still firm, about 45 minutes when skinned. Add salt and pepper to taste. Cover again and let the peas rest until needed.

Prepare the couscous. Dissolve the salt in the water. Following the instructions given on page 328, but at the beginning, when the grain is first spread, use the same technique to incorporate the oil into it, before incorporating the salted water. After these liquids are absorbed, let the couscous rest for 1 hour on the serving plat-ter, not a cotton towel. For the steaming, use just salted water and seal the 2 parts of the *cuscusera* with the dough (see page 328).

While the couscous is resting and steaming, prepare the vege-tables. Clean the artichokes, cut them into quarters, then place in a bowl with cold water with the lemon halves squeezed in. Place the other vegetables together in a second large bowl of cold water and soak for 30 minutes. When ready, heat the oil in a stockpot over medium heat. Drain all the vegetables and add them to the pot, first the carrots, then the artichokes, fennel, and onions. Sauté for 1 minute without stirring, then add enough water to completely cover the vegetables. Season with salt and pepper to taste, cover, and simmer without mixing until they are cooked but still firm; this will take about 30 minutes. Transfer the vegetables to a crockery bowl and cover the bowl with aluminum foil to keep them warm until needed. Reduce the vegetable poaching water by half.

Meanwhile prepare the chicken. Heat the oil in a large skillet over high heat, then add the chicken pieces in a single layer. Sauté for 10 minutes until golden brown all over. Sprinkle the scallions over; season with salt, pepper, and saffron, then cover with a layer of tomatoes. Cover with lid, lower the heat, and cook for 20 minutes.

Meanwhile, arrange the chicken on a serving dish. Reheat the chick-peas and the vegetable poaching water. Transfer the prepared couscous to a large serving platter and start adding the broth from the chick-peas, always mixing it thoroughly into the grain. When all the broth is absorbed, add the chick-peas and mix very well. Form a mound and make a well in it. Place the cooked vegetables in the well. Each serving should be arranged with the grain on the bottom of the plate, then the vegetables and chicken with its sauce on top. Some of the reduced vegetable poaching broth should then be added.

10 medium-sized scallions, white and green parts, coarsely chopped
Salt and freshly ground black pepper
2 generous pinches ground saffron
2 pounds ripe, fresh tomatoes, cut into quarters and seeded; or 2 pounds canned tomatoes, drained and seeded

FREGOLA O FREGULA

SARDINIAN BOILED COUSCOUS

FOR THE COUSCOUS GRAIN:
1 pound couscous (not instant)
½ cup cold water
2 extra-large egg yolks
½ teaspoon salt
2 large pinches ground saffron

FOR THE FISH:
½ pound squid (calamari), cleaned
½ pound octopus
Coarse-grained salt
1 sea bass (about 2½ pounds), cleaned, with head and tail left on
1 whiting (about 1½ pounds), cleaned, with head and tail left on

FOR THE SAUCE:
1 large red onion, peeled
1 medium-sized stalk celery
2 large cloves garlic, peeled
¾ cup olive oil
1 cup dry white wine
Salt and freshly ground black pepper
2 large pinches hot red pepper flakes (optional)

FOR THE BROTH:
3 cups cold water
1 cup dry white wine
6 tablespoons tomato paste
Salt and freshly ground black pepper

*Fregola is another coarse grain with historical connections. It is interesting to speculate that **Pasta grattugiata**, which is made by grating dough that has been allowed to dry, is a later way of approximating **Fregula**, particularly since it swells up when boiled, as does the Sardinian couscous.*

The couscous grain can be prepared up to 3 days in advance. Preheat the oven to 375 degrees. Place the couscous on a large serving platter and spread it all over. Start adding the cold water drop by drop in the center, incorporating some of the grains surrounding it. Keep pouring in the water, incorporating more grains until all the grains have absorbed the water and all the water has been used. At that point, start rubbing the grains between your hands so the water is absorbed uniformly and the grains remain separated as they swell. Spread the grains out over the platter again. Mix the egg yolks, salt and saffron in a small bowl and repeat the previous procedure, using the eggs instead of water. When all the egg is incorporated, the grains will have swelled to a much greater thickness.

Transfer the couscous to a cookie sheet and spread it out again. Place the cookie sheet on the middle shelf and bake for 10 minutes. Turn off the oven but leave couscous inside for 3 hours, with only the pilot left on. (Note: If using an electric oven or an oven without a pilot, bake the couscous for 10 minutes, remove the cookie sheet from the oven, lower oven to minimum, and wait 20 minutes. Then repeat this procedure twice.)

Remove the couscous from the oven and set aside to cool for about 2 hours. The couscous can be stored in a jar, tightly closed, until needed.

Prepare the fish (see page 130). Cut the squid into 1-inch rings and the octopus into 1-inch pieces, and put them in a small bowl with cold water and a little coarse salt. Cut off the heads and tails of the fish, then cut the bodies into 1½-inch slices. Place the heads and tails in a bowl with cold water and a little salt; soak the fish slices in a second bowl of salted water.

Start the sauce. Finely chop the onion, celery, and garlic together on a board. Heat the oil in a medium-sized flameproof casserole over low heat; when the oil is warm, add the chopped vegetables and sauté for 5 minutes. Drain the squid and octopus, rinse under cold running water, and add to the casserole. Cook for 20 minutes, stirring every so often with a wooden spoon.

Start the broth. Heat the water with the wine in a medium-sized saucepan and bring to a boil. Drain the fish heads and tails, rinse under cold running water, and add to the pan. Simmer for 20 minutes, adding salt and pepper to taste.

Return to the sauce. Add the wine to the squid and octopus in the casserole, and let the wine evaporate for 15 minutes. Add some lukewarm water if the fish is not soft and tender.

Finish the broth. Strain the broth and discard the heads and tails. Dissolve the tomato paste in the hot liquid. Combine the broth with the sauce, taste for salt and pepper, and put in the red pepper flakes if you are using them. Cover and cook for 30 minutes.

Bring a large stockpot of cold water to a boil. Warm a large serving platter. When the water in the stockpot reaches a boil, add coarse salt to taste, then add the *fregola* and boil for 10 minutes, stirring every so often with a wooden spoon. Meanwhile, drain the fish slices, rinse under cold running water, and add to the casserole. Cook, covered, for 5 to 6 minutes.

Drain the *fregola* into a colander lined with cheesecloth. Spread it out over a warmed platter. Pour over the sauce, and arrange the fish pieces in the center. Sprinkle with parsley and serve.

NOTE:
Commercial *fregola* can be bought. It requires a longer cooking time, up to 25 minutes.

TO COOK THE
COUSCOUS:
Coarse-grained salt

TO SERVE:
**25 large sprigs Italian
parsley, leaves only**

FROM REGGIO-
EMILIA

SERVES 6 TO 8

1 ½ cups unbleached all-
purpose flour
¼ cup very fine semolina
flour
¼ cup freshly grated
Parmigiano cheeese,
grated very fine with no
lumps
3 extra-large eggs
Salt to taste
Large pinch of freshly
grated nutmeg
2 quarts defatted chicken
or beef broth, preferably
homemade

TO SERVE:
Freshly grated Parmigiano
cheese

PASTA GRATTUGIATA *OR* PASTA GRATTATA *OR* PASTA RASA
GRATED PASTA IN BROTH

Pasta grattugiata exists in different parts of Italy under a variety of names. While this kind of pasta is homemade, it has even been adapted to commercial dried pasta under the name of grandinine or pastine, and in modern times is used mostly in broth.

Arrange 1 cup of the flour in a mound on a board. Make a well in the flour, then place the semolina in the well. Mix the Parmigiano and eggs in a small bowl and season with salt and nutmeg. Pour the mixture into the well, then use a fork to start incorporating the egg mixture into the flours. Keep mixing until a homogeneous ball of dough is formed.

Begin kneading, incorporating more flour, until the ball of dough is very hard, about 15 minutes. Wrap the dough in plastic and freeze for 45 minutes; this replaces several hours of drying.

Place a 4-sided hand cheese grater on a well-floured surface. Use the large-hole side to coarsely grate the hard ball of dough, letting the pieces fall onto the flour so they do not stick together. When all is grated, bring the broth to a boil in a large pot over medium heat. While the broth is heating, place the *pasta grattugiata* and the remaining flour in a colander and shake very well, both to coat the pasta and to remove the excess flour. Add the pasta to the broth and cook for 1 to 3 minutes depending on dryness. Serve with some Parmigiano sprinkled over each portion of broth and pasta.*

VARIATIONS
1. Nutmeg can be omitted from the dough.
2. Black pepper can be added to the dough, with or without nutmeg.

* This pasta can be prepared even 3 or 4 days in advance.

GRAN FARRO *OR* MINESTRA DI FARRO

FROM TUSCANY

TUSCAN BEAN SOUP WITH WHEAT BERRIES

SERVES 8 TO 10

*Farro, an ancient form of wheat called "spelt" in English, is still treasured in certain Italian dishes. In this, whole grains of soft wheat are used, cooked in a way that is very suggestive of the coarsely milled harder wheat of couscous. In the mythic Neapolitan dessert for the coming of spring and Easter, **Pastiera,** soft spring-wheat grains are used and must have originated in ancient times with farro. The dish that most strongly survives is **Gran farro** in Tuscany, a thick minestrone incorporating the whole grains of **farro,** which probably dates back to the days when Etruscan wheat was prized.*

Soak the beans in cold water overnight. The next morning, coarsely chop the carrots, onion, celery, and garlic all together on a board. Cut the *pancetta* or *prosciutto* into small pieces. Drain and rinse the beans and put them in a medium-sized stockpot, preferably terra-cotta, along with the chopped ingredients, *pancetta* or *prosciutto,* and broth. Place the pot over medium heat (if using terra-cotta, place a Flame Tamer between the burner and the pot) and heat, uncovered, until the broth reaches a boil. Cover the pot and simmer for 1½ hours (the beans should be very soft). Pass the contents of the pot through a food mill, using the disc with the smallest holes, into a second pot over medium heat. Taste for salt and pepper. After the broth reaches a boil, simmer for 5 minutes.

Rinse the *farro* under cold running water, then add it to the broth, stir very well with a wooden spoon, and cook for 25 minutes, stirring every so often; the *farro* should open and be cooked. Remove the soup from the heat and let it rest, covered, for 10 minutes before serving. Place a teaspoon of oil and a twist of black pepper on each serving. The soup can also be served at room temperature after a few hours, or reheated, adding an additional cup or so of lukewarm broth.

NOTE:
Farro is a type of soft wheat berry, also called *spelt*. It is available in Italian groceries or natural food stores.

1 cup dried *cannellini* (white kidney beans)
2 medium-sized carrots, scraped
1 medium-sized red onion, peeled
1 large stalk celery
1 medium-sized clove garlic, peeled
4 ounces *pancetta* or *prosciutto,* in 1 piece
3 quarts cold chicken broth, preferably homemade, or water
Salt and freshly ground black pepper
1 cup *farro* (see Note)
8 to 10 teaspoons olive oil

Nidi di carnevale: The only sweet use of the Tuscan
chocolate pasta that is really traditional is in the
nests made for carnival season, with the chocolate
pasta embellished with chopped nuts and honey.

DESSERT PASTAS

Yes, there even are pasta desserts! The simplest, but very popular is the deep-fried, crisp little pastry snacks sprinkled with sugar—called, amusingly, *cenci* or "rags," meaning leftover bits. Some rum is added to the pasta dough, not only for flavoring but for the crisper result created by the alcohol. Dessert *tortelli*, filled with a stuffing of ricotta, raisins, rum, egg yolks, and sugar, are fried, sprinkled with more sugar, and finally flamed with rum (see Recipe Appendix).

Some dishes in other parts of this book might seem sweet enough to be desserts. I refer to Plum-Filled *Gnocchi* (page 226) and Fine *Lasagne* with Poppy Seeds from Trieste (page 224). But in their hometowns, they are first courses, a holdover of the earlier centuries when sweet and savory dishes could be mixed in the same course.

The *Torta di taglierini* here is an ambitious pasta torte made with almonds, walnuts, Amaretti, cocoa, Marsala, and very thin pasta such as *capellini*.

And though the conversation-piece chocolate pasta is not normally a sweet dish, it is utilized for a dessert in carnival season in Tuscany, when the pasta is arranged in little nests and fried, then covered with a sauce of honey, brandy, and almonds.

These are all serious traditional desserts, not strange concoctions, and I encourage you to try them.

NIDI DI CARNEVALE
CHOCOLATE PASTA DESSERT "NESTS"

FROM TUSCANY

SERVES 6

Prepare the pasta with the ingredients and quantities listed, placing the cocoa and sugar in the flour well along with the other ingredients (see page 14). Stretch the pasta dough to about 1/16 inch thick, on the pasta machine take to the next to last notch, then cut into 6 equal sheets and let rest on dish towels until a thin film forms on the pasta. At that moment, cut the sheets of pasta into *taglierini* (see page 34), which will be a little thicker than usual (about 1/16 inch). Make 6 separate mounds, and place the mounds on cotton dish towels to rest until the oil is hot. Do not allow the *taglierini* to become very dry or they will break while frying.

Put the oil in a deep-fat fryer and set over medium heat. Line a large cookie sheet with paper towels. When the oil is hot (but not more than 375 degrees), place 1 mound of *taglierini* in a small wire strainer (not more than 5 inches in diameter and 3 inches deep). Insert the strainer into the hot oil and hold it until the pasta turns lightly golden and looks very crisp, about 2 minutes. Remove the strainer and invert the fried pasta nest to that the rounded bottom is now up. Repeat the same procedure with the other 5 nests.

When the baskets all are cooked, place the honey in a heavy saucepan, add the brandy, mix very well, and put the pan over low heat, continuously stirring with a wooden spoon until the brandy is completely incorporated and the honey reaches a boil. Simmer for 2 minutes, then remove from heat and set aside until lukewarm.

Coarsely chop the almonds on a board. Transfer the nests, bottom down, onto 6 individual plates; sprinkle the chopped almonds over them and use a small ladle to coat them with the lukewarm honey. Serve. (The nests, the honey sauce, and the almonds can all be prepared several hours in advance and assembled just before serving.)

FOR THE PASTA:
2½ cups unbleached all-purpose flour
2 extra-large eggs
Pinch of salt
2 tablespoons semi-sweet cocoa powder
4 teaspoons granulated sugar

TO FRY THE PASTA:
2 quarts vegetable oil

FOR THE SAUCE:
1 pound honey
6 tablespoons brandy
4 ounces blanched almonds

FROM MANTUA
(LOMBARDY)

SERVES 8

FOR THE PASTA:
Coarse-grained salt
**4 ounces dried *capellini*,
    preferably imported
    Italian**
**2 tablespoons olive or
    vegetable oil**

FOR THE BATTER:
**4 ounces blanched
    almonds**
2 ounces walnuts
2 ounces Amaretti cookies
**8 tablespoons (4 ounces)
    sweet butter, at room
    temperature**
1¼ cups granulated sugar
3 extra-large eggs
**½ cup unsweetened cocoa
    powder**
1 teaspoon orange extract
**⅓ cup dry Marsala or dry
    Vermouth**

FOR THE CAKE PAN:
**1 tablespoon (½ ounce)
    sweet butter**
**4 tablespoons unbleached
    all-purpose flour**

TORTA DI TAGLIERINI
PASTA TORTE WITH CHOCOLATE

Bring a large pot of cold water to a boil, add coarse salt, then add the pasta and cook for only 4 minutes. Fill a large bowl with cold water and add the 2 tablespoons of oil. Drain the pasta and add it to the bowl with oil and set aside until needed.

Prepare the batter. Put almonds, walnuts, Amaretti, butter, and 1 cup sugar in a blender or food processor and grind until very fine. Add the eggs, cocoa, and orange extract; process again. The ingredients should be completely blended.

Preheat the oven to 375 degrees. Drain the pasta and place it in a large crockery or glass bowl. Add the remaining ¼ cup sugar and Marsala, and mix very well. Butter and flour an 8-inch spring-form cake pan. Transfer the thick batter to the bowl with the pasta and, using 2 forks, combine the batter thoroughly with the pasta; transfer the mixture to the prepared pan and bake for 1 hour.

Remove torte from the oven, transfer to a rack, release the form, and set torte aside to cool for at least 30 minutes. Transfer the torte to a round serving platter and serve it cut into wedges.

NOTE:
This torte cannot be reheated. It is best served within 4 to 5 hours of baking.

VARIATIONS
    1. Eggs can be omitted.
    2. The cocoa can be reduced to 2 tablespoons.
    3. Fresh *taglierini*, made with flour, eggs, and salt, can be used in place of the *capellini*.

Cuscus dolce

DESSERT COUSCOUS

In Sicily, couscous is even a dessert, incorporating the age-old Mediterranean almonds, rosewater, pistachio nuts, candied citron, and orange peel as well as chocolate and custard cream, which most likely were added in later centuries.

Prepare the custard cream. Blanch the pistachio nuts in a pan of boiling water with coarse salt added (otherwise the nuts will turn yellow). Dry the nuts with paper towels, then finely chop them on a board or grind them in a food processor. Place the egg yolks in a medium-sized crockery or glass bowl, add the sugar, and use a wooden spoon to mix the sugar into the yolks until they turn a lighter color. Slowly add the cream, then the lukewarm milk, mixing steadily. Add the chopped nuts and the rosewater, and mix very well. Place in the top of a double boiler.

Bring water to a boil in the bottom of the double boiler. When the water begins to boil, insert the top, making sure the water does not touch it, and stir constantly with a wooden spoon, always in the same direction. When the cream coats the spoon, just before it boils (absolutely do not allow the cream to boil), remove the top of the double boiler from the heat and continue to stir the contents for 1 minute more. Transfer the custard to an empty wine bottle (to keep skin from forming), cork it, and refrigerate until needed.

Prepare the couscous with ingredients and quantities listed, following the procedure on page 328 but using just salted water for the steaming. Let the couscous rest for 1 hour until cool.

Mix the granulated and confectioners' sugar with the vanilla in a large bowl. Cut the chocolate into pieces the size of half an almond. Cut the toasted almonds in half and the candied fruit into pieces the same size. Add the couscous, chocolate, and almonds to the bowl with the sugar and mix very well. Transfer the couscous to a large serving platter and arrange it in one thick layer. Pour the cooled custard cream over the couscous and serve, spooning out the sweet grain topped with custard sauce.

FOR THE CUSTARD CREAM:
60 pistachio nuts
Coarse-grained salt
5 extra-large egg yolks
8 tablespoons granulated sugar
1 cup cold heavy cream
½ cup lukewarm milk
2 tablespoons rosewater

FOR THE COUSCOUS:
1 pound couscous (not instant)
1 cup cold water
½ teaspoon salt

FOR THE STEAMER:
3½ cups unbleached all-purpose flour
1 cup cold water

TO FLAVOR THE COUSCOUS:
2 tablespoons granulated sugar
1 teaspoon confectioners' sugar
5 drops vanilla extract
2 ounces semisweet chocolate
3 ounces toasted almonds
2 ounces candied citron
2 ounces candied orange peel

Some typical Italian cheeses. Top right: Homemade
ricotta. Notice the molded shape produced by a
basket. This solid, dry, second curd (not a true
cheese) works best for cooking. Bottom right:
Homemade mascarpone, useful for many desserts
and stuffings.

HOMEMADE INGREDIENTS

FROM ALL OVER
ITALY

MAKES 2 CUPS

RICOTTA

**3 quarts whole- or part-
skim milk**
3 drops lemon juice
**1 cup (8 ounces) plain
yogurt**

Pour the milk into a crockery or glass bowl and stir in the lemon juice. Let the mixture rest, covered, for 36 hours in a cool place or on the bottom shelf of the refrigerator. Add the yogurt and mix with a wooden spoon until it is completely incorporated, then transfer to a large saucepan. Bring to a boil over medium heat, stirring constantly with a wooden spoon, then boil for only 1 minute. Remove pot from heat and drain the ricotta in a large colander lined with a cheesecloth. Tie the cheesecloth at the top with string and let it hang free above a bowl for 1 hour. Ricotta is then ready to use.

FROM ALL OVER
ITALY

MAKES 8 OUNCES

MASCARPONE

**1 quart heavy cream (not
ultrapasteurized)**
**¼ teaspoon tartaric acid
(see Note)**

*This method produces **mascarpone** as fresh as that found in Italy, and therefore very sweet.*

Pour the cream into a glass casserole, then place the casserole into a larger flameproof casserole containing some cold water, making an improvised *bagnomaria (bain-marie)*. Place the *bagnomaria* over medium heat and bring the cream to a temperature of 180 degrees, mixing every so often with a wooden spoon. Check carefully with a candy thermometer. As soon as the cream reaches the exact temperature, remove *bagnomaria* from heat, add the tartaric acid to the cream, and stir with a wooden spoon for 30 seconds. Then remove the insert containing the cream from the water bath and stir for 2 minutes more.

Line a fine-mesh basket with thick cheesecloth and pour in the cream mixture. Let the mixture stand for 12 hours over a bowl in a cool place or on the bottom shelf of the refrigerator. Prepare four 9-inch squares of thick cheesecloth. Place one-fourth of the *mascarpone* in the center of each piece of cheesecloth, then fold it like a package, without tying it. Place the package on a plate and refrigerate for 12 hours before using it.

NOTE:
Mascarpone is called for in the *Tortelli con la coda*, page 246. Tartaric acid, one of the most common vegetable acids and similar to cream of tartar but more acidic, is found in berries and tamarind

seed. It is used in making baking powder, effervescent drinks, and homemade wines, and can usually be purchased in pharmacies or available through Caswell-Massey, 518 Lexington Avenue, New York, N.Y. 10017; store telephone (212) 755-2254; for mail order, call (212) 620-0090.

Concentrato di Pomodoro

TOMATO PASTE

FROM ALL OVER ITALY

YIELDS 1½ CUPS

2 pounds ripe, fresh tomatoes; or 2 pounds canned tomatoes, preferably imported Italian

Tomato paste is a concentrate of pure tomatoes. It has sometimes been misused as a quick substitute for tomatoes or tomato sauce, and it is sometimes wrongly added to tomatoes, thickening the sauce and making it unpleasantly acidic. However, it is a mistake to think of this concentrate negatively. Though it must not be thought of as a substitute for whole tomatoes, because it has quite a different taste, it is a legitimate ingredient of certain dishes. Of course, you must use a high-quality tomato concentrate. Best of all is home-made tomato paste, really quite easy to make and easier to pre-serve in modern-day ice-cube trays than through the older canning methods.

If using fresh tomatoes, cut them into pieces. Place fresh or canned tomatoes in a medium-sized flameproof casserole and sim-mer over medium heat for 35 minutes. Pass tomatoes through a food mill, using the disc with smallest holes, into a crockery or glass bowl. Pour the sauce into a clean, heavy saucepan and re-duce it over low heat for 1 hour, mixing every so often with a wooden spoon and taking care that it does not scorch on the bot-tom. It should emerge very thick and homogeneous.

Transfer the sauce to a crockery or glass bowl to cool com-pletely, about 1 hour. Pour the concentrate into ice-cube trays with their dividers, and put in the freezer until completely hard. Remove the cubes from the tray and store in freezer bags. When needed, remove the necessary number of cubes from the freezer a day before using, and let them defrost slowly but completely in a small covered bowl on the bottom shelf of the refrigerator. Add the to-mato paste as an ingredient only when it is completely defrosted. Remember that salt and aromatic herbs must be added indepen-dently, since the tomato paste does not contain them.

ACKNOWLEDGMENTS

Of those to whom I owe thanks for their help on this labor of love, first I wish to thank my knowledgeable, helpful, and sympathetic editor Carole Lalli and her assistant Kerri Conan. And I am grateful to Frank Metz and Eve Metz of the Art and Design Departments for their graciousness and understanding.

For help on the photos, special thanks to: Mario Buccellati of New York, for their elegant silver and flatware; Tessilarte of Florence, Italy, for all the tablecloths and napkins; Cristallo di censo, colle Val d'Elsa, for the crystal glasses; Sardinia Export Inc., for help with Sardinian products and props; Associazione Ceramiche Faenza, for Faenza (faience) ceramics; Commune di Bologna, for help with the photos in that city; Jeffrey Toppel, my cooking assistant, for the photos; Ann Nurse, colleague as cooking teacher, and always generous with her help; Eleanor Kremen, in whose wonderful kitchen I made some of these recipes; and, again, to Henry Weinberg, for the kind of help without which this book could not have been done.

INDEX

Have BETTER HOMES AND GARDENS® magazine delivered to your door. For information, write to:
MR. ROBERT AUSTIN
P.O. BOX 4536
DES MOINES, IA 50336

ABOUT THE AUTHOR

Giuliano Bugialli has always been interested in wine and food. Born and raised in Florence, Italy, his family enjoyed traditional cooking and lively gatherings. Although he studied languages in Florence and Rome, he maintained an interest in cuisine and word of his talent spread.

Bugialli came to the United States to teach languages, but he found himself cooking professionally more and more. As his reputation grew, he focused completely on cuisine. In 1972, he began teaching, and founded schools in New York and in Florence. He now attracts students from around the world.

In 1980, Bugialli won Italy's prestigious Caterina di Medici award for his outstanding contribution to Italian cuisine. He is the author of *Classic Techniques of Italian Cooking*, *The Fine Art of Italian Cooking*, and *The Foods of Italy*.